A ROYAL DESTINY

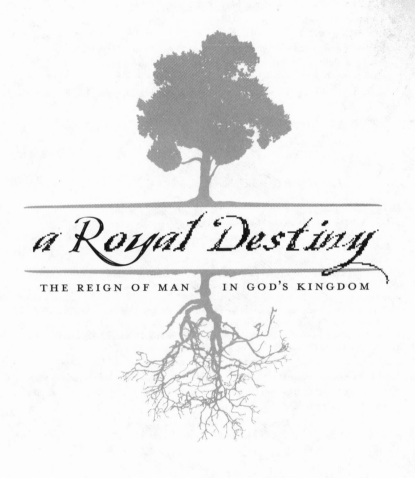

a Royal Destiny

THE REIGN OF MAN IN GOD'S KINGDOM

THURMAN WISDOM

BOB JONES
UNIVERSITY PRESS

www.bjupress.com

Library of Congress Cataloging-in-Publication Data

Wisdom, Thurman, 1931-
  A royal destiny : the reign of man in God's kingdom / Thurman Wisdom.
    p. cm.
  Summary: "Traces the theme of the kingdom of God, and man's reign in that kingdom,
as the Bible develops it from Genesis to Revelation"—Provided by publisher.
  Includes bibliographical references and index.
  ISBN 1-59166-687-2 (perfect bound pbk. : alk. paper)
  1. Kingdom of God—Biblical teaching. 2. Theological anthropology—Biblical teach-
ing.   I. Title.
  BS680.K52W57 2006
  231.7'3—dc22

                                                                        2006011090

Cover Photo Credits: © 2006 iStockphoto Inc.

ESV: Scripture quotations marked (ESV) are from The Holy Bible, English Standard Version, copyright © 2001
by Crossway Bibles, a division of Good News Publishers. Used by permission. All rights reserved.
NASB: Scripture quotations marked (NASB) are taken from the NEW AMERICAN STANDARD BIBLE®,
Copyright ©1960, 1962, 1963, 1968, 1971, 1972, 1973, 1975, 1977, 1995 by The Lockman Foundation. Used by
permission.
NIV: Scripture quotations marked (NIV) are taken from the HOLY BIBLE, NEW INTERNATIONAL
VERSION®. Copyright © 1973, 1978, 1984 International Bible Society. Used by permission of Zondervan. All
rights reserved.
The "NIV" and "New International Version" trademarks are registered in the United States Patent and Trademark
Office by International Bible Society. Use of either trademark requires the permission of International Bible Society.
The fact that materials produced by other publishers may be referred to in this volume does not constitute an en-
dorsement of the content or theological position of materials produced by such publishers.

The fact that materials produced by other publishers may be referred to in this volume
does not constitute an endorsement of the content or theological position of materials
produced by such publishers.

A Royal Destiny: The Reign of Man in God's Kingdom
Thurman Wisdom, PhD

Design by Craig Oesterling
Composition by Michael Boone

© 2006 BJU Press
Greenville, South Carolina 29614

Printed in the United States of America
All rights reserved

ISBN 1-59166-687-2

15 14 13 12 11 10 9 8 7 6 5 4 3 2 1

To my beloved children
by birth and by marriage
and to my beloved grandchildren
living and, by God's grace, yet to live

With this volume I open my heart
that you may see the springs from which my love for you flows
and that, above all, you may drink abundantly
from those, the purest of springs.

TABLE OF CONTENTS

Part Four
THE FINAL WAR

INTRODUCTION

"HERMAN WHO?"

"Herman Who?"

"Hermeneutics."

"How do you spell it?"

"H-e-r-r . . . I'm not sure, but it comes from the Greek."

With due reverence, Scott's eyes widened at the word *Greek*. "I'd better listen to this guy," he thought. "He knows stuff that comes from the *Greek*. So what if he can't spell? Lots of smart people can't spell."

"So what system of Bible study do you use?" the inquisitor asked.

"System," thought Scott, rummaging frantically for something intelligent to say, "system . . . I gotta have a system?"

By now, the eyes of his Inquisitor had narrowed; and his roommate (the one he had just impressed with the news that he was going to take Accounting 101 in his freshman year) had a noticeable smirk on his face.

"Well," stammered Scott, hoping a moment of inspiration would somehow fill the vacuum, "I . . ." (His words came out reluctantly, each one sounding dumber than its predecessor.) " . . . just . . . read."

"*Just read?*" The words of his inquisitor rang with judgment and disbelief.

Then a remarkable thing happened. The eyes of the inquisitor began re-forming to a look of *pity* . . . and maybe even a tinge of *concern*. "Wonderful," sighed Scott, "he has the gift of mercy. He hasn't let the fact that he knows stuff that comes from the *Greek* go to his head."

Scott is a senior now, but he still remembers the warm glow he felt when he saw that look of pity. He and the guy he (later) nicknamed "The Inquisitor" have become best of friends. "Good ol' Inquisitor," he thinks, "he taught me a lot of really neat stuff. Hermeneutics stuff like how to do pre-Bible-study aerobics, how to kick the spiritualizing habit, and how to recognize a *hapax legomenon* when you see one. He even loaned me his own personal copy of *The Complete Idiot's Guide to the Bible*. (That touched me deeply.) And just think, here I am graduating! Ready to launch out into the deep. And ready at last to begin reading my Bible intelligently."

SO WHY NOT JUST READ?

The saga of Scott may seem a little silly to you, but be wary of first impressions. Some names and circumstances in the story were altered to protect the guilty, but the story itself is more in touch with reality than you might think. Ever since the beginning of the church, our tendency to rely heavily on "Bible scholars" to feed and enlighten us has been a sign of spiritual decline. Even as we grip our Bibles and dogmatically affirm the priesthood of the believer, we look for other "priests" to tell us when to read the Bible, why it doesn't really say what we think it says, and how we can integrate biblical things we haven't thought about much into our default lifestyle. When at last we open our study Bibles, we often find ourselves looking at a page that appears to warrant the ascription "The Pentateuch, by Scofield, with notes by Moses."

Don't get me wrong, please! I am not advocating book burning. I am totally in favor of Bible teachers, hermeneutics classes, theological guides, and study Bibles (to say nothing of the prospect of selling this book). But for all that, to keep a bit of balance in our thinking, we need periodically to remind ourselves that David became a man after God's own heart without a *Life Application Study Bible*.

I fear we have drifted into a when-all-else-fails-read-the-Instruction-Manual mentality toward the Word of God. Christian scholars, electronic technicians, and commercial entrepreneurs have done about everything imaginable to make the Bible accessible and intelligible. They have translated it, analyzed it, outlined it, defined it, illustrated it, dramatized it, and wrangled over it. The one thing remaining for us to do is read it—and this has become the great omission of the church. Even the mistranslation, misinterpretation, and misapplication of the Word are innocuous when compared with this sin of disregard.

But if we just pick up our Bibles and start reading, how are we going to know what is really going on? What will keep us from getting waylaid by some hidden meaning? On the human side, we have a built-in filter, including an immune system, in the natural laws of language.

THE LAWS OF LANGUAGE

One of the best yet most neglected axioms for Bible study is "Read the Bible as you would read any other book; read the Bible as you would no other book." The heavenly side of this paradox cautions us to look into this Book reverently and to weigh its words carefully, for it is unique, inerrant, and infallible. On the earthly side, the paradox invites us to open its pages and read it as we would read a newspaper or a letter. Christian scholars once dabbled with the notion that the biblical languages were special, divine languages. Now, of course, all recognize that the human authors of Scripture communicated to the people in the language of the common people. The Hebrew and Aramaic of the Old Testament were the languages of shepherds, farmers, and merchants. The Greek of the New Testament was the *koine*, the common language—the kind a housewife would use at the fish market. The messages of these books were communicated, as oral speech is generally, in accordance with the natural laws of language.

And exactly what are these "natural laws of language"? Actually, it's something of a stretch to call them *laws*, though the dictionary has left an opening that allows them to squeeze through. The *American Heritage Dictionary* gives as one definition of *law* "a rule of conduct or procedure established by custom, agreement, or authority." Our word gets through on the "custom" part. The rules of language, of communication, go with the flow of human customs. They are very user-friendly (not to be confused with the rules of English Grammar 101). They are wonderfully flexible and multifaceted. They not only allow the words in their custody to play their own typecast parts, but they allow them often to substitute for each other and even sometimes to play opposite roles.[1]

This is not to say that we, like the Queen of Hearts in *Alice in Wonderland*, can make words mean whatever we want them to mean. The magistrate who keeps order in the world of language is Context. No word can live—really live—without Context, and those that try have to spend their lives incarcerated in dictionaries. Realtors say that the first three imperatives for good real estate are location, location, location. For Bible readers, the imperatives are context, context, context. These three governors look with hearty favor on commoners. They are "of the people, by the people, and for the people" types. So even the commoner who knows the context well will be light (and enlightened) years ahead of the person who knows the original languages but has a wimpy grip on context.

We should, therefore, read our Bibles as we would read any other book. If we do that long enough and consistently enough, we won't have any problem recognizing the heavenly side of our axiom. The same communication principles that apply to the reading of a newspaper article, a weather report, or a short story apply to the reading of the Bible. How many hermeneutical headaches the saints would have saved themselves had they consistently followed this simple principle! Seminary classes in hermeneutics have become necessary largely because Christians have strayed from, or have been lured from, the fundamental laws of communication.

Nevertheless, many an overprotective gardener of truth, in his zeal to ward off hermeneutical trespassers, has littered the landscape with warning and directional signs. Do I, for example, really need to know what *brachylogy* ("a condensed expression") is in order to understand Paul's admonishment to Gentile Christians: "Boast not against the branches. But if thou boast, thou bearest not the root, but the root thee" (Rom. 11:18)? And when I hear a new twist on words, like "snowplows, lathering up to shave the night's growth off the streets," do I mentally go through a five-step process to immunize myself against the danger of "overspiritualizing"? (1) snowplows have no consciousness of the need to shave; (2) a snow plow is not self-motivated; (3) lathering has no clear relevance to snowplows; (4) snow does not grow on streets, it falls; and

---

[1] Take, for example, the word *bad*. In certain contexts, it can mean "good." The same is true even of some biblical words. The Hebrew word translated by such expressions as *mercy, kindness,* and *goodness* (*chesed*) can mean "shameful thing or wicked thing" (e.g., Lev. 20:17).

(5) snowplows are incapable of concern for streets. Therefore, the author must be using symbolism or a mystical form of speech understandable only to the initiate. Isn't it true, instead, that life's experiences trip intuitional triggers that allow us to understand even obtuse imagery? The best way, then, to become reasonably adept at handling symbolic language is simply to live—and pay attention. If you live long enough, eventually your experiences and associations will be able to gang up on linguistic nuances that masquerade as symbols and such.

If we go back to the first statement about man in the Bible—that God made man in His own image—we must assume that built into the very nature of man was the capacity for communication. Evolutionists would have us believe that early man learned gradually to communicate through grunts and groans that eventually evolved into language. Biblical revelation, though, tells us that God communicated with man and man with God from the very first.

So why don't we just read the revelation of God? Even in His so-called general revelation, God is continuously "uttering speech" and "showing knowledge" (Ps. 19:1–6). It is our responsibility, then, to "consider" His heavens (Ps. 8:3) and to hear His word. "Holy Scripture cannot make its true impression unless it be read in continuity . . . again and again . . . The best posture for receiving light is not that of an umpire among contending interpreters. . . . Suppose some errors are picked up, as they will be, in individual cases; these will be gradually corrected by the confluent light of many passages."[2]

DIVINE REVELATION: A SUBLIME SELF-DISCLOSURE

Unfortunately, the word *revelation* has something of a theological cadence to it. It's the kind of word you expect to see in religious processions with robed choirs, stately anthems, incense, and such. Most people don't

---

[2] J. W. Alexander, *Thoughts on Preaching* (Carlisle, PA: Banner of Truth Trust, reprint 1975), 179. Some may be suspicious that these are the words of a frustrated PhD candidate—a man bent on crushing the current philosophy of education with his wounded pride. In fact, James Waddel Alexander (1804–1859) was at once a scholar's scholar and a man of the people. A rare combination indeed! He was the oldest son of Archibald Alexander, who organized and became the first professor of Princeton Seminary. His brother, Joseph A. Alexander, was a renowned theologian and Oriental scholar. Though J. W. Alexander taught at Princeton for three years, he devoted himself chiefly to the pastoral ministry. Charles Hodge said of him, "No minister in our Church was a more accomplished scholar."

use it much, perhaps because ordinary people like things that are down to earth—and *revelation* is definitely not a down-to-earth type of word. So when we speak (in theological circles) of the revelation of God, exactly what are we talking about? On this word, the dictionary seems to belabor the obvious; but when you think about it, it helps some. Revelation, says the *American Heritage Dictionary*, is "the act of revealing or disclosing." In theology, the same source tells us, the word refers to "a manifestation of divine will or truth."

We could say that God's revelation is a sublime act of self-disclosure. Or we might say that divine revelation is the process by which God tells us all about Himself—that is, all we can comprehend and handle profitably. On the human level, we tend to communicate most freely with those we know best. To our best friends we reveal our highest dreams, our deepest needs, and our greatest fears. To strangers, news hounds, and telemarketers—and anyone we suspect might be interested merely in using us—we tend to be rather close-mouthed. On the divine level, the same principles apply to God's self-disclosure. God communicates most freely with His best friends—those who are most in tune with Him and most compatible with His nature (e.g., John 14:21; I Sam. 3:15; Ps. 74:9; Amos 8:11–12).

The people of the world are Athenians at heart. They like to think of the Supreme Being as the Unknown (and unknowable) God (Acts 17:23). Such ignorance is blissful in a world bent on ignoring God. (Note that *ignore*—to refuse to pay attention to, to disregard—is the root of this type of ignorance.) Though ignorance is no excuse in earthly courts for the violation of human laws, people of the world blissfully suppose that ignorance of God will neutralize their accountability in the heavenly courts.

In fact, God has gone out of His way to reveal Himself to man, even to rebellious man. "The heavens declare the glory of God; and the firmament sheweth his handywork. Day unto day uttereth speech, and night unto night sheweth knowledge. There is no speech nor language, where their voice is not heard" (Ps. 19:1–3). Throughout the world, in every language, God is communicating daily with man:

Because *that which is known about God is evident within them; for God made it evident to them.* For since the creation of the world His invisible attributes, *His eternal power and divine nature, have been clearly seen, being understood* through what has been made, so that they are without excuse. For even though *they knew God*, they did not honor Him as God, or give thanks; but they became futile in their speculations, and their foolish heart was darkened (Rom. 1:19–21, NASB).

Note my italicized words: even to a degenerating pagan world that willfully and impudently rejected Him, God actively and continually revealed Himself.

THE INWARD WITNESSES OF GOD'S SELF-DISCLOSURE

The self-disclosure of God also has inward witnesses:

For when the Gentiles, which have not the law, do by nature the things contained in the law, these, having not the law, are a law unto themselves: which shew the work of the law written in their hearts, their conscience also bearing witness, and their thoughts the mean while accusing or else excusing one another (Rom. 2:14–15).

These verses teach that all people have within them an invisible law by which they have the intuitive power to discern right from wrong. Furthermore, they have an inward judge (conscience) which condemns them when they break the law within and commends them when they conform to it. Whether or not these verses explain the nature of the discernment imparted through the Tree of Knowledge, they confirm that man has within his nature the power to discern right from wrong. Tragically, man does not have within him the moral power to always choose the right and deny the wrong; but he has residing in his being the standards inherent in God's nature and—through conscience—the judgments by which God condemns and justifies mankind.

It is true, of course, that men have twisted and ignored this inward unwritten law, and that they have defiled and largely obstructed the work of conscience. But they have done the same thing to the written law of God and to divinely appointed judges. The fact remains that God has revealed Himself universally, abundantly, and clearly. Furthermore, though the divine law and conscience may be misused, they cannot be obliterated. Societies and nations have established and sought to enforce laws that contradict the law of God; but they have never succeeded in abolishing God's law.

And the same is true of conscience. In Bunyan's *Holy War*, after Diabolus had taken the city of Mansoul, he sought to "put out of place and power" the

> Lord Mayor, whose name was my Lord Understanding, and Mr. Recorder, whose name was Mr. Conscience.... As for Mr. Recorder, before the town was taken he was a man well read in the laws of his King, and also a man of courage and faithfulness to speak truth at every occasion. Now this man, Diabolus could by no means abide, because—though he gave his consent to his coming into the town—yet he could not, by all the wiles, trials, stratagems and devices that he could use, make him wholly his own.[3]

The word *conscience* appears over thirty times in the New Testament, but the inspired writers never explained it. They did not have to. They correctly assumed that all people, in all cultures, were painfully aware of this inflexible judge. In fact, perhaps the best way to think of conscience is to personify it as an internal judge who holds court in the soul of man. Written indelibly on the walls of man's soul is the divine law, and our internal, impartial judge rules in accordance with this law.

This judge will also make rulings based on other laws imposed upon it; but these laws—whatever temporary power they may have—can never supersede or erase the divine law written in the heart. A man's conscience may be weak because the principles of the law of God are not well ingrained and enforced in his soul (I Cor. 8:12). It may become defiled and—as a judge who has been bribed—become temporarily unclear in its judgments. And a man's conscience may also be "seared with a hot iron" (I Tim. 4:2)—that is, so branded by Satan that it becomes insensitive to truth and judgment. But in none of these cases can Satan make conscience "wholly his." The ancient laws of God are still embedded indelibly on man's soul. Conscience still "remembers" these laws, and it rules in accordance with their standards.

THE ELOQUENT SILENCE OF SCRIPTURE

There is profound eloquence in well-placed silence. "And the Lord turned, and looked . . . and Peter went out, and wept bitterly" (Luke 22:61–62). "Be still, and know that I am God," the psalmist exhorts us

---

[3] John Bunyan, *The Holy War* (Chicago: Moody, 1978), 74–75.

(Ps. 46:10); and Elijah found the Lord, not in the sound and fury of the wind or the earthquake or the fire, but in the still small voice.

In fact, the stately silence of the writers of Scripture often testifies more effectively of its divine nature than scholarly argumentation could. Consider how many wrong things these writers could have said. However much intelligence we ascribe to these thirty or so men, they were all creatures of their own time and culture. They, as all of us, shared in a defective cultural and educational process. What kept them from committing these errors to the written page? Consider the example of Clement of Rome. A scholar of classical culture, Clement as a young man knew the apostle Paul and later became the senior pastor of the church of Rome. Around AD 95 (about the time John wrote Revelation), he wrote a letter to the Corinthian church. To illustrate the Resurrection in this letter, Clement refers as fact to the myth of a miraculous bird called the phoenix that regenerated itself every five hundred years.

In silence, the inspired writers separate the wheat from the chaff, the sublime from the mundane, the glorious things of heaven from the merely great on earth. Think of the marvelous splash in earthly history made by Alexander the Great. If your name is Alexander or Alex or Sasha or Sandra or Sandy, you have been influenced by this Macedonian warrior who lived twenty-three centuries ago. Even after Alexander's death and the dissecting of his empire, the brazen claws of the Greek culture he spread[4] cut into the heart of Roman society and from there into the world at large. Yet for all that, Alexander the Great appears in the Bible only as a horn on a goat (Dan. 8:5, 21)!

The scriptural writers pass in tortuous silence by great empires that have risen and fallen and been laid in glorious dust—the authors fearful, it seems, of losing sight of the glories of heaven above and a little splinter of Mediterranean shore below. But even when they turn their attention toward the Messiah, their gaze is so riveted on the Cross and its consequences that they seem almost oblivious to the wonders in the early life of the God-man. Turn to the Gospel of John and leaf through its pages. On the very first page you find yourself within three years of the Cross. And when you arrive at chapter twelve, little more than halfway through

---

[4] It is interesting, in this connection, that the fourth beast in Daniel's vision (the Roman Empire), which had teeth of iron, had nails of brass (7:19).

the Book, you are greeted with the words "Then Jesus six days before the passover"—and you are standing now within one week of the Crucifixion.

Why this profound silence? The heart of the psalmist moves us toward the answer: "My heart is inditing [stirring in] a good matter: I speak of the things which I have made touching the king: my tongue is the pen of a ready writer" (Ps. 45:1). The Spirit of God riveted the hearts of the inspired writers on the lofty themes by which man comes to know God. "Holy men of God spake as they were moved by the Holy Ghost" (II Pet. 1:21*b*).

THE SCRIPTURAL STORY AS HISTORY

To some students, history is a chamber of horrors, littered with the dead bodies of yesteryear's heroes and villains, stifling with the dust of centuries, and gorged with insipid dates.

In fact—and I hope you are ready for this—history is life. So if you enjoy life you should enjoy history. I say *should* with caution, knowing full well that there is a great chasm between *should* and *would*; but if you could somehow bridge that chasm, you would find in history all of the pulsing sensations of life. This is why it was inevitable that the Word of God should be also a book of history. God is the Author of Life; and His revelation—His Self-disclosure—is for real people who live in real places in real time.

So when you find in the Bible "boring" lists of people, you are finding nothing that you haven't already found in life. When you walk through a mall, when you sit in a doctor's office, when you stand in line at a supermarket, you see crowded "lists" of people—nameless, faceless, inscrutable, boring people.

When Jesus asked the blind man at Bethsaida what he saw after the first stage of healing, the man responded, "I see men as trees, walking" (Mark 8:24*b*). As with that blind man, most of us haven't reached the second stage of the healing process. We generally see men as objects, not as people. Some time ago, I walked into a secretary's office to pick up a note from the printer. Sitting at one of the desks was a student I knew, so I greeted him with "How are you doing?" He responded, and I rejoined, "Great!" A while later, I walked into the same office, and the laughing secretaries asked, "Did you hear what that student said when you asked how he was doing? He said, 'Miserable'!" No, I really didn't hear what he said, because I hadn't actually seen him as a person. I saw him as an interest cue, as a reminder that I should be interested in people, that I should be concerned about how they are doing; but for all that, he was to me—at that time, at least—nameless and faceless and feeling-less.

God, on the other hand, is a people Person to the nth degree. He never sees simply rosters of people, nor does He see people simply as prospects. He doesn't even see them simply as tools for His agenda—though He alone has the right to see people that way. And He (amazing grace!) never even gets bored with people. His Word, therefore, is about people, people He knows, not just people on His lists.

As a holy book, the Bible is unique in its interaction with history. No other holy book, no other religion, is comparable—anywhere near comparable—with the Bible in this feature. This is not mere religious rhetoric. This is a fact that will bear up under the most suspicious scrutiny. Listen to the words of Paul L. Maier, professor of ancient history at Western Michigan University.

> Of all religious beliefs in the world, past or present, none have more thoroughly based themselves on history than Judaism and Christianity. The divine-human encounter in the biblical faiths always involves claims about *real* people, living in *real* places, who acted in *real* events of the past, many of which are also cited in secular ancient history. . . .
>
> Because Judeo-Christianity has so thoroughly influenced Western culture, we are prone to imagine that all other world religions have a similarly solid historical base. This is by no means the case. It can, in fact, be argued that *every* religious system before or since Judaism and Christianity has avoided any significant interaction with history, and instead has asked its followers to believe, by sheer faith alone, the claimed revelations of its founder(s). . . .
>
> Or, whenever links with genuine history *are* claimed—as in several modern belief systems today—these are never verified by secular history or the findings of archaeology.[5]

Dr. Maier's words ring in harmony not only with the facts of history but with the experiences of life. Thieves, deceivers, and counterfeits—whether religious or otherwise—have no greater ally than obscurity. So

---

[5] *In the Fullness of Time* (New York: HarperCollins, 1989), xv, emphasis original. Dr. Paul L. Maier is the author, translator, and editor of numerous works relating to the history of Christianity. His published works include modern translations of Josephus and Eusebius and two popular historical novels, *Pontius Pilate* and *The Flames of Rome*.

when a rascal is confronted in cross-examination about his nefarious deeds, he invariably calls up his reserves from the murky swamps of willful ignorance. "Where were you last Saturday night, the seventeenth of June?" "I'm not sure." "Not sure? Just three days ago?" "Well, sometimes on Saturdays, I go to a friend's house, but not every Saturday." "What's the name of this friend?" "I don't remember which friend I was with. I've got lots of friends." "Is George C. Brown your friend?" "That all depends on how you define *is*." And on and on it goes. Deceivers are spooked even by the oncoming shadows of reality, including innocuous reality, for they never know when some meddlesome fact is going to do them in.

Not so the inspired writers. With daring frankness, the authors of Scripture interweave their writings with names, places, times, incidents, and anecdotes chronicled or alluded to in secular history—each one carrying an invitation to skeptical and suspicious antagonists to scrutinize and dismantle Scripture's claims.

And don't think they haven't tried! At each convergence of secular and sacred history, the scribes of the scholarly set have staked out their sifting rights and unloaded their dissecting tools. Acknowledging on the one hand that their aggregate anthology of ancient history has, by necessity, multiple blank pages in it, these scribes have nevertheless found a way to read in these blank pages the most devastating contradictions to Christianity. We often find these scholars trumpeting the news that their painstaking research compels them to say that history knows nothing of this or that incident or this or that personality in the Bible. Then at length we find them, a bit red-faced but not a bit repentant, announcing that a certain brilliant scholar with a shovel or a not-so-bright Bedouin with a goat has uncovered some ancient pottery that will help us fill in some of our empty pages; and, lo, it so happens that the biblical writers had this one right after all.[6]

MY APPROACH TO THE BIBLICAL STORY

As a story, the Word of God reflects, depicts, and reacts to the realities of life. The Word, in fact, not only depicts life, it is life (Heb. 4:12). Perhaps this is why God chose to reveal His thoughts to us in story form.

---

[6] The existence of the Hittites is a relatively well-known case in point; the existence of writing before the time of Moses is another.

Stories live on. Outlines and analyses turn yellow and die when exposed to the breath of life. Analytical studies have their place, of course, but only as organ donors for the living. It may be unsettling to think this way; but outlines, paradigms, and critical analyses of Scripture have basically the same function in the religious world as cadavers have in the medical field. Their value lies wholly in the patterns of knowledge they yield that can be taken from the morgue to the world of the living.

My approach to this study is governed by the dominant need I sense as I enter the Holy Oracle of God—the need to experience what I see in that sacred place. My plan, then, is more to follow the pulsations of the Word than simply to analyze them. My overriding desire is to lead the reader into the experiences and sensations I feel in this Holy Oracle. My method, in general, will be to tell what I have seen and felt as the Reader has narrated His Story to me—much, I would hope, as the brethren of Malachi's burden who "feared the Lord," when the Oracle was opened to them, "spake often one to another" of their experiences in the beauty of the Holy of Holies (Mal. 3:16).

An essential element in this approach—and, in my opinion, in any experiential approach to the Word of God—is imagination. To some of God's people, *imagination* has an irreverent tone to it. They see in it hues of the curse in Revelation on those who add to or take from the words of the Book. As a matter of fact, imagination—our picture-making facility— is a gift from God and is an essential ingredient of thought. Though some may be more visual than others in their thoughts, it is impossible for anyone to think without using this God-given facility; and, consequently, it is impossible for anyone to read the Bible experientially without imagination. In the Bible, the "most customary way of expressing God's truth is not the sermon or theological outline but the story, the poem, the vision, and the letter, all of them literary forms and products of the imagination."[7]

As I seek to follow the escalating drama of the Word, I would like to involve my readers in all the major segments of the drama; but by necessity, I will be highly selective in the illustrative scenes I show. The method I have chosen will not allow me, in most cases, to give reasons and refutations concerning interpretations; and it will not allow me to get involved

---

[7] Leland Ryken, *The Christian Imagination* (Grand Rapids: Zondervan, 1981), cited by Warren W. Wiersbe, *Preaching and Teaching with Imagination* (Wheaton, IL: Victor, 1994), 40.

in technical, linguistic, and theological arguments—though I will pay some deference to this feisty side of truth in the footnotes.

One other matter demands some comment. By the time a person reaches a milepost in life beyond his allotted threescore and ten (as I have), his list of creditors in the thought arenas of life has grown far beyond manageable proportions. And since the new thoughts have been warmly received by the natives and have mingled freely with them, the whole cerebral population can at times appear indigenous. Consequently, in my credits, I may have overlooked some of the creditors to whom I am deeply indebted. Not too long ago, while I was meditating on a certain subject, an exciting thought occurred to me. As the thought developed, I formulated in my mind a paragraph I just knew I could use to good effect in a sermon. "Thank you, Lord," I said to myself, "for the gift of creativity." A while later, I picked up a copy of Oehler's *Theology of the Old Testament*—and there was that "original" thought, a venerable centenarian, couched almost line for line in the same words!

If therefore it appears to you that I may have pilfered someone's well-earned cogitations, please call me before you call the police. I promise that, as much as lies within me (no pun intended), I will make it right.

I invite you, at last, to join with me in heart and experience as we survey the Holy Oracle. I want to share with you something of the song of songs that plays in my heart as a result of my visits to this place.

PART ONE

FOUNDATIONAL MATTERS

. . . inherit the kingdom prepared for you from the foundation of the world.

Then shall the King say unto them on his right hand, Come, ye blessed of my Father, inherit the kingdom prepared for you from the foundation of the world.

Matthew 25:34

THE FIRST ELEVEN CHAPTERS OF the Bible are foundational to the entire written revelation of God. A foundation provides the parameters and basis for the edifice. In effect, it is a herald of things to come; and as a herald, its purpose—its reason for being—is to support the edifice. The ultimate "message" of a structure is in the edifice, but the basis and guideline for that message is the foundation.

By its nature, a foundation tends to be sublimated, ignored, and even violated. Foundational problems abound in human structures. The most famous of these is the Leaning Tower of Pisa. Begun in AD 1173 as the final stage of Pisa's cathedral complex, this elaborate bell tower, reaching 185 feet into the sky, was designed to call the citizens of the city to worship. It became instead a curiosity, a tourist attraction, and a wrangling point for engineers.

What went wrong? In brief, the engineers failed to conform the edifice to its foundational parameters. The problem developed early in the construction process, and work was suspended several times. Nevertheless, a century of finagling did nothing to solve the problem. From the fourteenth century, when the tower was finally completed, to the twentieth, it continued in its refractory ways—basking in the attention it was getting. By 1990, the tower, in danger of collapse, was closed, and engineers worked for a decade to achieve a more respectable slant.

Bible students could learn a thing or two from the Leaning Tower. Over the centuries, many clever and creative biblical architects have constructed ornate, impressive towers on the holy place of scriptural revelation. In varying degrees, many have gone the way of the wonderful Tower of Pisa. Some have fallen of their own weight, but others have been so propped and perfected that their slant is hardly perceptible to the typical observer.

Our natural inclination when we examine a foundation is to view it in light of its edifice instead of vice versa. This, I think, is a greater danger for Bible students than it is for students of secular literature. By the time the typical Bible student gets around to seriously examining foundational matters, he already has strong, emotionally laden perceptions concerning the edifice that houses the oracle of God. Typically, he was quite oblivious to the foundation when he first experienced the life-giving power of this temple; and his new life has developed and grown in direct proportion to the accuracy of his perception of the temple's Resident.

The answer to this problem of unduly favoring our predispositions is constant realignment. We must get in the habit of constantly making sure we are still aligned with the foundation of the divine revelation. This section examines the understructure of the kingdom "prepared . . . from the foundation of the world."

CHAPTER ONE

IS THERE A UNIFYING THEME IN THE BIBLE?

UNITY IN THE DIVERSITY
OF THE BIBLE

IN MANY RESPECTS, THE DIVERSITY in the Bible is its most obvious feature. Rather than presenting His Word in one dramatic moment of history and one neatly outlined volume, God chose to give it to us in two volumes and sixty-six installments over more than fifteen hundred years. And rather than writing this sacred revelation with His own finger or communicating its words through angels, He chose to engage more than thirty human authors from different countries and cultures and whose occupations ranged from herdsman to king. And rather than creating a heavenly, sacredly static language to communicate His revelation, God chose to speak through three very human languages—languages whose words were jostled and shaped by the cultures in which the authors lived. And rather than dictating His words verbatim, He chose to form and filter them through those men's own experiences and personalities. Furthermore, in our well-meaning efforts to "organize" the Bible, we have divided it into 1,189 chapters and 41,173 verses. No wonder the typical Christian tends to read his Bible as the writer of Hebrews describes the Old Testament revelation—"at sundry times and in divers manners"!

But the wonder of the diversity of the Bible makes its unity all the more amazing. Given the same set of circumstances by which the Bible came into existence, what other book, sacred or secular, can claim anything comparable to the unity of the Bible? Over a century ago, Henry Rogers offered this challenge:

> By no process, let us shuffle the more copious existing materials as we may, or exercise the most discriminating arts of selection, could we compile a *mélange* equal in bulk to the Bible, that could for a moment cheat any ordinary mind into the belief that it formed an organic whole.[1]

No less compelling are the words of A. T. Pierson:

> The unity of the Bible is absolutely unique. Never elsewhere have so many different treatises, historical, biographical, ethical, prophetical, poetical, been combined together, making one Book, as all the hewn stone and timber make one building, or better still, as all the bones, muscles and ligaments combine in one body. This again, while indisputable as a fact, is unparalleled in literature, all the conditions being, humanly speaking, not only unfavourable, but fatal to such a combination.[2]

Virtually all believing Bible scholars have recognized the unity of the Bible; but even some liberal theologians have acknowledged it. For example, the renowned Old Testament scholar Dr. John Bright acknowledged that "while the complexity of the Bible is by no means to be minimized, there nevertheless runs through it a unifying theme which is not artificially imposed."[3]

DIVERSITY IN THE SEARCH FOR UNITY

But exactly what is the central theme of the Bible? The inspired writers compare the Bible to food (Deut. 8:3; Heb. 5:13–14; I Pet. 2:2), and most of us tend to use our Bibles as we use daily food. We look for spiritual nourishment, something to satisfy the needs of our souls. Our default approach to the Bible is more analytical than comprehensive. As with our table food, we take our spiritual nourishment in small bites. Except when we are preparing Sunday school lessons or sermons, most of us don't even stop to think of the Bible's dominant themes, much less of

---

[1] Cited by Newman Watts, *The Incomparable Book* (New York: The American Tract Society, 1940), 75.

[2] Ibid.

[3] John Bright, *The Kingdom of God* (New York: Abingdon-Cokesbury Press, 1953), 10.

its overall message. Unfortunately, the same is largely true of Bible commentators. Focused on the details, particularly of the difficult or controversial passages, they generally relegate discussion on the overall message of the Bible to a line or two—or, worse yet, to a pronouncement—in the introduction.

When pressed, conservative Bible scholars readily agree that there is a unifying theme; but they disagree as to precisely what that theme is—or at least as to how to express the theme. As strange as this circumstance may appear, it is not that unnatural in human experience. It is quite common, for example, for a person to recognize a general truth without understanding the dynamic components of that truth. For example, virtually everyone perceives that the body is a united organism; but how many can identify the mysterious catalysts that harmonize the functions of the body?

The Bible, likewise, is a living organism (John 1:1–4; 6:50–51; Heb. 4:12; I Pet. 1:23). Each part of the Word is organically connected with the whole, and the whole supports each part. As with the body, we may marvel at the power and beauty of the Word in its various parts. But we cannot truly comprehend its full message unless we see and treat it as a living organism—with an ultimate purpose as well as many subsidiary ones.

Scholars who discuss the unifying theme of the Bible often propose one of the following three: Christ, Redemption, or the kingdom of God.[4] These three proposals are merely different aspects of one grand theme. If we focus on any one of these proposals, each could lay claim to being a dominant theme in the Bible.

Christ as a Prominent Theme in the Bible

In John 1:1, Christ is called the *Word* (*logos*). Whatever else this expression may connote, it identifies Christ with the Word of God—the revelation of the mind of God to man (John 1:18; Matt. 11:27; Heb. 1:3). To the Jews Jesus said, "You search the Scriptures, because you think that in them you have eternal life; and it is these that bear witness of Me," suggesting that in their avid searching of Scripture, they had missed the whole point—Christ.[5] And during His four-hour walk to Emmaus

---

[4] The glory of God is another commonly proposed theme.

[5] John. 5:39, NASB. In the Greek, the opening words of this verse could be translated either as a command, as in the KJV, or as a statement of fact. The context supports the latter approach.

with Cleopas and his friend, the risen Savior "expounded unto them in all the scriptures the things concerning himself" (Luke 24:27*b*; cf. Acts 27:32–35). Paul testified that the veil by which the Jews were blinded as they read the Old Testament is "done away in Christ" (II Cor. 3:14*b*), for the key to understanding the Scriptures is Christ.

Redemption as a Prominent Theme of the Bible

The story of the Bible is the story of man's redemption. There can be no serious question that Redemption is a dominant theme in the Bible. At the Triumphal Entry, the multitudes chanted praise to Christ from Psalm 118, "Hosanna to the Son of David: Blessed is he that cometh in the name of the Lord; Hosanna in the highest" (Matt. 21:9; Ps. 118:25–26). The word *Hosanna*, borrowed from the Hebrew, means "Save now!" Though later developments exposed the ambivalence of this crowd, their words on this occasion are tantamount to an official recognition of Jesus of Nazareth as their Messiah and Savior. After announcing that Mary was to bear a son as a virgin, the angel instructed Joseph, "Thou shalt call his name JESUS: for he shall save his people from their sins" (Matt. 1:21*b*). From the very introduction of sin into the world, God promised that the seed of the woman would defeat Satan and bring salvation (Gen. 3:15). Throughout the Bible, the Lord is repeatedly called—and repeatedly identifies Himself as—Savior (e.g., II Sam. 22:3; Ps. 106:21; Isa. 43:3; 60:16). And in the grand finale of the Bible, the book of Revelation, the conclusion of the age is announced in words that focus on the work of redemption: "And I heard a loud voice saying in heaven, Now is come salvation, and strength, and the kingdom of our God, and the power of his Christ: for the accuser of our brethren is cast down, which accused them before our God day and night" (Rev. 12:10).

The Kingdom of God as a Prominent Theme of the Bible

At the judgment of the nations in the end times, the King says to those on His right hand, "Come, ye blessed of my Father, inherit the kingdom prepared for you from the foundation of the world" (Matt. 25:34*b*). In this awesome context of judgment, it is easy to overlook the striking statement that the kingdom of the righteous has been in preparation "from the foundation of the world." John's announcement of the conclusion of the age also focuses on the coming of this kingdom: "And I heard a loud voice saying in heaven, Now is come salvation, and strength, and the kingdom of our God, and the power of his Christ."

Furthermore, the inspired writers make it abundantly clear that John the Baptist (the forerunner of the Messiah) and the Messiah Himself both focused on the kingdom of God. John the Baptist introduced his preparatory ministry with the words "Repent ye: for the kingdom of heaven is at hand" (Matt. 3:2). Mark summarizes the preaching ministry of Jesus as "preaching the gospel of the kingdom of God" (Mark 1:14; cf. Matt. 4:17, 23).

The focus in the Gospels on the kingdom of God only confirms and expands the focus of the Old Testament. It could well be said that the entire ministry of the Old Testament prophets was to prepare for the coming kingdom of God. When our Lord included the petition "Thy kingdom come" in His model prayer (Matt. 6:10; Luke 11:2), He was echoing a well-established Jewish tradition. In fact, ancient rabbis had decreed, "That prayer in which there is no mention made of the kingdom of heaven, is *not* a prayer."[6]

The Unifying Theme: A "Threefold Cord"

These three dominant themes—Christ, Redemption, and the kingdom of God—are inseparably interwoven throughout the Bible. They are really one theme. **The Bible is the story of the redemption and reign of man in God's kingdom through Christ, the Savior and King.**

Whenever any one of these is in view the other two are implicit. The appearance of Christ in His sovereignty presupposes His work in salvation. The coming of the kingdom depends on the coming of the King. The citizens of the kingdom are the redeemed who have submitted themselves to the King.

In ancient times, it was natural to think of a savior and a king as one and the same. Human nature being what it is, people were commonly in need of a savior—someone strong and wise enough to rescue them from their troubles and to maintain their freedom through strong (if not equitable) leadership. Consequently, early in Israel's history the inspired writers present God, not simply as Savior or as King, but also as Savior-King. "For God is my King of old, working salvation in the midst of the earth" (Ps. 74:12). "For the Lord is our judge, the Lord is our lawgiver, the Lord is our king; he will save us" (Isa. 33:22). "I will be thy king: where is any other that may save thee in all thy cities? and thy judges of whom thou

---

[6] Albert Barnes, *Notes on the Old Testament* (Grand Rapids: Baker, 1961), at Matt. 6:10.

saidst, Give me a king and princes?" (Hosea 13:10; cf. Ps. 25:5; 27:9; Mic. 7:7).

This concept of a savior-king applied quite naturally to men as well. The Hebrew word for *save, savior* (*yasha*) is used of judges in Israel who, after saving the people from their enemies, ruled over them (Judges 3:9, 3:15; 8:22); and the word is later used of human kings (e.g., II Kings 13:5). As would be expected from the general use of the term, *savior* was often used as a title of honor for secular kings in ancient times. Even "savior of the world" was ascribed to Julius Caesar and to later Roman emperors.[7]

To say simply that Christ is the unifying theme of the Bible is fine so long as we give credit to Christ where credit is due. Likewise, some say that Redemption or salvation is the unifying theme. This is fine so long as we recognize that salvation is integrally interwoven with Jesus Christ—and only with Him. Even to say that the kingdom of God is the theme is fine, as long as you recognize this term in the full orb of its biblical setting. Christ is the King, He is the reason for the existence of the kingdom, and He is the fulfillment of the kingdom.

MY FOCUS ON THE KINGDOM OF GOD

This study will focus on the Bible's developing story of the kingdom of God, emphasizing God's purpose for man to reign with Him in that kingdom. As I have intimated in the discussion above, we might utilize one aspect of this "threefold cord" to represent the whole. We might say, for example, that Christ is the unifying theme of the Bible; but if our view of Christ is unscripturally narrow, our "unifying theme" will be inaccurate. If we see Christ only as Savior, either we will miss much of the Bible's message or our interpretation will be skewed; for Christ is also the King and Judge of His Father's kingdom.

I have chosen to focus on the kingdom of God for these reasons: (1) since this aspect of the unifying theme of the Bible has been widely neglected in Bible study, Bible students commonly miss much of the Bible's contextual message; (2) without question, the kingdom of God

---

[7] Erich Sauer, *The King of the Earth* (Grand Rapids: Eerdmans, 1962), 133.

is a dominant subject in the Bible that interplays in some way with virtually everything the inspired writers tell us; (3) if we fail to recognize the importance of this dominant subject, we will inevitably have a deficient perception of Christ—for God has chosen to present His Son, the Messiah, in the context of His kingdom. Man's redemption through Christ, his Savior and King, is for the ultimate purpose of his reigning in His kingdom; and (4) the Creator's announced purpose for man to fill and dominate the earth (Gen. 1:26–28) is integrally tied to His kingdom. The dominance of mankind over the earth will be accomplished, through the work of Christ, in the context of God's eternal kingdom.

If indeed reigning with God in His kingdom is an integral part of the unifying theme of the Bible (as I believe it is), there should be interplay throughout the Bible on this sublime concept. "If a work consists of one idea, although that one idea is very comprehensive and has many ramifications, then the only way in which it can be set forth is as an organism. The whole idea will be in every part. The beginning cannot be properly understood unless you know also the end."[8]

Does this idea—the dominance of the kingdom of God in the Bible—sound radical or even unorthodox to you? Perhaps you're saying, "I never heard this before," or (worse) "Are you the only nut who thinks this way?"

Let me assure you that many others (not other nuts!) have come to the same conclusions. Let me give you a few statements from recognized Bible scholars of various theological persuasions. Alva J. McClain, in his classic work, *The Greatness of the Kingdom*, says concerning the essence of Old Testament prophecy,

> Nothing is clearer, according to Old Testament prophecy, than that the great goal of the Lord's people was centered in the arrival of God's Kingdom on earth.[9]

In another classic work, *The Life and Times of Jesus the Messiah*, the Jewish-Christian scholar Alfred Edersheim says this concerning the Old Testament foundation for New Testament expectations:

> The most important point here is to keep in mind the organic *unity* of the Old Testament. Its predictions are not isolated, but features of one grand prophetic picture; . . . its history, not loosely connected events, but an organic

---

[8] Adolph Saphir, *Divine Unity of Scripture* (Grand Rapids: Kregel, 1984), 199–200.

[9] Alva J. McClain, *The Greatness of the Kingdom* (Winona Lake, IN: BMH Books, 1974), 335.

development tending towards a definite end . . . . The idea, underlying all, is God's gracious manifestation in the world—the Kingdom of God.[10]

Referring to the theme of the Gospels, the same author says,

> Just as the Old Testament gives neither the national history of Israel, nor the biography of its heroes, but a history of the Kingdom of God in its progressive development, so the Gospels present not a "life of Christ," but the history of the Kingdom of God in its progressive manifestation.[11]

The renowned Scottish theologian James Orr sees the doctrine of the kingdom of God as rooted in the first chapter of Genesis and as the central idea in Old Testament revelation.

> The real basis for the idea of the kingdom of God is already laid in the Creation history. . . . The Creation narrative . . . with its delegation to man of "dominion" over the creatures (cf. Ps. 8), already lays down this doctrine . . . . The history of OT revelation, therefore, is simply . . . the history of the developing kingdom of God. . . . from the first a kingdom of grace and salvation. Herein, from the biblical point of view, lies the key to all historical developments, the explanation of all arrangements and movements of Divine providence.[12]

George N. H. Peters (1825–1909), author of *The Theocratic Kingdom*, a benchmark work on this theme, declared that "the Scriptures cannot be rightly comprehended without a due knowledge of this kingdom." He notes that a number of writers in his day, while differing from his premillennial viewpoint, "correctly make the kingdom of God *the central* topic around which all other doctrines logically arrange themselves . . . apprehending the kingdom of God as the guiding idea." Peters says about the New Testament apostles,

> The entire tenor of the New Test. impresses us, that their superior qualifications as teachers arises from their acquaintance with the doctrine of the king, resulting from the personal instructions received from Christ, and the subsequent special guidance of the Spirit.[13]

---

[10] *The Life and Times of Jesus the Messiah* (Grand Rapids: Eerdmans, repr. 1974), 1:160, emphasis original.

[11] Ibid, 1:570.

[12] "Kingdom of God," in *A Dictionary of the Bible*, James Hastings, ed. (New York: Charles Scribner's Sons, 1911).

[13] *The Theocratic Kingdom* (New York: Funk and Wagnalls, 1884; Grand Rapids: Kregel, 1988), 1:29, 141, emphasis original. Citations are to the Kregel edition.

Biblical Aspects of the Kingdom of God

As McClain observes, the expression *kingdom of God* is a biblical term, and we must therefore define it by its scriptural usage. He suggests, further, that the concept of a kingdom assumes at least three essential elements: a *ruler* with authority and power; a *realm* of subjects; and a *reign*, the actual exercise of sovereign power.[14] When the scriptural writers refer to the kingdom of God, they always assume these three essential elements. Though they refer to it in various contexts and with a variety of emphases, their references can nevertheless be grouped under two basic scriptural perceptions of the kingdom of God.

The Universal Kingdom of God

The scriptural writers recognize that God is, always has been, and always will be the supreme Sovereign of the universe. "Thy kingdom is an everlasting kingdom, and thy dominion endureth throughout all generations" (Ps. 145:13). As Creator and supreme Commander, God puts whom He will on the thrones of the world—and removes them at His pleasure.

> This matter is by the decree of the watchers, and the demand by the word of the holy ones: to the intent that the living may know that the most High ruleth in the kingdom of men, and giveth it to whomsoever he will, and setteth up over it the basest of men (Dan. 4:17).

> I have made the earth, the man and the beast that are upon the ground, by my great power and by my outstretched arm, and have given it unto whom it seemed meet unto me (Jer. 27:5).

> For there is no power but of God: the powers that be are ordained of God (Rom. 13:1*b*).

To godly believers, this universal rule of God as supreme King was a present reality. It affected the way they thought and reacted in a world dominated by kings and kingdoms antagonistic to the people of God and their earthly kingdom. David recognized this principle when he penned Psalm 2.

> Why do the heathen rage, and the people imagine a vain thing? The kings of the earth set themselves, and the rulers take counsel together, against the Lord, and against his anointed, saying, Let us break their bands asunder, and cast away their cords from us. He that sitteth in the heavens shall laugh: the

---

[14] *The Greatness of the Kingdom*, 16–17.

Lord shall have them in derision. Then shall he speak unto them in his wrath, and vex them in his sore displeasure. Yet have I set my king upon my holy hill of Zion (vv. 1–6; cf. Acts 4:25–28).

The Earthly Covenant Kingdom of God

The earthly covenant kingdom of God is in reality an aspect of the universal kingdom. The preparations for man to inherit this kingdom began at the foundation of the world, when God made man in his image and ordained that he should have dominion over the earth (Matt. 25:34; Gen. 1:26–28).

Through His covenant with Abraham, God ordained that the descendants of this Patriarch, the people of Israel, would represent this aspect of His kingdom in the land of Canaan. Through Abraham's promised Seed, the Messiah, this earthly kingdom would ultimately fulfill God's purpose for man to reign with Him.

This covenant kingdom could be referred to as the coming kingdom or the millennial kingdom. It will be established in the last days when its King, the Messiah, returns to earth with His glorified saints.[15]

After the Messiah's millennial reign, when all His enemies are put under His feet, He will give His kingdom over to the Father; and it will take its place in the universal, eternal kingdom of God. "Then cometh the end, when he shall have delivered up the kingdom to God, even the Father; when he shall have put down all rule and all authority and power. For he must reign, till he hath put all enemies under his feet" (I Cor. 15:24–25).

Following the universal laws of language, the inspired writers sometimes use terms like *the kingdom of God* to describe the earthly people of the kingdom, professed believers in all ages. For example, Paul speaks of God delivering us from the power of darkness and translating us "into the kingdom of his dear Son" (Col. 1:13). Though earthly saints have not yet received their full inheritance, they are, even on earth, kingdom citizens. Paul, when persecuted and mistreated in the Roman world, could claim the privileges of a Roman citizen and appeal to the emperor for justice.

---

[15] McClain uses the term *Mediatorial Kingdom* as a convenient designation for the earthly covenant kingdom of God. He bases this term on the idea that the method of rule in this phase of God's kingdom is through an earthly mediator, "a divinely chosen representative who not only speaks and acts for God but also represents the people before God." The adjective "universal," he says, refers to the extent of rule; "mediatorial," to the method of rule. *The Greatness of the Kingdom*, 21, 41.

Likewise, the believer as a citizen of the covenant kingdom can appeal to his King and expect in time to receive his full inheritance.

Orchestration of the Unifying Theme

Considered as a whole, the Bible is a story—the grandest of all stories, but nevertheless a story. As other writers often do, the inspired writers draw on many forms of communication to develop their message. Interwoven into the story of the Bible are narratives, speeches, poems, explanations, exhortations, illustrations—whatever is necessary to get the message across—but all these instruments of communication are orchestrated to sound through the depths of man's soul to a grand finale. If we follow this musical score through all of its intonations and modulations to its climax, we will see the overwhelming impact of its message.

We do this with other good literature. As we read through a well-written book, we almost intuitively gather elements that will play into the impact of the conclusion. Consider, for example, Charles Dickens' *A Tale of Two Cities*. The opening words of this classic are among the most famous in English literature:

> It was the best of times, it was the worst of times, it was the age of wisdom, it was the age of foolishness, it was the epoch of belief, it was the epoch of incredulity, it was the season of Light, it was the season of Darkness, it was the spring of hope, it was the winter of despair, we had everything before us, we had nothing before us, we were all going direct to Heaven, we were all going direct the other way.

To many a beleaguered lit student, these are just words to memorize or to match with "one of the guys we have to know." To the thoughtful reader, these words contain in embryonic form the message of the entire book. In the end, Sydney Carton, a ne'er-do-well, a man who had incriminated himself with the words "I care for no man on earth," goes to the guillotine for the husband of the woman he loves. As he climbs the stairs to meet his fate, he utters these words, "It is a far, far better thing that I do, than I have ever done; it is a far, far better rest that I go to, than I have ever known"—so, it was the best of times, it was the worst of times.

If we expect this type of development in uninspired literature, should we not expect it in the inspired Volume? And indeed, when we open our divine Book, we find it to be a Book wrought out in human experience—in the dramas, the delights, the disappointments, and the depressions of life. So it should come as no surprise to us, when we look at the first pages of our Book, to find in embryo a theme that—though its features may not be yet fully discernible—will play into our souls and through our experiences, preparing us for the grand finale.

In Genesis the serpent appears, subtle and supple, perversely pleasing to his unwary victims. In Revelation he is the dragon, "that old serpent," now vicious and gargantuan with the blood of the victims of the ages. In Genesis there is the Tree of Life, guarded by the fiery sword of cherubim. In Revelation, the tree is open to all for the healing of the nations. Christ appears as the Alpha and Omega, the beginning and the end—a reminder that the Redeemer Who was present during the first black night of sin will be there to exult in the new day, having written in His blood the final letter in the story of Redemption.

Between Eden and the Isle of Patmos, the biblical theme plays its chords through the story of mankind, always in harmony with the first notes of the piece and always, with sound of trumpets, moving toward the last. Even if we find ourselves captured at times by some variant melody, it is only to discover eventually that the variation is not deviant after all but in tune with the rest of the great symphony of God.

CHAPTER TWO

"FROM THE FOUNDATION OF THE WORLD"

THE FIRST "READERS" OF THE BIBLE

IT WAS TO UNLIKELY PEOPLE in an unlikely place that the work began of inscribing the revelation of God's plan for man. The unlikely place was the wilderness of Sinai. Barren, foreboding, presiding imperiously over its wasteland domain, Mount Sinai was far removed in time and space—and in character—from the Garden of Eden. There, in the first sanctuary of God's revelation to man, the very atmosphere must have breathed benedictions on the communion between heaven and earth. On Mount Sinai, as far as the eye can see, all seems brindled with hues of the curse. Even the living creatures in this wasteland speak more of death than of life. A bit of movement on a barren rock turns out to be a snake or tumbleweed. In the sky, circling vultures mark a rude new gravesite. Even the sun seems to glare angrily at the doleful creatures it illuminates. Forty years later, Moses described this meeting of God with Israel with the words "He found him in a desert land, and in the waste howling wilderness" (Deut. 32:10).

The unlikely people for this written revelation were the people of Israel. Until recently, they had been slaves in Egypt. Over four centuries before, the nation had been transplanted in embryonic form to Egypt. Shepherds by trade and tradition, they were viewed by the Egyptians as the offscouring of humanity (Gen. 43:32; 46:34)—a people to be ostracized, except as they could be used to serve higher levels of humanity.

Strange as it may seem, the Egyptians' disdainful demeanor was the very reason God brought the sons of Jacob to Egypt in the first place. In Canaan, the land destined to be their inheritance, the sons of Jacob were becoming Canaanites. Anger, envy, lust, treachery—all the noxious qualities indigenous to Canaan—had settled into the culture of the children of Jacob. Reuben, the firstborn and heir apparent, had violated his father's bed. Of Simeon and Levi, next in line for inheritance rights, the prophet Jacob said, "Instruments of cruelty are in their habitations. . . . Cursed be their anger, for it was fierce; and their wrath, for it was cruel" (Gen. 49:5b, 7a). Judah, who proved to be one of the nobler sons of Jacob, had through Canaanite licentiousness been lured into incest. With one exception, all were guilty of rejecting the spiritual light that came through Jacob; and all but the youngest were guilty of cruel treachery against the one exception, Joseph.

By necessity then, God arranged to transplant these budding Canaanites. Had the Lord left them in Canaan, the people He had ordained to preserve and proclaim His message would have been absorbed into Canaan's culture and condemnation. In Egypt, however, cultural (if not moral) separation would be forced upon the children of Jacob. Through the contrary winds of favor and disfavor in the land of Goshen, Israel could maintain its ethnic identity through four centuries in Egypt.

But though Egypt would not digest Israel, Israel developed a taste for Egypt (Exod. 32:8; cf. I Kings 12:28). No wonder, really. For the ordinary mortal, the lure of Egyptian life, philosophy, and religion was overwhelming. Herodotus said of the Egyptians, "They are religious to excess, beyond any other nation in the world."[1] Their temples were magnificent and awe-inspiring. Graffiti of an ancient tourist visiting Djoser's Step Pyramid reveals something of the reverent wonder these shrines inspired: "The scribe, Ahmose, son of Iptah, came to see the temple of Djoser. He found it as though heaven were within it, Re [the ancient Egyptian sun god] rising in it."[2]

---

[1] *Herodotus: The Histories* (New York: Penguin, 1972), 143.

[2] Gilbert M. Grosvenor, ed., *Ancient Egypt: Discovering Its Splendors* (Washington, DC: National Geographic Society, 1978), 9. Some scholars believe that this scribe, Ahmose, may have been a contemporary of Moses. Whatever the case, Djoser's Step Pyramid would have been built centuries before the time of Moses or Ahmose.

In Egypt, as in ancient Athens, it must have sometimes seemed easier to find a god than a man.[3] Everywhere you looked, there was a god or a representation of a god. Even human beings were prospective gods.[4] As with most pagan religions, devotees viewed certain gods as presiding over specific realms of life or conditions in life. If a woman were pregnant, she would appeal to the god of fertility. When a man traveled by sea, he would seek help from the god of the sea. If a man were doing business in a certain town, he would court the favor of that town's god. So well ingrained was this ritual of deference to territorial deities that when a king conquered enemy territory, he didn't destroy the defeated gods of that land; he sought instead to win their favor.

So the unlikely people to whom this revelation was addressed were in legacy and looks, Israelites; in heart, Canaanites; and by culture and practice, Egyptians.

Foundational Principles for Reigning with God

It is in this historical, geographical, and cultural context that we must seek to understand this first revelation of God in the Bible. To these rescued slaves in the wilderness, what exactly did God reveal about Himself and about His plans that would serve as a foundation for their new lives? The salient points of this foundational revelation call for man to recognize three interdependent principles. If he is to fulfill his purpose in life, he must recognize (1) that God is absolutely sovereign over all realms of life in the universe; (2) that God made man in His image to reign with Him over His earthly kingdom; and (3) that the Creator is the Master we must imitate.

---

[3] Petronius, a traveler in the first century AD, wrote this of Athens. Barnes's *Notes* relative to Acts 17:16.

[4] "They saw their gods every hour of the day and night, in sun and moon and stars, in the Nile and its cliffs, in flowers and in animals. And in human beings, for the goal of their religion was the transformation of human beings into gods—or gods into human beings." Virginia Lee Davis, "Pathway to the Gods" in *Ancient Egypt*, 154. "There seems to have been a god linked to or representative of nearly everything in the world, from the physical facets of nature to abstract notions of the human condition. . . . There were plenty of gods to go around to suit any given occasion, and two or more gods could even be combined." Donald P. Ryan, *The Complete Idiot's Guide to Ancient Egypt* (Indianapolis: Alpha Books, 2002), 74.

Recognize God's Sovereignty over All of Life

The central revelation of the Creation story (Gen. 1:1–31) is that God alone is the Source and Sustainer of every realm of life. Instead of simply telling us that God created all things, the inspired writer leads us step by step through six realms of life—realms commonly attributed to the gods of this world—and tells us that God alone is sovereign. There is no god of light to whom we owe allegiance. Nor is there a god of the sea to whom we should pay respect, nor a god of the land we should worship. God is sovereign over all of life, the Source and Sustainer of all. Therefore, we should appeal to Him and Him alone for our needs and desires in all aspects of life—and He alone should be the object of our worship.

The people of Israel could not have been totally ignorant of this foundational truth about God. Their fathers from Abraham on had passed down the truth of the Creator God from generation to generation. Even those outside the favored nation of Israel, including the Egyptians, had heard of the one true God, the Creator of all.[5]

But the people of Israel had gotten Egyptian hearts. They had absorbed the philosophy of the world and, like the people of the world, had developed a capacity to ignore the true God. This opening revelation, therefore, while not a totally new revelation to the people of Israel, was a call for them to recognize anew the true God as the Author and Sustainer of all life. They needed to recognize that Elohim is the Absolute Sovereign over every realm of life. There are no other gods responsible for various spheres of the universe. There is no sun god or moon god. There is no god of the sea or of agriculture. There is not a particular god to whom man should appeal if he changes his status in life or if he needs help with a decision or if he encounters difficulties. In every circumstance, in each realm of life, he is to look to Elohim alone as his Source and Sustainer. Elohim alone is sovereign in the universe, and He is absolutely sovereign.

The message that the people of God were to receive by this revelation is that however variegated the vicissitudes of life's domains may be, there is only one God Who is truly sovereign over every dominion. As we enter into new and sometimes fearful realms of life, there is no legitimate—or profitable—appeal we can make to "the powers that be" in that realm.

---

[5] For documentation and striking illustrations of the knowledge of the true God among pagan people, see Don Richardson, *Eternity in Their Hearts* (Ventura, CA: Regal Books, 1984).

This message, which those of us in the New Testament era tend to relegate to the idolatrous high places of the distant past, is meant for all. It was to New Testament saints that the apostle John wrote, "Little children, keep yourselves from idols" (I John 5:21; cf. I Cor. 10:17; II Cor. 6:16–17). This message is foundational in the Bible because it is foundational to man's purpose in life.

Fundamentally, our pilgrimage involves a divinely ordained discipleship program that leads us successively through new realms of potential spiritual enlightenment and new realms of spiritual testing. The issue in each case is whether we are going to bow to the established gods of these new realms or look to the true Sovereign of the domain. The battle of life, in each case, is whether we should submit to the gods entrenched in the new realm or look for new light and wonders from the God of all realms. Each time we set foot on new territory, we face anew Solomon's test of spiritual wisdom,

> Trust in the Lord with all thine heart; and lean not unto thine own understanding. In all thy ways acknowledge him, and he shall direct thy paths. Be not wise in thine own eyes: fear the Lord, and depart from evil (Prov. 3:5–7).

Recognize That Man Is Destined to Reign with God

It is in the context, then, of God's absolute sovereignty over all realms of life that He reveals His plan and purpose for man:

> And God said, Let us make man in our image, after our likeness: and let them have dominion over the fish of the sea, and over the fowl of the air, and over the cattle, and over all the earth, and over every creeping thing that creepeth upon the earth. So God created man in his own image, in the image of God created he him; male and female created he them. And God blessed them, and God said unto them, Be fruitful, and multiply, and replenish the earth, and subdue it: and have dominion over the fish of the sea, and over the fowl of the air, and over every living thing that moveth upon the earth (Gen. 1:26–28).

John Bunyan, in his poetic "Apology" for Pilgrim's Progress, depicted the development of the theme for his classic work with these quaint lines:

> *For, having now my method by the end,*
> *Still as I pulled, it came; and so I penned*
> *It down; until it came at last to be,*
> *For length and breadth, the bigness which you see.*

In his own inimitable fashion, Bunyan might have said something similar about the "thread" of Genesis 1:26–28. If one pulls carefully on this thread, the whole message of the Bible will unfold. The passage tells us that God made man in His image to have mankind reign with Him over His earthly kingdom. In some way, everything in the Bible relates to this profound statement of God's design of man and His plan for man.

We are tempted to say that the fall of man negated the promise of this passage. But aside from the fact that these words—written thousands of years after that tragedy—were addressed to fallen Israel, this passage gives us the immutable purpose of God. Though marred and defiled by the Fall, man is still a creature made in the image of God (Gen. 9:6); and God's purpose—to be fulfilled through His redemptive work—is still for man to reign with Him (Rev. 1:5–6; 20:4). Through prophetic insight, David recognized that this divine purpose includes the literal fulfillment of the command for man to "have dominion over the fish of the sea, and over the fowl of the air, and over every living thing that moveth upon the earth." He asked,

> What is man, that thou art mindful of him? and the son of man, that thou visitest him? For thou hast made him a little lower than the angels, and hast crowned him with glory and honour. Thou madest him to have dominion over the works of thy hands; thou hast put all things under his feet: all sheep and oxen, yea, and the beasts of the field; the fowl of the air, and the fish of the sea, and whatsoever passeth through the paths of the seas (Ps. 8:4–8).[6]

According to some interpreters, the writer of Hebrews (in 2:6–9) applies Psalm 8:4–8 exclusively to Christ; but even those who favor this interpretation[7] acknowledge that the context of Psalm 8 requires that these words be applied to man. In fact, David's words evidently refer to the promise of Genesis 1:26–28. In their context, the words in the Hebrews quotation "but now we see not yet all things put under him" are the writer's comment on David's words concerning God's promise that man is to have dominion over all created creatures (Heb. 2:8; Ps. 8:6); and the writer's use of the expression "not yet" reveals that he fully expected all things to be subjected to redeemed man eventually.

---

[6] Remarkably, the Hebrew literally reads "a little lower than Elohim." The reading *angels* is from the Septuagint translation, which the writer of Hebrews follows (Heb. 2:7).

[7] For example, Albert Barnes.

The key to interpreting the Hebrews passage lies in the phrase "but we see Jesus" (Heb. 2:9). In essence, the writer of Hebrews is saying, "God promised through David that He would put all things in subjection under man's feet. We have not yet seen this promise fulfilled in man, but we see Jesus, the Captain and Forerunner of our salvation. Through His redemptive work, He provided for the fulfillment of the promise that we will have dominion over all the works of His hands."[8]

If we look now at this statement of man's created nature and destiny (Gen. 1:26–28) in the light of the general context of this section, we see this principle forming: **man's royal destiny is integrally related to his recognition of God's absolute sovereignty.** To the extent that man recognizes the sovereignty of God in every realm of life, to that extent he will reign with Him.

Recognize the Creator as the Master to Imitate

The work of creation culminates—rather strangely, it appears to some—in a day of rest for God:

> Thus the heavens and the earth were finished, and all the host of them. And on the seventh day God ended his work which he had made; and he rested on the seventh day from all his work which he had made. And God blessed the seventh day, and sanctified it: because that in it he had rested from all his work which God created and made (Gen. 2:1–3).

Three striking features arrest our attention in this first revelation of the Sabbath: (1) why is the revelation of the Sabbath a part of the Creation story? (2) if the Sabbath was designed for man's rest, why does this first revelation of it speak of God resting? (3) why, even before the fall of man, was a whole day each week set aside for its observance?

---

[8] It is noteworthy, in this connection, that the inspired writer uses the human name Jesus (without any accompanying designation) for the Savior here. This is contextually very significant. As Westcott observes, "The personal name Jesus . . . always fixes attention on the Lord's humanity." *Epistle to the Hebrews* (Grand Rapids: Eerdmans, n.d.), 45. By his emphatic use of *Jesus* here, the inspired writer is calling attention to the fact that Christ in His manhood fulfilled God's original plan for man to reign over all nature and, by so doing, He opened the way for all redeemed mankind to reign with Him. "In 'the Son of man' (Jesus) then there is the assurance that man's sovereignty shall be gained." Ibid. "From this passage it appears, that with the single exception of Him who is to put all things under him, i.e., God, all things are to be put under man." John Brown, *An Exposition of Hebrews* (repr., Fort Washington, PA: Banner of Truth Trust, 1961), 94.

Part of the Creation Story?

The Creation story clearly extends through 2:3, which includes the account of God resting on the seventh day. What is the significance of these three sentences as a part of the Creation story? In what way do these statements support the message of the Creation story—that God is the Source and Sustainer of all life? And in what way do these words interact with God's purpose for man—that he should reign with Him over His earthly kingdom?

These words in this opening revelation tell us that the concept of the Sabbath is foundational to God's plan. Because of Jewish, cultic, and even Christian misuse of the Sabbath principle, we are naturally inclined to react against such statements. Nevertheless, the biblical revelation concerning the importance of the Sabbath in God's plan is compelling. Not only does the Lord present the Sabbath to us in His foundational revelation of creation, but He presents it again in the Ten Commandments, His revelation of His foundational laws for mankind.

Furthermore, the prophets clearly saw keeping the Sabbath as essential to the spiritual health of Israel. During his lifetime, Isaiah witnessed the fall of Israel and was called upon to visit his beloved nation Judah in the intensive care unit, her "whole head . . . sick, and the whole heart faint" (1:5b). So what was the prophet's counsel during this desperate time?

> Thus saith the Lord, Keep ye judgment, and do justice: for my salvation is near to come, and my righteousness to be revealed. Blessed is the man that doeth this, and the son of man that layeth hold on it; that keepeth the sabbath from polluting it, and keepeth his hand from doing any evil (Isa. 56:1–2).

Of all the potential cures he could have mentioned, he told them, in effect, that keeping the Sabbath was a key to their recovery (cf. Isa. 58:13–14; Jer. 17:24–25; Ezek. 20:20).

God Resting?

Why does this passage speak of God, rather than man, resting? This opening passage of the Bible reveals that just as God is the Author and Sustainer of all life, He is also the finisher of all (cf. Heb. 12:2). He "rests" in the sense that He is satisfied with His completed work—much as a master artist rests satisfied after he puts his final touches on a painting. Nothing can be added to what the Creator has done, and no one can keep His created work from fulfilling His ultimate purpose. Following the double announcement that the work of Creation was finished, the statement that God rested on the seventh day tells us that He was satisfied with the created universe—that it fulfilled His purpose.

But fundamental to our understanding God's purpose in establishing the Sabbath is what our Lord proclaimed in the face of ritualistic violation of the divine plan: "The sabbath was made for man, and not man for the sabbath" (Mark 2:27). God clearly has man in view when he proclaims that the seventh day is blessed and sanctified. The children of Israel were familiar with the Sabbath requirement before they reached Mount Sinai (Exod. 16:23ff.). Therefore, they knew that God expected them to rest on that day. This first revelation of the Sabbath suggests that man should imitate God and rest on that day in satisfied contemplation of the completed work of Creation.

The writer of Hebrews (4:1–10) suggests that the concept of the Sabbath is essentially related to man's faith in God.[9] In essence, the Sabbath was to be man's declaration of his absolute confidence in and satisfaction with his Creator. This confidence and satisfaction would include, of course, the works of the Creator. The man who has a satisfying confidence in his Creator will be satisfied also with the realm his Creator has chosen for him. This principle applied even to Adam and Eve before the Fall. (In fact, it was the violation of this principle that produced the Fall.) Man's development in the image of God depended fully on his willingness to rest confidently in the judgment and benevolent plan of his Sovereign Creator.

---

[9] Interpreters differ as to whether the "rest" of Hebrews 3:11–4:11 refers to celestial (eternal) rest or whether the term includes the rest (the peace, joy, etc.) that comes to the believer through the gospel. To me, the latter interpretation is more consistent with the argument of the passage. The writer of Hebrews knows that among his recipients are professing Christians who, under the pressure of persecution, are thinking of forsaking their profession of Christianity and returning to "the faith of their fathers." In effect, the inspired writer declares that this action would indeed be comparable to the professed faith of some of their fathers; for in the day of temptation in the wilderness, they hardened their hearts against the Lord and His Word and, by unbelief, refused to enter into the rest God had prepared for them. Was this "rest" the land of Canaan? The writer declares that it was not. Joshua could not provide the rest of which the writer is speaking. Only Jesus can provide such rest. The rest the author is speaking of is attained by faith in the Messiah, and it is rejected by unbelief (Heb. 4:2–3, 6, 10–11). Note that the inspired writer declares that the gospel was preached to both Old Testament and New Testament saints (4:2). Those who received it by faith entered into God's rest; those who did not believe did not find rest. The rest of which the inspired writer is speaking, then, is "a general name for that happiness, whether enjoyed on earth or in heaven, on the possession of which men enter when they believe the Gospel." Brown, *Hebrews*, 198. Essentially, however, all agree that the "rest" of this passage comes only through the finished work of Jesus Christ.

A Whole Day?

Why, even before the Fall, was a whole day set aside for the Sabbath? In the Garden, man was not yet under oppressive labor nor afflicted by physical infirmities. He could also rest and be refreshed each night. Why then did he need a whole day of rest each week from his ordinary labors? The answer may be found in the admonition of a well-known hymn: "Take time to be holy." The call for man to rest with God is a call for him to enter into the joy and satisfaction of his Creator.

In his response to Job, the Lord asks, "Where wast thou when I laid the foundations of the earth? . . . when the morning stars sang together, and all the sons of God shouted for joy?" (Job 38:4, 7). Why did the Lord point out that the angels shouted for joy? Because Job had violated the Sabbath principle. Had he entered into the joy and satisfaction the Lord feels over His creative activities—as the angels did—he would not have complained as he did.

The Sabbath was designed to periodically remind man of the wonder of the Lord's works and of the fact that only through his Lord can he have satisfaction and fulfillment. There is no "Plan B" for man. He cannot hope to add to his joy and fulfillment by going beyond his Creator's purpose for him.

Even in earthly relationships, it takes time to develop empathy. When you commune with your most intimate friend, you absorb something of that friend's personality. Not only do you see new dimensions in that friend's personality, but you also find that the two of you are thinking and feeling in harmony. So it is as we fellowship with the Lord. With each time of communion, we see new dimensions in His personality, and we find ourselves entering into His joys and sorrows. This takes time. The words of the psalmists express this principle: "I wait for the Lord, my soul doth wait, and in his word do I hope" (130:5). "Be still, and know that I am God" (46:10).

Even before the Fall, then, the Sabbath served a vital purpose in man's development. By observing the Sabbath—resting from his own works— man reminded himself that his entire being and development depended wholly on his Lord. Each Sabbath, as he progressively developed in the knowledge of God, he would have new areas in which his enlarged confidence in the Lord could rejoice. After the Fall, the dimension of salvation had to be added, but the fundamental principle remained the same. The Sabbath is still God's ordained means for man to enlarge his confidence in his Creator and Savior as he develops in his knowledge of God. It is significant, in this connection, that in the revelation of the Ten Commandments, the inspired writer gives a twofold basis for the observation of the Sabbath: the rest of God at Creation (Exod. 20:11) and the redemption of Israel from the bondage of Egypt (Deut. 5:15).

Does the Sabbath principle apply to the New Testament era? Yes! In the church age, the day of observation was changed to the first day of the week as a memorial of the resurrection of Jesus Christ—the event that publicly sealed God's work of redemption.

After all, the sabbatical concept is a fundamental part of the inspired record of Creation. If the decree to create man in the image of God applies to us, then joining in the rest of the God we mirror applies to us as well. It is true, of course, that the Jews misused and misapplied the

In the Millennium, the Sabbath will again be observed on the seventh day (Ezek. 44:24; 45:17; 46:1, 3–4, 12). Why? That question is not easy to answer. We could say simply (as some interpreters do) that in the Millennium, now-converted Israel will again become the vehicle for God's revelation—largely by a new temple and its rituals. But even aside from the fact that this response does not address the central issue in the change from the seventh to the first day—is not the Resurrection the seal of salvation for all believers?—Ezekiel envisioned a number of dynamic changes in the Mosaic legislation. Why not include a change in the day of sabbatical observance?

The answer, perhaps, is traceable to the nature of the first Sabbath. The Creator established it and sanctified the first Sabbath to represent the fulfillment of His purpose for creation. That He "rested" on the seventh day reveals His full satisfaction with every aspect of His creative work. His purpose for creation had been completely fulfilled. However, with the fall of man, salvation became a necessary aspect of God's fulfilled purpose. The Resurrection completed and verified the saving work of the Lamb of God, but God's divine purpose for creation was not yet completed. It was appropriate, therefore, that the church, commissioned to preach the completed work of salvation to all nations, should take Resurrection Day as its memorial Sabbath. But in the Millennium, the Messiah's reign on earth, the seventh day—representing the fulfillment of God's Creation purpose—is the appropriate symbol.

Sabbath by over-legalizing it. But legalistic excesses never justify licentious extremes.

In this connection, do not we in the New Testament era have some pharisaical robes of our own to discard? If indeed the purpose of the Sabbath is to provide time for the child of God to contemplate the wonder and works of his Lord, to what extent are we accomplishing this goal in our observance of the Lord's Day? It seems to me that as with Martha, we are so often "cumbered about with much service" in our churches that we rarely devote much time for the "good part" for which the Lord commended Mary. In His admonition, the Lord told Martha that the good part Mary had chosen "shall not be taken away from her." The Martha activities of our churches come and go, adding little to the spiritual health of the church. But when the people of God choose to devote the Lord's Day to the Lord, the spiritual benefit they gain will "not be taken away."

As originally designed, the Sabbath was an exercise in faith for man. By ceasing work and resting on this day, man would join God in satisfaction with His completed works. The Sabbath principle, then, became a key element in God's primeval "school" for man. By entering into God's work six days a week and contemplating God's finished work on the seventh, man would develop in the knowledge of God, preparing himself to reign with God.

GRADUATION FROM GOD'S ROYAL SCHOOL

The Process in God's Program

When do we graduate from God's royal school? Educational programs commonly include a graduation day in the distant future. So it is with God's program. The command for man to subdue the earth looked toward the distant future. It evidently involved a process by which mankind would eventually spread beyond the Garden of Eden to the ends of the world.

When was this process to be completed? Evidently, when mankind had completed the assignment to fill the earth and subdue it. We speculate about what would have happened had there been no Fall. Ordinarily such speculation serves no good purpose, but here it helps round out the picture of God's purpose for man.

Ultimately, mankind, multiplying in an ideal environment, would fill the earth. What then? Evidently, if man was destined to reign with God, he would have to reach a state in which he was no longer capable of dying. In effect, he would need to reach a state of glorification. Later revelation confirms that man must be glorified before he will fully inherit the kingdom of God and reign with Him on earth (e.g., Rom. 8:17–23). But even at this state in God's revelation, it must have been clear to man that the culmination of God's program for him was yet in the distant future.

This suggests that man was to develop in his knowledge of the nature of God and His works (Rom. 1:19–20; Pss. 19:1–6; 33:6–8) as he fulfilled God's command to "replenish the earth, and subdue it." By spreading throughout the earth and mastering the laws of life in God's creative works, man would increase in his knowledge of God and so conform more and more to the likeness of his Creator—again preparing himself to reign with Him.

The idea of a man being sinless and at the same time improvable tends to ruffle the human brain, but there is really no need for such unseemly wrinkles. Luke tells us that Jesus "increased in wisdom and stature, and in favour with God and man" (2:52; cf. 2:40). The sinless Son of Man had the capacity to increase intellectually, physically, spiritually, and socially. The unimpaired development of the Son of Man illustrates the potential for the development of sinless mankind.[10] Of course, this passage nowhere implies that Jesus was ever lacking in favor with God, but rather that each stage of His development fulfilled the joyful favor of His Father. The Son of Man, then, illustrates what should have been for the first Adam and his descendants.

If we look at these two divine decrees for man—the one stated, the other implicit—that man is to fill and subdue the earth and that, periodically, he is to rest with God in contemplation of His finished work, we see two foundational ways for man to fulfill his destiny. He is on the one hand to be constantly enlarging the borders of his experience with God.

---

[10] Note that this fourfold development includes spiritual development—even for the sinless Son of Man! How could this be? How are we to understand the statement that Jesus "increased . . . in favour with God"? Literally, the word translated *increased* (*prokopto*) means "to progress or go forward." The word *favour* (*charis*) is generally translated *grace* in the KJV. Grace (*charis*) has a wide range of connotations. Commonly the word is used, as it is in Luke 2:52, to depict the approval of another; but the connotation includes the thought of that which brings joy, pleasure, or delight. Online Bible definition; see also Colin Brown, ed., *The New International Dictionary of New Testament Theology*, (Grand Rapids: Zondervan, 1976), 2:115–124.

As he enters new realms of experience with God, he must constantly exercise submission and supervision. Each new realm calls anew for him to recognize God's sovereignty, and it calls for enlarged requirements of responsibility, or supervision, on his part.

On the other hand, he must repeatedly practice resting with his Creator. Doing this constantly reminds him that all depends on his faith—his confidence—in the Lord. Nothing can be added to the Lord's perfect work, and nothing more than the Lord Himself is necessary to fulfill His plan. There should be no "if only" in the life of the child of God—if only I had this or that or if only God had done this or that. He has all he needs in his Lord, in the gifts the Lord has entrusted to him, and in the circumstances in which his Creator has placed him.

The People in God's Program

God's declaration of His purpose for man intimates a process of development for mankind: "God said unto them, Be fruitful, and multiply, and replenish the earth, and subdue it: and have dominion over the fish of the sea, and over the fowl of the air, and over every living thing that moveth upon the earth." He promised dominion to all mankind, not just to the first man or to any individual.

When God made man in His own image, He gave man the power to reproduce in his own image. He made countless other creatures—the angels, for example—with no such power; but He made man with the ability to produce a society of creatures like himself.

This fact provides a dynamic that we simply cannot overlook—though we human types often try. Each person in God's plan is an individual, unique and wonderful in his own right; yet each is a part of the community of mankind. God holds each man accountable for his own thoughts and actions. But every individual also has some influence on others. God holds him accountable for this influence, and He holds society responsible for its response.

There is a mystery in this. The human race has been bound inextricably to its first parents to share their legacy—whether good or bad. "Wherefore, as by one man sin entered into the world, and death by sin; and so death passed upon all men, for that all have sinned" (Rom. 5:12). "For since by man came death, by man came also the resurrection of the dead. For as in Adam all die, even so in Christ shall all be made alive" (I Cor. 15:21–22).

How does this principle—that of individual sanctity balanced with human unity—apply to God's design for man to reign with Him? If man is to reign with God, he must, as his Maker does, assume responsibility both for the individual and for the race. He must constantly have his eye on both. He can neither forfeit his individual responsibilities for society's sake nor sacrifice society on the altar of his individual need. He cannot develop in the image of God by isolating himself from society; nor can he develop in God's purpose for him by entering fully into the flow of his society.

If we would imitate our Maker, then, in this dual responsibility, we must follow the example of Immanuel, God in the flesh. When Nicodemus, a Pharisee and ruler of the Jews, came to Jesus at night, our Lord focused on him as an individual and spoke to him in the context of his particular culture and viewpoint. Yet even as He made an intensely personal appeal to one man, Jesus had His eye on the world. He concludes His conversation with the amazing comment that anyone who believes on the Messiah of the Jews will have eternal life. And years later John adds, as a reflection of the heart of his Master, "For God so loved the world, that he gave his only begotten Son, that whosoever believeth in him should not perish, but have everlasting life."

CHAPTER THREE

THE ORIGINAL PATTERN OF GOD'S KINGDOM

THE FOUNDATION BLOCKS OF GOD'S REVELATION

THE FIRST ELEVEN CHAPTERS OF Genesis are foundational to understanding the central message of the Bible and God's central purpose for man. Consider for a moment the chronological structure of the Bible. If we assume that Creation took place about 4000 BC, then the first eleven chapters of the Bible (about eleven pages in a standard edition of the Bible) cover about two thousand years. The rest of the Bible, from Genesis 12 through the book of Revelation, deals with events that took place in the same amount of time! Imagine all the fascinating information God could have given us about the first two thousand years of Earth's history. He chose instead to give us just a bare sketch, just a few incidents, of this fascinating period. Why? These incidents were all He needed as foundation blocks for His written revelation.

Speaking of building blocks, let's look briefly at the form and layout of these foundational blocks. The inspired writer has marked them clearly with expressions such as the one we find in Genesis 2:4, "These are the generations." The word *generations* (*toledoth*) as used in Genesis was the ancient expression for *history*.[1] Thus the words "These are the generations" could be translated "This is the history."

So if we use these *generations* notations as our guide, can we see in this eleven-page introduction a foundational pattern on which to build the entire written revelation of God? I think we can.

The first building block (Gen. 1:1–2:3) could be viewed as the prologue to the Bible, the introductory remarks that tell the reader the basis for understanding all that follows. This section establishes that God, the Creator and Source of all, is absolutely sovereign in all aspects of life, and that He created man to reign with Him in His earthly kingdom.

In Genesis 2:4 the first *generations* statement appears, suggesting that, properly speaking, the history of the universe begins here. This second foundational block (2:4–4:26) tells us of the embryonic formation of two antagonistic kingdoms in the earth, the kingdom of God and the kingdom of the world. The third foundational block (5:1–6:8) describes the corruption and condemnation of the entire earthly realm as the two kingdoms intermingle. The fourth section (6:9–9:29) tells us that God, rather than allowing mankind to destroy His earthly kingdom, established an everlasting covenant of redemption by which the realm could eventually be restored. The fifth foundational section (10:1–11:9) describes in brief the makeup, philosophy, and methods of the kingdom of the world in its antagonistic struggle to control God's earthly realm. The final foundational section (11:10–26) traces the line of Redemption through the descendants of Seth. Following in outline form, with some explanatory comments, are these foundational sections except for the final one, which could be viewed as a prelude to the story of Abraham.

1. Prologue: God's Sovereignty over All Aspects of Life the Foundation for Man's Reign with Him (Gen. 1:1–2:3)

   God, the Creator, Source, and Sovereign of all aspects of life in the universe, created man in His image so that mankind might, after a probationary period, reign with Him in His earthly kingdom.

2. Embryonic Kingdoms: The Formation of Two Kingdoms (Gen. 2:3–4:26)

   Deceived by Satan, however, man forfeited his potential for unmitigated progress toward his destiny by grasping for a sovereignty

---

[1] In modern Hebrew this word is used for *history*. See Ernest Klein, *A Comprehensive Etymological Dictionary of the Hebrew Language for Readers of English* (New York: Macmillan, 1987), 694.

independent of his Creator. In response to man's rebellion, the Lord revealed a gracious plan for man's redemption, based on his willingness to disavow his rebellion and trust his Lord and Savior. From that time on, mankind divided into two antagonistic kingdoms, the kingdom of God and the kingdom of the world.

3. Corruption and Condemnation: The Corruption of God's Kingdom Through Compromise and the Condemnation of the Human Race (Gen. 5:1–6:8)

These two kingdoms with diametrically opposed life principles continued to develop in the earth. However, degenerative wickedness eventually infected all mankind, and the children of God became entangled in marital alliances with the children of the world— resulting in universal corruption and divine condemnation.

4. God's Covenant for the Redemption of Mankind (Gen. 6:9–9:29)

But God graciously preserved the light of righteousness in the earth and provided a deliverer. Through this man, and particularly through his son Shem, the Lord established a covenant to preserve mankind in the earth and to work redemption for the people of God.

5. Babel: God's Control of the Rebellious People of the Earth (Gen. 10:1–11:9)

Though God's covenant with Noah and his descendants was designed to preserve the light of righteousness in the earth, the nations largely followed the pattern of rebellion that had dominated before the Flood. The ambition of mankind in general has been the same as that of fallen man in the Garden of Eden. He desires to be "like God, knowing good and evil" (Gen. 3:5b, NASB); that is, he desires to be a Sovereign in his own right, independent and self-sufficient, operating on the basis of his own judgment of good and evil.

Ideally, man might like to live as simply a good neighbor of God. That is, he would like to live quite independently of God, perhaps occasionally inviting Him over or seeking His advice. As a good Neighbor, though, God would respect his privacy and not interfere with his life; and he, of course, would do the same.

As long as this good-neighbor policy seems to be in effect, the man of the world can maintain a relatively congenial attitude toward God. Problems develop, however, when God begins to manifest His sovereignty. The Bible characterizes unregenerate men as "haters of

God" (Rom. 1:30; cf. 8:7), and they are indeed all that this expression implies. But their hatred is only as clear as their perception of the absolute sovereignty of God—the jurisdiction He has over them. Our Lord declared, "Me [the world] hateth because I testify of it, that the works thereof are evil" (John 7:7; cf. 15:24).

The Tower of Babel illustrates the ultimate ambition of man. His desire—the desire of the ages, really—is to establish a universal kingdom over the earth, independent of God, for the glory of mankind.

The Formation of Two Kingdoms (Gen. 2:4—4:26)

When we follow the pattern suggested by the *toledoth* headings, we find that the writer evidently intended Genesis 2:4 through 4:26 to be viewed as a unit, for the next heading is at Genesis 5:1. We should therefore avoid the common practice of dividing this section into topical segments and look instead for a unified message in the entire passage.

As with narratives generally, the conclusion of the story of this section tells us the focus and theme of the writer. This section climaxes with the formation of two antagonistic kingdoms. The central focus of this primeval history of the universe, then, is the beginning of a titanic warfare: the life-or-death conflict between the kingdom of light and the kingdom of darkness. This is to be a dominant theme throughout the Word of God. In fact, there is a sense in which the rest of the Bible develops and culminates the story of the war between these two kingdoms.

The message of this section develops in three stages: the original character and pattern of the earthly kingdom man is to inherit from God (2:4–25), the attack and victory of Satan over the heirs of the earthly kingdom (3:1–24), and the formation and pattern of two antagonistic kingdoms in the earthly domain God has willed to man (4:1–26).

The Original Pattern of God's Kingdom (Gen. 2:4—25)

God created man as the heir apparent of His earthly kingdom. This account describes the formation of the man and woman for their position as joint heirs of God's earthly kingdom, and it outlines the character and conditions relating to their realm. We have here the original pattern for the kingdom of God: God's people in His appointed place under His rule, preparing to reign with Him. The inspired writer presents this part of the narrative in three stages: the formation of the heir of God's earthly kingdom (vv. 4–7), the realm of the heir (vv. 8–17), and the formation of the joint heir of God (vv. 18–24).

The Formation of the Heir of God's Earthly Kingdom (Gen. 2:4–7)

The writer introduces this part of his narrative with the remarkable announcement that "these are the generations of the heavens and of the earth when they were created, in the day that the Lord God made the earth and the heavens" (v. 4). That is tantamount to saying, "This is the primeval history of the universe, beginning with the time of creation." This statement is striking because of the scope of the writer's narrative. He describes his story as the history of "the heavens and the earth"—the history of the entire created universe! He will focus on the earth (as suggested by the reversal of the words "heavens and the earth" to "earth and the heavens" in v. 4b) and eventually narrow his focus to Israel. Nevertheless, this opening announcement tells us that the cataclysmic conflict the writer is introducing will involve the entire created universe.

This striking announcement also introduces a new designation for the divine Being: the "Lord God" (*Yahweh Elohim*). The designation *Yahweh* (literally, an imperfect verb meaning "He is") "points out the Divine Being as moving, pervading history, and manifesting Himself in the world. . . . He is the personal God in His historical manifestation. . . . This movement of the personal God in history, however, has [special] reference to . . . the salvation of man."[2] *Yahweh* is the preeminent covenant name for God in the Old Testament. In its various forms, the name appears over 6800 times in the Old Testament, more than twice as many times as the next most common designation for God, *Elohim*.

Elohim designates God as the awesome "mighty One," the Creator of the universe.[3] Grammatically, *Elohim* is the plural of *Eloah*, a term for God that appears less than 60 times in the Old Testament. (*Elohim* occurs as a designation for the true God over 2300 times.) Hebrew scholars

---

[2] C. F. Keil and Franz Delitzsch, *The Pentateuch* (Grand Rapids: Eerdmans, n.d.), 1:75.

[3] There is wide disagreement among scholars concerning the etymology of *Elohim* and its related words. The most frequently given suggest that the word is rooted in the concept of power or of fear. R. Laird Harris, ed., *Theological Wordbook of the Old Testament* (hereafter *TWOT*), 2 vols. (Chicago: Moody Press, 1981), 1:42.

commonly designate this use of the plural as a "plural of majesty," a plural used not to denote number but to intensify the characteristics inherent in the word. "In this intensive sense Elohim depicts the one true God as the infinitely great and exalted One, Who created the heavens and the earth, and Who preserves and governs every creature."[4]

The combination "Lord God" (*Yahweh Elohim*) appears twenty times in chapters two and three, which is close to half the total number of times it appears in the entire Pentateuch. Why this strong emphasis at this point in the written revelation of God? It was extremely important for Israel (the target audience of this initial revelation) to see at the outset that their covenant Lord was the same as the Creator of the universe. They were not to think of Yahweh as simply the God of Israel. We know from later revelation that they had imbibed much of the spirit of Egypt. It would have been easy, almost natural, for them to think of Yahweh as a tribal deity. In using this combination, the inspired writer is jealously guarding—and inculcating in his listeners—the awesome nature of the Author and Sustainer of all life, the Lord Who had visited them to redeem them.

Moses emphasizes three features in his account of the formation of man as the heir apparent of God's earthly kingdom.

(1) The words "there was not a man to till the ground" (Gen. 2:5) emphasize the need for man in God's creation order. Man, as the potential master of the earth, was an intrinsic part of God's plan from the very beginning. Without him, the earth would have been incomplete and perpetually imperfect.

(2) The description of the process of man's creation declares that God "formed man of the dust of the ground" (Gen. 2:7). It is interesting and most significant, particularly after the initial revelation that God made man in His own image, now to emphasize the fact that God formed man from dust. The Lord's design in this was evidently that the substance from which man was made would serve as a constant reminder of his need for humility (cf. Job 4:19; Gen. 18:27; I Kings 16:2). Even before the Fall, this revelation was important for man. His place of potential sovereignty over the earth demanded his awareness of his total dependence on his own Sovereign.

---

[4] Keil and Delitzsch, *The Pentateuch*, 1:73. The writer's intention in using *Elohim* is generally made clear by his use of singular verbs, adjectives, and pronouns with it.

(3) God also "breathed into his nostrils the breath of life; and man became a living soul" (Gen. 2:7). Of the animals, the writer declares that God simply spoke and they came into being (1:24); but of man, he says God *breathed* His own life into him. This action describes man's receiving the breath of life—that is, becoming a living creature; but the fact that the writer pictures God Himself breathing into man suggests a profound difference between man and the animals. "God breathes directly into the nostrils of the one man, in the whole fulness of His personality, the breath of life, that in a manner corresponding to the personality of God he may become a living soul."[5]

On the one hand, then, God expects humility from the man He formed from the dust of the earth. On the other hand, He expects dignity. These two features were in perfect balance before the Fall; but ever since then, man has been overemphasizing one or the other. Though it might seem that the pride of fallen man would cause excessive dignity, this is not necessarily the case. Try as he may, man cannot escape from the oppressive consciousness of his own weakness. And here the "dust" aspect of his constitution becomes a handy tool. His plea for his weakness—and wickedness—commonly translates into the excuse "I'm only human."

Furthermore, the high priests of evolution have provided a dogmatic rationale for man's groveling and degrading actions. If man indeed evolved from lower life, then his primeval constitution may explain—and even justify—a lifetime of degrading actions. Here then is one of the great ironies of history. Evolution, which professes to promote man's upward development, is in fact a prime tool for his degradation. Consequently, unregenerate man is constantly toggling between the reality of his weakness and his inordinate ambition for exaltation. Only through Christ can the delicate balance of man's constitution be restored, for Christianity humbles without degrading and exalts without inflating.

The Realm of the Heir Apparent (Gen. 2:8–17)

For the heirs of His earthly kingdom God designed a realm for physical, mental, and spiritual development. Their first school would be the Garden of Eden. God even formed Adam outside the Garden then put him in it—as if allowing him to see something of the territory he and his

---

[5] Ibid., 1:80.

descendants would ultimately inhabit and subdue before giving him his immediate assignment.

The inspired writer presents the Garden of Eden as the source—from both a geographical and a spiritual standpoint—for the ultimate development of the entire earthly realm of man. He depicts the river that watered the Garden as parting after leaving Paradise into four rivers that ensured the fruitfulness of all areas of the earth. He points out the potential for riches in one of these areas, suggesting by extension that primeval Earth had abundant potential in riches. Since God had commanded mankind to fill the earth and subdue it (1:28), He evidently intended for Adam and Eve's descendants to spread from the Garden of Eden throughout the whole earth. Ultimately, their goal would be to turn the whole earth into a "Garden of Eden."

But the whole earth, beginning at Eden, was preeminently a school for man's spiritual development. As he fulfilled his assignment to subdue the earth, as he served and managed Earth's plant and animal life, he would enlarge his knowledge of the Lord.

At this point in his experience, the only basis for man's knowledge of good and evil was the Word of God. All that God had made was "very good"; everything God designed fulfilled the purpose for which He made it. However, at this time, man had no intuitive ability to discern good from evil. He had to rely wholly on God for such judgments. What God allowed was good, and what God forbad was evil, though the forbidden fruit itself might (in appearance and original design) be "good."

The two trees in the midst of the Garden represented the key issue in man's spiritual development. Would he seek to reach his royal destiny by trusting his Creator for everything that happened in life? Or would he seek to reign by means of the knowledge available in the Tree of the Knowledge of Good and Evil?

The Tree of Life represented man's choice to trust wholly in the Lord for life and all that goes with life—including knowledge.[6] It is impossible for man to live without gaining knowledge. Even in a largely unregenerate world, the heavens are constantly declaring the glory of God and showing His handiwork (Ps. 19:1); and certainly in the pristine conditions of the Garden, Adam and Eve were daily gathering knowledge of their Maker, of

---

[6] Evidently, Adam during his probation time never sensed a need to eat from the Tree of Life, though the Lord had told him he could eat freely of every tree in the garden except the Tree of

As we all well know from experience, there are many things in life that may be intrinsically good, that are not necessarily good for us. The word *good* in the context of Genesis 1 means "that which fulfills God's purpose." When God pronounced a work of creation good, He was, in effect, saying, "This fulfills My purpose." On the same basis, the problem of distinguishing between what is intrinsically good and what is good for us can generally be settled by asking the question, "Does this fulfill God's purpose for me?" Adam and Eve took fatal fruit from a tree that in itself was intrinsically good because they failed to ask this question.

His works and His standards. The knowledge that comes through trust develops gradually and steadily as man matures in his walk with the Lord.

The Tree of Knowledge, on the other hand, represented the Prodigal Son's choice. It depicts man's decision to demand his promised inheritance now. In making this decision, man assumes that by the knowledge of good and evil he can reign over the earth in his own power. He will be independent of his Maker, a "god" in his own right.

The Lord God's warning against this was emphatic and terrifying: "But of the tree of the knowledge of good and evil, thou shalt not eat of it: for in the day that thou eatest thereof thou shalt surely die" (Gen. 2:17). Since he lived hundreds of years after his fateful decision, interpreters often say that Adam died spiritually that day while God's grace preserved his physical life for many years after that. This is true, but it doesn't tell the whole story. Indeed, when man declared his independence from God, he severed himself from life itself—from God, the only Source of true life in the universe, "in whose hand is the soul of every living thing, and the breath of all mankind" (Job 12:10; cf. Acts 17:25, 28; John 11:25; Col. 1:17).

In addition, when man gained his own intuitive knowledge of good and evil, he thereby lost his sense of total dependence on the Lord in a very

---

Knowledge (2:16–17). This seems to have been providential. Had Adam and Eve eaten of the Tree of Life, their time of probation would have ended. They would have received a divine quality of life ("eternal life") that would have rendered them impervious to sin and death. An effective probation demands at least two viable choices, and it also requires time. Furthermore, the nature of divine revelation demands time. God reveals Himself to man in stages over extended periods of time; and it is unthinkable that He would have not done so with Adam and Eve before He would have allowed Satan to present them with such a fateful decision.

critical area of his life: moral judgment. The fundamental criterion for determining good and evil is not the intrinsic value of the thing in question. As we learned from Genesis 1, good and evil are tied to the Creator's purpose. Consequently, though fallen man may have an intuitive knowledge of good and evil, attempting to act independently of God's purpose skews his moral judgments. Even the sacrifice of the wicked is an abomination to the Lord (Prov. 15:8; 21:27). Man's judgment concerning the moral good of sacrifice might be right; but going against the purpose of God wholly negates the good.

The Formation of the Joint Heir of God's Earthly Kingdom (Gen. 2:18–25)

"And the Lord God said, It is not good that the man should be alone; I will make him an help meet for him" (v. 18). God's creation process reveals something of the order and government of His kingdom. In this sixth day of creation, after calling the animals into existence, God has prepared a garden eastward in Eden for His climactic creative act: forming, in His own image, the joint heirs to His earthly kingdom.

The Lord's plan calls for creating the man first, outside the garden of Eden. The New Testament informs us that this order conveyed the divine order of authority, including the woman's dependence upon the man—not to suggest her inferiority but to impress upon the man and the woman the order in God's program. Paul wrote Timothy, "Let the woman learn in silence with all subjection. But I suffer not a woman to teach, nor to usurp authority over the man, but to be in silence. For Adam was first formed, then Eve" (I Tim. 2:11–13).

So God entrusted to Adam the revelation of man's commission and restriction:

> And the Lord God took the man, and put him into the garden of Eden to dress it and to keep it. And the Lord God commanded the man, saying, Of every tree of the garden thou mayest freely eat: but of the tree of the knowledge of good and evil, thou shalt not eat of it: for in the day that thou eatest thereof thou shalt surely die (Gen. 2:15–17).

As the "priest" of his home, Adam would be expected to communicate God's revelation to his wife.

After this revelation, "the Lord God said, It is not good that the man should be alone; I will make him an help meet for him" (2:18). The word *good* here denotes the fulfillment of God's purpose. It did not fulfill God's purpose for the man to exist alone. Literally, the expression *help meet* is "a help as before him or corresponding to him." When God created the woman, Adam would see in her a helper who was his counterpart—a person who fulfilled his needs and completed him as a human being.

Then the Lord God, instead of immediately creating the woman, brings before Adam the animals and birds of the Garden and requires him to name them one by one. Why? It was important that the man see the need for the woman, not only that he might fulfill God's purpose to multiply and fill the earth but that he might also, with his partner and joint heir, govern the earthly kingdom. Naming the creatures required Adam to discern the nature and characteristics of each and to designate them accordingly. Thus the Lord again and again impressed upon Adam that there was no living creature on earth that corresponded to his nature.

Only then did the Lord God begin creating the woman. The process by which He created her is very instructive. He had "formed" Adam from the dust of the ground; but when He made the woman, He caused Adam to fall into a deep sleep and took from him a rib from which He "built" (*banah*) the woman. This revelation (that God made the woman from the man's rib) establishes once and for all the dignity of the woman as equal to the man in nature and in the image and likeness of God. This revelation also establishes the unity of the human race. Since all mankind descended from this couple, all share equally in their nature and dignity.

> The woman was created, not of the dust of the earth, but from a rib of Adam, because she was formed for an inseparable unity and fellowship of life with the man, and the mode of her creation was to lay the actual foundation for the moral ordinance of marriage.[7]

The Lord God Himself, as the Father of the bride, "brought her unto the man"; and Adam immediately recognized that "This is now bone of my bones, and flesh of my flesh: she shall be called Woman [*ishah*], because she was taken out of Man [*ish*]" (2:23). These are man's first recorded words in Scripture. Significantly, they are in the form of poetry—evidently uttered extemporaneously by Adam. The inspired writer utilized his poetic expressions (or a translation of them) to suggest something of the beauty and the intense emotion of the occasion. A more literal rendition of this poetical outburst, though its crassly literal English sacrifices the beauty of the Hebrew parallelism, will give some idea of the

---

[7] Keil and Delitzsch, *The Pentateuch*, 1:89.

There can be no such thing in humanity as a naturally inferior race. Families, tribes, and nations can become degraded, but no ethnic group can legitimately be viewed as inherently inferior. Even in the context of violence and bloodshed, the requirement that man execute any fellow human being guilty of murder is based on the principle that man was created in the image of God (Gen. 9:6).

intense emotion Adam felt as the Lord presented his bride to him. Note in this rendition the vast contrast he sees in his bride and the animals he has just named: "This one, this time—bone from my bones and flesh from my flesh! This one is to be called *ishah*: for from *ish* this one was taken."

Then, lest future generations should reason that the principles of marriage in Paradise would not apply to people after the Fall, the narrator reveals a fundamental principle of marriage for all mankind: "Therefore shall a man leave his father and his mother, and shall cleave unto his wife: and they shall be one flesh" (2:24).

This first wedding ceremony says nothing specifically of love. The expressions used instead are the words *leave* and *cleave*. Marriage as God ordained involves an intimate relationship that goes infinitely beyond even the filial relationship of a son or daughter to parents. Though this new relationship doesn't obliterate filial connections, it nevertheless completely supersedes them and goes far beyond them in intimacy—for in marriage the two become one flesh.

The word translated *cleave* (*davaq*) is a very strong Hebrew word. The Old Testament uses this word of things that adhere or cling tightly together. Job, for example, speaks of his bones cleaving to his skin (Job 19:20); and the inspired writer describes the mighty warrior Eliezer as smiting the Philistine "until his hand was weary, and his hand clave unto the sword" (II Sam. 23:10). Scriptural writers use the expression in both a good sense and a bad. They use it to denote adhering devotedly and loyally to the Lord (Deut. 11:22), but they use it also of illicit love relationships (Gen. 34:3; I Kings 11:2).

The inspired writer makes the marriage relationship virtually synonymous with the expression "They shall be one flesh." Establishing a "cleaving" relationship in marriage produces a oneness in soul and body—so that our Lord, dealing with the question of severing such a relationship, declares, "They are no more twain, but one flesh" (Mark 10:8*b*).

The joint heir of God's earthly kingdom, then, was designed to be one with her husband. This principle is fundamental to God's plan for man— to reign with Him.

CHAPTER FOUR

THE SUBTLE SERPENT—THE SEEKING SAVIOR

W E ARE STILL DEALING WITH the primeval formation of two antagonistic kingdoms, each claiming inheritance rights to God's earthly kingdom. In the preceding chapter, we saw the formation of the kingdom's ordained joint heirs and the realm they were to inherit. In this chapter, a titanic, aeonian battle begins between Satan, depicted here as the subtle serpent, and the Lord, Who appears here for the first time as the seeking Savior.

THE SUBTLE SERPENT (GEN. 3:1—8)

Of our enemy Satan, Paul declared, "We are not ignorant of his devices" (II Cor. 2:11*b*). These eight verses constitute a veritable instruction manual concerning the devices of Satan in warfare. No other single passage in the Bible so specifically outlines the strategy of our supreme enemy.

The Subtlety of Satan Declared (Gen. 3:1*a*)

This "manual" emphasizes the subtlety of our adversary. This quality is our first word of caution concerning our enemy: "Now the serpent was more subtil than any beast of the field which the Lord God had made" (referring to the creature Satan used as an instrument[1]). The word *subtle* here refers to the serpent's craftiness and prudence (cf. Matt. 10:16). Serpents show great skill and caution ("prudence") in avoiding danger and in catching their prey, largely through their ability to move gracefully and quietly without detection. Before the Fall—and the curse by which the serpent's form was changed—it was undoubtedly this characteristic of graceful, subtle movement that distinguished this creature.

The Subtlety of Satan Displayed (Gen. 3:1b–5)

Satan displayed his craftiness in his choice of the form in which he appeared, in his choice of the time and place for the attack, and in the means he used to create doubt in the woman.

In Choosing the Form in Which to Appear

Satan cultivated an aura of weakness and vulnerability in his first appearance to the woman. He appeared to her, not as an angel, but in the form of a small, subordinate creature—a beautiful and graceful creature that would naturally appeal to the woman. Likewise, the serpent spoke as an apparently inferior creature who seemed to be following the woman rather than leading her. He addressed Eve as an inquirer requesting enlightenment about something he did not understand: "Yea, hath God said, Ye shall not eat of every tree of the garden?" (v. 1b). The statement expresses surprise and an apparent misunderstanding of the nature of the prohibition: "Is it really true that God has said you can't eat of any of the trees of the garden?"[2]

In Choosing the Time and Place for the Attack

"Now those skilled in war must know where and when the battle will be fought . . . . Those skilled in war bring the enemy to the field of battle and are not brought there by him."[3] Satan, an absolute master at the art of

---

[1] It is clear from this passage and others (John 8:44; II Cor. 11:3, 14; Rom. 16:20; Rev. 12:9; 20:2) that Satan communicated through the serpent. Nevertheless, the fact that the inspired writers later use the word *serpent* as a designation for Satan suggests that the nature of this creature communicates a message concerning the nature of temptation. The statement that the serpent was more subtle than any beast of the field evidently refers to the created animal. See Matt. 10:16 where the term *wise* (*phronimos*) characterizes the serpent as prudent and discreet.

[2] The Hebrew could be translated "every tree," but the context, including the response of the woman to the question, supports the translation "any tree."

[3] Sun Tzu, *The Art of War*, trans. Samuel B. Griffith (New York: Oxford University Press, 1963), 99, 96.

war, carefully chose the time of his attack and the field of combat; then he patiently waited for his enemy to come to the field of battle.

He chose a time when the when the woman was alone in the center of the spacious, park-like garden. It was important that she be near the forbidden fruit, and doubly important that she be alone at the time of attack. His strategy hinged on persuading her to act independently of her husband, her immediate authority. The man's immediate authority was God Himself. An appeal to the man to rebel could more easily be perceived as a direct assault on God. For the woman to act independently of the man would appear to be a relatively small step in autonomy compared to what the man would have to do.

In Creating Doubt in the Woman

If you were the Devil, how would you go about getting the first man and woman to sin? They lived in a perfect environment. They had no physical infirmities or moral deficiencies he could exploit. There were no social problems. There could be no such thing as inordinate ambition in such a place—or could there? In fact, ambition turned out to be a door of opportunity. Here he had something to work with, something to exploit. Ambition, by definition, is a strong desire to achieve something; and built into man's nature by virtue of his commission at creation was a desire to achieve something—to subdue the earth and to reign over the earthly kingdom. It was by the door of that ambition that Satan entered the hearts of the man and woman. But in order to be successful, he had to engineer a subtle change in the door of legitimate ambition. He had to find a way to make the woman see the door of opportunity as a door of dissatisfaction. Once she entered that door, he was able to lead her to another door—the door of pride.

The door of dissatisfaction. How could anyone become dissatisfied in the garden of Eden? Adam and Eve had been given certain duties: they were to dress the garden and to keep it. But as yet there was no hard labor involved in this. It was delightful labor. The earth and the elements cooperated fully with their masters. The trees and plants yielded abundant fruit. The flowers blossomed beautifully and their fragrance filled the air.

But there was one restriction, one prohibition. They were not to eat of the Tree of the Knowledge of Good and Evil. Why? They hadn't been told. They had only been warned that in the day they ate of that tree they would surely die. Here was the serpent's opportunity. Only one prohibition! But

Satan found a way to magnify that one prohibition until it festered into dissatisfaction.

His method of magnifying it was wonderfully subtle. He ventured no confrontation, offered no direct contradiction. He simply inquired. He was in search of knowledge. He had heard something and wondered if it was true. "Yea, hath God said, Ye shall not eat of every tree of the garden?" he said. "Did I hear this right? Did God say you cannot eat of any of the trees in the garden?"

In that day, Adam and Eve must have felt a certain empathy with creation, and particularly with the animals of creation. Creation had not yet rebelled against its earthly masters, and it was not yet groaning impatiently for better lords and a better day (Rom. 8:22–23). Satan designed his question to play on this natural sympathy. His question implied that God's restriction seemed unreasonable. Eve responded sympathetically to this creature's apparent need of enlightenment: No, God hasn't restricted us from all the trees. "We may eat of the fruit of the trees of the garden."

Fine so far; he had struck two mildly discordant notes. The first she corrected through her apparently superior knowledge; but the second touched a sympathetic—and ultimately fatal—chord. "But of the fruit of the tree which is in the midst of the garden, God hath said, Ye shall not eat of it, neither shall ye touch it, lest ye die" (Gen. 3:3). With these words, Eve legitimized the serpent's implication. His inquiry had magnified the prohibition. Eve's response confirmed his suspicions by promiscuously adding another prohibition: "Neither shall ye touch it." Then, having followed the serpent's twisted reasoning that God's prohibition was unreasonable, Eve proceeded naturally to the implication of that reasoning. If the prohibition is unreasonable, then punishment cannot be certain or strictly enforced. So the Lord God's fearful warning, "In the day that thou eatest thereof thou shalt surely die," became in Eve's thought "lest ye die," or "you might die."

Satan now had the opening he had been looking for. Eve had modified the word she had heard from the Lord, adding a questionable condition to it and omitting key words in the warning. Satan now, in a direct assault against the word of God, picked up—as if it were a discarded weapon—one of the words she had omitted. "Ye shall not *surely* die," he said (emphasis mine). Then, as the climax of his appeal, he added some words of his own: "For God [*Elohim*] doth know that in the day ye eat thereof, then your eyes shall be opened, and ye shall be as gods [*Elohim*], knowing good and evil."

And where is the lie in this climactic statement? There is no falsehood in these words! Ironically, this was the climactic appeal of God as well. He had made man in His own image that man might reign with Him. The conflict was not in the announced goals for man. The conflict was in the means of achieving the ultimate fulfillment of those goals. Man's sin stemmed not so much from his desire to be "like God" as from his accepting Satan's method of achieving God-likeness.[4]

In Satan's scheme, the key to the highest form of life was knowledge—specifically the knowledge of good and evil.[5] In God's plan, the key to mature knowledge was life. Satan's plan promised immediate deification; God's plan required patient waiting and development. God's plan required submission to Him as the Creator and Lord of every realm of life. Satan's plan declared independence from God; built into his scheme was a spirit of antagonism toward God. Essentially, it was man's rejection of God's Word that brought about the conflict between God and man.

As the serpent's words stand, they are an expression of the truth. But the context in which they were uttered holds an insidious implication: God forbad you from eating of that tree because He doesn't want you to be like Him, knowing on your own how to distinguish between good and evil. He doesn't really have your best interests in mind. He wants you to be totally dependent on Him for every move you make. Under these circumstances, will you ever indeed reign over the earth as He has promised?

The door of pride. "And . . . the woman saw that the tree was good for food, and that it was pleasant to the eyes." This seems to agree with the serpent's comments, she must have thought. If the tree is evil, why does it produce good fruit? And why is it so beautiful? Mesmerized now by the tree's beauty and delectable fruit, Eve may have thought, *Even God calls*

---

[4] The Hebrew word *elohim* could be translated "gods" or "God," depending on the context or syntax.

[5] The full name the inspired writer gives the tree of forbidden fruit is "the tree of the knowledge of good and evil" (Gen. 2:9, 17). In fact, Keil suggests that Jeremiah (22:16) regarded the phrase "knowledge of good and evil" as one word. *The Pentateuch*, 1:81 (see chap. 3, n. 2). This suggests that the focal point of the power of this tree was not on knowledge per se but on the ability to discern between right and wrong. This ability marks the distinction between maturity and immaturity (Deut. 1:39; I Kings 3:9) and is a quality inherent in true godliness (Gen. 3:5, 22; II Sam. 14:17). The sin was not in desiring this ability. The sin was in seeking it before God was ready to give it. Essentially, the sin of Adam and Eve was the same as that of the Prodigal Son. They demanded their inheritance before they were really entitled to it.

this tree the Tree of the Knowledge of Good and Evil. What could be wrong with having the knowledge of good and evil? Here is a creature—a beautiful creature—who seems to know things that neither Adam nor I know. What are we missing out on? What wondrous new things could we have and enjoy if we had this knowledge—knowledge that is there for the taking?

"And when the woman saw that the tree was good for food, and that it was pleasant to the eyes, and a tree to be desired to make one wise, she took of the fruit thereof, and did eat, and gave also unto her husband with her; and he did eat" (Gen. 3:6). Here in primal form is a triad of sin's promises that have formed the sordid pillars of society in the kingdom of the world: the lust of the flesh, the lust of the eyes, and the pride of life (I John 2:16). The word translated *lust* (*epithumia*) in that passage is used elsewhere in the New Testament to describe legitimate desire. Legitimate desires become sinful lusts when we seek to fulfill them outside the will of God. Even intense desires are not in themselves wrong. (See Luke 4:2; 22:15; I Thess. 2:17.) When Eve saw that the tree was good for food, she felt what must have seemed to be a legitimate desire for physical pleasure. In fact, the desire for food or for physical pleasure in general was not in itself wrong. It became so only when she chose to fulfill it outside God's will.

Eve saw the tree also as delightful, desirable, to the eyes. The fundamental meaning of the word translated *pleasant* here is "desirable." In this case, the tree's beauty made it delightful to look at; and what is delightful to the eyes naturally becomes desirable as the soul longs to possess the delightfully aesthetic experience the object creates—to make that beauty a part of itself. Again, the desire itself was not wrong. It became so when she sought to fulfill it outside the will of God (cf. Josh. 7:21; Luke 4:5–8).

To Eve, the tree was also "a tree to be desired to make one wise." As with the word translated *pleasant*, the word *desired*, though a different Hebrew word, refers to that which a person longs for or wishes to possess. Again, nothing was wrong with her desiring to be wise; God's entire program for man included the daily development of wisdom and discernment. But her desire for wisdom became wrong when she sought fulfillment outside the will of God. The apostle John calls this desire "the pride of life" (I John 2:16). The word translated *pride* (*alazoneia*) refers to a braggart. Fundamentally, a braggart is an impostor who lives in a make-believe world where he is the star. The vice of such a person centers "in self and is consummated in his absolute self-exaltation. . . . Such 'vainglory,' such a false view of the value of our possessions, belongs to life . . . in its present concrete manifestation and not to life in its essential principle."[6] In partaking of this tree, Adam and Eve left the world of reality where God is sovereign and man is the heir apparent of His earthly kingdom, and they entered an illusory world of imagination where man is the star and God is simply a part of the supporting cast.

The words "with her" obviously do not mean that Adam had been with her during the temptation. The whole context demonstrates otherwise. We would expect Adam and Eve not to be apart for very long at any time. Perhaps as no couple since the disruption that came through the Fall, this original couple had become one flesh. They were one in spirit and soul. But apparently, in one of their brief times of separation, Satan found his opportunity to deal with the woman alone.

Now having joined her, Adam finds her holding fruit from the forbidden tree. No doubt she explained her marvelous experience, testifying to the fruit's delicious taste and to the potential it offered for a new and better life. Then she extended her hand and urged her husband to share this wonderful experience. Here the words "with her" take on a deeper connotation, for her husband was not just with her in body. He was with her in spirit and soul. She had become so much a part of him that he could not imagine life without her. "Adam was not deceived" (I Tim. 2:14), but he realized immediately that his wife had been thoroughly beguiled by the serpent and had eaten the forbidden fruit.[7]

And so he took the fruit she offered and ate it. "And the eyes of them both were opened, and they knew that they were naked; and they sewed fig leaves together, and made themselves aprons" (Gen. 3:7). How can we speak of this man and woman as suddenly "knowing" they were naked? And why, though they were man and wife, were they suddenly ashamed of their nakedness (cf. 2:25; 3:10)? Shame results from a sense of guilt or from a sense of weakness and inadequacy. Before the Fall, the first man and woman would have felt neither.

But surely, you may say, though they may not have felt guilt, they must have sensed their inadequacy compared to God or even the stronger animals!

---

[6] B. F. Westcott, *The Epistles of John* (1883; repr., Grand Rapids: Eerdmans, 1960), 65.

[7] These contrasting words and word forms lay special stress on the serpent's complete deception of Eve. More literally, I Tim. 2:14 reads, "And Adam was not deceived [*epatethe*, passive verb of *apatao*], but the woman having been completely deceived [*exapatetheisa*, passive participle of an emphatic form of *apatao*] became involved in transgression."

Not really. Your sense of adequacy or inadequacy is directly related to the task required of you. If you were asked to trim a bush or pick fruit from a tree you would feel no such sense. It is only when we are expected to do something beyond our power that we have a sense of inadequacy and the shame that goes with it. Before the Fall, Adam and Eve felt no shame because they had been created fully equipped to fulfill all the tasks God expected of them. But when sin entered—when they took upon themselves the impossible task of being *Elohim*—they became ashamed, for they knew they were inadequate.

And they knew this—that they were inadequate to fulfill their destiny to reign over the earth—even before they had acknowledged their sin and felt the full impact of their guilt. Man's sin-infected nature is such that probably even then they entertained a hope that the serpent's promises would somehow be fulfilled. Yet they could not escape a vague sense of guilt, a feeling—undefined and uninvited—that there was something about them or in them that was unclean. It is perhaps for this reason that the inspired writer describes the fig-leaf coverings they made for themselves as "loin coverings" (NASB). They felt the need to cover the parts of their bodies from which impurities are removed.

So now they are "as *Elohim*, knowing good and evil"—just as the serpent had promised. In their newfound independence, they had seen a need (their nakedness) and they had coped with it. Using their newly acquired knowledge, they had made fig-leaf coverings for themselves. But what of God's warning? That thought must have been hanging over them on that fateful day, particularly over Adam, who had not been deceived by the serpent's promises. Then "they heard the voice of the Lord God walking in the garden in the cool of the day: and Adam and his wife hid themselves from the presence of the Lord God amongst the trees of the garden."

THE SEEKING SAVIOR
(GEN. 3:9–24)

It is very easy for us to think of this part of the narrative strictly in terms of judgment. But had God been thinking strictly in those terms, He would have executed the death sentence at the moment of the sin. He is coming here not primarily as Judge but as Savior. He is seeking redemption for Adam and Eve and ultimately for the human race. This passage provides a preincarnate revelation of the seeking Savior probing for the source of sin (vv. 9–13); providing for victory over sin (vv. 14–15); punishing sin (vv. 16–19); witnessing His promise and provision received (vv. 20–21); and, finally, protecting the eternal soul of mankind (vv. 22–24).

The Savior Probing for the Source of Sin (Gen. 3:9–13)

Adam and Eve had been awakened anew to their guilt when they heard the voice of the Lord as He walked in the Garden in the cool of the evening.[8] Perhaps the Lord God had been meeting daily with the man and the woman, appearing in human form. Whatever the case, meeting with the Lord, as Adam had done previously (2:15–19), must have seemed quite natural in that day—until now. Now everything has changed; and Adam and Eve, hearing the voice of the Lord as He approaches, hide themselves.

Jehovah's Interrogation—To Awaken Guilt (Gen. 3:9–11)

The Lord God, addressing Adam as the original recipient of His revelation, called, "Where art thou?" The Lord knew where Adam was. His question was designed to awaken Adam to his spiritual condition. Indeed, the question "Where art thou?" goes far beyond Adam. It is a question that applies to all men in all eras everywhere. It is a question that probes to the heart of the matter of life. Where are you in your relationship with your Creator? Are you rightly related with Him? If so, why does He have to seek you out? Why are you hiding?

Adam's response is the prototype of man's response to God throughout the ages, "I heard thy voice in the garden, and I was afraid, because I was naked; and I hid myself" (v. 10). Over the centuries, much ink has been devoted to scholarly treatises dealing with such subjects as "Man's Quest for God." But, in reality, man searches for God—that is, the true God—as a mouse searches for a cat.

---

[8] Though the word translated *voice* (*qol*) in the KJV can be rendered *sound* or *noise* (e.g., I Kings 14:6), the context suggests that the word *voice* should be retained here. It does not seem natural to me that Adam and Eve, on hearing a noise among the trees, would immediately conclude that this was the Lord. Would they not tend to associate such noises with animals? Furthermore, it does not necessarily follow that because the Lord is described as walking, *qol* must refer to the sound He made as He was walking. The sentence could be translated, "And they heard the voice of the Lord God as He was walking about [the Hebrew word for *walking*, *halak*, is a reflexive participle here] in the garden." In v. 10, Adam said, "I heard thy voice in the garden," with no reference to the sound of the Lord's walking. Adam and Eve had sinned because they had not listened carefully enough to His words. Now, when He seeks them, He engages them anew with His words.

Man's first hiding place was really quite simple. He thought he found refuge behind some foliage in the garden. He was totally unsuccessful in his first attempt to hide, and every attempt since that time has resulted in miserable failure. But that has not deterred him. In fact, every failure to hide from God has only inspired man to construct more and more elaborate hiding places: whole systems of thought and movements of men, all devoted to the one objective perceives as essential for his peaceful existence on earth—obliterating any consciousness of the Creator out of his life.

In response to Adam's reply, the Lord said, "Who told thee that thou wast naked? Hast thou eaten of the tree, whereof I commanded thee that thou shouldest not eat?" This question—strangely, yet not so strangely—resulted in a series of accusations from the man and the woman.

Man's Accusations—To Escape Guilt (Gen. 3:12–13)

Again, man's efforts to escape the guilt are prototypical. They present a pattern man has used ever since. When faced with his guiltiness, man tends to blame others, ignorance, or circumstances; but in all these efforts he is in reality blaming God.

He blames others. "The woman whom thou gavest to be with me, she gave me of the tree, and I did eat." Having exposed an insidious cover-up in his son, the father thunders, "Learn to handle your faults like a man!" Seeking clarification, the beleaguered boy responds, "Blame them on Mom?" Sadly, the history of mankind largely testifies in behalf of the boy. Some philosophical wag has offered this polemical plum to the list of matrimonial advantages: "Everyone should be married. After all, there are some things you can't blame on the government."

He blames ignorance. But in this prototypical case, the woman has someone to blame also. "And the Lord God said unto the woman, What is this that thou hast done? And the woman said, The serpent beguiled me, and I did eat." In effect, she blamed her sin on ignorance. To deceive is to mislead concerning truth and reality. At the bottom of her excuse was the proposition, Had I known the facts, I would not have done this. But remember, the word *ignore* lurks somewhere in the root system of much that we call ignorance. Eve sinned, not because of a deficiency in information, but because she ignored the knowledge that was available.

He blames circumstances. "The woman . . . thou gavest to be with me . . . the serpent beguiled . . ." In turn, both the man and the woman allude to conditions in the context of their fatal decision, conditions that had a modifying affect on them. If this woman had not been with me or if the serpent had not been there at that time, this might not have happened. This was tantamount to claiming that in fact, God was responsible for what had happened. It was the Lord Who ordained or allowed the circumstances that conspired against us. Actually, the circumstances overwhelmingly favored the man and the woman. The circumstances were designed for their development and ultimately for the fulfillment of God's purpose for them. It was on the basis of this principle—that God designs all providential circumstances for our benefit—that David exclaimed, "Against thee, thee only, have I sinned, and done this evil in thy sight: that thou mightest be justified when thou speakest, and be clear when thou judgest" (Ps. 51:4).

The Savior's Provision for Victory over Sin (Gen. 3:14–15)

In the midst of this interrogation and in tones of judgment, the Lord pronounces a curse that paradoxically contains both the promise of life and victory over sin. The curse was upon Satan under the symbolism of the serpent. The promise was of a Savior Who would eventually get total victory over the serpent.

The Curse of the Serpent (v. 14)

As a symbol and illustration of His curse upon Satan, the Lord pronounced a curse upon the creature Satan had used as his instrument. "And the Lord God said unto the serpent, Because thou hast done this, thou art cursed above all cattle, and above every beast of the field; upon thy belly shalt thou go, and dust shalt thou eat all the days of thy life." As the Creator and Owner of all living things, the Lord chose, for man's sake, to make this creature an illustration for all ages of the curse and degradation that comes through Satan, the Adversary of God.

The Promise of the Savior (v. 15)

"And I will put enmity between thee and the woman, and between thy seed and her seed; it shall bruise thy head, and thou shalt bruise his heel."

It is striking to see that this first gospel promise is directed, not to Adam and Eve, but to the serpent. In the first instance, it is a warning to the prince of this world, this would-be king, that his ultimate doom is sealed. Furthermore, his defeat will come from a most unlikely source. He had found the woman vulnerable to his attractive and subtle powers. But now God will put in the woman, and in her seed, hatred and hostility toward the serpent; and the serpent, in consequence, would hate the woman.

We are not dealing here with a woman's hostility toward snakes. The inspired writer is dealing with a divinely implanted spiritual hostility toward Satan. The "seed"—of the woman and of the serpent—refers in this passage to spiritual descendants, and the woman's seed who crushes the head of the serpent refers to Christ (Gal. 3:16; cf. Matt. 13:38; John 8:44; I John 3:8–10). This brief passage foresees an escalating hostility between two branches of the human race, a war that will culminate in the Seed of the woman crushing the head of the serpent. Thus man, through a coming Redeemer-Man, will fulfill his destiny to reign with God in His earthly kingdom.

The Savior's Judgment of Sin (Gen. 3:16–19)

Our minds tend to form a dichotomy between a savior and a judge. In the Scriptures, and in ancient times generally, there was no such dichotomy. The inspired writers repeatedly present the Savior of the world as also its Judge (e.g., John 5:22, 26–30; II Thess. 1:7–8; Rev. 19:11–16). Those who refuse to recognize Christ as Savior will ultimately meet Him as Judge, but there is a judgment role He assumes in salvation as well. His saving work involves the judgment—and control—of sin (John 3:3–6; 4:15–26; 9:39). In this case, the Savior's judgment of the man and the woman opens the way of salvation for all of mankind.

In the Woman (Gen. 3:16)

As a part of the disciplinary judgment of the woman, she was to have pain and sorrow in childbirth. "Unto the woman he said, I will greatly multiply thy sorrow and thy conception; in sorrow thou shalt bring forth children." The second word translated *sorrow* (*etsev*) has connotations of both physical pain and emotional sorrow.[9] With each new life born into the world, she would experience the pain and sorrow associated with death. From now on, each new child will contain the seeds of death. These sorrows and pains that attend both childbearing and the physical conditions necessary to make it possible are actually instruments of God's grace. By afflictions and sorrows "the heart is made better" and more receptive to salvation (Eccles. 7:2–3; Job 33:19–24; I Cor. 11:32; I Tim. 2:15).

---

[9] *TWOT*, 2:687–88 (see chap. 3, n. 3).

In addition to her sorrow in childbirth, the woman now will be more completely subject to the man than she had previously been. Before the Fall, the woman was to be subjected to the man as a matter of divine order (I Tim. 2:12–13); but now this subjection will be intensified. "And thy desire shall be to thy husband, and he shall rule over thee." Eve had fallen into sin (and had led Adam into sin) by seeking to fulfill her desire independently of her husband. Now women will have to depend more and more on their husbands. In general, a woman succeeds or fails to the extent that her husband does; and her goals and ambitions are integrally connected with those of her husband. Furthermore, the rule of the husband, aggravated by conditions relating to sin, will become more and more oppressive and burdensome to bear.

In the Man (Gen. 3:17–19)

As the man, the intended lord of the earth, had rebelled against his Lord, he would now find that the realm over which he had been appointed would rebel against him:

> And unto Adam he said, Because thou hast hearkened unto the voice of thy wife, and hast eaten of the tree, of which I commanded thee, saying, Thou shalt not eat of it: cursed is the ground for thy sake; in sorrow shalt thou eat of it all the days of thy life; thorns also and thistles shall it bring forth to thee; and thou shalt eat the herb of the field; in the sweat of thy face shalt thou eat bread, till thou return unto the ground; for out of it wast thou taken: for dust thou art, and unto dust shalt thou return.

As his wife will suffer sorrow and pain in bringing new lives into the earth, so the man will suffer in his efforts to bring life from the earth; and even the life he brings forth, bearing as it often does thorns and thistles, will speak of pain and resistance. Furthermore, his production of life from the earth will constantly remind him of death. As he eats his bread to gain strength for life, the sweat on his brow will remind him of the pain it took to wrest this bit of life from the earth. As he returns to the earth to plow again in the hope of more and better life, he will be reminded that one day he will return to earth once and for all—for he was made of dust, and to dust he will return.

The Savior's Promise and Provision Received (Gen. 3:20–21)

Did Adam and Eve respond to the Savior's overtures? The closing words of this somber narrative hint that they did. These verses contain an indication of Adam's faith and an illustration of the salvation of Adam and Eve.

An Indication of Adam's Faith (Gen. 3:20)

In His judgment, God remembered mercy. He had cursed and pronounced inevitable doom on the tempter, but for the tempted He opened a door of hope. Through the Seed of the woman, He said, mankind will eventually triumph over the serpent. Adam revealed his faith in the Savior's promise by calling his wife Eve ("living") because she was the mother of all living. He might have concluded that she was the mother—the source—of death, for it was through her that death came into the world. But instead he chose to believe God's promise.

An Illustration of the Salvation of Adam and Eve (Gen. 3:21)

"Unto Adam also and to his wife did the Lord God make coats of skins, and clothed them." Even before the Savior had approached them, Adam and Eve had sensed the shame of their sinful condition—vainly attempting to cover themselves and hide from God. Now, through the work of the Savior in their behalf, they find that the death of an innocent animal has to occur before they can be adequately covered. Did they witness the death of this animal? The inspired writer doesn't tell us, but they had to know when they saw the animal skins that an innocent creature had died in their behalf. Thus the first death on earth—apart from the spiritual death that took place in the first man and woman—was a sacrificial death.

> Thus that clothing at the *outset* of human history became a prophecy in symbol of the *central* point of the history of salvation, of the cross of Golgotha, and at the same time a suggestion of the blessed *end* when God will at last have clothed His chosen with the resurrection body and the wedding garment of glory (Phil. 3:20, 21; II Cor. 5:2–4; Rev. 19:8).[10]

The Savior's Protection of the Way of Life (Gen. 3:22–24)

And the Lord God said, Behold, the man is become as one of us, to know good and evil: and now, lest he put forth his hand, and take also of the tree of life, and eat, and live for ever: Therefore the Lord God sent him forth from the garden of Eden, to till the ground from whence he was taken. So he drove

---

[10] Erich Sauer, *The Dawn of World Redemption* (Grand Rapids: Eerdmans, 1963), 60–61, emphasis original.

out the man; and he placed at the east of the garden of Eden Cherubims, and a flaming sword which turned every way, to keep the way of the tree of life.

Here is a strange paradox; in order to have life, man must be subjected to death. If he does not die, he cannot live. For if man in his sinful condition were allowed to eat of the Tree of Life, he would eventually find that what appeared to be eternal life was in fact eternal death—"the second death" (Rev. 20:14; 21:8; 14:10). And as with men in general, so it would be with the Savior, the Son of Man: "And Jesus answered them, saying, The hour is come, that the Son of man should be glorified. Verily, verily, I say unto you, Except a corn of wheat fall into the ground and die, it abideth alone: but if it die, it bringeth forth much fruit" (John 12:23–24).

CHAPTER FIVE

THE FORMATION OF
TWO ANTAGONISTIC KINGDOMS

A FTER THE PROLOGUE (GEN. 1:1–2:3) has established that God, the Creator and Sustainer of all life, formed the man and woman to have dominion over the earth as heirs of His earthly kingdom, the story of the Bible begins with an account of how, in the very dawn of history, two antagonistic kingdoms developed on earth—the kingdom of the world and the kingdom of God (2:4–4:26). The formation of these two kingdoms unfolds in three stages: (1) the original pattern and conditions for the life and destiny of God's heirs in His earthly kingdom (2:4–25); (2) Satan's subtle attack and victory over God's appointed heirs, and the response of the Savior to this attack (ch. 3); and (3) the development of an antagonistic spirit against God that eventually led to the formation of two opposing kingdoms (ch. 4).

This climactic section of primeval history presents the story of two diverse sons (4:1–15) who became, representatively, the patriarchs of two divisions of mankind (4:16–26).

THE TWO SONS (GEN. 4:1–15)

From the very beginning, the inspired writer highlights the differences in these two sons. The circumstances of their births were different; their interests were different—one was a shepherd, one a farmer; their offerings were different; their natures were different; and their destinies were different. Though some of these dissimilarities appear to be incidental, the author's emphases leave the cumulative impression that we are seeing here the first rivulets of two divergent streams of humanity.

Their Diverse Births and Interests (Gen. 4:1–2)

Literally, the opening statement in this paragraph reads, "And the man knew Eve his wife; and she conceived, and bare Cain, and said, I have gotten a man, the Lord!" These words, taken just as they read without assuming an ellipsis (with an understood expression such as "from" or "with the help of"), express the idea that Eve thought that the "man" she had received was the Lord, the promised Seed.

Could this be? Is it possible that Eve, at the very dawn of history, recognized that the promised Seed would be the Lord Himself? It seems to me that in its context the passage reveals that message. In order to see the contextual development of the story here, we need to forget the chapter divisions in our modern Bibles, and we need to empathize as much as possible with the perceptions and experience of Eve.

Just a few lines before this account of the birth of Cain, the inspired writer tells us of the Lord's promise that the Seed of the woman would crush the head of the serpent. By now, she clearly recognized that the serpent was simply the tool of a supernatural creature; and the revelation that a child taken from her own body would crush this creature was also a revelation that this child would be supernatural. Adam and Eve had seen the Lord, apparently in human form; and, from their vantage point, it would not be unnatural for them to conceive of the Lord taking human form as their Savior. It may be, in fact, that the Lord's occasional appearances in human form (e.g., Gen. 18:1–2; 19:1–2) were part of man's preparation for the Incarnation.

Would it then be unnatural for them to think that this, the first child ever born into the world, would be the promised Seed? Eve's description of the child is striking. "I have gotten a man (ish)," she says. Commonly, the Scriptural writers describe a newborn baby with terms such as son, male, or child—not as ish, a term that is sometimes used in Scripture to denote a noble or great man (e.g., Pss. 49:2; 62:9; I Sam. 26:15; Isa. 2:9).

The concept of the Lord coming to earth appears very early in biblical history and even (though in twisted form) in ancient traditions of the secular world. For example, Enoch, who would have lived and prophesied

I nterpreters who object to this interpretation of Eve's words in Genesis 4:1 commonly do so on the basis of what could be termed the progressive revelation of the messianic promise in the Bible. They assert that only gradually did the inspired writers reveal the nature, including the deity, of the Messiah. I readily acknowledge that the revelation of God the Son unfolds progressively in Scripture (as does the revelation of God the Father and God the Spirit), but I feel that there is another dynamic involved here. Parallel with the progressive revelation of God in history, there has been a progressive degeneration of man's capacity for divine revelation. To the extent that spiritual dullness has atrophied man's capacity to know God, to that extent an expanded and intensified revelation is necessary for a man to arrive at the goals God has for him.

Think about the dynamics involved here. A dull child in the sixth grade may have been exposed to more factual evidence than a brilliant child in the fourth grade but at the same time have considerably less insight into the nature of what he has studied than the little genius two grades below him does. On the basis of the same principle, it may well be that the first men and women on earth had considerably more insight into the true nature of God's revealed truth than those in succeeding generations who had the advantage of more light. As Hosea discovered when he attempted to proclaim God's revelation to his people, "Harlotry, wine, and new wine take away the understanding" (Hosea 4:11, NASB). As sin developed and progressed in the earth, how much of divine revelation became so twisted and distorted in the minds of men that God, in consequence, had to limit certain aspects of the original divine light lest even they become blinders? For example, once polytheism became virtually universal in the ancient world, a revelation of the triune nature of God in the Old Testament period would have been a stumbling block to the people of Israel.

while Adam was still alive, spoke of the Lord's coming to earth to judge sinners (Jude 14–15).

Whatever the case, Eve clearly had great hopes for this newborn child. She called him *Cain* ("possession") because she saw him as a most precious possession. Little could she have known in that blessed moment that the first baby born into the world would grow up to be a murderer, and that his name would come to represent the philosophy of untold generations following him—for "the way of Cain" (Jude 11) is the path of greed and self-centeredness, seeking your own at whatever cost.

By the time their second child came along, Adam and Eve were already much older and wiser in the realities of the sin nature, for they named him *Abel* ("vanity"). Apparently, by this time they had seen something of the emptiness and fruitlessness of life; and to their utter dismay, they had seen that their hopes that had rested in their first human possession were vain.

These brothers, whose births depicted differing circumstances, also had different interests. Abel was a keeper of sheep, Cain a tiller of the ground. Both were working within the sphere of God's original plan for man; but, as in all things, a person's pursuit of his interests is governed by his philosophy of life. Abel, in accordance with his philosophy, could see the importance of the sheep submitting to and following the shepherd. Cain, governed by his view of life, could see his own prowess and works wringing fruit out of a divinely cursed earth.

Their Diverse Offerings and Natures (Gen. 4:3–8)

And in process of time it came to pass, that Cain brought of the fruit of the ground an offering unto the Lord. And Abel, he also brought of the firstlings of his flock and of the fat thereof. And the Lord had respect unto Abel and to his offering: but unto Cain and to his offering he had not respect.

The expression translated *in the process of time* (literally, "at the end of days") indicates that a good deal of time had lapsed.[1] There is a sense in which the offerings of the two brothers emanated naturally from their occupations. Each brought a part of what he had labored to produce. But the inspired writer describes Abel's offering as "of the firstlings of his flock and of the fat thereof," whereas he describes Cain's offering as "the fruit of the ground"—not the first fruits of the ground but merely the fruit. Furthermore, the reference to the "fat thereof" indicates that Abel did not merely dedicate this animal to the Lord but also slew it.

When we consider the time we are dealing with in the revelation of God, it is remarkable that Abel felt compelled to slay the animal he was offering to the Lord. Meat was not used as food until after the Flood;

---

[1] Seth, whom God appointed as "another seed instead of Abel" (4:25), was born 130 years after creation (5:3). If we assume that Seth's birth took place not long after the murder of Abel, about 125 years had lapsed since creation. Of course, we don't know how long Adam and Eve were in the Garden before their fall, nor of how long after the Fall Cain and Abel were born. However, it seems reasonable to assume that about 100 years had lapsed since their births, for Cain has a wife and fears potential avengers of blood (4:14).

therefore, the thought of slaying an animal must have been entirely foreign to the mindset of that day. It must be that the Lord revealed the need for sacrifice—perhaps at the time He provided animal skins for the clothing of Adam and Eve.

> The idea of expressing religious feelings, or of expiating sin, by shedding the blood of animals, could never have entered into the mind of man. We read that God clothed our first parents with the skins of animals; and by far the most probable account of this matter is, that these were the skins of animals which He had commanded them to offer in sacrifice.[2]

It is undoubtedly for this reason—that God had revealed the need for sacrifice—that the writer of Hebrews declares, "By faith Abel offered unto God a more excellent sacrifice than Cain" (11:4). Abel's sacrifice was more excellent because it was an expression of his faith in the Lord and His word. The Lord rejected Cain's offering because it was not an expression of faith in the Lord. He was not trusting in the Lord when he came with his offering. He came, perhaps, in recognition of the Lord's power and to solicit His blessing; but, as his reaction to rejection indicates, his offering was an expression of his confidence in himself and in his works.

"And Cain was very wroth, and his countenance fell." Here Cain reveals both his nature and his mindset. He had come to worship the sovereign God, his Creator and Judge. Yet he rejected the judgment of the Lord he had allegedly come to worship. Why? Evidently because in his own judgment, his offering was fine. After all, he had the knowledge of good and evil, and by virtue of this knowledge was essentially a god in his own right. Why should he accept the judgment of this God Who claimed sovereignty over him?

The writer's description of Cain's anger is instructive as a characteristic of the "way of Cain." He describes him as raging (literally, "burning greatly") within, but as expressing this rage outwardly only with a downcast look of displeasure. This is a picture of utter frustration—the kind of frustration that results from the feeling that you've been denied something you have a perfect right to, and there's nothing you can do about it. Cain knew that the judgment of the Lord would stand. It was unfair, he thought, but there was nothing he could do to overturn it. He was left, then, with seething resentment (cf. Ps. 2:1; John 7:7; Rom. 8:7).

---

[2] Brown, *Hebrews*, 492–93 (see chap. 2, n. 8).

Graciously, the Lord appealed to Cain as to a willful child. His words (here expanded somewhat and interpreted) combine a compassionate appeal with an ominous warning of the danger that lurks in the nurtured folds of his anger: "If you make this matter right, shall not your countenance be joyfully lifted up? But if you do not make it right, sin crouches at the door of your heart; and your desire for blessing, rather than being fulfilled, will be under sin's control. It should not be this way: you should and can rule over sin."[3] The context suggests that the "lifting up" (translated *accepted* in the KJV) of verse 7 is the counterpart to the "fallen" countenance of Cain (vv. 5, 6). As a fallen countenance depicts a gloomy or sullen spirit, a lifted countenance pictures a joyful, open spirit (cf. Job 10:15; 11:15; 22:26).

Cain answered the Lord with sullen silence—a silence that enshrouded and insulated his soul from the light of true life.

Their Diverse Destinies (Gen. 4:9–15)

The Character of Cain

Even an embittered soul observes a certain respectful protocol toward power, and so it was with Cain. In the presence of the Lord, he stifled his anger and maintained an aura of silent reverence; but he felt no such need, either for silence or respect, toward his brother. In striking contrast with his stubborn silence toward the Lord, "Cain talked with Abel his brother." What did he talk with him about? The writer chooses not to tell us. Instead, he simply attaches this cryptic account of Cain's words with his brother to the crime he committed against him—and in so doing he makes the words accessories to the crime.

The words *when they were in the field* suggest the possibility of some premeditation on Cain's part—if not premeditation, at least a sense of freedom from accountability. He may have invited him to go with him out in the field,[4] perhaps his own field, under the guise of seeking help from one who had found a way to please God. Undoubtedly, he told Abel that the Lord had rejected his gift. If his case was typical, he probably

---

[3] The Lord's appeal for Cain to do well (literally "good") cannot be an appeal for him to begin living right, though the Lord, of course, knew that he had been living wickedly (I John 3:12). This would have been an appeal for him to earn favor with God by his good works—to say nothing of the fact that a sudden change of lifestyle by Cain would not erase the sins of his past. The Lord's appeal was for Cain to make this matter right by repenting of his sin.

[4] The LXX reads, "And Cain said to Abel his brother, Let us go out into the plain," and the Latin Vulgate has, "Let us go abroad."

expected his brother to sympathize with him and to wonder with him at the unfairness of it all. When his brother, instead of sympathizing and agreeing with him, took up the cause of the Lord, his words turned intense, then accusatory, then angry: "And it came to pass, when they were in the field, that Cain rose up against Abel his brother, and slew him."

What drove Cain to commit such a heinous act? We're inclined in our day to blame acts of violence on "the times," but Cain was not living in a time of violence. Violence was virtually unheard of in his day; and, evidently, deliberately taking another person's life was unthinkable—so much so that Cain feared that people everywhere would call for his blood (4:14). Furthermore, Cain's murderous action was not simply a crime of passion. The circumstances of the murder reveal no such thing as uncontrolled rage, and there is no evidence whatsoever of a feeling of regret afterwards. For some reason, Cain had a compulsion to get rid of his brother—to blot him out of his life. Why?

To find the answer, we must trace Cain's sinful nature to its root. Adam and Eve first sinned because they wanted to be like Elohim—to be gods in their own right. By eating of the Tree of the Knowledge of Good and Evil, man declared his independence from God. Ever since that day, the goal of mankind has been independence and self-sufficiency: "Let us break their bands asunder, and cast away their cords from us" (Ps. 2:3).

Of course, man found that Elohim was infinitely superior to him in knowledge and power. Therefore, it became necessary to appeal to Elohim for help and blessing—and some humbled themselves fully before the Lord and looked to Him alone for salvation and fulfillment. But those (like Cain) who refused to humbly acknowledge the sovereignty of the Lord learned to hate God and His followers. God and His followers represented a threat to their own godhood. Cain knew that he could not get rid of God, his supreme Protagonist. But he thought he could ignore Him, and he could certainly rid himself of Abel, Elohim's representative on earth.

In his hatred of God and the people of God, Cain is a prototype of the people of the world. Jesus told His disciples, "If ye were of the world, the world would love his own: but because ye are not of the world, but I have chosen you out of the world, therefore the world hateth you" (John 15:19).

The Condemnation of Cain

"And the Lord said unto Cain, Where is Abel thy brother?" These are words of grace, designed to awaken a slumbering conscience. The words *thy brother* add a poignant touch to the question. Twice at the time of the murder, the inspired writer emphasizes the words *his brother* to show the unnatural wickedness of this crime. Now the words fall from the mouth of the Lord Himself—as if to see whether Cain held even a vestige of the filial love he once shared with his brother. Cain's response is shocking in its impudence and hardness. "I know not: am I my brother's keeper?" These words are almost as strange as they are impudent. Did he really think he could hide his dark secret from the omniscient God, the Creator Who had spoken the world into existence? Was he indeed announcing to the Judge Himself that he had no responsibility for the welfare of his brother? It is strange, also, that he who had been so reticent before could now speak so boldly and critically.

Cain's unrepentant and hardened spirit confirmed, the Lord pronounces sentence upon him:

> What hast thou done? the voice of thy brother's blood crieth unto me from the ground. And now art thou cursed from the earth, which hath opened her mouth to receive thy brother's blood from thy hand; when thou tillest the ground, it shall not henceforth yield unto thee her strength; a fugitive and a vagabond shalt thou be in the earth (vv. 10–12).

The divine sentence begins with an exclamation of the enormity of the crime committed: "What hast thou done!" Then the Judge presents the evidence: "The voice of thy brother's blood crieth unto me from the ground." The cry of the blood symbolizes the cry of murdered Abel for justice (cf. Rev. 6:9–10). And the Judge responds to the cry by issuing Cain a decree of poetic justice: the earth that absorbed the lifeblood of Abel shall for you be cursed in its ability to produce life. And you, in your search for the enhanced life you thought shedding blood would bring, are doomed instead to wander restlessly, unfulfilled, during your days on earth.

The vacuum created by impudent self-confidence is filled naturally and easily with despair. The severity of the judgment quickly deflates Cain's shameless bravado, and now he whines pitifully before the bar of justice, "My punishment is greater than I can bear. Behold, thou hast driven me out this day from the face of the earth; and from thy face shall I be hid;

Why did the God Who later commanded the execution of murderers preserve the life of unrepentant Cain? Did God's law change as the times changed? To deal with this question, we must first establish some biblical principles. According to God's eternal law, all sin deserves the death penalty. In fact, this penalty will ultimately be executed on all sinners. Therefore, all extension of life is a matter of God's grace, related to His plan of salvation; and all earthly penalties for sin are matters of God's saving grace. The Lord's earthly penalties for sin correspond to earthly sinners' needs related to His plan of salvation. Cain's fear of outraged avengers of blood indicates that at this early stage of history, God did not need to impose the death penalty as a teaching tool or controlling factor. Only later, after violence had increased inordinately, did an earthly death penalty become necessary. Based on His nature, God's eternal law has never changed and never will change. Nevertheless, He may, in His gracious plan of salvation, choose to change the earthly penalties for violations of His law.

and I shall be a fugitive and a vagabond in the earth; and it shall come to pass, that every one that findeth me shall slay me."

His plea is characteristic of an unrepentant sinner facing judgment. He laments the unfairness of the troubles he will face as a result of the punishment, yet he begins with a formal acknowledgment of his sin. Literally rendered, his opening line is "My iniquity is greater than I can bear."[5] With these words, Cain becomes the prototype for one of the most common of the semantic ploys in the sinner's repertoire. He willingly, even glibly, takes the word *sin* on his lips while his whole verbal supporting cast laments the troubles sin brings, not the wickedness of the sin itself.

The thrust of the next sentence is "If this is indeed the case, then I will surely be slain by an avenger of blood."[6] He complains that the Lord is

---

[5] In fact, this sentence could be translated, "My iniquity is greater than can be forgiven." The word translated *bear* (*nasa*) means "to lift up or bear (carry)," but it is sometimes used in the Old Testament in the sense of "to take away or forgive." The translation *bear* seems to fit the context of Gen. 4:13 better. In Ps. 38:4 and Isa. 24:20, the inspired writers speak of iniquity as a great burden. Nevertheless, an argument could be made for contextual support of the other translation as well. With his claim that he would be hidden from the presence of the Lord, Cain may have been reemphasizing the notion that he could never be forgiven. As strange as it seems, sinners sometimes find twisted comfort in the notion that God will not forgive them. This relieves them (so they think) of the responsibility of dealing with the most compelling fact of life—that God would have all men to be saved.

[6] The word translated *behold* (*hen, hinneh*) can, if it introduces a condition, have the significance

driving him "from the face of the earth." In other words, the decree of unfruitfulness means that he will be forced to leave the fruitfulness and civilization near Eden—which would also mean being hidden from the protective presence of the Lord. Evidently, before the Flood, the Garden of Eden continued to serve as a holy place, a sanctuary from which the Lord manifested Himself. Cain apparently viewed the presence of the Lord as limited to this Garden area or its adjoining territory where worshipers came before the Lord.

Cain's appeal is driven by fear—fear for his own life. Was forgiveness and restoration possible for this murderer? He had to be aware of the fact that God had been wonderfully gracious and forgiving toward his parents, though it was through their sin that the curse of death had come to the human race. But Cain has no real desire for reconciliation. His attitude toward God has not changed. He is at enmity with Him, and reconciliation would involve submitting to his Enemy as his Savior and Sovereign. He stands as a condemned murderer pleading for his life before the bar of justice. He finds no real fault with his own action toward his brother. He finds fault instead with God's judgment. God has overlooked one problem, he suggests, in the implementation of His judgment: it will not restrict others from doing to him what he himself has done to Abel.

Nevertheless, though the Lord knew all this about Cain, He set a mark of protection upon him. "And the Lord said unto him, Therefore whosoever slayeth Cain, vengeance shall be taken on him sevenfold. And the Lord set a mark upon Cain, lest any finding him should kill him."[7] The

---

of *if* (e.g., II Chron. 7:13; Job 13:15). In Gen. 4:14, Cain is lamenting that the condition, or circumstances, of his judgment will make him constantly vulnerable to any outraged relative who feels he should be executed.

[7] The word translated *mark* (*owth*) is the general Hebrew word for *sign*; and, as with our English word, it covers a wide range of concepts. In the Old Testament, the word is used to denote a miracle or wonder (e.g., Exod. 4:8–9; Deut. 11:3); but it is used also to depict an identifying symbol, standard, or flag (e.g., Num 2:2; Deut. 11:18; cf. Gen. 9:12–13; 17:11). Therefore, we can't say confidently on the basis of the word itself (as some interpreters do) that the sign was a heavenly wonder of some sort to assure Cain that he would be protected from violence. The contextual drift of the narrative suggests that the Lord must have put a physical mark on Cain. Aside from the question of why Cain—before whom the Lord Himself was evidently standing—would need or benefit from a miracle, we should remember that Cain's plea arises from fears concerning his future wanderings in the earth, wanderings that might involve several hundred years. As the earth increased in population, people far and wide would know of Cain's heinous act, would be outraged against him, and would be concerned that his presence would endanger the welfare of their family members. These people needed some physical indication that God, in His grace, had ordained that Cain should not be executed.

mark, whatever it was, served both as a warning and as evidence of God's abundant grace in preserving the life of this murderer.

As with his bereft and grieving parents, the death penalty would fall on Cain. But for now, he and his descendants will be allowed to live—in accordance with the Lord's gracious plan for the salvation of mankind.

THE TWO DIVISIONS OF MANKIND (GEN. 4:16–26)

And thus, it would seem, ends the tragic story of two sons. But, in fact, this is only the beginning. From these two sons eventually developed two divisions of mankind—two kingdoms, really. Cain and his "way"—his philosophy of life—set the stage for the development of the kingdom of the world, one dominated and energized by the Serpent. Abel, and the path of life he chose, set the stage for the development of God's earthly kingdom, a kingdom antagonistic in spirit and philosophy to the kingdom of the Serpent.

The Ungodly Line of Cain (Gen. 4:16–24)

"And Cain went out from the presence of the Lord, and dwelt in the land of Nod, on the east of Eden." Cain's move eastward took him from the place of the Lord's manifestation—His "presence"—at the sanctuary in Eden; but there is much more involved here. The physical distance he put between himself and the presence of the Lord reflected his spiritual distancing from the Lord. In effect, the geographical barrier solidified and crystallized the spiritual barrier he had established by his life of wicked deeds.

The name Nod is from the same root as the word translated vagabond (vv. 12, 14) and signifies wandering. Even as Cain sought to establish himself in one place and neutralize the curse, he still dwelt in the land of restless wandering (Isa. 48:22; 57:20–21).

It may have been centuries later that Cain began building a city; and he called his new city Enoch after the name of his son. Enoch means "to dedicate or inaugurate." To Cain, and undoubtedly to his descendants, this new city represented a new beginning, the establishment of a new civilization. From the standpoint of scriptural revelation, Enoch was the first capital of the kingdom of the world. Succeeding centuries would bring other capitals for this kingdom, but the genius—the spirit and character—of the kingdom would remain the same. Its sovereign, the Serpent, would remain the same.

With Lamech, the seventh from Adam, the character of the Cainite line surfaces. As Cain had exemplified the free reign of passion, so did Lamech—only Lamech legalized his passions at the marriage altar: "And Lamech took unto him two wives: the name of the one was Adah, and the name of the other Zillah." Cain had sought to neutralize the curse of his sin in the stability and security of a city. Lamech through his children added beauty, power, and wealth to the City of Destruction: "And Adah bare Jabal: he was the father of such as dwell in tents and have cattle. And his brother's name was Jubal: he was the father of all such as handle the harp and pipe. And Zillah, she also bare Tubal-cain, the forger of every cutting instrument of brass and iron: and the sister of Tubal-cain was Naamah" (Gen. 4:20–22, ASV).

The curse of Cain had included restlessness and wandering. Jabal, the son of Adah, made the nomadic way of life a means of gaining earthly possessions.[8] Cain brought discord and tension into the milieu of life; but Jubal's music neutralized and even beautified the dissonance. Cain's act of violence caused him to fear retribution from his fellow man. But Tubal-cain's forging of sharp weapons of brass and iron neutralized fear.

Cain might well have gloried in his violence had he not been arraigned for judgment so soon after the crime. But Lamech has no such problem. In a poetic ecstasy, he tells his wives—and his posterity—about the "justifiable homicide" of a young man who had accosted and wounded him:

And Lamech said unto his wives, Adah and Zillah, Hear my voice; ye wives of Lamech, hearken unto my speech: for I have slain a man to my wounding, and a young man to my hurt. If Cain shall be avenged sevenfold, truly Lamech seventy and sevenfold.

Quite appropriately, this piece of martial poetry has been called "Lamech's Sword Song." Tubal-cain had pioneered in the forging of all types of brazen and iron cutting instruments—undoubtedly including weapons. A young man had wounded Lamech; and in self-defense (so reads his elegy), he drew his shiny new filial gift and killed the offender.[9]

---

[8] The name Cain (*Qayin,* "possession") and the word translated *cattle* are from the same root (*qanah,* "to get," "possess"). In ancient times, a person's possessions were commonly determined by the number of cattle he had.

[9] The language here allows for the possibility that Lamech is boasting of what he would do if he were attacked; but the interpretation reflected in such translations as the KJV and the NASB is

The last line of Lamech's elegy vents the overweening arrogance that underlay his godless spirit. "If Cain shall be avenged sevenfold, truly Lamech seventy and sevenfold." Cain had appealed to God for protection, and the Lord had promised strict judgment on those who would harm him. Lamech imagines himself beyond the need of divine help. He himself will wreak vengeance on anyone who ventures to attack him—a vengeance more fearful than God Himself would execute.

Lamech's insolent and profane spirit was evidently pandemic in the earth at this time. Judging from the life spans given in Genesis 5, Lamech would have lived about the time of godly Enoch. According to the account of the godly line (if we allow for no genealogical gaps in years), Enoch would have been raptured almost one thousand years after Creation, about six hundred years (less than one full generation) before the Flood. Enoch characterized the people of his day as godless and impudent:

> And Enoch also, the seventh from Adam, prophesied of these, saying, Behold, the Lord cometh with ten thousands of his saints, to execute judgment upon all, and to convince all that are ungodly [asebes, "without reverence, profane, ungodly"] among them of all their ungodly deeds which they have ungodly committed, and of all their hard speeches which ungodly sinners have spoken against him (Jude 14–15).

By this time, the philosophy and spirit of the kingdom of the Serpent dominated the world. People generally had lost all reverence toward God. Cain's insolent attitude and hard words toward the Lord ("Am I my brother's keeper?") had fully blossomed in his descendants.

The Godly Line of Seth (Gen. 4:25–26)

This primeval history of the development of two antagonistic kingdoms (2:4–4:26) began with an account of the original pattern and conditions in God's earthly kingdom (2:4–25) and with the story of the Serpent's attack on the heirs of the kingdom and of the Lord's redeeming work in their behalf. The climax of this narrative introduces two diverse brothers who personify the two kingdoms. Now the potential godly heir to the kingdom has been slain; and the ungodly line of Cain, in spite of the divine curse, seems to be dominant in the world.

---

more consistent with the wording of the poem. The word translated young man (yeled) refers even when used of an adult to an inexperienced, younger person. In a fictional portrayal of himself as an avenging master of martial arts, a person such as Lamech would not boast of killing an inexperienced opponent.

What has become of God's plan for mankind? What of His redemptive plan? Did not God make man in His image to reign with Him in the earth? How will this be accomplished? Through the Tree of Knowledge, the Cainite civilization now controls the earthly kingdom.

Now we see the two kingdoms in vivid contrast. In the kingdom of the Serpent, we expect to see sorrow, frustration, unfruitfulness, and loneliness. Instead, we see civilization, prosperity, culture, refinement, and power. On the other hand, we see no such advancement in the kingdom of God. Seth ("appointed one") is born to take the place of Abel. Is the kingdom of God to develop from this infant? As they watch the kingdom of the world develop apace, the people of God have no choice but to wait and hope.

After a full century, a child is born to continue the godly line of Abel. But with the joy of the birth of Enosh, there must have also been disappointment and fear. *Enosh*, one of the names for man in the Bible, depicts man as weak and frail.[10] Perhaps the child Enosh was weak and sickly, an unlikely instrument for establishing a godly line of heirs for God's kingdom. Whatever the case, his name reveals an awakening to reality that drove the children of God to begin anew "to call upon the name of the Lord."

On such realities the kingdom of God is built. "The kingdom of heaven is like to a grain of mustard seed, which a man took, and sowed in his field: which indeed is the least of all seeds: but when it is grown, it is the greatest among herbs, and becometh a tree, so that the birds of the air come and lodge in the branches thereof" (Matt. 13:31–32). "Therefore I take pleasure in infirmities, in reproaches, in necessities, in persecutions, in distresses for Christ's sake: for when I am weak, then am I strong" (II Cor. 12:10).

The next episode of the story of mankind (Gen. 5:1–6:9) will continue the story of the development—and the tragic decline and compromise—of the godly line from Adam through Seth to Noah.

---

[10] Hebrew scholars differ concerning the root of *enosh*, but I agree with Leupold and others that contextual evidence in numbers of passages supports the idea that the word is related to *anash*, "to be weak, frail, sick." This passage (Gen. 4:26) seems to be associating men's perceiving themselves as weak with a revival of "calling upon the name of the Lord." At the same time, the writer seems to be contrasting the last-mentioned person in the Cainite line, Lamech (who saw himself as powerful), with the last-mentioned in the godly line. Other references in which *enosh* is related to weakness include Job 4:17; 10:4–5; 33:12; Ps. 8:4 (where *enosh*, "weak man," is used synonymously with *adam*, "man from dust"); Ps. 103:15; and II Chron. 14:11.

CHAPTER SIX

COMPROMISE AND CORRUPTION

WITH DIAMETRICALLY OPPOSED LIFE PRINCIPLES, these two kingdoms continued to develop in the earth. However, encroaching and degenerative wickedness eventually infected all mankind, and the children of God became entangled in marital alliances with the children of the world—a disastrous compromise that resulted in universal condemnation.

DEVELOPMENT AND DECLINE IN GOD'S KINGDOM (GEN. 5)

The title, "The Book of the History of Adam," has an air of formality. It is the only one of the dozen or so historical ("generations") introductions in Genesis that is called a "book." This suggests that we are dealing here with an important document, perhaps a written account with which Moses was familiar.

The next statement is something of a subtitle, or explanatory enlargement, of the designation for this history: "In the day that God created man, in the likeness of God made he him; male and female created he them; and blessed them, and called their name Adam ["man"], in the day when they were created." With these words, the inspired writer adds an element of focus to his history. He is going to tell us the history of Adam in light of God's original plan for man. God created man in His own image; and by creating them male and female and blessing them, He evidently intended for mankind to increase and develop in accordance with His original plan.

It seems almost an afterthought—and an unnecessary one at that—when Moses adds "and called their name *adam*, in the day when they were created." Why was it necessary for him to say this? We are already well acquainted with the first man and with the designation *adam* for mankind. It was necessary as a reminder of the humble substance from which God chose to make man. "And the Lord God formed man [*adam*] of the dust of the ground [*adamah*] .... For dust thou art, and unto dust shalt thou return" (Gen. 2:7; 3:19).

God made man in His own image to reign with Him—the writer emphasizes this anew with the words "Adam ... begat a son in his own likeness, after his image" (5:3)—but though He made man in His image, He chose also to make him of the dust of the earth. Herein lies the key to the ultimate fulfillment of man's destiny. In order to reign with God, man must recognize his true relationship with His Maker. This will bring him both humility and dignity: "But now, O Lord, thou art our father; we are the clay, and thou our potter; and we all are the work of thy hand" (Isa. 64:8); "Humble yourselves therefore under the mighty hand of God, that he may exalt you in due time" (I Pet. 5:6).

And how did man prepare for his destiny? Did he recognize his true relationship with his Creator—made in the image of God, yet made of dust? Did he prepare for his destiny by humbling himself under the mighty hand of his Maker? We know that one division of mankind, the Cainite branch, chose instead to eat heartily of the Tree of Knowledge; and by this means—by exercising their ability to choose for themselves what was good for them—they would (they supposed) fulfill their destiny and reign over the earth.

At this point in the narrative, it appears that the program of the Cainites was succeeding. They were apparently more numerous than the Sethites and were clearly far ahead of them in prosperity, culture, and power. Deprived of proximity to Paradise, they were building their own. Little did they know, little did they care, that all their efforts were mere embellishments, deceptive gilding on the curse. Inexorably, they were heading for disaster.

Interpreters, including many conservatives, commonly assume that the genealogies of Genesis 5 and 11 have chronological gaps in them that allow for the addition of many years and that make it impossible to determine the number of years from Adam to Noah and from Shem to Abraham. It is true that the biblical writers, in accordance with the requirements of their messages, often omit names in genealogical lists (e.g., Ruth 4:18–22; Matt. 1:1–17). However, it is difficult to see how the structure of Genesis 5 and 11 allows for such chronological gaps in these passages. It is true also that in ancient times terms like *begat*, *father*, and *son* were used with greater latitude than they are today. But in these genealogies, even if we assume that a certain father-son relationship may in fact be a grandfather-grandson relationship, the chronology remains intact. For example, from the standpoint of a Jew in biblical times, I could legitimately say that my grandfather lived forty-three years and begat me—that is, he was forty-three years old when I was born into my father's household.

Though the chronology of Genesis 11:10–32 is not as detailed as that of Genesis 5, the same principle holds true. In this case, we know that Luke (evidently following the LXX) inserts the name *Cainan* between Arphaxad and Salah (Luke 3:35–36; Gen. 11:12–13). Some conservative Bible scholars feel that since *Cainan* is not in the Hebrew text or the oldest Greek manuscripts, it should be viewed as spurious. But the case for the chronological consistency of Genesis 11 does not hinge on this question. If the name Cainan is valid, the more consistent contextual approach would be to assume that Arphaxad, at age thirty-five, was the grandfather of Salah.

The first part of "The Book of the History of Adam" (Gen. 5), with its account of the development of the godly line, leads us to the brink of this disaster. The decline of the power and influence of the children of God is virtually imperceptible in this part of the story. We are impressed, instead, with the longevity of these ancient patriarchs; and we tend to think that longevity—and the multiplication of the race that results—is a sign of blessing and of growing power.

Nevertheless, already among the sons of God there had been some hints of decline and of the infiltration of the world's philosophy. Even the encouraging words "then began men to call upon the name of the Lord" (4:26b) suggest that before this time, men had not been doing so. Enosh was born 235 years after creation, when Seth was 105 years old.

Thus, in only two generations, devotion to God had declined—even among the sons of God. As the words of Jude (14–16) reveal, by the time of Enoch, four generations later, the spirit of rebellion and irreverence had virtually permeated society before Adam had passed off the scene.[1]

About seventy years after Enoch was raptured, Noah ("comfort") was born. His father, Lamech, prophesied that his son was so named because "This same shall comfort us concerning our work and toil of our hands, because of the ground which the Lord hath cursed" (Gen. 5:29b). The word *comfort* seems hardly an appropriate representation of the cataclysmic judgment that was to come in Noah's day. But indeed the judgment would bring comfort and rest. The curse of Cain had reached its full blossom in the burdened, insecure, and restless antediluvian society. "But the wicked are like the troubled sea, when it cannot rest, whose waters cast up mire and dirt. There is no peace, saith my God, to the wicked" (Isa. 57:20–21).

CORRUPTION THROUGH COMPROMISE

"Since, therefore, the giant [Diabolus] could not make him [Mr. Conscience] wholly his own, what doth he do but study all that he could to debauch the old gentleman, and by debauchery to stupify his mind and more harden his heart in the ways of vanity."[2] With the sons of God in the primeval world, Diabolus followed the same strategy. Though he could not make them "wholly his own," he could find ways to defile them.

For a few generations, the descendants of Cain must have been isolated somewhat from the descendants of Seth. "Cain went out from the presence of the Lord, and dwelt in the land of Nod, on the east of Eden"; he moved from one physical location to another. This suggests that the expression *the presence of the Lord* represents the place of God's manifestation, the first "temple" of the Lord. This must have been the Garden of Eden, where God had previously met with Adam and Eve. Sinful man could no longer live there, and cherubim guarded the way of the Tree of

---

[1] Enoch would have been 308 years old when Adam died. Enoch's prophecy is clearly eschatological. He is speaking of the final coming of Christ to execute judgment on the sinful. But Jude includes the apostates of his day in this judgment, and certainly the apostates of Enoch's day should be included as well. The prophets were messengers first to their own generation. When they by divine inspiration envisioned final judgment, they proclaimed this judgment to their contemporaries.

[2] Bunyan, *Holy War*, 75 (see Introduction, n. 3).

Life. But evidently, man continued to meet with God nearby until the Flood, when all (including Eden) was destroyed.

Whatever the case, Cain had moved "east of Eden" and begun building a city and a civilization some distance from this primeval temple and from the people who worshiped there. However, as "men began to multiply on the face of the earth," there had to be contact and interaction between the two societies. It has been conservatively estimated that the population of the earth at the time of the Flood must have been not less than twelve billion.[3] The necessity of a universal flood indicates that by that time there must have been people dwelling in all parts of the earth. Consequently, there had to be contact and interaction between the descendants of Cain and the descendants of Seth.

"And it came to pass, when men began to multiply on the face of the earth, and daughters were born unto them, that the sons of God saw the daughters of men that they were fair; and they took them wives of all which they chose" (Gen. 6:1–2). Perhaps in earlier days the family of Seth, dwelling in the land of Eden, had looked with foreboding at Cain's growing family in the distant east. After all, these people were under a special curse from God. According to God's Word, they were doomed to a life of restlessness and fruitlessness. Word must have eventually reached the Sethites of the Cainites' growing violence and promiscuity. But word must also have come of their cultural advancement. There were musicians, poets, and artists among them. There seemed to be good people among these Cainites. They weren't all murderers, as Cain had been; nor were they all bigamists, as Lamech had been. And it wasn't as if they were all devoid of the knowledge of God. After all, Cain himself had been a worshiper of God.

It must have been relatively easy for sons of God to convince themselves that they could legitimately and safely intermarry with Cainite women. "The sons of God saw the daughters of men that they were *good.*" It is interesting that the inspired writer chose to use the word *good* (*tov*) here. This word can be translated *fair* or *beautiful* (e.g., Gen. 24:16; II Sam. 11:2), but its primary meaning is much broader. This is the same word the opening chapters of Genesis use to describe God's creative work and God's marriage plans for man. There the word *good* means "appropriate, fulfilling God's purpose." The rationale of man undoubtedly included

---

[3] Alfred M. Rehwinkel, *The Flood* (St. Louis: Concordia, 1951), 28ff.

these thoughts, but in fact, the context of Genesis 6 indicates that the sons of God were driven more by sensuality than by thoughts of fulfilling God's will. The words "they took them wives of all which they chose" carry the tones of willfulness and rashness.

Oblivious now to the words and will of God, man is driven instead by his own impulses. Could he but hear heaven speak, he would hear ominous words: "My spirit shall not always strive with man, for that he also is flesh: yet his days shall be an hundred and twenty years" (Gen. 6:3). The sons of God, dominated by carnal considerations in their choice of life partners, demonstrate that man is indeed flesh and that further degeneration is inevitable.

While the children of God maintained separation from sin and sinners, corruption could not become thoroughly pervasive; but now all hope of the preservation of purity is gone. In one generation, one hundred twenty years, mankind will be ripe for judgment. The "salt of the earth," having lost its savor, "is thenceforth good for nothing, but to be cast out, and to be trodden under foot of men" (Matt. 5:13b). "Therefore, the law is ignored and justice is never upheld. For the wicked surround the righteous; therefore, justice comes out perverted" (Hab. 1:4, NASB).

Genesis 6:4 further proves the pervasive wickedness of this civilization—now unhindered by the influence of the godly: "Tyrants were in the earth in those days—and also after that when the sons of God came in unto the daughters of men and bore children to them—these tyrants were the heroes of ancient times, men of renown" (6:4, private translation).[4]

---

[4] Interpreters often assume that this passage presents the *nephilim* as coming from the union of the sons of God and the daughters of men; but, in fact, the passage teaches that the *nephilim* were in the earth before the intermarriage took place. "To the unprejudiced mind, the words, as they stand, represent the *Nephilim*, who were on the earth in those days, as existing before the sons of God began to marry the daughters of men, and clearly distinguish them from the fruits of these marriages." Keil, *The Pentateuch*, 1:137.

The Hebrew word *nephilim*, translated *giants* by the Septuagint and the Authorized Version, is probably from a root meaning "to fall, or to fall upon" (i.e., to attack, kill). Keil, ibid.; H. C. Leupold, *Exposition of Genesis*, 2 vols. (Grand Rapids: Baker, 1960), 1:258. The only other place *nephilim* appears in the Old Testament is Numbers 13:33, where the context provides some justification for the translation *giants*. However, as Leupold notes, this translation in the Genesis passage "directs attention away from the moral issue (wicked bandits) to a physical one (tall stature)." Ibid., 1:259. In Genesis, the inspired writer further identifies the *nephilim* as *gibborim* ("mighty ones, heroes") and as *men of renown*. The root of the Hebrew word *gibborim* and its derivatives appear over three hundred times in the Old Testament, and cognates of this root appear commonly in other Semitic languages of the Middle East. *TWOT*, 1:148 (see chap. 3, n. 3).

I believe the context and the language require that the "sons of God" in Genesis 6 be viewed as professed believers (Sethites) who intermarry with unbelievers (Cainites). The term *son(s) of God* appears only six times in the Old Testament (Gen. 6:2, 4; Job 1:6; 2:1; 38:7; and Dan. 3:25). Interpreters who hold that the sons of God were fallen angels generally claim that the Old Testament uses this term only of angels, sometimes claiming also that the concept of a man or woman being a child of God was unknown in the Old Testament. The expression *sons of God* in Job 1:6; 2:2; and 38:7 certainly refers to angels. But there is no scriptural evidence that this expression is ever used of fallen angels. In fact, the concept of being a son (or child) of God in both Testaments presupposes spiritual harmony and favor with God. (See Deut. 14:1; 32:5; Ps. 73:15; Prov. 14:26; Jer. 3:19; 31:1, 9; Hosea 1:10; John 1:12; Rom. 8:14–16; II Cor. 6:18; Gal. 3:26.) The New Testament writers use terms such as *sons of God* and *children of God* without explanation—as designations familiar to their readers and hearers who had yet only the Old Testament revelation. Biblically, a "son of God" would be any creature (whether supernatural or human) who is in spiritual harmony with God.

The preceding unit in Genesis (2:4–4:26) climaxed with telling about the establishment and character of the Cainite civilization (the kingdom of the world) and the renewal of the Sethite civilization (the kingdom of God). The next unit, 5:1–6:8 (as marked by the *toledoth* introductions), shows the genealogical links in the godly line from Adam to Noah. It was by Noah that God would deliver the Sethite civilization from the encroaching wickedness that had engulfed all mankind. This leads naturally to the view that Genesis 6 describes the intermarriage of the people of God with the people of the world.

Likewise, the language of Genesis 6 supports this view as well. Advocates of the fallen-angel interpretation hold that these creatures committed the unnatural sin of lusting after earthly women and committing fornication with them (Jude 6–8; II Pet. 2:4–10). However, as Keil has well observed, the statement Moses used for taking wives (Gen. 6:2) "is a standing expression throughout the whole Old Testament for the marriage relation established by God at creation," and is never applied to fornication or simply to physical relations. *The Pentateuch*, 1:131 (see chap. 3, n. 2).

Furthermore, saying that the sons of God were attracted to certain "daughters of men" by their beauty conflicts with Christ's words about the nature of angels (Matt. 22:30; Mark 12:25; Luke 20:36). How can asexual supernatural creatures with no capacity for reproduction be sexually attracted to earthly women and through them produce children? Saying (as some interpreters do) that our Lord's words refer to angels in heaven—good angels—does little to answer this. We are dealing here with the nature of angels, who are asexual spirit beings. Unless we are prepared to say that rebellion is inherently related to sexuality, how can we say that the apostasy of certain angels made them sexual creatures?

Advocates of the fallen-angel view generally take their cue from Jude's comparison of fallen angels with Sodom and Gomorrah:

> And the angels which kept not their first estate, but left their own habitation, he hath reserved in everlasting chains under darkness unto the judgment of the great day. Even as Sodom and Gomorrha, and the cities about them in like manner [to these (*toutois*)], giving themselves over to fornication, and going after strange flesh, are set forth for an example, suffering the vengeance of eternal fire (Jude 6–7).

These interpreters observe that since the word "these" (*toutois*) is masculine and the word "cities" is feminine, *toutois* could not refer to the cities of the plain, as some claim. It must refer to the angels. But Jude may be referring back to the "ungodly men" of verse 4 (where he began this discussion of apostates). Or he may have used the masculine because he had in mind the inhabitants of the cities, saying that the cities did not commit fornication, the inhabitants did. Furthermore, even if *these* refers to the angels, it by no means follows that the angels must have "given themselves over to fornication." The point of comparison is the degeneration and degradation of apostates. As the angels left their place of dignity and descended into a lowly sphere, so did the people of Sodom and Gomorrah. The emphasis of verses 5–7 is on the departure of apostates from one sphere to another.

We might add that the expression *strange flesh* (*sarkos heteras*, "different flesh"), which is used to support the fallen-angel view, actually clashes with it. This expression applies to human beings who practice unnatural sex, but it does not apply to spirit beings who unite with creatures of flesh. The fallen-angel theory calls for spirit beings simply to follow after flesh, not *different* flesh. The Bible speaks of Jesus as having come "in the flesh" (e.g., I John 4:2–3; cf. John 1:14). It would be inappropriate (as well as theologically inaccurate) to speak of Christ as coming in "different flesh."

The context of Genesis 6:4 clearly presents the *nephilim* as key players in the degeneration of the antediluvian civilization. The spirit of violence that Cain introduced grew until "the earth was filled with violence" (Gen. 6:11*b*). In such a civilization, the most powerful (the *gibborim*) become the heroes and "saviors" of society (cf. Gen. 10:8–10; Dan. 11:38).

The universal dominance of the kingdom of the Serpent demanded the destruction of the world. The world, lying in the lustful embrace of the Evil One (I John 5:19), was given over wholly to corruption.

> And God saw that the wickedness of man was great in the earth, and that every imagination of the thoughts of his heart was only evil continually. And it repented the Lord that he had made man on the earth, and it grieved him at his heart. And the Lord said, I will destroy man whom I have created from the face of the earth; both man, and beast, and the creeping thing, and the fowls of the air; for it repenteth me that I have made them (Gen. 6:5–7).

Here is a marvelous and sublime mystery—an expression of grief from the omniscient, omnipotent Creator of the universe! It is better to bask in the wonder of such realities than to attempt to adjust infinity to the reason-bound dimensions of our little minds. "Such knowledge is too wonderful for me; it is high, I cannot attain unto it" (Ps. 139:6).

At the same time, if we are to be guided in our thinking by God's own written revelation, we must let the Scriptures establish our parameters. On another occasion the Lord said to His prophet, "It repenteth me that I have set up Saul to be king." Yet later, the prophet said to Saul, "the Strength of Israel will not lie nor repent: for he is not a man, that he should repent" (I Sam. 15:11, 29).

In all of these passages, the word *repent* is based on the concept of sorrow. But the word's connotation in each case must be determined (as with all words) by its context. In his proclamation to Saul, Samuel uses *repent* synonymously with *lie*, his message being that God will not deal falsely with His own word and His own nature. His eternal plan can be fulfilled only in accordance with His holy nature and word. When these are violated, God will not allow His sorrow to move Him to change His plan.

In the other two passages, the inspired writers are depicting the Lord's sorrow for the objects of His infinite love. Theologians classify such statements as anthropomorphic—as attributing human characteristics to God; and, of course, the principle involved here is an inherent aspect of communication. Any communication, to be effective, must be conformed to the nature and capacity of its recipients. But our best means of understanding the mystery of divine sorrow is to view God Himself, in His incarnate form, as He interacts with the earthly objects of His love. When He saw Mary weeping, Jesus "groaned in spirit" and "wept." One week before His crucifixion, when He saw Jerusalem from the Mount of Olives, He burst into tears—at the thought, it seems, of what might have been (John 11:33–35; Luke 19:41; cf. Heb. 5:7).

As God pronounces judgment on the corrupt antediluvian civilization, the wonder is not that He expresses His grief. The wonder is that there is no record here of His anger—for surely He must have been outraged at the corruption He saw everywhere in His creation. "But Noah found grace in the eyes of the Lord."

THE LIGHT IN THE CLOUDS

"And now men see not the bright light which is in the clouds" (Job 37:21). God's love for man demands that His immutable purpose for him be fulfilled. "Noah was a just man and perfect in his generations, and Noah walked with God," but it was grace that formed the basis for his redemption—and for the redemption of the world (Gen. 6:8, 9). Against the awesome blackness of universal condemnation, God's gracious redemptive purpose shines with the promise that ultimately man will reign with God in His kingdom.

God's purpose for man was that he might reign with Him—through the recognition of the absolute sovereignty of God in every realm of life, and through the knowledge of God that comes through submission to Him. Man universally violated both of these principles. "Professing themselves to be wise, they became fools" (Rom. 1:22). Having chosen to eat of the Tree of Knowledge, they thought themselves capable—through their internal knowledge of good and evil—to choose "the good life" for themselves. They saw no compelling need, apparently, to depend on God.

Having rejected God and His government, the antediluvian civilization was ruled by the gods it produced—the *nephilim*. These tyrants, "mighty ones," were heroes in the eyes of the common people (Gen. 6:4). They ruled, it appears, by their personal power and popularity. The people of the world evidently saw them as benefactors of humanity. We saw this pattern suggested in the Cainite Lamech. He gloried in violently disposing of a person he saw as a threat, but his legacy brought cultural and material benefits (Gen. 4:17–23). We will see this pattern later in Nimrod.

In fact, this is the pattern for the kingdom of the world through the ages (Luke 22:25).

The last verse in this section shines a ray of redemptive light in a world under the ominous, dark cloud of condemnation, "But Noah found grace in the eyes of the Lord." The words that precede this statement are, strange as it may seem, the equivalent of the first part of John 3:16, "For God so loved the world." For when the inspired writer says, "It repented the Lord that he had made man on the earth, and it grieved him at his heart," he is declaring, in human language, that God's infinite love for mankind brought infinite pain to His heart. This is the language of unfathomable love.

CHAPTER SEVEN

A NEW ORDER

JUDGMENT: PREPARATION FOR THE NEW ORDER

THE UNIVERSAL DOMINANCE OF THE kingdom of the world demanded the destruction of the world. "The earth also was corrupt before God, and the earth was filled with violence. And God looked upon the earth, and, behold, it was corrupt; for all flesh had corrupted his way upon the earth" (Gen. 6:11–12).

By necessity, the Savior of the world must also be its Judge. We saw this pattern even in the Garden of Eden. After their first sin, when the eyes of Adam and Eve were opened and they experienced their first sense of shame, they "heard the voice of the Lord God walking in the Garden in the cool of the day: and Adam and his wife hid themselves from the presence of the Lord God amongst the trees of the Garden" (Gen. 3:8). Why did they hide themselves? Because they saw God as their Judge coming to condemn them and to impose on them the punishment He had promised. In fact, the Lord was coming to them as Savior and as Judge. In order to save them, He had to judge them (cf. John 5:22-24; Matt. 25:32; Rom. 2:16; Acts 10:42; 17:31).

God mercifully gave a 120-year period of grace before this judgment. But once it began, He took a full year to execute it. The period of grace was the result of "the longsuffering of God" (I Pet. 3:20), but why did God choose to take a full year to execute and complete His judgment on earth? Why did He not destroy the condemned suddenly and begin immediately rebuilding the new order? We must remember that the Lord designs His judgments more for the surviving witnesses than for the condemned. "Smite a scorner," the Wisdom of God tells us, "and the simple will beware" (Prov. 19:25). The scorner himself will not learn from judgment, but a simple person who witnesses it may. Those who survived the Flood needed to learn something about the devastating results of sin. If future generations were to benefit from this judicial action, these surviving witnesses would have to pass the fearful story of judgment on to their descendants.

In general, sinful people have cultivated a willing ignorance concerning the judgment of the Flood (II Pet. 3:5–6), as they have concerning all divine judgments. Josephus tells us that Nimrod said "he would avenge himself on God for destroying their forefathers!" *Antiquities* 1.4.2. The virtually universal tradition of mourning for dead ancestors observed at the disappearance of the Pleiades at the end of October or beginning of November, at the same time the Flood began (Gen. 7:11), seems to reflect the spirit Josephus attributes to Nimrod. As observed throughout the world, the custom follows the natural sinful tendency of sympathizing with those being punished rather than empathizing with the righteous Judge. The Bible specifically warns God's people against this (e.g., Deut. 7:16; 13:8; 19:13). Additional information and illustrations of the custom of mourning for the dead are in Rehwinkel's *The Flood*, page 169 and following (see chap. 6, n. 3). The earth itself became a witness to future generations, for it was never the same after the Flood. Much of the territory that had been fruitful in the past was covered with the dark waters of the oceans—gloomy reminders of God's judgment—and great tracts of land became barren and bleak wildernesses.

A COVENANT WITH MANKIND

The judgment is past, and God now establishes a new order for the world in a solemn covenant—the first the Bible mentions (Gen. 6:18; 9:9ff.). The word *covenant* is used eight times in connection with the new order God establishes through Noah. The Bible's uses of the word refer to a binding agreement between two or more parties. Such an agreement would naturally involve promises, obligations, and conditions. The same word is used both of human covenants (e.g., Gen. 21:27–32; 31:44–55) and of divine (e.g., Gen. 6:18; 15:18).

This covenant with Noah forms God's basis for dealing with the human race—and His redemptive purpose for man—for the rest of human history. The Lord calls it an "everlasting covenant" (Gen. 9:16). In other words, it is never to be abrogated. Its provisions apply all through human history. God is guaranteeing that He will fulfill His purpose for mankind, the plan He announced at creation (Gen. 1:26–27).

Thus a covenant establishes and solemnly ratifies the new order. What should we expect now? Intuitively, we expect a dramatic break from all that plagued mankind in the past and a new life of fulfillment for man in the future. We find instead that though the form of government changes, sinful man does not change—and so the afflictions of mankind continue.

Every change God imposes on man merely furthers His purpose for man. He has chosen to make man in His image that mankind might ultimately subdue the earth and reign over it with Him (Gen. 1:26–27). Inevitably, God will fulfill His redemptive purpose.

A NEW PROMISE

By the time of the Flood, sin's encroaching power had taken such control of man that "every imagination of the thoughts of his heart was only evil continually" (Gen. 6:5b). Remarkably, it is because of this power that God promises not to destroy the earth again with a flood: "I will not again curse the ground any more for man's sake; for the imagination of man's heart is evil from his youth; neither will I again smite any more every thing living, as I have done" (Gen. 8:21b). In God, there is "no variableness, neither shadow of turning" (James 1:17b). Neither His attitude toward sin nor His principles of judgment changed after the Flood.

God's promise not to destroy the human race and the new order He established for mankind are based on His redemptive purpose. So intent is God on fulfilling His purpose for man that He establishes the rainbow as a universal sign of His benevolent promise. "And God said, This is the token of the covenant which I make between me and you and every living creature that is with you, for perpetual generations: I do set my bow in the cloud, and it shall be for a token of a covenant between me and the earth" (Gen. 9:12–13). The words of Franz Delitzsch depict the message of the symbolism in the rainbow:

> Springing as it does from the effect of the sun upon the dark mass of clouds, it typifies the readiness of the heavenly to pervade the earthly; spread out as it is between heaven and earth, it proclaims peace between God and man; and whilst spanning the whole horizon, it teaches the all-embracing universality of the covenant of grace.[1]

On earth, Erich Sauer observes, we see only half the rainbow—picturing our presently imperfect experience of redemption (I Cor. 13:9–12; I John 3:2)—but eventually we will see the complete bow encircling the throne, a symbol of redemption completed to the glory of God (Ezek. 1:28; Rev. 4:3).[2]

New Restrictions

God's new governmental order provided the basis for His new promise to preserve mankind from future destruction. To the extent that man loses the capacity to govern himself, to that extent he needs external restrictions imposed upon him. When God judged Cain for the murder of his brother, Cain feared that "Every one that findeth me shall slay me" (Gen. 4:14), suggesting that at this stage in the antediluvian civilization, all men were outraged by the sin of murder. Cain's fear was that this general outrage would lead men everywhere to seek justice against him. By the time of the Flood, however, "the earth was filled with violence." The heroes of that civilization were the *nephilim*, the "violent ones" (Gen. 6:4, 11, 13). Consequently, God established after the Flood a universal law of capital punishment, entrusting man with the authority and responsibility for its implementation.

In His original order, God gave man dominion over the animals, which evidently included harmony and voluntary submission (Gen. 1:26–27; 6:19–20; 7:2–3). Now, in God's new order, man's dominion over the animals would mean fear and antagonism, and animal meat would strengthen man's declining physical constitution (Gen. 9:2–5).

---

[1] *The Pentateuch*, 1:154–55 (see chap. 3, n. 2).

[2] *World Redemption*, 74 (see chap. 4, n. 10).

God also dramatically restricted man's life span. Those born within one hundred years or so of the Flood lived only about half as long as their antediluvian forefathers. Then the earth was "divided," apparently at the time of the building of Babel, and man's life span was cut in half again (Gen. 10:25; 11:12–25, 32). Though this decline reflects the degenerative physical effects of man's sinfulness, we must never forget that it is the Lord alone Who gives and takes life (Job 12:10; Ps. 90:3). The pre-eminent reason is redemptive, therefore, for the decline in man's allotted years. Had man continued to enjoy the health and longevity of his antediluvian ancestors, he would have become hardened even more against redemption (Job 21:7–15; Eccles. 8:11).

New Divisions

Inevitably, sin leads to division (Isa. 57:20–21). Lamech prophesied that his son Noah ("rest") would "comfort us concerning our work and toil of our hands, because of the ground which the Lord hath cursed" (Gen. 5:29b). This suggests that as the sinfulness of the antediluvian civilization escalated, the curse on mankind became increasingly aggravating, resulting in a restless society devoid of comfort.[3] The divisions in the budding new postdiluvian society were a direct result of sin. Our concern is with how these divisions interplay with God's redemptive plan.

A Place for God in the Divisions (Gen. 9:18–27)

By its very nature, God's redemptive plan plays against the backdrop of man's sinfulness. What appears at first to be an anticlimactic revelation of Noah's character sets the stage for a momentous announcement concerning God's future relationship with humanity.

The first revelation in this story is a surprising reminder of man's inherent sinfulness. After being introduced to Noah as a man who "walked with God"—one of only two in the Bible described this way (Gen. 5:24; 6:9)—we are shocked to find him shamefully drunk. Why did the writer include this flaw in the life of a man whose godly character was virtually unique in his generation? Is Noah's drunkenness an essential part of the story of Ham's insolence? Here we must remember that the purpose of

---

[3] The word translated *comfort* (*nacham*) is not a direct derivative of the Hebrew word for *Noah* (*Noach*). As was quite common with prophets, Lamech utilized the resemblance in sound of the two words to express his message.

divine revelation is to reveal God's redemptive plan for mankind. Essential to this plan is the exposure of the insidious nature and power of sin.

The revelation of Noah's drunkenness reminds us of the foundation for his righteousness, "grace in the eyes of the Lord" (Gen. 6:8). His drunkenness gives us a vignette of what Noah was like apart from the grace of God—and in spite of the grace of God. For Ham, his father's drunkenness provided a rationale for insolence. Had he accidentally seen his father naked but not drunken, he would have had no real basis for gloating to his brothers.

In a sense, Noah's prophecy (9:25-27) simply revealed the ultimate results of the moral tendencies already developing in his three sons. Even apart from inspiration, a discerning parent can sometimes predict mature qualities of budding characteristics he sees in his children. By inspiration, God gave Noah heightened insight into the inevitable result of the moral characteristics he saw in his sons. Keil's observations are again worthy of special note here:

> To understand the words of Noah with reference to his sons (vv. 25–27), we must bear in mind, on the one hand, that as the moral nature of the patriarch was transmitted by generation to his descendants, so the diversities of character in the sons of Noah foreshadowed diversities in the moral inclinations of the tribes of which they were the head; and on the other hand, that Noah, through the Spirit and power of that God with whom he walked, discerned in the moral nature of his sons, and the different tendencies which they already displayed, the germinal commencement of the future course of their posterity, and uttered words of blessing and of curse, which were prophetic of the history of the tribes that descended from them.[4]

The fact that Ham had no share in Noah's blessing suggests that the entire Hamitic branch of Noah's descendants might somehow partake in the curse on Ham's sinful characteristics. However, the curse itself specifically denounces Canaan, Ham's youngest son. Evidently the sensual inclinations that Ham displayed had become prominent characteristics in Canaan. Ham's insolence is simply another side of his sensuality. A person who disdains the controls of decency will often also be disrespectful of authority. Solomon's description of the harlot testifies of this principle: "She is loud and stubborn . . . with an impudent face" (Prov. 7:11, 13).

---

[4] *The Pentateuch*, 1:156–157.

The seed of the curse was in the sin that would ultimately dominate this branch of humanity. The curse Noah uttered actually foretold the inevitable results of the sin Ham and his sons had embraced. Ham's disrespect toward his father lost—for himself and his posterity—the promise of divine blessing that comes with respect for authority (Exod. 20:12; Eph. 6:2–3) and brought instead the deterioration that such sin ultimately brings (Prov. 20:20; 30:17). By allowing the sensual in his nature to dominate, Ham planted for his posterity the seeds of degradation and subjugation (Gen. 49:4; Hosea 4:11).

Ironically, the very qualities destined to bring about the Hamites' subjugation were in the short term the means by which they dominated. Stubborn and willful people often have an aura of strength that allows them to temporarily dominate the less assertive. Likewise, those who themselves are dominated by the flesh tend to dominate others in the physical arenas of life. Even in the secular world, however, the spirit eventually conquers the flesh. Those who are strong in inward qualities will inevitably prevail over those whose strength is merely outward. The history of the Hamites demonstrates the validity of these principles. Early in history, Hamitic civilizations were aggressive and dominant. Eventually, however, they were brought under subjection by Shemites and Japhethites. The specific fulfillment of the curse of Canaan began with the subjugation of the Canaanites by Joshua, and it culminated with the Romans' subjugation of Carthage.

Against the dark hues of this awful curse, Noah pronounces a far-reaching blessing on Shem and Japheth that has messianic overtones. The inspired writer heightens the significance of this twofold blessing by introducing it with a fresh *and he said* and by using the expression "and Canaan shall be his servant" after each stage of the blessing. Furthermore, the form of Shem's blessing is immensely significant. Rather than directly pronouncing a blessing on Shem, Noah praises the God of Shem with the words "Blessed be the Lord God of Shem" (Gen. 9:26; cf. Deut. 33:20). This expression calls special attention both to the magnitude of God's blessing on Shem and to the gracious work of the Lord in his life. Shem's respect for his father was not simply a matter of his upbringing but fruit of his personal relationship with the Lord.

It is significant, also, that the blessing uses the name *Lord* (*Yahweh*). *Yahweh*, the most frequent designation for God in the Old Testament, commonly refers to God's covenant relationship with His chosen people (e.g., Gen. 15:18; Exod. 24:7–8; 34:28). The name therefore connotes an established personal relationship with God. The name *Yahweh* is combined in the blessing with the more general term for God, *Elohim*, suggesting the general application of the blessing through Shem to the world at large. This special blessing looks back to the promised Seed of Genesis 3:15. As Luther well says, Noah "did not speak of any earthly benediction but of the blessing of the promised Redeemer, whom he regarded as so glorious that He could not be (*fittingly*) described in words."[5]

Of Japheth Noah prophesied that God would "enlarge" him, and that he would "dwell in the tents of Shem" (Gen. 9:27*b*). The enlargement speaks of expansion and prosperity. In this context, the dwelling of Japheth in the tents of Shem must speak of Japheth's participation in the special blessings pronounced on Shem. Referring to God as "the Lord God of Shem" is comparable to recognizing Shem as a man of God—and consequently as having influence over others in the communication of the knowledge of God (cf. Gen. 31:53). It is natural, therefore, to think that Shem must have influenced his brother in the action they took to cover their father. In this same sense, the Seed of Shem will have spiritual influence among the descendants of Japheth.

The Redemptive Plan of God in the Divisions

The curse of Cain was that he would be "a fugitive and a vagabond" and that the ground would not henceforth yield him its strength (Gen. 4:12). In apparent resistance to this divine pronouncement, Cain "builded a city," seeking to establish himself and his descendants in a state of blessedness—in spite of the curse of God. The "way of Cain" was man's way of fulfilling God's original plan for mankind to reign over the earth. It became obvious soon after the Flood that the way of Cain was destined to continue.

To Restrict the Influence of the World's Mighty Ones (Gen. 10:8–12)

Before the Flood, the *gibborim* were the heroes of the world—the *nephilim* who dominated by personal power and popularity. Within one hundred years of the judgment of the Flood, another mighty one appears, Nimrod, a son of Cush.[6] Nimrod's influence emanates from a very small

---

[5] *Commentary on Genesis* (repr., Grand Rapids: Zondervan, 1958), 1:176.

[6] According to Gen. 10:25, in the days of Peleg "was the earth divided." This is evidently a reference to the Tower of Babel, and it may refer to geological changes in the land as well. Most apply the statement that the earth was divided only to the division of nations, but the wording may point beyond the nations to the earth itself—to physical changes that would provide stronger natural

base in the Bible. The King James Version allots him only five verses (eighty-two words, Gen. 10:8–12). Yet his influence reaches to eternity. As with most tyrants, he first appears as a benefactor of society (cf. Luke 22:25). "He began to be a mighty one [hero] in the earth." He gained his fame, evidently, as "a mighty hunter before the Lord."

The inspired writer connects the expression "before the Lord" to the heroic activity of Nimrod. After the Flood, wild animals became a menace and a danger (Gen. 9:5). Nimrod fought these creatures with such skill and bravery that a thousand years later, in the time of Moses, Nimrod's heroism was proverbial: "Wherefore it is said, Even as Nimrod the mighty hunter before the Lord." Whether or not *before the Lord*, in this case, depicts Nimrod as consciously rebellious toward God and defying the curse He had imposed upon man, it seems clear that the people did not view him this way. To them he was the greatest of heroes, one whose activities were a blessing to mankind and approved by God.

As the perception of Nimrod's beneficence increased, his influence over men did too. Undoubtedly, discerning people saw rebellion in the attitude and actions of Nimrod. But heroism is a matter more of emotion than of mind. There is a raging spirit of rebellion in mankind that needs only a strong leader's hand to give it direction and body.

Not surprisingly, Nimrod eventually became an object of worship. According to George Rawlinson, worship of the deified Nimrod has continued into modern times under such titles as *Bel-Nimrod*, "the god of the chase" or "the great hunter."[7] However secular history may enhance our knowledge of Nimrod, we must remember that the biblical record, though it may seem agonizingly brief, is sufficient for the divine message it contains. From the standpoint of the unfolding message of the Bible, these five verses give us important information concerning the developing war between the kingdoms.

These verses tell us that even after the universal judgment of the Deluge, in which all who were openly rebellious against God were destroyed, the kingdom of the Serpent continued and, in fact, flourished. Before the Flood, there were renowned and popular "mighty ones,"

---

boundaries between the nations. The dramatic change in life span beginning with Peleg supports the possibility of strong physical changes in the earth at that time.

[7] *The Seven Great Monarchies* (New York: John B. Alden, 1885), 1:100. A footnote on p. 527 of this work notes that "the identification of Nimrod with Orion is noted by Greek writers" and that "Orion is a 'mighty hunter' even in Homer."

tyrants, ruling in the earth. After the Flood, these same features were destined to continue.

After the Flood, however, God limits the power and influence of this earth's mighty ones by dividing earthly kingdoms. God has done this, the inspired writer informs us, for redemptive purposes. The Lord

> hath made of one blood all nations of men for to dwell on all the face of the earth, and hath determined the times before appointed, and the bounds of their habitation; that they should seek the Lord, if haply they might feel after him, and find him (Acts 17:26–27).

To Frustrate the Union of Man Against God (Gen. 11:1–9)

Inherent in man is a desire for union in spirit with his fellow man. But unity in spirit is possible only as man, made in the image of God, maintains his spiritual relationship with God. The story of Noah's curse and blessing indicates that, at a very early stage after the Deluge, the brotherly unity of man had deteriorated—essentially because of differences in the brothers' relationships to God.

Immediately after the Flood, God had reiterated His command that man should "be fruitful, and multiply, and replenish [fill] the earth" (Gen. 9:1b). But men by this time had evidently sensed a need to form an outward bond in order to maintain the inward unity they were losing. "Go to," they say, "let us build us a city and a tower, whose top may reach unto heaven; and let us make us a name, lest we be scattered abroad upon the face of the whole earth" (Gen. 11:4). Their proud ambition was evidently to establish a magnificent memorial to themselves ("let us make us a name") as the founding fathers of the new civilization that would be recognized in future generations as the way the human race had maintained its unity and power.

Ancient tradition suggests that the Hamites instigated the rebellion against God. Having been excluded from Noah's prophetic blessing, they sought (as Cain had) to provide for themselves by their own power. According to Josephus,

> It was Nimrod who excited them to such an affront and contempt of God. He was . . . a bold man, and of great strength of hand. He persuaded them not to ascribe it to God as if it was through his means they were happy, but to believe that it was their own courage which procured that happiness. He also gradually changed the government into tyranny—seeing no other way of

turning men from the fear of God but to bring them into a constant dependence upon his power.[8]

The statement "And the Lord came down to see the city and the tower, which the children of men builded" (Gen. 11:5) is a striking anthropomorphic expression of God's judicial intervention in the affairs of man. The confusion of tongues was poetic justice in the sense that it revealed outwardly what had already taken place within man.

If language is the audible expression of emotions, conceptions, and thoughts of the mind, the cause of the confusion or division of the one human language into different national dialects must be sought in an effect produced upon the human mind, by which the original unity of emotion, conception, thought, and will was broken up. This inward unity had no doubt been already disturbed by sin.[9]

In His judgment of rebellious man, "the Lord scattered them abroad from thence upon the face of all the earth" (11:8)—and thus forced them to fulfill His benevolent purpose. Henceforth the place proposed as a memorial to man's greatness would be known by discerning men as a place of confusion and false hope.[10]

---

[8] *Antiquities* 1.4.2.

[9] Keil, *The Pentateuch*, 1:174–175.

[10] The spelling *Babylon* is from the Greek rendition of the Hebrew word *Babel*, the word consistently used in the Old Testament to depict the city of Babylon. According to the standard Hebrew lexicons, the word seems to be derived from *bab-ilu*, an Akkadian word meaning "Gate of God." According to Louis Goldberg, the inspired writer may have intended a word play, perhaps on the Hebrew word *balal*, "to confuse" (cf. Lev. 18:23; 20:12). *TWOT*, 1:89 (see chap. 3, n. 3).

THE FOUNDATIONAL PILLARS

The foundation of the written revelation of God, unlike other foundations, is not a substructure designed to provide hidden support for the edifice—and therefore of special interest only to architects and technicians. It is in fact an integral part of the edifice. The foundational pieces of God's Word are more like the pillars of ancient Greek temples. These columns supported the edifice, but their artistic beauty was meant to be seen. This chart highlights these pillars of divine revelation.

God Alone Is the Source and Sustainer of All Life

The very first thing God tells us about Himself is that He alone is the sovereign Creator of all. His throne is a throne of unparalleled antiquity; it was established in the timeless past. His domain extends to the boundless edges of the universe. All that follows in the divine revelation—all the issues, all the questions, all the failures, all the successes—are related to this opening revelation.

God Made Man in His Own Image to Reign with Him

"And God said, Let us make man in our image, after our likeness: and let them have dominion over . . . all the earth" (Gen. 1:26). Man is destined to reign with God over His earthly kingdom. But this divine proclamation of man's destiny is in the context of God's sovereignty. In order to reign with God, man must recognize Him as his Sovereign and rely on Him as the only Source and Sustainer of his life. Thus the fulfillment of man's destiny to reign over all earthly life depends wholly on his full subordination to the Sovereign God of the universe.

God Made Man to Develop in His Likeness

Implicit in the triune God's creation plan for man is an extended time period. His plan calls for mankind to multiply, fill the earth, and subdue it. This will involve a period of development for man. There must be a time of probation when man will mature in his knowledge of God. The heir must be prepared for his inheritance.

The Original Plan for Man's Development

"And the Lord God took the man, and put him into the garden of Eden to dress it and to keep it." "And God blessed the seventh day, and sanctified it: because that in it he had rested from all his work which God created and made" (2:15; 2:3). We might summarize God's plan for man's development with three words suggested in these passages: serve, supervise, and submit.

OF DIVINE REVELATION

Man's duties in the garden involved serving the basic needs of the place to which God had assigned him. He was also to develop judgment, creativity, and organization by supervising in his assigned place. Then he was to develop his knowledge of the Lord by submitting, resting, and communing with Him, enjoying His finished work on the Sabbath.

The Key Issue in Man's Development

The choice between the Tree of Knowledge and the Tree of Life represents the key issue in man's development. Choosing to eat of the Tree of Knowledge meant declaring independence from God—saying that man's own discernment could fulfill his destiny to reign over the earth. On the other hand, the Tree of Life represented man's total commitment to the Lord for life and all that goes with it—including knowledge—which was the way he could ultimately come to reign with God.

God Will Fulfill His Plan Through the Redeemer

Though man fell into sin, God will fulfill His plan for man to reign with Him. In the abysmal darkness of the Fall, God held before Adam and Eve the promise of a Redeemer Who was to come from the seed of the woman: "And I will put enmity between thee and the woman, and between thy seed and her seed; it shall bruise thy head, and thou shalt bruise his heel" (Gen. 3:15). The issues and the foundational pillars remain the same, but now man must be redeemed. The sovereign King becomes the Saviour.

God's Plan Calls for Conflict Between the Kingdoms

In the last day, at the judgment of the nations, the King will declare to the righteous, "Come, ye blessed of my Father, inherit the kingdom prepared for you from the foundation of the world" (Matt. 25:34b). At the dawn of history, the inspired writer tells us of the formation of the kingdom of the Serpent (Gen. 2:4–4:26). By their very nature, these two kingdoms are destined to be perpetually at war. The goal of both kingdoms is to reign over the earth. Through the Tree of Knowledge and the sinful nature of man, the kingdom of the Serpent dominates the earth. But through the power of the Redeemer, the kingdom of God will ultimately prevail.

God's Plan Includes Periodic Judgment

Seven times in the opening chapter of the Bible, God saw something He had made and evaluated it as "good." As the omniscient Judge of the universe, God must evaluate what He sees. Since He is of purer eyes than to look with toleration upon evil (Hab. 1:13), He must periodically judge between good and evil.

PART TWO

THE DEVELOPING STORY OF THE KINGDOM

And beginning at Moses and all the prophets. . .

And beginning at Moses and all the prophets, he expounded unto them in all the scriptures the things concerning himself.

Luke 24:27

WHAT A BIBLE STUDY THAT must have been! The seven-mile trip to Emmaus would have taken close to four hours, and our Lord's exposition of "the things concerning himself" may well have occupied most of that time. As the master communicator, He must have dealt with the Old Testament revelations about Himself in the context of the disciples' expectations. They had said to this Stranger, "We trusted that it had been he which should have redeemed Israel" (Luke 24: 21).

In their perception, the Old Testament revealed the Messiah as the Redeemer of Israel and the Restorer of the kingdom. Their perception wasn't necessarily incorrect, but it was incomplete. To complicate matters, they were typical Bible students, saddled with prejudices that made it difficult for them to see contrarian light.

This section seeks to follow our Lord's example and survey the Holy Oracle from the Garden of Eden to the Isle of Patmos, in order to see how the entire Bible develops the themes established in its opening pages.

CHAPTER EIGHT

THE PROMISE AND ESTABLISHMENT
OF THE KINGDOM

A GOOD ARCHITECT DESIGNS THE FOUNDATION with the edifice in view, and we would certainly expect the Architect of God's Word to have done this in His revelation. As he prepared to pass into eternity, Joshua testified, "Ye know in all your hearts and in all your souls, that not one thing hath failed of all the good things which the Lord your God spake concerning you; all are come to pass unto you, and not one thing hath failed thereof" (Josh. 23:14b). Yet Joshua was speaking of only one stage in God's plan for mankind.

At the beginning of our study, I suggested that three dominant themes—Christ, Redemption, and the kingdom of God—are inseparably interwoven throughout the Bible, and that in reality, these three themes are simply different aspects of one grand theme, a threefold cord that unifies the story of the Bible. We can say, then, that the Bible is the story of **the redemption and reign of man in God's kingdom through Christ, the Savior and King.**

The foundational passage in which the Lord reveals His purpose for man to reign with Him over His earthly kingdom is Genesis 1:26–28:

> And God said, Let us make man in our image, after our likeness: and let them have dominion over the fish of the sea, and over the fowl of the air, and over the cattle, and over all the earth, and over every creeping thing that creepeth

upon the earth. So God created man in his own image, in the image of God created he him; male and female created he them. And God blessed them, and God said unto them, Be fruitful, and multiply, and replenish the earth, and subdue it: and have dominion over the fish of the sea, and over the fowl of the air, and over every living thing that moveth upon the earth.

Though this revelation is part of the story of Creation, it was given to fallen men—and God has never rescinded it. In fact, He has reaffirmed it repeatedly (e.g., Ps. 8:4–8; 115:15–16; Luke 12:32; Matt. 25:34; I Cor. 6:2–3; II Tim. 2:12; Rev. 1:6; 2:26–27; 20:6; 22:5). All of this tells us that the concept of man reigning with God in His earthly kingdom is a dominant concept in the Bible.

If this is the case—that God's eternal purpose is for man to reign with Him in His earthly kingdom—we would expect to see virtually everything in the inspired revelation playing into this divine purpose. In fact, this is what we do see.

From the very beginning, we see the earthly kingdom of God forming. As we progress through the Bible, we see that kingdom developing, warring against the kingdom of the world, declining, occasionally reviving, and finally (it appears) disintegrating. But never do the inspired writers allow us to lose sight of the kingdom of God. When it appears all is lost in the earthly kingdom, the prophets tell us no, all is not lost. The kingdom of God will prevail, and the citizens of that kingdom will reign with God just as He promised.

But what of the preeminent Personality of Scripture, the Messiah? From the very first, the divine revelation presents Him as King. We must view Him first as one with His Father in Creation, for "the same was in the beginning with God. All things were made by him; and without him was not any thing made that was made" (John 1:2–3). So the One Who walked with Adam and Eve in the Garden appears first as their Sovereign—the Creator and King over every earthly realm they were commanded to subdue. From the beginning, mankind's prospect to reign over the earth fully depended on recognizing and submitting to his sovereign Creator.

When Adam and Eve fell into sin, their King revealed Himself as their Savior—still the only way for mankind to fulfill God's purpose of reigning over the earth. Rather than annulling His original plan, God with redeeming grace provided for its ultimate fulfillment.

How then should man prepare to fulfill his royal destiny? By the same means revealed to Adam and Eve. He must recognize and submit to his Creator as his absolute Sovereign in every realm of life. As man progresses from realm to realm in conquering the earth, he progresses also in his knowledge of God. Thus he gains, in God's time, the knowledge of good and evil—knowledge inherent in the forbidden Tree of Knowledge—and ultimately he becomes "as God," knowing good and evil, and ready to reign with Him.

FROM RUIN TO REIGN: THE MAKING OF KINGS

Destined for royalty? Can that be? Indeed it can and is! The story of the Bible is the story of God's developing plan to bring man into his royal inheritance as a king in His kingdom. We can see this more clearly if we look at the broad movements of this story as it unfolds in the Bible.

We see seven successive stages to this grand story:

(1) The prologue of the Bible, the first eleven chapters of Genesis, leads us step by step to the revelation that God chose Abraham as the channel through which He would accomplish His purpose—for man to reign in His earthly kingdom with Him.

(2) After the foundational principles given in the prologue, the story of the covenant kingdom of God—the people through whom God will accomplish His purpose—begins. This patriarchal period focuses on the promise of the covenant kingdom.[1]

(3) The next stage of the story begins with the call of Moses and concludes with his death. This Mosaic period reveals the establishment of the covenant kingdom.

(4) The next movement in the story could be called the prophetic stage. During this period, the prophets admonished Israel concerning the decline, death, and revival of the covenant kingdom. In general, I am following the Hebrew classification of the prophets for this period. The Jews designate the books of Joshua, Judges, Samuel and Kings as "Former Prophets," and the books of Isaiah, Jeremiah, Ezekiel,

---

[1] For the stages in the Old Testament story beginning with Abraham, I am largely following Keil's analysis. See his "Prolegomena on the Old Testament and its Leading Divisions," *Biblical Commentary on the Old Testament* (Grand Rapids: Eerdmans, n.d.), 1:9–15.

and the Twelve (the Minor Prophets) as the "Latter Prophets." Some of the books the Jews classify under the heading "The Writings" (e.g., the Poetic Books, Daniel, Ruth, Ezra, Nehemiah, Esther, and Chronicles) I will also use as part of the prophetic stage.

The final movements in God's developing plan for His earthly kingdom are in the New Testament:

(5) The Gospels show the coming kingdom presented to and rejected by Israel.

(6) Then after His resurrection, the rejected King commands His disciples to go and make disciples in all nations. These disciples had witnessed their King present His coming kingdom and be rejected by the chosen people. Now, included in the commission of their King is the promise that the coming kingdom will be preached and received through the ministry of the church. To this ministry the New Testament writers devote twenty-two books (Acts–Jude), but only about the same amount of space as the four Gospels.

(7) In the final movement of the story, the Lord reveals to the apostle John the culmination of the coming kingdom: the final victory of the Lamb over the Dragon and the reign of the saints as kings of the earth.

The Scriptures develop the theme of the kingdom of God all the way from God's promise to Abraham, who "looked for a city . . . whose builder and maker is God," to the fulfillment of that promise in "the holy city, new Jerusalem, coming down from God out of heaven."

THE PROMISE OF THE
COVENANT KINGDOM

The Lord's call established the Abrahamic covenant—a covenant requiring faith in the Lord and submission to His word—as the way He would accomplish His purpose for mankind. This covenant promised that through the descendants of Abraham, the Lord would bring the Seed through Whom redeemed mankind would reign with God. The Lord's promises to Abraham, Isaac, and Jacob laid the foundation for the future development of the kingdom of God. Their experiences revealed Him as their sovereign Lord, all-sufficient to fulfill the covenant promises entrusted to them.

Everything in the stories of the Patriarchs relates in some way to the Abrahamic covenant. For example, it is on the basis of the covenant promise that God gave Canaan to the descendants of Abraham. Paradoxically, it is also on the basis of this covenant that the Lord took the descendants of Jacob out of the Promised Land to live some four hundred years in Egypt. Since the sons of Jacob were fast becoming Canaanites in heart and spirit, the Lord isolated His people—thus protecting the line of the promised Seed—in the land of Goshen.

At the same time, the experiences of the Patriarchs give us both positive and negative principles by which the child of God may prepare to fulfill his destiny. The experiences of the Patriarchs illustrate the practical outworking of God's command to multiply, fill the earth, and subdue it. As with the Patriarchs, each child of God is given a realm on earth to conquer, possess, and establish dominion over. As with the Patriarchs, each new experience brings with it new revelations of God and, potentially, better knowledge of God—which brings an enlarged capacity to reign with Him.

THE ESTABLISHMENT OF THE COVENANT KINGDOM

This second stage begins with the call of Moses and ends with his death. In this period the Lord reveals (1) the redemption of Israel from the house of bondage; (2) the adoption of Israel to expand the covenant kingdom; (3) the Law of God to govern the covenant kingdom; and (4) the need for the life-giving presence of God in communion with man.

Redemption from the House of Bondage

God's gracious work of redemption as depicted in the Pentateuch lays the foundation for the national life of Israel as the redeemed people of God. Redemption is essentially a matter of the heart, and God's revelation of the need for redemption appeals first to the heart. In the center of the New Testament revelation of salvation stands the Cross—an intensely emotional symbol. And the story of an innocent Man being delivered by wicked men to die an agonizing death is an intensely dramatic story. Not until the New Testament reader has experienced this drama do the inspired writers begin to explain its theological implications.

This principle holds true throughout the revelation of God. Our Lord's appeal to man is first and preeminently an appeal to the heart. It is no surprise then, when we open the book of Exodus, to find Moses introducing the profound subject of redemption with a nation's deliverance from slavery. After the drama of this deliverance, the inspired writer presents the basis by which God could justly deliver sinful Israel from slavery in the symbolic ritual of the sacrificial system.

The rescue of Israel from slavery in Egypt serves as a prototype of God's redemptive grace in the world (Deut. 7:8–10; Hag. 2:5–9; II Cor. 10:1–4; Heb. 3:15–19). In order for Israel to be an instrument of God's redemptive grace and a royal priesthood for God in the world, they needed to experience God's redemptive work in their behalf.

At least a dozen times in Scripture the inspired writers call Egypt "the house of bondage." It was indeed a house of physical bondage for Israel, but the scriptural writers mean a form of slavery that goes infinitely beyond physical bondage: the bondage of the soul to sin. They speak, for example, of the Lord *redeeming* the people of Israel from the house of bondage and making them His people. "And what one nation in the earth is like thy people Israel, whom God went to redeem to be his own people, to make thee a name of greatness and terribleness, by driving out nations from before thy people, whom thou hast redeemed out of Egypt?" (I Chron. 17:21; cf. Deut. 8:14; 13:5, 10).

The Lord used His redeeming work during the Exodus against the gods of the world system (Exod. 12:12) to fortify the soul against the lure of apostasy (Deut. 8:10–18; 13:5, 10). The Exodus also revealed the Lord's awesome power to overcome all obstacles for His people and became the basis for godly attitudes and actions throughout all of life (Deut. 9:26; Mic. 6:3–8).

The inspired writers use two Hebrew words (and their derivatives) to picture God's redemptive work. The word used most often in the Old Testament for *redemption* or *redeemer* is *gaal*. This word, with its derivatives, appears in the Old Testament 118 times. Though it is generally translated in the King James Version by words such as *redeem, redemption,* or *redeemer*, sometimes it is translated *kinsman* and sometimes *revenger* or *avenger*. This range of translations reflects the scope of the duties and responsibilities of the *gaal*. The word depicts the action and practice of a responsible kinsman to redeem and restore his relatives from difficulties and danger.[2]

---

[2] Keil, *Commentary on the Old Testament*, 1:144.

The other Hebrew word the inspired writers used to depict Redemption is *padah*. This word, with its derivatives, appears 69 times in the Old Testament. In the KJV, *padah* is generally translated by words such as *redeem*, *ransom*, or *deliver*. The word was originally a commercial term dealing with the transfer of ownership through payment or substitution.[3]

The Lord as Kinsman-Redeemer

"Whoever finds me will kill me" (Gen. 4:14*b*, NASB). Cain's words may seem to express an inordinate and unreasonable fear. But the Lord's response to Cain demonstrates that his fear was neither unnatural nor irrational. The Lord issued a stern warning of retribution against anyone who killed Cain, and He set a mark of protection on him. Even if we allow for the relative innocence of that early society, this passage testifies of man's inherent outrage at the thought of his own flesh and blood being dishonored or violated—and at that early stage in history, all would recognize their kinship with one another. Both Scripture and history prove that in ancient civilizations God utilized this principle of man's natural concern for the welfare and honor of his kin to maintain law and order.

In the ancient world, with many predominantly rural or isolated populations and no organized police force, the kinsman-redeemer (or avenger of blood) was the guardian of civil justice. Given the nature of man, kinsman-redeemer justice was susceptible to misuse—as with any human system of justice. However, it provided a deterrent to crime and oppression that otherwise would have been impossible in many ancient communities.

The inspired writers present God as the ultimate Kinsman-Redeemer, and the actions of a worthy kinsman-redeemer depict the Lord's work in Redemption. The kinsman-redeemer assumed the responsibility for the welfare and honor of the members of the family, including the extended family (Lev. 25:49). This responsibility might extend to a wide range of circumstances. For example, if a relative in financial straits had sold his property or had sold himself as a slave, it was the kinsman-redeemer's responsibility to buy back the property or to buy the person out of slavery (Lev. 25:25, 47–48). If a relative were murdered, the kinsman-redeemer was responsible for executing the murderer (Num. 35:19). Indirectly, the

---

[3] *TWOT*, 2:716 (see chap. 3, n. 3).

kinsman-redeemer's obligations might even include the marriage of his brother's widow (Deut. 25:5–6; Ruth 4:4–5).[4]

According to this analogy, the work of Redemption is wonderfully broad and comprehensive—infinitely more so than most Christians recognize. God's redeeming work deals not only with the salvation of the soul, but with the difficulties and distresses of the soul—including the difficulties that result from our own sinfulness and foolishness. After a life filled with trouble, much of which was his own making, Jacob speaks of the Angel of the Lord as having "redeemed me from all evil" (Gen. 48:16; cf. Ps. 78:33–35; 103:4).

To many Christians, the comparison of the kinsman-redeemer with the Savior breaks down when the *gaal* becomes the "avenger of blood" (e.g., Num. 35:19); but the same inspired writers who describe the Messiah as the gentle Savior present Him also as the wrath-filled Judge. In fact, our Lord declared during His earthly ministry that "the Father judgeth no man, but hath committed all judgment unto the Son" (John 5:22). One day, terrified sinners will seek to hide from the "wrath of the Lamb." They will see the sacrificial Lamb of God not as an object of scorn but as an object of terror (Rev. 6:16; cf. II Thess. 1:7–9; Matt. 25:31–46; Rev. 19:11–15).

The Lord as Deliverer from Bondage

Although the Hebrew word *padah* was originally a commercial term, the word came to be used to express ransom or deliverance. In the Old Testament, the word is generally translated by a word such as *redeem, ransom,* or *rescue.*

The inspired writers sometimes use the two words for redemption synonymously, even in the same sentence (see Jer. 31:11; Hosea 13:14). But their choice of words would connote different emphases to their hearers and readers. For example, on different occasions when Moses spoke to the people of Israel, he used both *gaal* and *padah* to depict the Lord's deliverance of Israel from bondage (Exod. 6:6, *gaal;* Deut. 7:8, *padah*). But, as the context of these passages indicates, his emphasis on these occasions

---

[4] In Scripture, the levirate marriage (Deut. 25:5–10), the requirement that a single brother marry his widowed sister-in-law, is not clearly presented as an obligation of a kinsman-redeemer. Nevertheless, the concept of the levirate marriage, which was practiced in ancient times before the Mosaic law was revealed (Gen. 38:8), was consistent with the kinsman-redeemer's responsibilities. In general, a kinsman-redeemer was expected to do anything within his power to restore the honor and well-being of an afflicted relative (cf. Ruth 3:9–4:12).

was on different aspects of the Redeemer's work. In the Exodus passage, the officers of Israel were discouraged and angry with Moses. His message to Pharaoh had brought increased oppression rather than deliverance (Exod. 5:19–21). When Moses took these complaints to the Lord, He responded,

> I have also heard the groaning of the children of Israel, whom the Egyptians keep in bondage; and I have remembered my covenant. Wherefore say unto the children of Israel, I am the Lord, and I will bring you out from under the burdens of the Egyptians, and I will rid you out of their bondage, and I will redeem you with a stretched out arm, and with great judgments: and I will take you to me for a people, and I will be to you a God: and ye shall know that I am the Lord your God, which bringeth you out from under the burdens of the Egyptians" (Exod. 6:5–7).

This passage emphasizes the Lord's kinsman-redeemer relationship with His people.

On the other hand, forty years later when Moses addressed a new generation of Israelites, he emphasized the mighty work of redemption itself:

> But because the Lord loved you, and because he would keep the oath which he had sworn unto your fathers, hath the Lord brought you out with a mighty hand, and redeemed you out of the house of bondmen, from the hand of Pharaoh king of Egypt. Know therefore that the Lord thy God, he is God, the faithful God, which keepeth covenant and mercy with them that love him and keep his commandments to a thousand generations (Deut. 7:8–9).

As with *gaal*, the use of the word *padah* in Scripture demonstrates that the redeeming work of the Lord is wonderfully broad. The psalmist speaks of the Lord's redemption as "plenteous"—so much so that the Lord will redeem Israel from all his iniquities (Ps. 130:7–8). But the Lord's work as Deliverer, as His work as Kinsman-Redeemer, extends beyond salvation from sin into the trials of life. The mighty Redeemer stands ready to plead the cause of the fatherless against thieves and oppressors (Prov. 23:10–11). David testified that the Lord had redeemed him from all the "distress" he had experienced in life (I Kings 1:29).

The Festival of Redemption

The establishment of the Passover climaxed the Lord's deliverance of Israel from the house of bondage and it prepared the people of God for the revelation of the final Passover Sacrifice. It was by faith that Moses, representing the true people of God, kept the Passover. It was also by faith that the children of Israel experienced the power of God in their escape from Egypt at the Red Sea (Heb. 11:28–29). By faith Isaiah saw the Messiah as the Lamb of God (Isa. 53:7), anticipating the announcement of John the Baptist, "Behold the Lamb of God, which taketh away the sin of the world" (John 1:29).

The Sacrifice as the Basis for Redemption

The concept of animal sacrifices depicted in the Passover was already well known, not only in Israel but in the entire ancient world. When Adam and Eve first fell into sin, "the Lord God [did] make coats of skins, and clothed them" (Gen. 3:21b). This divine action at the dawn of human history involved animal sacrifice. But this initial sacrifice was made only after the Lord had promised a Redeemer (Gen. 3:15) and had value only as it represented faith in the Redeemer (Heb. 10:4; Ps. 50:13–14; 51:16–19). By the special revelation of an authorized sacrificial system in Leviticus, the Lord entrusted Israel with the protection and proclamation of the Redeemer's work.

The first six chapters of Leviticus present requirements for the five types of offerings that serve as the basis of the covenant nation's sacrificial system. These five sacrifices present a fivefold portrayal of the sacrificial work of the Redeemer. They can also be applied to the believer (Rom. 12:1; Matt. 16:24; I John 4:17). Our Savior's sacrifice on the cross was comprehensive and infinite in its potential and in its effects—much too powerful and wonderful to be depicted symbolically in one type of sacrifice. Therefore, the inspired writer sets before the believer five different sacrifices to suggest (if only feebly) the wonder and power of the expiatory work of Christ.

The first problem the condemned sinner faces is "How can God's wrath be appeased?" Once the grace of God settles this problem, the sinner faces another problem: "How can I, a sinner by practice, please a holy God?" The sacrifice of Christ fully responds to both these problems, and the five Levitical sacrifices depict the Lord's response to this twofold need.

The first three sacrifices (the burnt, peace, and meal offerings) address the sinner's need to please God in his actions and attitude. The last two offerings (the sin and trespass offerings) address the need to satisfy God's righteous anger against sin and the sinner. It might appear that the order of the sacrifices in Leviticus is the reverse of logical sequence. It would seem that the sinner has to appease God's wrath (the work represented in the sin and trespass offerings) before he can offer sacrifices depicting God's pleasure. If we keep in mind, however, that these sacrifices represent the work of Christ the Redeemer, the order in Leviticus will appear quite natural. Christ first pleased God in everything (Matt. 3:17). Then, having fulfilled the law in every detail, He became the perfect sacrifice.

The burnt offering (Lev. 1; 6:8–13). The distinctive feature of the burnt offering was that the animal, except for its skin, was entirely consumed on the altar. This was true of none of the other offerings. The ritual called for the one offering the sacrifice to lay his hands on the animal and then to slay it "before the Lord" (Lev. 1:4–5). By laying his hands on the head of the animal, the offerer was identifying himself with the animal. In effect he was saying, "Today I am dying to myself and giving myself wholly to God." It was undoubtedly this offering Paul had in mind when he wrote to the Roman believers, "I beseech you therefore, brethren, by the mercies of God, that ye present your bodies a living sacrifice, holy, acceptable unto God, which is your reasonable service" (Rom. 12:1).

Preeminently, the burnt offering is a picture of the Son of Man, Who gave Himself fully and freely to the Father that sinful men might become living sacrifices to God. Secondarily, this offering pictures a believer who senses a need in his life for full consecration.

The meal offering (Lev. 2; 6:14–23). The "meat" offering was the only one of the five that did not include flesh. When the King James Version was translated, the word *meat* meant food. Modern translations generally call it a meal, grain, or cereal offering. This sacrifice was essentially an offering of flour, bread, or grain, with oil, salt, and generally incense added. None could be offered with leaven or with honey. Under certain circumstances, the meal offering could be given separately (e.g., Lev. 5:11; 7:12; Num. 5:15), but as a general rule it was brought in conjunction with the burnt and peace offerings.[5] The ritual called for a handful of the meal offering to be burned on the altar, and the rest was given to the priests as "a thing most holy" (Lev. 2:3) to be eaten in the sanctuary (Lev. 6:18).

Consisting as they did of food offered before the Lord and sanctified by special restrictions, the meal offerings symbolized the spiritual food of Israel, the Word of God (Deut. 8:3; Matt. 4:4). Oil, a scriptural symbol of the Holy Spirit (Zech. 4:2–6), was to be added to the offerings, picturing the life-giving power of the Word in God's people. The salt that was added to this (as well as to all other sacrifices) depicted the power of the

---

[5] Alfred Edersheim, *The Temple: Its Ministry and Services* (Grand Rapids: Eerdmans, 1963), 136–37.

Word to preserve from the corrupting influence of sin. Therefore, both honey and leaven, symbolizing the corrupting influences of such sins as hypocrisy and malice (Luke 12:1; I Cor. 5:8), were forbidden. The incense added to the offerings symbolized communion with God and God's pleasure (Ps. 141:2; Rev. 8:3–4).

As the Word of God, as the Bread of Life, Christ is the life, the spiritual nourishment of the people of God (John 1:1; 5:39–40; 6:51, 53–58). To many of the professed disciples of Jesus, the statement "Except ye eat the flesh of the Son of man, and drink his blood, ye have no life in you" was a "hard saying" (John 6:53, 60). Their problem, stemming from their carnal, worldly spirit, was unbelief (John 6:63–64).

But for the believer, what does it mean to "eat the flesh of the Son of man"? Just as food nourishes and sustains us physically, so Christ nourishes and sustains us spiritually. That is the general truth: Christ provides and maintains our spiritual life. But if I want to strengthen the quality of my spiritual life, how can I improve my spiritual "eating habits"? Perhaps an analogy will help. When we spend a good deal of time with a close friend—sharing experiences, hopes, dreams, and fears—that person becomes a part of us. We digest and assimilate into our life something of his life. In human experience, such close friends often begin acting and reacting alike.

The same is true in the spiritual realm. When we spend time with Christ—considering the thoughts He shares with us, sharing with Him our thoughts, our experiences, our desires, our fears—we cannot help but digest and assimilate into our life something of His life. This is more than simply reading the Word and saying our prayers. It is consciously communicating with Him, listening to His voice as we read His Word and holding conversation with Him.

When we read the Word, it's easy to fall into the habit Christ addresses with the Jews when He says, "You search the Scriptures, because you think that in them you have eternal life; it is these that testify about Me; and you are unwilling to come to Me so that you may have life" (John 5:39–40, NASB). The Jews to whom Christ was speaking knew the Scriptures well but were missing Scripture's whole point. They thought that in *them*, in the laws of Scripture, they had eternal life; but the Scriptures' constant testimony was of Christ. They had so focused on the facts of Scripture that they had missed its grand Subject.

Preeminently, then, the meal offering pictures Christ as the Bread of Life, the spiritual nourishment of the believer. Secondarily, the meal offering pictures the believer in the sense of II Corinthians 3:2–3: "Ye are our epistle written in our hearts, known and read of all men: forasmuch as ye are manifestly declared to be the epistle of Christ ministered by us, written not with ink, but with the Spirit of the living God; not in tables of stone, but in fleshy tables of the heart." As Christ is, so the believer, imitating his Master, is a copy of the Word of God "known and read of all men." Without question, the believer's inheriting the attributes of his Savior is one of the most amazing features of the work of divine grace (cf. Rom. 8:29; John 17:22–23; II Cor. 3:18). The Scriptures declare, "As he is, so are we in this world" (I John 4:17b), and they attribute what is true of Christ to the believer. As He is the Light of the World, so is the believer (Matt. 5:14; John 8:12). As Christ took up His cross, so should His followers (Mark 8:34). As Christ will rule with a rod of iron, so will the believer (Ps. 2:9; Rev. 2:26–27).

The inspired writers consistently present the meal offerings with the burnt offerings—almost as if they were part of the burnt offerings (Lev. 23:18; Num. 7:87; 8:8; 15:24; 28:27–28; cf. Ezek. 46:13–14). The combination of the burnt offering and the meal offering embodies the concepts of total consecration, involving death to self and living anew to God (Rom. 6:11–13), and of continuous sanctification—the sustaining of a living relationship through the words of the living God.

The peace offering (Lev. 3; 7:1–17; 7:11–34). The distinguishing feature of the peace offering was that the offerer and his family ate part of the sacrifice. The law called for parts of other offerings (the meal, sin, and trespass) to be eaten by the priests, but the peace offerings included a sacrificial meal for a layman. It was the most joyous of the five sacrifices, for it depicted "a season of happy fellowship with the Covenant God, in which He condescended to become Israel's Guest at the sacrificial meal, even as He was always their Host."[6] For the individual believer, his peace offering meant that he had accepted Christ's invitation of Revelation 3:20, "Behold, I stand at the door, and knock: if any man hear my voice, and open the door, I will come in to him, and will sup with him, and he with me."

---

[6] Ibid., 134.

The root idea of the Hebrew word commonly translated *peace* (*shalom*) is completion, wholeness, or fulfillment. For example, the inspired writers often use this word, or a variation of it, to depict the completion of a building project or the fulfillment of a certain season (e.g., II Chron. 5:1; Neh. 6:15; Isa. 38:12; 60:20). Consequently, the peace offering pictured much more than the absence of hostility between the Lord and the worshiper. It pictured the restoration of a full and harmonious relationship.

As with the meal offering, the peace offering commonly accompanied the burnt offering, as if closely connected with it. In fact, the daily ritual of the tabernacle and temple suggests that this was the natural order. The daily burnt offerings, which had to be consumed entirely on the altar, would burn most of the day and sometimes all day. Consequently, the fat portions of the peace offerings were laid on the burnt offerings (Lev. 6:12). However, even with voluntary sacrifices, worshipers who offered burnt offerings frequently gave peace offerings with them (e.g., Exod. 24:5; Judges 20:26; I Sam. 10:8; 13:9; II Sam. 6:17; I Kings 3:15). Total consecration was the prerequisite for a full and harmonious relationship of peace with the Lord.

The sin offering (*Lev. 4:1–5:13; 6:24–30*). The distinguishing feature of the sin offering was that blood from the sacrifice was put on the horns of the altar or, in special cases, taken into the sanctuary and sprinkled "before the Lord" toward the veil. The horns were the altar's most prominent feature. As the horns of an animal speak of its power, so the horns of the altar symbolized the altar "as a place of the saving and life-giving power of God."[7]

The sin offering provided atonement for sins committed "through ignorance" (Lev. 4:2, 13, 22, 27). The Hebrew word (*shagagah*) translated *ignorance* means "to go astray, err." It does not necessarily mean that the sinner is totally unaware of his offense. The word is used of those who cause the blind to "wander out of the way" and of sheep who wander "through all mountains" (Deut. 27:18; Ezek. 34:6). It addresses, therefore, man's chronic inclination to stray from the commandments and standards of the Lord.

The requirements of the sin offering varied according to the sin's potential for influence in the congregation. If the high priest sinned "so as to bring guilt on the people" (Lev. 4:3, NASB)—that is, in his official

---

[7] Keil, *The Pentateuch*, 2:191 (see chap. 3, n. 2).

capacity as high priest—he was to lay his hands on the head of a young bullock, kill the animal "before the Lord," sprinkle the blood seven times "before the Lord" toward the veil in the sanctuary, and put some of the blood on the horns of the altar of incense in the holy place. The remainder of the blood had to be poured at the bottom of the brazen altar, the fat of the animal was to be burned on the altar, and the rest of the animal (including the refuse) was to be burned in a clean place outside the camp. The same sacrifice and ceremony was required if the "whole congregation" had committed such a sin (Lev. 4:3–21).

If a ruler sinned, he was to offer a male kid of the goats. The ritual for his sacrifice was essentially the same as that for the high priest and the whole congregation, except that it was all carried out at the brazen altar. Blood was not taken into the holy place and sprinkled toward the veil or put on the horns of the altar of incense (Lev. 4:22–26). If any of the common people sinned, he was to bring a female kid of the goats or a female lamb. The ritual was essentially the same as that for a ruler (Lev. 4:27–5:13). As an essential part of the ceremony, the attending priests were to eat the flesh of the sin sacrifice in the court of the tabernacle, except when the sin offering was for the high priest or the whole congregation. In those cases the meat was to be consumed in fire (Lev. 6:26, 29–30).

The trespass offering (Lev. 5:14–6:7; 7:1–6). The distinguishing feature of the trespass offering was that it involved money, or its equivalent. The trespass offering addressed the harm done by the sinner in violating the rights of the Lord or of another, and it called for monetary restitution to the person violated or in certain cases to the priest.

The Hebrew words used in connection with the trespass offering emphasize the guilt (*asham*) of the sinner for unfaithfulness or treachery (*maal*). The Hebrew word often translated *trespass* (*maal*) in the King James Version almost always refers to an act of treachery or unfaithfulness in violation of the law of God.[8] Almost half of the sixty-four times this Hebrew word for treachery appears in the Old Testament, it is connected with the expression "against the Lord" or an equivalent (e.g., "against Me"). All sin is ultimately against the Lord (Ps. 51:4), and any kind of unfaithfulness—including, for example, the disloyalty of a husband to his wife—stems from treason against God.

---

[8] *TWOT*, 1:519–520 (see chap. 3, n. 3).

One of the most painful results of sin is the knowledge of the harm sin does to others. A man who has been unfaithful to his wife may repent and be reconciled to her, but how does he deal with the harm he has done to her and to the children? Often a person who is guilty of such a sin has great difficulty accepting God's forgiveness. His difficulty is complicated by the fact that there are always repercussions to sin—even forgiven sin. That reconciled husband may find his wife overly suspicious of him when he is away from home, or he may find his children disrespectful toward him.

But the trespass offering symbolizes the magnificent truth that Christ's sacrifice covers not only the sin but also the harm done by the sin. David suggests this concept in his song of praise for God's mercy: "Who forgiveth all thine iniquities; who healeth all thy diseases" (Ps. 103:3). Indirectly, all disease is the result of sin. By coupling God's forgiveness of all iniquity with His healing of all diseases, David is prophesying that the redemptive work of the Messiah will cover the effects of sin as well as sin itself.

The Adoption of Israel

After delivering Israel from the bondage of Egypt, the Lord formally adopted the nation to be His special people for the fulfillment of His kingdom purposes.

> Ye have seen what I did unto the Egyptians, and how I bare you on eagles' wings, and brought you unto myself. Now therefore, if ye will obey my voice indeed, and keep my covenant, then ye shall be a peculiar treasure unto me above all people: for all the earth is mine: and ye shall be unto me a kingdom of priests, and an holy nation. These are the words which thou shalt speak unto the children of Israel (Exod. 19:4–6).

And the people, accepting this blessed promise (Exod. 19:7–8), became the valued treasure of the Lord "above all people" of His earth. There is no contradiction here with "God so loved the world." In fact, the special value the Lord has chosen to place on Israel is related to His calling for the nation to be a "kingdom of priests," a royal priesthood that would bring the world to God. The Lord chose Israel as a special treasure in the same sense that He called Paul to be "a chosen vessel unto me, to bear my name before the Gentiles, and kings, and the children of Israel" (Acts 9:15b). This promise, then, represents an extension and application of the original Abrahamic covenant—that through the Patriarch's seed all the families of the earth will be blessed.

That Israel is destined to be a kingdom of priests—or a nation of priests and kings—speaks again of God's purpose for man to reign with Him in His earthly kingdom. Ultimately this holy nation will include all who belong to Christ; for "if ye be Christ's, then are ye Abraham's seed, and heirs according to the promise" (Gal. 3:29). And so Peter, under inspiration, applies the promise of Exodus 19 to New Testament saints.

> But ye are a chosen generation, a royal priesthood, an holy nation, a peculiar people; that ye should shew forth the praises of him who hath called you out of darkness into his marvellous light: which in time past were not a people, but are now the people of God: which had not obtained mercy, but now have obtained mercy (I Pet. 2:9–10).

The Law to Govern the Covenant Kingdom

The concept of law has fallen on hard times in America—sadly, even in Christian circles. Somehow, coffee-shop "theologians" have managed to set the congenial cousins law and liberty at loggerheads. The lofty truth that man cannot be saved by the law has been transformed to mean that the law is to Christian living what Scrooge was to the spirit of Christmas. Law, allegedly, is the enemy of Christian liberty.

But the Bible teaches no such thing. Even Paul in the midst of his battle to establish the truth of Christian liberty exclaimed, "I delight in the law of God after the inward man" (Rom. 7:22); and in this he echoed the spirit of David and of all who, like him, are "after God's own heart" (Ps. 1:2; 119:97).

God designed the law to be a "schoolmaster" to bring people to Christ (Gal. 3:24). The Hebrew word *torah* comes from a root (*yarah*) that was commonly used to depict teaching.[9] The Law was intended as a teaching tool. Laws inform us of the nature of the lawmaker and tell us something about the lawmaker's view of the situation to which a law is applied. Our human nature being what it is, we might otherwise have a negative view of the lawmaker and his opinion concerning the situation.

Whatever the case, the law is informing us of something. If a driver barreling down a highway at 70 mph suddenly sees a sign that says "Caution! Reduced speed zone ahead," he is nevertheless being informed of something he otherwise would not have known. The wise motorist will generally take heed to this new information and adjust his speed accordingly.

---

[9] Ibid., 1:403.

The law of God has the same function in the life of the believer. God's law teaches the believer something about God's nature and about what God thinks of certain actions, thoughts, and attitudes in human experience.

The natural question of a people being rescued from Egyptian culture and religion is "What is God—the God of our fathers—like?" The answer the inspired writer gives is "God is holy." In order for man to conform to the image of God and fulfill God's purpose to reign with Him, he too must be holy (e.g., Lev. 11:44–45).

The Hebrew words for *holy* appear in the last four books of the Pentateuch over 250 times, about 40 percent of the times they appear in the entire Old Testament. Though the Hebrew word for *holy* in the Old Testament carries the connotation of purity (e.g., Exod. 19:14; Lev. 16:4, 24; 22:6), the inspired writers generally emphasize the concept of separateness or being set apart for special use. The first time the word is used in the Bible it has this meaning: "And God blessed the seventh day, and sanctified it [made it holy]: because that in it he had rested from all his work which God created and made" (Gen. 2:3; cf. Exod. 3:5; 13:2).

The Lord's command to Moses after judging the rebellious Korahites is a striking example: "The censers of these sinners against their own souls, let them make them broad plates for a covering of the altar: for they offered them before the Lord, therefore they are hallowed: and they shall be a sign unto the children of Israel" (Num. 16:38). Though these men had acted in sinful rebellion, the priests were to view their censers as holy because they had been consecrated to the Lord.

This emphasis suggests that conformity to the image of God is at its root a matter of being wholly devoted to Him. As God is set apart—unique in His purity—so must we be (II Cor. 6:17–18; II Cor. 7:1). As God is totally unlike the sinful world, so must His people be.

In order to conform to the image of God, then, man must be holy. But the word *holy* gives us only a general concept of what God is like. He is pure. He is separate. He is unique. But how does His separateness apply to life? What thoughts, attitudes, and actions in the everyday course of life make a man holy? God answers this question by introducing man to His law. The laws of God reveal in specific detail what God is like and how man may bring his life into conformity to His image.

The Presence of God for Conformity to His Image

From the beginning, God's evident plan was to dwell with man. The nature of God and the original nature of man demanded such a union. Man was made in the image of God, and the omnipresent God was everywhere in that pristine world of the first man and woman. Since Adam and Eve were like God in spirit, they must have sensed His presence often—like a child who knows his mother is in the room even without seeing her. Beyond this, the inspired writer suggests that God periodically manifested Himself to the physical senses of Adam and Eve and walked with them in the garden "in the cool of the day" (Gen. 3:8).

Ultimately, likeness in nature demands communion. Elihu's profound words to Job suggest this mystical union between the spirit of man and God, even during man's fallen state: "But there is a spirit in man: and the inspiration of the Almighty giveth them understanding" (Job 32:8). Elihu is undoubtedly alluding to Genesis 2:7, "And the Lord God formed man of the dust of the ground, and breathed into his nostrils the breath of life; and man became a living soul." According to Elihu, man's spirit of life, creatively wrought by the Spirit of God, gives man the potential for spiritual understanding (cf. John 1:9). In his unfallen state, man could commune with God unhindered. The presence of God would have been a reality inwardly as well as outwardly.

Our Lord told His disciples that His ultimate plan for them was to dwell with Him: "And if I go and prepare a place for you, I will come again, and receive you unto myself; that where I am, there ye may be also" (John 14:3). But even on earth, before this perfect union takes place, God's plan for man—His work of developing His own image in man—requires that God and man dwell together. For example, Christ's call and training of the twelve disciples required that they be "with Him" (Mark 3:14). As Jesus prepared His disciples for His departure, He assured them that He would continue revealing Himself to them by dwelling with them. "If a man love me, he will keep my words: and my Father will love him, and we will come unto him, and make our abode with him" (John 14:23). The nature of man and the development of man in the image of God demands the presence of God in man's life—that man dwell with God and that God dwell with man.

The concept of the tabernacle of God is built upon this principle. The tabernacle (and later the temple) was an integral part of the covenant of God because God's presence among His people was an essential part of

His covenant relationship.[10] At the beginning of the instructions concerning the tabernacle, the Lord told Moses that His fundamental purpose for the tabernacle was that He might dwell among His people: "And let them make me a sanctuary; that I may dwell among them" (Exod. 25:8). Later, in His instructions to Aaron and his sons concerning their ministry in the tabernacle, the Lord impressed anew upon them the fact that the tabernacle and sacrifices were designed so that He could meet with and dwell with His people. Note the emphases (my italics) in these words (Exodus 29:42–46):

> This shall be a continual burnt offering throughout your generations *at the door of the tabernacle of the congregation before the Lord: where I will meet you, to speak there unto thee.* And there *I will meet with the children of Israel, and the tabernacle shall be sanctified by my glory.* And I will sanctify the tabernacle of the congregation, and the altar: I will sanctify also both Aaron and his sons, to minister to me in the priest's office. *And I will dwell among the children of Israel,* and will be their God. And they shall know that I *am* the Lord their God, that brought them forth out of the land of Egypt, *that I may dwell among them:* I am the Lord their God.

Even the names for the tabernacle emphasize the Lord dwelling in the midst of His people. Of the four names ascribed to the tabernacle, three directly refer to its fundamental purpose.[11]

(1) *Mishkan,* the Hebrew word commonly translated *tabernacle* in the King James Version, is the most general name for this sanctuary. This term means "dwelling place," emphasizing God's intimate association with His people.

(2) *Ohel moed,* "tent of meeting," appears well over one hundred times in the Pentateuch (e.g., Exod. 27:21). The KJV generally translates this expression "the tabernacle of the congregation." This designation signifies not merely an assembly of people but the meeting of the Lord with His people.

(3) *Ohel haeduth* is translated as "the tent of the testimony" (Num. 9:15) or "the tabernacle of witness" (e.g., Num. 17:7). The words *testimony* and *witness,* in these passages, refer to the tables of the Decalogue that were put in the ark (Deut. 10:2), which, consistent with this usage, is called

---

[10] The importance of the tabernacle in God's covenant relationship with man is evident from the emphasis on its description and establishment. Almost 40 percent of the book of Exodus (chs. 25–31, 35–40) details the establishment, maintenance, and proper use of this sanctuary.

[11] For a good discussion of these terms, see Geerhardus Vos, *Biblical Theology* (Grand Rapids: Eerdmans, 1959), 165–68.

"the ark of the testimony" (e.g., Exod. 25:22) and "the ark of the covenant" (e.g., Num. 10:33). The tables of the Decalogue represent the entire Word of the Lord. In fact, in addition to the tables within the ark, a copy of the entire Law of God was placed beside the covenant (Deut. 31:26). Furthermore, the innermost sanctuary, the holy of holies, was also called the "oracle" (from *davar*, "word," e.g., II Sam. 16:23; I Kings 6:20), signifying that this is the sanctuary where God communicates with His people. All of this suggests that the designations "tent of the testimony" and "tabernacle of witness" speak also of God's desire to dwell among His people—with a special emphasis on His desire to communicate with them.

(4) *Mikdash*, generally translated "sanctuary" in the KJV, designates the tabernacle as a holy place. This term may seem not to relate to the presence of God, but in fact it does. The fact that the place of God's appearing on earth is supremely holy speaks of God as He really is: infinitely pure, separate from sin and sinners. Since true fellowship is based on likeness of natures, any fellowship is defective to the extent that the people involved fail to conform and commune inwardly. The term *mikdash* announces the nature of the tabernacle's Resident and invites those of like nature to commune with Him.

We humans often base our fellowship with others not on who they really are but on who we think they are or on how they appear to conform to our philosophy and agenda. The same is true of much of what we call fellowship with God. God made man in His own image, but fallen man seeks to make God in his own image. Consequently, man's worship tends to be the worship of "God" not as He really is but as the worshiper thinks He should be. The tabernacle was designed to conform the worshiper to God's nature in order to fellowship with Him.

God calls sinners to come to the sanctuary that they might be conformed to His nature and His purpose for them (II Chron. 30:8–9). If any sinner should think it impossible for him to come to a holy God without incurring His wrath, the Lord invites into His presence all who will humble themselves:

> For thus saith the high and lofty One that inhabiteth eternity, whose name is Holy; I dwell in the high and holy place, with him also that is of a contrite and humble spirit, to revive the spirit of the humble, and to revive the heart of the contrite ones. For I will not contend for ever, neither will I be always wroth: for the spirit should fail before me, and the souls which I have made (Isa. 57:15–16).

CHAPTER NINE

THE DECLINE, DEATH, AND REVIVAL OF THE KINGDOM

THE FOURTH MOVEMENT IN THIS marvelous story we could call the prophetic stage. It covers the period from the death of Moses to the close of Old Testament revelation with Malachi. Following (loosely) the Hebrew classifications, we will survey this period by focusing first on the Former Prophets and then on the Latter Prophets.

The Former Prophets (the books of Joshua, Judges, Samuel, and Kings) chronicle the decline and disintegration of the kingdom under the old covenant. The Latter Prophets (Isaiah, Jeremiah, Ezekiel, and the twelve minor prophets), though they cry out against the sins of the covenant nation, focus largely on the promised revival of the kingdom under the new covenant.

THE FORMER PROPHETS: DECLINE AND DISINTEGRATION UNDER THE OLD COVENANT

I never did like the idea of peeking at the last page of an exciting story to see how it comes out—except in the Bible. Frankly, if I didn't know how the divine revelation turns out, much of my Bible reading experience, especially in the Old Testament, would be of the Slough-of-Despond variety.

Consider, for example, the developing story of the kingdom of God in the books of Joshua, Judges, Samuel, and Kings. By the time we arrive at Joshua, we have already been through a wilderness variety of the Slough of Despond. We have seen strewn in that wilderness the bones of an entire generation of rebellious kingdom citizens. Even the younger generation who by God's grace survived the wilderness wanderings carried the seeds of kingdom disintegration. As he prepared to proclaim his final prophetic message, Moses said, "For I know thy rebellion, and thy stiff neck: behold, while I am yet alive with you this day, ye have been rebellious against the Lord; and how much more after my death?" (Deut. 31:27).

So when at last we get to Joshua, we're more than ready to emerge from our depressing slough, and we're saying to ourselves, Now at last the kingdom will come into its own. And we do see victory and a certain amount of fulfillment in Joshua, but even the glow of victory shows a few ominous signs of coming failure. Joshua has to rouse his people from lethargy: "How long are ye slack to go to possess the land, which the Lord God of your fathers hath given you?" (18:3*b*). His people could not drive out certain enemies (15:63; 17:12), and he became aware before his death that some of the kingdom citizens had become idolaters (24:23).

Then in Judges, defeat and disintegration become a dreary reality, until finally in the book of Ruth we see a rainbow of hope in the promise of David. Before we reach David, our rainbow of hope first glistens a bit with the prophetic ministry of Samuel, then disappears in clouds of disappointment in the folly of Saul. Then at last David comes to the throne, and we start saying again, Now the kingdom of God will come into its own. And when Solomon takes the throne, it appears for a while that we have arrived.

But then more disappointment. Solomon falls, the kingdom is divided, and it's all downhill from there—relieved only occasionally by a reviving rise in the terrain that slows, but does not stop, the precipitous descent—until at last we see the temple in flames and the citizens of the kingdom being led away in chains.

The saga just recorded is actually the saga of the people of God throughout the ages. We are still asking the question the disciples asked their risen King: "Lord, wilt thou at this time restore again the kingdom?"

We have not listened well to our King's admonishment, "It is not for you to know the times or the seasons" (Acts 1:7*b*); nor have we really caught the drift of Elisha's words to Gehazi, "Is it a time to receive money, and to receive garments, and oliveyards, and vineyards, and sheep, and oxen, and menservants, and maidservants?" (II Kings 5:26*b*).

Abraham, the father of all who "wait for the kingdom of God" (Mark 15:43), was content to live in tents as a sojourner in the Promised Land because his faith looked for a distant city "whose builder and maker is God" (Heb. 11:10*b*).

From the very beginning, the promise of reigning with God has been a distant promise the believer must grasp by faith. Even with Adam and Eve this was the case. The original promise contemplated mankind filling the earth and subduing it—which would take time. It was the serpent who introduced the notion that you don't really have to wait or even rely wholly on God: you can reach godhood on your own just by eating from the Tree of Knowledge. By its nature, faith is farsighted and inherent in the nature of unbelief is nearsightedness (Heb. 11:13; II Pet. 1:9).

WHY "FORMER PROPHETS"?

If the term "Former Prophets" for the books Joshua through Kings seems antiquated or perhaps too "Jewish" for you, you may not like my next comment. The designation "Former Prophets" is actually a much better title for these books than our standard "Historical Books" is. Were these books (and Ruth, Ezra, Nehemiah, Esther, and Chronicles, which we commonly lump with them) really designed to give us an inspired "History of Israel"?

Consider for a moment what a sketchy history of Israel this would be. The time period covered by these books extends from about 1400 to 430 BC, almost a thousand years. Yet only about four hundred pages (in many standard copies of the Bible) are devoted to this extended time period—and about a hundred of these four hundred pages (Chronicles) give parallel and sometimes duplicate accounts of the "history" recorded elsewhere. Furthermore, if we are in the history mode when we examine these pages, we will notice that whereas some accounts of important historical incidents are tantalizingly skimpy, in other cases the writers go into grand detail about matters that historically are relatively incidental.

Do the inspired writers themselves call this material a history of Israel? As a matter of fact, they do just the opposite. For example, repeatedly in the accounts of the kings you find yourself reading statements like, "And the rest of the acts of . . . and all that he did . . . are they not written in the book of . . . ?" (e.g., I Kings 11:41; 14:19, 29; II Kings 24:5; cf. Josh. 10:13; II Sam. 1:18; I Chron. 9:1; 29:29; II Chron. 9:29). These statements say: If you want more details, go to the history books.

Each of these books is a message from a spokesman of the Lord, and in that sense each writer was a prophet. A biblical prophet was primarily a messenger of God, an authoritative and infallible proclaimer of God's word. He was more of a *forth-teller*, one who speaks forth publicly in behalf of God, than a *foreteller*.[1] Though God has chosen not to reveal the names of these inspired authors, their messages prove that they were indeed prophets in the biblical sense.

THE MESSAGE OF THE FORMER PROPHETS

Seen in the Experience of Hannah

Is the message of the Former Prophets consistent with the farsighted faith of our father Abraham? Weren't the messages of these prophets just instructive accounts of past events, recorded under inspiration for our admonition and profit (I Cor. 10:11)? They were all that, but they were much more. The patterns for admonition in these books are interwoven with the covenant principle of farsighted faith. If we are simply gaining helpful devotional thoughts from the positive and negative examples in these books, we may be missing the heart of their messages. At the heart of Christ-like living—development in the image of God to fulfill the purpose of God—is farsighted faith.

---

[1] Because of man's natural curiosity about the future and because prophets did sometimes make striking predictions concerning the future, it is easy for the Bible reader to think that the prophet was primarily a foreteller of events. The serious Bible student must disabuse himself of this notion, or he risks missing the vitally important messages of the biblical prophets. Even more seriously, he risks missing the significance of the threefold office of Christ as *prophet*, priest, and king. Among the many good references on this subject are *The Prophets of Israel* (Grand Rapids: Baker, 1979), by Leon J. Wood, and *The Prophets and the Promise* (Grand Rapids: Baker, 1963), by Willis Judson Beecher.

The song of Hannah (I Sam. 2:1–10) gives us an example of the essential message of these prophets, as well as of how this message plays into the experience of an "ordinary" citizen in the kingdom of God.

The well-known story of Hannah begins with an intensely personal look at a frustrated and angry woman. She has been suffering for some years the reproach of barrenness, a reproach that had connotations of divine disapproval. She might have borne the subtle insinuations in silence, but her adversary gave strident voice to her secret doubts and fears.

Peninnah, the other wife of Elkanah, had a different reason for being frustrated and angry, and she expressed it in a different way. She had good reason, she thought, to be frustrated. She had been a good mother in Israel, favored of the Lord with sons and daughters; yet her husband had chosen not to favor her. Instead he had bestowed his favor on barren Hannah—in an obvious and insulting fashion. Even at the feasts of the Lord, when he should have been demonstrating his special gratitude for his children and their mother, Elkanah chose to give barren Hannah the "worthy portion" of the sacrificial meal (I Sam. 1:4–5).[2]

The peace offering was supposed to be the most joyous of the sacrifices. Its rituals signified the restoration of fellowship with the Lord and His people. But it was anything but that for the two wives of Elkanah. No doubt Peninnah pretended to be happy, but inwardly she was burning with jealous anger. She expressed her "joy" with provocative comments, couched perhaps in words of "gratitude" to the Lord for the children He had given her. As she did this year after year (v. 7), her toxic words sank deeply into Hannah's soul and began to fester.

The inspired writer uses eight different Hebrew expressions to describe the emotional turmoil raging in Hannah at the climax of this insidious process. She couldn't get Peninnah's gloating innuendos out of her mind. She turned them over and over again. Especially grievous was the insinuation that it was the Lord Who had cursed Hannah with barrenness ("because the Lord had shut up her womb," v. 6), perhaps because of

---

[2] Peninnah and her children could not have failed to feel the weight of this insulting favoritism, though Elkanah may have rationalized that he was only trying to pacify Hannah during a time when she might have been tempted to be bitter rather than thankful to the Lord. Elkanah, a Levite (I Chron. 6:22–28, 33–38), would have been particularly sensitive and knowledgeable about the choice portions of the sacrificial meal. The best portions were to be given to the priests (Lev. 7:30–34) and, by custom, the choicest portion of the meat eaten by the worshipers would be given to the most honorable person in the gathering (e.g., I Sam. 9:24).

The word translated *provoked* and *grief* (*kaas*, I Sam. 1:6, 7, 16) means "to irritate to the point of anger." The word *fret* (*raam*, v. 6) means "to thunder or roar," suggesting intense, uncontrolled inward agitation—perhaps comparable to the exclamation "I felt like screaming!" The references to Hannah weeping (*bakah*, vv. 7–8) suggest continual bitter weeping that sometimes breaks into loud crying. The reference to the heart being *grieved* (v. 8, *yara*) connotes the idea of the heart trembling in grief, as we think sometimes of a person's lip involuntarily trembling when he is in deep sorrow. The expression *bitterness of soul* (*marah*, v. 10) speaks of an acrid internal feeling of gall—a gnawing pain in the pit of the stomach. The expression *sorrowful* (*qasheh*, v. 15) spirit speaks of an oppressed spirit, a spirit beaten and ill-treated by a cruel taskmaster. Hannah's explanation to Eli that she had spoken in the abundance of her *complaint* (*siyach*, v. 16) conveys the idea of a verbal cascade of the thoughts that were plaguing her.

some sin. She found herself alternating between bitter anger and abysmal grief, roaring within and weeping without.

In short, the whole process for Hannah was intensely personal. Yet when the Lord graciously answers her prayer and gives her a son, her song of praise is far from merely personal. Not once in this song (I Sam. 2:1–10) does Hannah specifically give thanks for the son she has received; nor does she speak specifically of the adversary who had caused her so much grief. Instead, she exults in the Lord Himself and His work in behalf of all of His people throughout His kingdom.

She praises the Lord for strengthening her against all of her enemies. She rejoices in His salvation. She sees Him anew as preeminently holy and as the only true Refuge. She sees Him now as overcoming the mighty ones of the earth, taking up the cause of the downtrodden and barren throughout His kingdom (vv. 1–7).

Through this personal, private experience of receiving the child she had prayed for, she has realized that the Lord will indeed fulfill His purpose for mankind. He will raise the poor from the dust, and "set them among princes, and to make them inherit the throne of glory" (v. 8). And how will He accomplish this purpose? The King He has appointed, the Messiah, will preserve His people in this life and ultimately judge His enemies to the ends of the earth.

He will keep the feet of his saints, and the wicked shall be silent in darkness; for by strength shall no man prevail. The adversaries of the Lord shall be broken to pieces; out of heaven shall he thunder upon them: the Lord shall judge the ends of the earth; and he shall give strength unto his king, and exalt the horn of his anointed (vv. 9–10).

This inspired account of an otherwise obscure Hebrew woman shows the saints of all ages how their personal experiences relate to the eternal kingdom of God. None are irrelevant. All are designed, directly or indirectly, to prepare the children of God for their royal inheritance and destiny.

Seen in the Experience of David

"Who am I, O Lord God? and what is my house, that thou hast brought me hitherto?" (II Sam. 7:18*b*). David was in a veritable ecstasy when he uttered these words. He was sitting "before the Lord" in the tabernacle at the time. The backdrop to his ecstasy, strangely, was the divine denial of a request that had been close to his heart.

At last, after many bloody battles, the Lord had established his kingdom. He now had some time to plan how best to secure the future of the kingdom God had given him. He had long before recognized that this was God's kingdom, and that its success depended wholly on God's dwelling in their midst as He had under Moses. So his first action in the process of establishing Jerusalem as his capital was to move the tabernacle to that city.

But he sensed the need for something more than a sacred tent for the manifestation of the Presence of the Creator of the universe. The King of kings should have a temple, a palace in which to dwell. We get the impression from David's words to Nathan (II Sam. 7:2) that the thought of building a temple occurred to him suddenly as he was sitting in his palace. But we learn from Psalm 132 that the idea of building a temple had fully occupied his mind for some time before he spoke to Nathan:

> Lord, remember David, and all his afflictions: how he sware unto the Lord, and vowed unto the mighty God of Jacob; Surely I will not come into the tabernacle of my house, nor go up into my bed; I will not give sleep to mine eyes, or slumber to mine eyelids, until I find out a place for the Lord, an habitation for the mighty God of Jacob (Ps. 132:1–5).

Such an intense desire! How then could the Lord's denial of this desire produce in David the ecstasy we just read of? The answer lies in the message that came with the denial. Nathan initially told David, "Go, do all that is in thine heart; for the Lord is with thee" (II Sam. 7:3*b*). Then he received a message from the Lord in the night that compelled him to return to David, bearing the news that it was not God's will for the king to build a temple.

But imbedded in this refusal was a message that turned disappointment to ecstatic joy. In effect, the Lord said, "You wish to build Me a house? No, I will build you a house!" (v. 11). Though David could not build a house for the Lord, his son would. Not only that, the Lord would establish the throne of his son's kingdom forever.

> I will be his father, and he shall be my son. If he commit iniquity, I will chasten him with the rod of men, and with the stripes of the children of men: but my mercy shall not depart away from him, as I took it from Saul, whom I put away before thee. And thine house and thy kingdom shall be established for ever before thee: thy throne shall be established for ever (vv. 14–16).

David was overwhelmed by this message. He had previously been almost obsessed with the thought of building a temple. Now he was possessed with higher and nobler thoughts—thoughts that transformed his entire outlook on life and that revitalized his perception of the Lord's purpose for him, for the kingdom of God, and for the world in which he lived. He could do nothing but go into the tabernacle and "sit before the Lord" and pour from his overflowing heart a song of praise to his God (vv. 18–29).

And why was David so ecstatic about this promise? Because the Lord assured him that his life and reign on earth were significant. It was wonderful, of course, that from his lineage the Messiah would come; but the promise also contained a suggestion that some of his royal descendants might turn from the Lord. He had seen firsthand the condemnation into which King Saul had fallen, and he knew all too well that some of the covenant people were in fact "sons of Belial" (e.g., II Sam. 23:6). What good would it be for him to have a "successful" reign as king, then pass the throne to another "mighty one" of this earth? Life's significance was not in his success as a leader nor even in the name he left for posterity. It was in his attachment to the Messiah, the King with whom he would reign.

David's example in leadership—for everyone. During an exciting game of trucks and cars and stuff, my four-year-old grandson, Nicholas, decided he needed to go downstairs and get another highway monster. Before he left, he gave me some strict instructions—designed, no doubt, to keep me from messing everything up in his absence. "Now, Grampa, you stay in that chair! And don't turn that light on!" I ventured a request for clarification on the chain of command: "Are you the big boss?" "Yes," he said. "Oh?" I answered, "Who made you the big boss?" "God!"

Well, little Nicholas was both right and wrong. He was right about what God had in mind for him. How do I know? God said so. He plans for His people to reign with Him. But Nicholas was also wrong. In fact, he erred where most of us err—in timing. When you think about it, most of our sins are timing problems. God's plan for His people includes all the things men fight and kill to obtain. If a man steals, he does so because he is not willing to wait for God to give him his desires. It is the same with all sins—and with all the passions and ambitions in which sin takes root.

A child of God who wishes to be king should not automatically be judged to be proud or overly ambitious—provided he is willing to wait for God's timing and follow God's program. In the case of my delightful little grandchild, he overstepped the boundary in timing—and I would have to admit (proud Grampa though I am) that his attitude resembled the attitude of the princes of this world. He must have sensed some of the problem himself, for right after his most authoritative commands, he began sucking his thumb.

It has often been said that these books (Joshua through Kings) focus largely on leadership, for it seems that in these narratives the fortunes of the kingdom of God rise and fall with the character of the man at the helm, whether general, judge, or king. I would agree, except (as suggested above) I see this focus having a much broader application than the special few we group in our minds under the connotative umbrella of "leader."

The Creator's original mandate was to all of mankind. Though from the beginning Eve was to be in subjection to Adam (I Tim. 2:11–13), the mandate for women as well as men was to subdue the earth and have dominion over it. "There is neither Jew nor Greek, there is neither bond nor free, there is neither male nor female: for ye are all one in Christ Jesus. And if ye be Christ's, then are ye Abraham's seed, and heirs according to the promise" (Gal. 3:28–29).

In God's plan, all people are in subjection to someone. At the same time, all are to rule over some realm. The Lord established this plan in Eden when he commanded the man and the woman to "dress" (*avad*, "serve") the garden and "keep" (*shamar*, "watch over, supervise") it. It was in this dual role of serving and supervising that they were to subdue the earth and have dominion over it. Of course, it was man's total submission to his sovereign Creator in accepting this dual role that would prepare him to fulfill his destiny of reigning with God.

Throughout the story of God's kingdom, the inspired writers emphasize the principle that humble service is at once the highest form of leadership and the best preparation for it. Leadership in the kingdom of God and the kingdom of the world are polar opposites. Like most of God's people, the apostles had a hard time absorbing this principle. Even under the shadow of the Cross, their Master found them quarreling over which one of them was destined for greatness in the kingdom.

He had admonished them once by setting a little child in their midst as a model for greatness. Now He set before them the striking difference between true greatness and the hollow "greatness" of the world.

> And he said unto them, The kings of the Gentiles exercise lordship over them; and they that exercise authority upon them are called benefactors. But ye shall not be so: but he that is greatest among you, let him be as the younger; and he that is chief, as he that doth serve. For whether is greater, he that sitteth at meat, or he that serveth? is not he that sitteth at meat? but I am among you as he that serveth (Luke 22:25–27).

What can we learn from David about reigning with God? Just a reminder: the word "we" here is an equal opportunity employer. I'm not just talking to natural leaders—the take-charge types who seem destined to set the pace for others. David and the other leaders in these books are all living illustrations of life's providential preparation for future princes in God's kingdom. And as with life in general, David's experiences give us both positive and negative examples.

The first realm in David's preparation for reigning in the eternal kingdom was the sheepfold. Here, in God's plan, he was to serve and supervise—and subdue this part of the earthly kingdom. It was during these "first ways" of David (II Chron. 17:3) that he established the pattern that made him a "man after God's own heart."

His renowned "Shepherd's Psalm" tells us why. He came to see himself as having no need ("I shall not want," 23:1–2) beyond that which his Shepherd could and would supply; and he saw his Shepherd as enabling him to overcome every obstacle in the path of life, whether internal or external (vv. 3–6). In short, he saw his Creator as sovereign over every realm of life. He learned at this early stage not to abandon his divinely ordained place of service, even in the face of powerful enemies. Through the Lord his Shepherd, he overcame the lion and the bear; by this the Lord prepared him for Goliath—and for other giants.

But from David we can learn some things to avoid as well. His astounding victory over Goliath thrust him not only into the public limelight but also to the forefront of the armies of the kingdom of God. And there for a few years he basked in the favor he had with God and men. Then suddenly he found himself out of favor with the king and fleeing for his life into the wilderness.

The Lord was still his Shepherd in the wilderness, but when he walked "through the valley of the shadow of death," he sometimes wondered, "Is the Lord indeed with me as He has been in the past?" One day, after a number of harrowing escapes in which the Lord had again and again proven Himself faithful, David nevertheless found himself saying that the people who had stirred Saul up against him "have driven me out this day from abiding in the inheritance of the Lord, saying, Go, serve other gods" (I Sam. 26:19).

As a matter of fact, neither these people nor Saul himself drove David from the Promised Land to serve other gods. His Shepherd had repeatedly "restored his soul" (e.g., through Jonathan, I Sam. 23:16–18 and Abigail, 25:26–33) and been with him through the valley of the shadow of death (e.g., I Sam. 24; 26:1–12). Somehow, in spite of God's promises and evidences of His protecting presence, David convinced himself that his best hope was beyond the borders of the Promised Land—though he had tried this before and had barely escaped with his life (I Sam. 21:10–15).

David was in Philistia for a year and four months (I Sam. 27:7), and those sixteen months may well have cost him ninety months as king over unified Israel. Before his sojourn in the land of the enemy, people everywhere in Israel, north and south, had recognized that the Lord had chosen David to be the next king (I Sam. 23:17; 24:20; 25:30; II Sam. 3:9, 18). But his near-fatal decision to seek refuge in the land of the enemy left many people wondering and gave ambitious Abner a foothold for the continuation of Saul's kingdom in the north. So after the death of Saul, only the tribe of Judah accepted David as king. He reigned in Hebron over this one tribe for seven and one-half years, ninety months, before he was able to take the throne of a unified nation.

After the fact, David apparently realized his error. Years later, when he was old, he recommended to all who would hear the truth he had so grievously violated, "Trust in the Lord, and do good; dwell in the land, and cultivate faithfulness" (Ps. 37:3, NASB).

THE LATTER PROPHETS: REVIVAL OF THE KINGDOM UNDER THE NEW COVENANT

More often than not, when a prophet appeared on the scene in ancient Israel, people were prone to ask, "What have we done?" Consider the experience of Samuel when the Lord sent him to Bethlehem. As he came into the little village, "the elders of the town trembled at his coming, and said, Comest thou peaceably?" (I Sam. 16:4; cf. I Kings 17:18; 22:8). In fact, the notion that prophets were characteristically conveyors of "heavy" messages became so widespread that even false prophets began to call their messages "the burden of the Lord" (Jer. 23:38).

In general, the characterization of the prophet as a man preaching against the evils of the day should not surprise us. The prophets presided over the decline and disintegration of the covenant kingdom—a decline brought about by the nation's spiritual decline.

Spiritual deterioration begins in the heart and works its way to the surface, and the process is generally slow and subtle. For years, all may seem well to the casual observer. The creeds and forms of worship continue as they were. Only an intangible "something" seems missing. Could it be the heart? But how could that be! The words of the worshipers seem so sincere, and the music, if anything, seems even better—more stately, more dignified, more appropriate for solemn worship.

Strange as it may seem, the outward aspects of worship may even seem to improve for a while. When the inward declines, people tend to compensate by putting more and more emphasis on the outward. Eventually, of course, deterioration of the inner being will lead to outward deterioration, but the process is serpentine—slow and subtle.

Israel followed this pattern of decline, but God, in His grace, would not let them go down that road in comfort. He sent prophets to dog their steps—warning, pleading, admonishing, and sometimes fulminating against them.

But the prophets were not simply troublemakers or signs of trouble. True, they came with weighty messages, but they came also heavily laden with promises. After calling thunderous storms down on recalcitrant

Israel, for the remnant who had a heart for God they had a message of hope, a covenant rainbow in the distant future.

Though there are many variations in the circumstances and emphases of these prophets (Isaiah–Malachi), their combined message is a revelation of the resurrection and reign of the kingdom of God under the new covenant. These prophets take the message of the fulfillment of the promise of the coming King and His kingdom to the highest pitch it reaches in the Old Testament.

It is no wonder then that we find in these prophets the principles established in the foundational prologue of the Bible. If man is to fulfill his destiny to reign with God, he must first humble himself by recognizing his Creator as absolutely sovereign over every realm of life. Constantly the prophets drum on this theme. Listen to Isaiah's preaching of the sovereign Creator's gracious work in behalf of the man who humbles himself:

> Hast thou not known? hast thou not heard, that the everlasting God, the Lord, the Creator of the ends of the earth, fainteth not, neither is weary? there is no searching of his understanding. He giveth power to the faint; and to them that have no might he increaseth strength. Even the youths shall faint and be weary, and the young men shall utterly fall: but they that wait upon the Lord shall renew their strength; they shall mount up with wings as eagles; they shall run, and not be weary; and they shall walk, and not faint (Isa. 40:28–31).

> That they may know from the rising of the sun, and from the west, that there is none beside me. I am the Lord, and there is none else. I form the light, and create darkness: I make peace, and create evil: I the Lord do all these things. . . . Woe unto him that striveth with his Maker! Let the potsherd strive with the potsherds of the earth. Shall the clay say to him that fashioneth it, What makest thou? or thy work, He hath no hands? . . . . I have made the earth, and created man upon it: I, even my hands, have stretched out the heavens, and all their host have I commanded (45:6–7, 9, 12).

> For thus saith the high and lofty One that inhabiteth eternity, whose name is Holy; I dwell in the high and holy place, with him also that is of a contrite and humble spirit, to revive the spirit of the humble, and to revive the heart of the contrite ones (57:15).

Let me remind you that we are dealing here with the first principles established in the opening pages of the Bible. In the account of Creation (Gen. 1), God reveals Himself as the Source and Sustainer of every realm of creation—the One sovereign over all. In the detailed account of man's creation, realm, and responsibilities (Gen. 2:4–25), the Lord reveals man as formed from the dust, yet made in the divine image by the very breath of God. Therefore, the basis of true life for him is humility, and the potential in him is divinity.

Another first principle in the opening pages of the Bible is that of the Sabbath. The revelation of the Sabbath, remember, is a part of the Creation story, signifying that it was intended as an essential element in the development of man in the image of God. The Creator set aside a whole day for man to memorialize His rest of satisfaction in His finished work of creation, and He ordained that man imitate his Creator and enjoy this rest in His finished work.

It is interesting to see how the prophets deal with this subject. The Sabbath is not, to them, simply another law of God. It is a fundamental principle, as it is at Creation. Why? Because entering into the rest of the Lord—His spirit of joy and satisfaction with His finished work—is the basis for our entire walk with the Lord. In a sense, it is foundational to the greatest commandment, to love the Lord with all our soul, mind, and strength; for love results from spiritual communion.

In the spirit of this principle, the Lord declares through Ezekiel that He gave His Sabbaths as a sign—with a special, significant message—between the Creator and His people, "that they might know that I am the Lord that sanctify them" (Ezek. 20:12b, 20; 31:13). When a man ceases from his own works and enters into the rest of his Creator's works, he discovers the truth that only the Lord can make him holy, conforming him to His own image and thus preparing him to reign with Him.

And what do the prophets say of man's destiny to reign with God in His earthly kingdom? The concept of the kingdom citizens reigning with God provides the backdrop for the prophetic message of the New Covenant kingdom's ultimate triumph and reign. The coming King, the Messiah, was to be a descendant of Abraham, as all of God's chosen people were. Those related to a king were of the royal family and in that sense reigned with the king.

The Lord promised to Abraham, and confirmed it with Jacob, that kings would come from his descendants (Gen. 17:6; 35:11). To some, this promise might apply only to the royal descendants of David. Would the prophets see beyond this narrow line?

As the prophets preached of the Lord's adoption of Israel as His chosen people, they would be reminded often of the preamble to that adoption ceremony—which included the promise that these people, the citizens of God's kingdom, would be a royal priesthood (Exod. 19:6). In the context of this promise, they could not help but think of Melchizedek, the king of Salem who was also the priest of the most high God. Then, too, they would know full well that David had spoken of their coming King as "a priest for ever after the order of Melchizedek" (Ps. 110:4).

It is against this broad backdrop of kingdom anticipation that Isaiah prophesies, "Behold, a king shall reign in righteousness, and princes shall rule in judgment" (Isa. 32:1). He is speaking of the anointed King to come and of the saints who will reign with Him as princes. These princes, Isaiah says, are to "rule in judgment." As the supreme King will reign according to the standard of righteousness, so His princes will rule according to the standard of justice. This suggests that the saints themselves will make judicial rulings during the millennial kingdom (cf. I Cor. 6:2).

The inspired author of Psalm 149, who may well have lived during the time of the Latter Prophets,[3] sees the saints also as participating in the actual judgment of the King's enemies.

> Let the high praises of God be in their mouth, and a twoedged sword in their hand; to execute vengeance upon the heathen, and punishments upon the people; to bind their kings with chains, and their nobles with fetters of iron; to execute upon them the judgment written: this honour have all his saints. Praise ye the Lord (Ps. 149:6–9).

As he felt the impulse of the Spirit to write these words, what Scriptures came to the psalmist's mind? Did he think, perhaps, of the fearful words of the Lord's judgment in the Song of Moses?

> If I whet my glittering sword, and mine hand take hold on judgment; I will render vengeance to mine enemies, and will reward them that hate me. I will make mine arrows drunk with blood, and my sword shall devour flesh; and that with the blood of the slain and of the captives, from the beginning of revenges upon the enemy. Rejoice, O ye nations, with his people: for he will avenge the blood of his servants, and will render vengeance to his adversaries, and will be merciful unto his land, and to his people (Deut. 32:41–43).

Certainly the psalmist would have been well aware of these words from Deuteronomy, for the Lord commanded Moses to teach this prophetic song to the people so that it would be passed on from generation to gen-

---

[3] Many interpreters feel that Psalm 149 was written after the return from the Babylonian Captivity, e.g., Albert Barnes.

eration. The two passages together depict the Lord as the supreme Judge and the saints as participating with and implementing His judgments on the enemies of the kingdom.

Daniel also saw the saints fulfilling their destiny to reign with God in His kingdom. One prophecy surged through Daniel's spirit with such power that he felt overwhelmed and emotionally drained by its revelations (Dan. 7:15, 28). It included visions of four great empires depicted as gigantic bloodthirsty beasts, a revelation of the Antichrist and his judgment, an awesome description of the Ancient of Days on the throne of judgment, and a description of the Son of Man, the Messiah, approaching the throne of His Father to receive His inheritance.

What is most remarkable after all this is that when Daniel asks for a summary of these visions ("the truth of all this," v. 16), the angelic interpreter makes one brief statement that focuses not on the great beasts or the brilliant personalities but on the lowly citizens of the kingdom: "These great beasts, which are four, are four kings, which shall arise out of the earth. But the saints of the most High shall take the kingdom, and possess the kingdom for ever, even for ever and ever" (vv. 17–18).

So awesome was the vision of the throne of the Ancient of Days that appeared before him that perhaps Daniel almost overlooked the other thrones in the heavenly scene:

> As I looked, thrones were placed, and the Ancient of days took his seat; his clothing was white as snow, and the hair of his head like pure wool; his throne was fiery flames; its wheels were burning fire. A stream of fire issued and came out from before him; a thousand thousands served him, and ten thousand times ten thousand stood before him; the court sat in judgment, and the books were opened (7:9–10, ESV; cf. Rev. 4:2–4).

This picture of thrones being placed near the throne of the Ancient of Days and of the "court" sitting in judgment gives the contextual background to the summary message of the angel that the saints of the Most High would receive the kingdom and take possession of it. This process will include infinitely more than just the enjoyment of kingdom blessings. For the saints, it will include the participating in the judgment initiated by their King—and reigning with Him on kingdom thrones.

CHAPTER TEN

THE COMING KINGDOM PRESENTED AND REJECTED

THE MESSAGE OF THE FORMER and Latter Prophets of the Old Testament begins to culminate with John the Baptist, a prophet whom few in the Old Testament equaled and none excelled (Matt. 11:11). Isaiah had testified that this man would be the forerunner of the Messiah, "the voice of him that crieth in the wilderness, Prepare ye the way of the Lord, make straight in the desert a highway for our God" (Isa. 40:3; Matt. 3:3).

The first recorded words of this preeminent prophet are "Repent ye: for the kingdom of heaven is at hand" (Matt. 3:2; cf. 4:17, where Christ said the same). It is immensely significant that his first message should draw attention to the kingdom of God and not directly to the King Himself. Why? Did not every believing Israelite have one overriding desire—that the Messiah would come to deliver the chosen people from their oppressors, to deliver the people from their woes, and to restore the nation to its promised glory? True, but to the prophets, the King and the kingdom were inseparably connected. They were one and the same.

The modern Western mind has difficulty understanding this. To us, the government and its leader are separate entities, comparable to a corporation and its CEO. In our system, a corporation may choose to hire a new CEO to give it (hopefully) new direction or improve its bottom line, but that corporation can exist without a CEO and continue to function while largely ignoring its CEO. This was not the case at all in ancient times. The king and the kingdom were one and the same. Daniel, referring to the kingdom of Babylonia, said to Nebuchadnezzar, "Thou art this head of gold" (2:38b).

The Baptist's words here tacitly reveal the central message of the Old Testament prophets, Former and Latter. He clearly saw no need to prepare people for the introduction of this subject, and he saw no need to explain what he meant by "kingdom of heaven" or "kingdom of God." His message was geared to the thought that dominated the hearts of all of God's people, for a genuine believer was one who "waited for the kingdom of God" (Mark 15:43).

This thought of the king and the kingdom being one and the same is the key to understanding the announcement that the kingdom of heaven was "at hand." When the Pharisees asked Jesus when the kingdom would come, He responded that the kingdom is not coming (at this time) "with signs to be observed. . . . The kingdom of God is in your midst" (Luke 17:20–21, NASB).[1] The kingdom was at hand, and in their midst, because the King Himself was present.

> Jesus presented the kingdom as being *at hand* in Himself. The Messianic kingdom, which in the Old Testament was in the future, had now come close to men in His own Person and work. In Him, it was now "in the midst of" them . . . . He Himself was the center and substance of the good news concerning the kingdom.[2]

WHAT IF?

"What if" questions can be precarious; but it might be helpful to consider two such questions to help complete our understanding of the passages we have been examining (such as Matt. 3:2, "the kingdom of heaven is at hand," and Luke 17:20–21, "the kingdom is in your midst").

---

[1] Later He told His disciples that in the last days the kingdom would come "with observation" (Luke 17:24ff.; Matt. 24:29ff.). The Lord here is drawing a distinction between the time of His first coming to fulfill the Passover sacrifice and the time of His Second Coming in the last days to establish His kingdom.

[2] D. Edmond Hiebert, *Mark: A Portrait of the Servant* (Chicago: Moody, 1979), 47.

What If Israel Had Accepted the Messiah?

What if Israel had received their King at His first coming? Would He have established the millennial kingdom at that time? A number of inter-preters hold that this is the only way we can legitimately interpret such passages as Matthew 3:2.[3] I do not agree. I feel that taken together and interpreted in accordance with the natural laws of language, the passages lead to another conclusion.

We should remember, for example, that the Lord's covenant with Abraham included the promise that through his seed all the families of the earth would be blessed. The adoption of the nation Israel as the cus-todians of God's earthly kingdom was not an end in itself, as the pream-ble to that adoption clearly indicates: "And ye shall be unto me a kingdom of priests" (Exod. 19:6). Israel, as a holy nation dedicated to God, was to be instrumental in teaching the nations of the world to know the Lord. According to the prophets, the millennial kingdom will include worship-ers of the Lord from all the nations of the world.

At the first coming of Christ, the evangelism of the Gentiles had not yet been accomplished. During His earthly ministry, the Lord focused His attention and preaching on the nation Israel. In fact, when He sent the Twelve and the seventy out, He sent them to the people of Israel, not to the nations (e.g., Matt. 10:5). Had Israel received their King at His first coming, there would still be much work to do, and many prophecies to be fulfilled, before the millennial kingdom could be established.

Would There Have Been No Sacrifice?

And what of the divinely ordained sacrifice of the Lamb of God? What if Israel had accepted their King when He came the first time? Wouldn't this mean that they would not have crucified Him, and that therefore there would be no sacrifice of the Paschal Lamb of God?

Without the sacrificial blood of the Lamb of God there could have been no remission of sin. Consequently, there could have been no millen-nial kingdom, for only the righteous can enter God's kingdom (Isa. 35:8, 10; 60:21; Ezek. 20:38; John 3:3; I Cor. 6:9).

It is true, of course, that the Father knew how His Son would die (Acts 2:23). But it is also true that God cannot be limited to one method in ac-

---

[3] For example, McClain in his classic work, *The Greatness of the Kingdom* (see chap. 1, n. 10), argues for this position.

complishing His eternal purpose. For example, had Israel received their King, could not God have fulfilled through the priests and the temple ritual the sacrifice of the Lamb? If Abraham, the father of the faithful, was willing to sacrifice his beloved son, believing he would be resurrected to fulfill God's promised purpose (Heb. 11:19), could not a believing high priest have done the same with God's Paschal Lamb?

Consider how God accomplished His purpose through men who were diametrically opposed to His will. Could He not have used people in believing sympathy with His will to do the same? Remember that the religious leaders of the Jews did everything in their power to avoid killing Jesus on a feast day (Matt. 26:5), and that the Romans, represented by Pilate, did not want to crucify Him (e.g., Matt. 27:18ff.). The "determinate counsel and foreknowledge of God" (Acts 2:23), therefore, included an infinite array of dynamic interplay with the will, emotions, and circumstances of men and movements so that the Lamb would be sacrificed at God's ordained time and in His chosen place.

THE KINGDOM AT HAND, THE KINGDOM FUTURE

Our Lord, Who called Israel to "repent, for the kingdom of God is at hand," also spoke of the kingdom as still future (e.g., Matt. 6:10; 7:21–22; Mark 9:47; Luke 22:18). He presented this dual message throughout His earthly ministry. Consider, for example, the following:

Proclamation of the Kingdom at Hand and the Kingdom Future in AD 31[4]

After Herod cast John the Baptist into prison, Jesus left Jerusalem and returned to Galilee: "From that time Jesus began to preach, and to say, Repent: for the kingdom of heaven is at hand" (Matt. 4:17; cf. Mark 1:14–15). In the same year, during the Sermon on the Mount, our Lord taught the disciples to pray, "Thy kingdom come" (Matt. 6:10). He later

---

[4] For the dates of Christ's earthly ministry, I am generally following those presented by Jack Finegan in his *Handbook of Biblical Chronology*, rev. ed. (Peabody, MA: Hendrickson, 1998), 367. These dates agree closely with those of Harold Hoehner, *Chronological Aspects of the Life of Christ* (Grand Rapids: Zondervan, 1977), a summary of which is presented by J. Dwight Pentecost, *The Words and Works of Jesus Christ* (Grand Rapids: Zondervan, 1981), 572. For the sequence of events in the life of Christ, I have largely followed the "Outline Harmony of the Gospels" of Samuel J. Andrews, *The Life of Our Lord upon the Earth* (repr. Grand Rapids: Zondervan, 1954), xxxiii–xxxix.

warns that many who profess to be believers "in that day" (in the future) will not be allowed to enter the kingdom of heaven (Matt. 7:21–22).

Proclamation of the Kingdom at Hand and the Kingdom Future in AD 32

When the Lord sent forth the twelve disciples to preach to the lost sheep of the house of Israel, He instructed them, "As ye go, preach, saying, The kingdom of heaven is at hand" (Matt. 10:6–7; cf. Mark 6:7–13; Luke 9:1–6; Luke 10:9, 11; 11:20). Yet in His instructions to the Twelve, our Lord evidently looked far beyond their immediate ministry to the ministry of disciples throughout the age (Matt. 10:16–23). He speaks of widespread persecution of His followers, of their being summoned before kings as a testimony to them and the nations (10:18, NASB, ESV). He concludes His instructions with a remarkable reference to the last days and the Second Coming:

> And ye shall be hated of all men for my name's sake: but he that endureth to the end shall be saved. But when they persecute you in this city, flee into another: for verily I say unto you, Ye shall not have gone over the cities of Israel, till the Son of man be come (Matt. 10:22–23; cf. Matt. 24:9,13).

Proclamation of the Kingdom at Hand and the Kingdom Future in AD 33

It was perhaps just two or three months before His crucifixion in AD 33 that the Pharisees asked Jesus when the kingdom of God would come. He responded, "The kingdom of God is not coming with signs to be observed, nor will they say, 'Look, here it is!' or 'There!' for behold, the kingdom of God is in the midst of you" (Luke 17:20b–21, ESV). Yet not long after, at the Passover supper, He "took the cup, and gave thanks, and said, Take this, and divide it among yourselves: for I say unto you, I will not drink of the fruit of the vine, until the kingdom of God shall come" (Luke 22:17–18). Thus He established the memorial of the Lord's Supper, anticipating a considerable time interval before the kingdom of God would be established.

The Message of the Kingdom at Hand and the Kingdom Future

The message in this dual proclamation is that where the King is, there, in essence, is the kingdom also. To a spiritually minded scribe who had been sent to test Jesus, the Lord said, "Thou art not far from the kingdom of God" (Mark 12:28–34; cf. Matt. 22:35–40). When a person receives the King, there is a sense in which he then enters the kingdom (see Matt. 23:13; John 3:5; Acts 14:22).

REIGNING WITH THE
ONCE-REJECTED KING

The Principle of Serving and Supervising Reaffirmed

In His message on the Mount of Olives, the Lord, after outlining events of the last days, admonishes His disciples concerning their responsibilities while they are awaiting His return to establish His kingdom. In one of these messages (Matt. 25:14–30), He compares the kingdom of heaven to a man who, in anticipation of a lengthy journey to a distant country, entrusts wealth for investment to his servants according to their abilities.

At length, when the master of the household returns, he calls his servants before him to give an account of their stewardship. When the servants to whom he has entrusted five and two talents each report a 100 percent gain on their investments, he commends each with the same words, "Well done, thou good and faithful servant: thou hast been faithful over a few things, I will make thee ruler over many things: enter thou into the joy of thy lord" (v. 21; cf. v. 23).

Here is an inspired illustration of the principle established in the opening pages of the Bible: the principle of serving and supervising. In Genesis, we found that man's perception of God was the key to his preparation for reigning with Him. To the extent he recognized his Lord's sovereignty and benevolence, to that extent he prepared for his royal destiny by serving humbly and supervising conscientiously. When the serpent planted in Eve's mind the thought that God's plan might not be benevolent, her perception of God changed; and, through the possibility of losing his wife, Adam's perception of the goodness of God became blurred—and together they fell into sin.

Our Lord's parable of the talents emphasizes this principle as well—the principle of man's perception of God. One of the stewards was so fearful of losing the talent entrusted to him that he hid it in the earth, stifling the possibility of his master's money either gaining interest or increasing by investment. His fear, rather than his prospects, controlled him. Why? Because of his perception of his master. "Lord, I knew thee," he said, "that thou art an hard man, reaping where thou hast not sown, and gathering where thou hast not strawed" (v. 24b). He saw his master as stern and harsh, and as having a certain mysterious power that lifted him above the natural laws of reaping and sowing. In short, he saw him as unreasonable and above reason—with no benevolent purpose for his servants in view. And his perception of his master paralyzed his preparation and made him ineligible to enter into his master's joy.

Open to Gentiles As Well As to Jews

In spite of the fact that the Lord's covenant with Abraham embraced the Gentiles as potential kingdom saints, the Jews, including even the disciples, had a very difficult time digesting this idea. They must, therefore, have been stunned at their Lord's reaction to the Roman centurion who said, "Speak the word only, and my servant shall be healed." The Lord "marveled," and what He said next left them marveling. "Verily I say unto you, I have not found so great faith, no, not in Israel. And I say unto you, That many shall come from the east and west, and shall sit down with Abraham, and Isaac, and Jacob, in the kingdom of heaven" (Matt. 8:9–11; cf. Luke 7:1–10).

For the Jews witnessing this poignant scene, the marvel was not that Gentiles would be converted. They knew full well that when the light and glory of the Lord had risen on Israel, the Gentiles, including even their kings, would come to that light (Isa. 60:1–3).

In fact, the scene as it was developing clashed with none of the Jewish preconceptions of Gentile conversion. According to Luke (7:1–10), the centurion was not so presumptuous as to appear in person before the illustrious Rabbi (7:7). Instead, he sent elders of the Jews to Him, and they described this centurion as "worthy" of help because of his favorable attitude toward the Jews. Then when Jesus went with the elders toward the centurion's home, the centurion sent friends with the message, "Lord, trouble not thyself: for I am not worthy that thou shouldest enter under my roof" (7:3–6). All this dovetailed well with Jewish notions of their future relationship with the Gentiles.

What must have shocked them beyond measure was Christ's saying that Gentiles from all regions of the dark pagan world would actually sit down with Abraham, Isaac, and Jacob—that they would have such places of honor at the kingdom feast. Could this ever be? Could it be that the Gentiles would actually be put on a level with the Jews? Perhaps this incident was part of the slow process of preparing Peter and the other disciples for the day when Jewish Christians would look with astonished wonder on the phenomenon of Gentiles actually receiving the Holy Spirit (Acts 10:45).

Our Lord's words concerning the centurion include nothing specific about reigning with God, but the implication is certainly there. In effect, His words reveal that the Gentiles would be heirs together with the Jews in God's kingdom. And His declaration that He had "not seen such great faith, even in Israel" proclaimed that if Jews are to reign with God, the Gentiles would too.

The Path to Greatness in God's Kingdom

It is about March, AD 33, one month before the Crucifixion. Jesus is on His last journey to Jerusalem. He has just been ministering across the Jordan in Perea. He and his disciples have now crossed the Jordan into Judea and have begun walking the five miles to their next stopping place at Jericho, six hours from Jerusalem. Luke tells us that while Jesus was yet in Galilee, several weeks before, He knew that the time for His sacrifice was drawing near and "stedfastly set his face to go to Jerusalem" (9:51).

Now as the shadow of the Cross loomed closer, He walked before His disciples rather than with them as He usually did. The disciples, seeing this, were astonished and became increasingly fearful. Then the Lord took His fearful and confused disciples aside

> and began to tell them what things should happen unto him, saying, Behold, we go up to Jerusalem; and the Son of man shall be delivered unto the chief priests, and unto the scribes; and they shall condemn him to death, and shall deliver him to the Gentiles: and they shall mock him, and shall scourge him, and shall spit upon him, and shall kill him: and the third day he shall rise again (Mark 10:32b–34).

Amazingly, it is at this point—after our Lord's instruction to His fearful disciples and description of the agonizing trial awaiting Him—that James and John draw the Lord aside from the other disciples and, with their mother serving as their spokesperson, present a special request.[5]

---

[5] Their mother, Salome, was one of the women who traveled with Jesus and the disciples from Galilee (Mark 15:40–41). Salome was the sister of Mary, the mother of Jesus (cf. John 19:25, Matt. 27:56, and Mark 15:40), and perhaps on this basis presumed she could win special favor speaking in behalf of her sons (Matt. 20:20–21).

"Grant that these my two sons may sit, the one on thy right hand, and the other on the left, in thy kingdom" (Matt. 20:21).

In response, the Lord gave the brothers an opportunity to apologize for their presumptuousness with an admonition and two questions. "Ye know not what ye ask. Are ye able to drink of the cup that I shall drink of, and to be baptized with the baptism that I am baptized with?" But the brothers answered, with unabashed self-confidence, "We are able" (Matt. 20:22). Before denying their request, the Lord sought again to correct their thinking (v. 23).

When the ten became aware of the request of James and John, "they were moved with indignation against the two brethren" (Matt. 20:24). But we have to ask here, Why were they indignant? Was it because of the pride the request revealed? Because of the presumptuousness of James and John? No, they were indignant because each thought he deserved one of the places the brothers had requested. They had all argued in the past about which one of them would be the greatest, and they would argue again about this in the future—on the very night of the Passover! (Luke 22:24; 9:46; Mark 9:34).

Then the Lord, with His eye on the distant future, called His followers all aside once again and instructed them concerning the path to greatness in God's kingdom:

> Ye know that the princes of the Gentiles exercise dominion over them, and they that are great exercise authority upon them. But it shall not be so among you: but whosoever will be great among you, let him be your minister; and whosoever will be chief among you, let him be your servant: even as the Son of man came not to be ministered unto, but to minister, and to give his life a ransom for many (Matt. 20:25b–28).

Remarkably (to some), the Lord did not condemn his disciples for their desire to be great in His coming kingdom. Properly exercised, this ambition is simply the desire of the true servant of God for more capacity to serve his Master. Far from discouraging such ambition, the Lord encouraged it, as He did in this lesson in true greatness (Luke 19:15–19; cf. Luke 6:23, 35; I Tim. 5:18; Heb. 11:6, 26; Rev. 22:12).

In this lesson, the Lord warned His followers that the type of leadership they were used to, that of the great ones of the world—people they sometimes found themselves admiring for their gifts and qualities—was in nature diametrically opposed to the spirit of the leader who would be great in God's eyes. If you would be great, if you would be first, He said, practice being a bond slave to your brethren. Don't allow yourself to rationalize that the type of "dynamic leadership" (in moments of truth, termed "dictatorial leadership") the rulers of this world exercise is the way you become a "benefactor" to your brothers and sisters in Christ (Luke 22:25).

The "Big Boss" Syndrome: The Path to Failure

Peter heard this timely instruction concerning the leadership style of the princes of the world, but he didn't hear. He had also heard the solemn words of his Lord that when He arrived at Jerusalem, rather than establishing His kingdom, He would be abused and crucified—but He would rise again. But Peter was very adept, as most of us are, at the art of selective listening. Some of his Master's words simply didn't register with him.

On the other hand, not long before these messages had passed undetected through his auditory system, Peter latched eagerly onto his Master's promise, "Verily I say unto you, That ye which have followed me, in the regeneration when the Son of man shall sit in the throne of his glory, ye also shall sit upon twelve thrones, judging the twelve tribes of Israel." The Lord had spoken these words in response to Peter's question, "Behold, we have forsaken all, and followed thee; what shall we have therefore?" (Matt. 19:27b–28).

Perhaps it was this thought of the disciples sitting on thrones judging the tribes of Israel that stimulated the strife as to who should be the greatest. Who would have the honor, for example, of reigning over the tribe of Judah? And whose throne would be placed closest to the Master's? Who had forsaken the most to follow the Master? And who had been most faithful to Him?

So a month or so later, it's no wonder that the strife breaks out again—though the occasion now, the Passover Supper, was even more solemn. And it's no wonder also that when the Lord warned, "All ye shall be offended because of me this night," Peter responds with such vehemence: "Although all shall be offended, yet will not I" (Mark 14:27, 29). The Lord has just spoken again of eating and drinking at His table in the kingdom, and of the disciples sitting on twelve thrones judging the tribes of Israel.

In the glow of this thought and the heat of the strife with his fellow disciples, Peter saw no possibility of his denying the Lord. After all, he had already forsaken all to follow his Master, and he was ready now to forsake his liberty and his life for his Lord.

He had gladly, and selectively, heard his Master's prophetic words concerning the twelve thrones; and he believed Him, since (as he would affirm) he believed all of his Lord's prophecies. But that night, he chose not to believe one of his Lord's prophecies: "Verily I say unto thee, That this day, even in this night, before the cock crow twice, thou shalt deny me thrice."

Once he had said to his Lord, "To whom shall we go? thou hast the words of eternal life" (John 6:68). And he would have been the first to argue that all of his Master's promises would be fulfilled—all, that is, except this one. In the face of this prophecy, "he spake the more vehemently, If I should die with thee, I will not deny thee in any wise" (Mark 14:31).

What happened here to Peter's logic circuit? One of the first things we should look for in cases like this is a timing problem. And if we look carefully at Peter's digestive system during this period—at the words he digested and the words he didn't—we'll find that timing was at the heart of his problem. He tried to take possession of his throne too soon; and this type of presumptuousness leads inevitably to the big-boss syndrome. Big bosses commonly become supremely confident in their own judgment calls, and what naturally comes with such confidence is green-eyed suspicion of contrary judgments—even if the contrary judgment is the Lord's!

CHAPTER ELEVEN

THE COMING KINGDOM PREACHED AND RECEIVED

NOT EVEN THE RESURRECTION SETTLED all the disciples' problems of perception. As most disciples do, they still had hang-ups and predilections that had to be coached and cajoled out of their system. One such problem was their perception of the Great Commission.

Christians often overlook the fact that all who heard our Lord's original proclamation of the Great Commission were Jews—Jews who for three years had been given such commands as, "Go not into the way of the Gentiles, and into any city of the Samaritans enter ye not: but go rather to the lost sheep of the house of Israel" (Matt. 10:5–6).

What perception did these Jews have of the Great Commission? Given their knowledge of the Old Testament, their cultural upbringing, and (shall we say it?) their prejudices, they must have thought of the Great Commission as something of a Great Concession. Yes, the prophets did speak of the conversion of Gentiles, but of course they would get in on the coattails of the Jews—hardly to be thought of as kingdom citizens and never holding places of honor.

It was indeed God's plan to use the chosen people of Israel as a kingdom of priests to bring the nations to Himself, but renegade priests, scribes, and Pharisees had so distorted this plan that it was hardly recognizable.

One writer suggests that the book of Acts, far from recording the apostles' obedience to the Great Commission, more accurately records their reluctance to obey it.[1] Peter, you remember, had to be practically dragged into the home of the Roman centurion Cornelius to present the gospel to an audience gathered for that purpose.

When Peter's Jewish brethren called him on the carpet about this, he explained his unprecedented action in detail (Acts 11:1–17). Three times the Lord had repeated His instructions to him in a vision. Then the messengers He had sent appeared at his door. And, said Peter, "the Spirit told me to go with them, making no distinction" (v. 12, ESV). The expression *making no distinction* (from *diakrino*) suggests the idea of not wavering through discrimination or because of personal preferences.

Furthermore, added Peter, I took these six brethren with me as witnesses. (He knew that an evangelistic foray into a Gentile home would be viewed as scandalous.) He concluded his detailed apology with an account of the Spirit of God falling on this gathering of Gentiles. Then the brethren, wide-eyed with wonder, made an amazing statement: "Then hath God also to the Gentiles granted repentance unto life."

Each time I read this dawning-light statement, I wonder if there was an angelic equivalent of "Duh" in response. What had the brethren really heard when the Lord announced His Great Commission? What did they think He meant when He said, "Go ye into all the world, and preach the gospel to every creature"? And of whom and to whom was He speaking when He told them the goal of the Great Commission, "that repentance and remission of sins should be preached in his name among all nations"? (Mark 16:15; Luke 24:47). But eventually, by degrees, the Great Concession and the Great Reluctance were transformed among the Jewish brethren into the Great Commission.

THE CHURCH AND THE KINGDOM

And what part did the church play in all this? Since the kingdom of God disintegrated and was disrupted under the Old Covenant, has the church under the New Covenant become a new, improved version of the

---

[1] Richardson, *Eternity in Their Hearts*, 197 (see chap. 2, n. 5).

kingdom of God? Such an idea has appeared in various doctrinal works, but its advocates invariably seek support for their thesis within the logical paradigm of a theological system rather than in the clear revelations of Scripture.

Never in Scripture are the church and the kingdom of God identified as one and the same. The word commonly translated *church* (*ekklesia*) in the New Testament appears 118 times. In none of these does a Scriptural writer use the word to designate the kingdom of God. In fact, John the Baptist and Jesus had preached the gospel of the kingdom of God for about three years before our Lord announced that He would (in the future) build something new, His church, an entity different from the kingdom—but designed for the purpose of promoting the divine goals for the kingdom.[2]

> And I say also unto thee, That thou art Peter, and upon this rock I will build my church; and the gates of hell shall not prevail against it. And I will give unto thee the keys of the kingdom of heaven: and whatsoever thou shalt bind on earth shall be bound in heaven: and whatsoever thou shalt loose on earth shall be loosed in heaven (Matt. 16:18–19).

On the other hand, the inspired writers consistently use the terms *kingdom of heaven* and *kingdom of God* to refer to the theocratic kingdom presented in the Old Testament and prophesied as coming through Christ in the last days. When John the Baptist and Jesus announced that the kingdom of God was at hand (Matt. 3:1–2; Mark 1:14–15), they took no time to explain what they meant by "kingdom of God" or "kingdom of heaven" because they knew that the Jews, versed in the Old Testament prophets, were well acquainted with these terms.

The Church an Instrument of Evangelism for the Kingdom of God

Though all of our Lord's words are equally inspired, the last words He spoke before He departed for heaven demand special attention, because they show what He obviously viewed as essential aspects of His message.

---

[2] Jesus traveled from Galilee to Jerusalem at the time of the Feast of Tabernacles (John 7), which took place Sept. 10–17 in AD 32. He announced that He would build His church after He had returned from Jerusalem to Cæsarea Philippi (Matt. 16:13–20), which was about thirty miles north of the Sea of Galilee (the northernmost point of His ministry). It is likely, then, that He instructed His disciples at Cæsarea Philippi about October, AD 32, five months or so before His crucifixion. John the Baptist began his ministry, announcing that the kingdom of God was at hand, in AD 28–29.

And what was the theme of His teaching in His last messages to His disciples?

To begin with, He gave His disciples a very important Commission. As apostles ("sent ones"), they were to go into all the world and make disciples of all nations, teaching them to take heed to and obey all He had taught them. For some reason, however, we in the Christian era often overlook the next part of our Lord's post-Resurrection ministry.

He had instructed His disciples to meet Him in Galilee (Matt. 28:7; Mark 16:7; John 21:1). There and later in Jerusalem, after giving them the Great Commission, He appeared periodically to them for forty days to give them His last earthly instructions. And what was the essence of His teaching during these forty days? Luke tells us that He spent that time "speaking of the things pertaining to the kingdom of God" (Acts 1:3).

These ten words tell us a great deal about the relationship of the church and the kingdom of God. Among other things, they tell us that we shouldn't think of the church's ministry as unrelated to the kingdom of God—as if the church and the kingdom were each destined to go their own ways, never to meet again until eternity.

On the contrary, these words tell us that the King's heart and mind is on His kingdom—and if His heart is there, where should ours be? The Lord was instructing His infant church. Just ten days or so after He completed His post-Resurrection messages, He would send His Holy Spirit to them in Jerusalem, and the church would be officially inaugurated.

It seems obvious from this that God designed the church as an instrument to promote and help fulfill His kingdom plans. What part is the church to play in the fulfillment of these ancient plans? His first assignment came in response to the disciples' question "Lord, wilt thou at this time restore again the kingdom to Israel?" He said,

> It is not for you to know the times or the seasons, which the Father hath put in his own power. But ye shall receive power, after that the Holy Ghost is come upon you: and ye shall be witnesses unto me both in Jerusalem, and in all Judæa, and in Samaria, and unto the uttermost part of the earth (Acts 1:7b–8).

The kingdom prophecies included the conversion of people throughout the nations of the world. When they receive the King, they are "translated" into His kingdom (Col. 1:13)—though, of course, their full inheritance will come when the King returns. Therefore, instead of asking when the kingdom would be restored, the disciples, after receiving the Holy Spirit, should act according to the nature of the kingdom promises and seek to fulfill the Great Commission.

The Church's Message Essentially of the Coming Kingdom

To the Ephesian elders Paul declared, "I kept back nothing that was profitable unto you. . . . I have not shunned to declare unto you all the counsel of God" (Acts 20:20, 27). What is it to preach "all the counsel of God"? Sandwiched between these affirmations of the completeness of his message, Paul summarized his ministry among the Ephesians in five words: "preaching the kingdom of God" (v. 25; cf. Acts 8:12; 19:8; 28:23, 31).

This is probably not the summary most Christians would have given of Paul's ministry, but it is an inspired summary. As such, it is profitable for correction, for instruction, and (in many cases) for reproof concerning our proclamation of the message of God (II Tim. 3:16).

But what of preaching Christ? To preach the kingdom of God as Paul preached it is to preach Christ, for He is the Savior and King without Whom there would be no kingdom. And what of preaching the plan of salvation? To preach the kingdom as Paul preached it is to preach "repentance toward God, and faith toward our Lord Jesus Christ" (Acts 20:21b), without which no one can enter into the kingdom of God.

At the same time, this summary tells us that "all the counsel of God" must include a focus that is often neglected in much modern preaching and teaching. The fact that the brief model prayer Christ gave His followers includes the petition "Thy kingdom come" should tell us something about the value of the kingdom focus in Christian living. The inspired writers maintained this focus in applying the truth of the coming kingdom to Christian conduct.

Our actions and attitudes should be consistent with the nature of the kingdom. Few issues have plagued the church more than questions, arguments, and divisions relating to Christian liberty. Even the ancient Roman church, a church respected "throughout the whole world" (Rom. 1:8b), had this problem. Some in the assembly, knowledgeable of the full implications of the gospel, took full advantage of their New Covenant freedom from the Mosaic dietary laws to "eat all things." Others simply couldn't understand how anyone could say that these biblical laws no longer applied (Rom. 14).

The more knowledgeable (though not necessarily more spiritual) believers, who seemed to be in the majority, were inclined to corner these "untaught" brethren, seeking to argue them into their "more enlightened" level of Christianity (v. 1). But when they found these saints unconvinced by their arguments (as is generally the case), they would consign them in their minds to an inferior status in the body of Christ. On the other hand, their "students," far from being impressed with the knowledge of these advocates of liberty, began to censure them for their refusal to obey the law of Moses (v. 3).

So how did Paul correct the problem? He called the majority to recognize anew the nature of the kingdom of God. "For the kingdom of God is not meat and drink; but righteousness, and peace, and joy in the Holy Ghost" (v. 17). The nature of the kingdom is the nature of its King—Christ. One who is Christlike in spirit is concerned preeminently with the spiritual qualities of true life. This appeal, though addressed primarily to the strong, applies to the weak as well. They tended to judge others based on outward observations rather than spiritual qualities.

Paul applied the same general principle to divisive brethren at Corinth who were judging his ministry on what they perceived to be negative outward circumstances:

> Now some are puffed up, as though I would not come to you. But I will come to you shortly, if the Lord will, and will know, not the speech of them which are puffed up, but the power. For the kingdom of God is not in word, but in power (I Cor. 4:18–20).

God's kingdom is a kingdom of great power. Therefore, in their relationships with fellow believers, true kingdom saints should seek to tap the spiritual power that works through their King, not the destructive power of words that undermine fellow kingdom citizens.

The same principle, that of acting consistently with the nature of God's kingdom, also applies to lifestyle questions. Throughout its history, the church has gravitated toward a sound-bite theology. We're not inclined to think things through, to look at the bigger picture, to consider the implications and ramifications of the truths we hear and read. Instead, we tend to latch on to catchy ten-second tidbits of truth and transform them into euphoric mantras for confident living.

One such truth that (though glorious in its natural setting) has been widely turned into a misleading mantra is the biblical doctrine of salvation by faith alone. The sound-bite application of this truth has lured Christians everywhere into assuming that a person's verbal testimony is the ultimate seal of approval. If he gets the formula right in his verbal testimony, any habitual lifestyle problems he may have can be attributed to backsliding, carnality, the company he keeps, or the need for enrollment in a discipleship program. Paul used the kingdom-of-God principle to deal—in a rather rugged fashion—with this problem also:

> Now the works of the flesh are manifest, which are these; adultery, fornication, uncleanness, lasciviousness, idolatry, witchcraft, hatred, variance, emulations, wrath, strife, seditions, heresies, envyings, murders, drunkenness, revellings, and such like: of the which I tell you before, as I have also told you in time past, that they which do such things shall not inherit the kingdom of God (Gal. 5:19–21; cf. I Cor. 6:9–10; Eph. 5:5).

These appeals all suggest the value of following Paul's example and not shunning to declare all the counsel of God. The Christian who has true knowledge of the nature of the kingdom of God will have more readily available to him the spirit and power of the King of that kingdom.

Our royal inheritance governs our attitude toward poorer brethren. The last place on earth you would (or should) expect to find an aristocracy is in the Christian church. But as a matter of fact, weeds and other noxious plants can grow even in the courts of the Lord's house. For example, our Christian *convictions* sometimes goad us into criticizing professed believers who (in our judgment) *lack the character* to earn a decent living.

The disciples, you remember, were astounded at our Lord's response concerning the departure of the rich young ruler, "Verily I say unto you, That a rich man shall hardly enter into the kingdom of heaven" (Matt. 19:23).[3] The disciples had evidently been caught in the version of "prosperity theology" that was common in the Jewish culture of their day. Certain passages in the Old Testament could be interpreted to mean that material prosperity is a sign of God's blessing on the righteous. After all, God had blessed the Patriarchs, David, and Solomon with prosperity.

---

[3] The Greek word behind Matthew's description of the disciples as "exceedingly amazed" (*ekplesso*, 19:25) denotes the idea of striking someone with such a blow that he is driven out or away. The word was commonly used of a statement that so shocked a person that he lost his sense of self-possession—or as we might say, "knocked him off his feet."

Consequently, to speak of a rich Jew having difficulty entering the king-dom of God seemed oxymoronic to them.

Sadly, this twisted theology became part of the cultural baggage con-verted Jews carried with them into the Christian church. It should not greatly surprise us, therefore, that James, writing to "the twelve tribes which are scattered abroad" (James 1:1b), had to deal with this problem. Believers were showing favoritism in their assemblies toward the rich and were treating poor brethren with pious contempt.

So how did James deal with this problem? He appealed to the prin-ciple of common inheritance all believers have in the kingdom of God: "Hearken, my beloved brethren, Hath not God chosen the poor of this world rich in faith, and heirs of the kingdom which he hath promised to them that love him?" (2:5).

Thus, balanced teaching and preaching concerning the kingdom of God will do much to rid the church of the deeply rooted plague of Christian aristocracy—the notion that our legacy allows us to look upon certain brethren as culturally or spiritually inferior. On the contrary, the legacy of the King has made some of these same brethren rich in faith and fellow heirs with the King Himself.

THE CULMINATION OF THE COMING KINGDOM

In the final movement in the biblical story of God's covenant kingdom, our Lord reveals the culmination of the war of the ages between the Dragon and the Lamb. To the complete surprise of the raging people and princes of this earth, our King reveals also who the real kings of the earth will be in His eternal kingdom.

THE COMING VICTORY

I was ten years old when America awoke Sunday, December 7, 1941, to find itself at war. I well remember that our troops were on the losing end of virtually every battle they entered in those early days of World War II. Nevertheless, you couldn't find an American who thought we were going to lose the war.

I remember seeing posters trumpeting the spirit of our people: "America Has Never Lost a War." The general attitude was "Just wait till we get rolling. You guys have had it!" It was largely human confidence, augmented somewhat by the notion that America had inherited the God's Chosen People mantle, that generated this attitude. Nevertheless, it so strengthened the resolve of the country that no defeat was final, that every failure was simply a steppingstone to ultimate success.

This is the proper kingdom spirit of the heirs of the King. Consider this announcement:

> And I heard a loud voice saying in heaven, Now is come salvation, and strength, and the kingdom of our God, and the power of his Christ: for the accuser of our brethren is cast down, which accused them before our God day and night (Rev. 12:10).

The author of these words was a Roman prisoner languishing on the barren island of Patmos. He addressed them to believers living under this mighty empire's dominating power. Though everything in his present situation spoke of defeat, John was anticipating victory—and telling other believers to do the same. He wanted God's people to know that there is strength for the soul, against all circumstances to the contrary, for the child of the King who recognizes his destiny—to reign with his King.

PART THREE

A PROTOTYPE OF THE KINGDOM SAINT

Abraham; who is the father of us all . . .

Abraham; who is the father of us all. . . . They which are of faith, the same are the children of Abraham. . . . So then they which be of faith are blessed with faithful Abraham. . . . By faith Abraham . . . looked for a city which hath foundations, whose builder and maker is God.

Romans 4:16; Galatians 3:7, 9; Hebrews 11:8, 10

THE INSPIRED WRITERS PRESENT ABRAHAM as "the father of us all." As the first eleven chapters of Genesis represent the foundation to the entire written revelation of God, the story of Abraham represents the ground floor of the edifice of God's Holy Oracle. If we are to understand the developing story of the Bible, then, we must get in on the ground floor.

We are dealing, remember, with the developing story of the fulfillment of God's purpose in His revelation to man. His purpose for man is that he should reign with Him in His kingdom (Gen. 1:26–28). How does the story of Abraham support God's announced purpose for mankind?

The story of Abraham gives an account of the roots of the believer's faith and, at the same time, provides for the people of God a prototype of the kingdom saint. The calling of Abraham introduces the covenant of the promised Seed through Whom all the nations of the earth will be blessed. The narrative of Abraham's pilgrimage and experiences is an inspired revelation of the outworking of this covenant-faith in the life of a believer.

In a sense, the story of Abraham, though it is based on the prologue of the first eleven chapters of Genesis, serves as the foundation to the developing story of the kingdom of God in the Bible. I have chosen, therefore, to devote several chapters to this foundational story. The inspired writers present the story of God's kingdom in the context of human life. My goal is to follow their example.

Chapter Twelve

The Making of a King

"You Are a Prince of God Among Us"

THESE WORDS (GEN. 23:6, ESV) reflect how the people of Canaan felt toward Abraham, but they also reflect his destiny. God Himself called Abraham His friend (Isa. 41:8; cf. II Chron. 20:7; James 2:23); and the Scriptures designate him as "the father of all who believe" (Rom. 4:11, ESV), the pattern for all believers.

It is through Abraham first that the free character of salvation is clearly announced (Gen. 15:6). It is through him that God reveals resurrection power as an integral part of salvation (Heb. 11:19). And it was to Abraham that God revealed the great culmination of salvation in the heavenly city (Heb. 11:10).[1]

Furthermore, it is to Abraham that the inspired writer announces the universal reach of salvation by the Seed that will bless all nations (e.g., Gen. 22:18). Consequently, it is through Abraham that God will ultimately fulfill His plan for mankind to reign with Him (Gen. 1:26–28). Though the promise of the kingdom is narrowed through Abraham to Israel, through him also it is expanded to the ends of the earth.

---

[1] See Sauer, *World Redemption*, 96–107 (see chap. 4, n. 10).

Know ye therefore that they which are of faith, the same are the children of Abraham. And the scripture, foreseeing that God would justify the heathen through faith, preached before the gospel unto Abraham, saying, In thee shall all nations be blessed. So then they which be of faith are blessed with faithful Abraham (Gal. 3:7–9).

The story of Abraham—and of the patriarchs who succeeded him—could largely be summarized with words wrought out in David's experience: "Trust in the Lord, and do good; dwell in the land and cultivate faithfulness" (Ps. 37:3, NASB). As Abraham trusted in the Lord and, fulfilling His purpose for him, dwelled in the land, he cultivated faithfulness. As he developed in faithfulness, the Lord increasingly blessed him. Abraham's original covenant blessing was based on this principle. For that matter, so is the whole Christian life.

THE PILGRIM'S PROGRESS

The Pilgrim's Progress is a classic largely because it so well reflects the spirit and drama of the original *Pilgrim's Progress* written by Moses. We know it as the story of Abraham. Paul uses Abraham as an example and prototype of a believer, but Abraham's testimony of salvation included much more than belief in God (John 8:39; James 2:21). The experiences of Abraham are characteristic examples of the walk of faith—an inspired *Pilgrim's Progress* by which the believer who studies it can prosper where Abraham prospered and avoid the pitfalls he stumbled into.

LIVES IN COUNTERPOINT

In his *Parallel Lives*, Plutarch compares and contrasts the strengths and weaknesses of certain Greek and Roman leaders who, he felt, had something to teach about life. A biblical version of such dual biographies might well be called *Lives in Counterpoint*—parallel lives that reveal contrasting elements in the overall theme. Early in the Bible story, for example, Moses sets before us Cain and Seth—lives in counterpoint—as the founding fathers of two diverse kingdoms. These two men had the same light of divine revelation, the same opportunities in life, the same advantages and disadvantages—and the same God-given desire to reign over the earth; but they took radically different approaches to fulfilling their desires.

Now, with a new civilization developing after the Deluge, the inspired writer presents two other men whose lives were destined to shape contrasting elements in the course of history: Nimrod and Abraham. Though very different in character, these two men had much in common. Both could be called founding fathers of the new orders in the kingdom of the world and the kingdom of God. Both ultimately won the admiration of a wide range of people, and the influence of both was destined to extend through time and into eternity. We have already looked briefly at Nimrod, but we want to look at him now as a contrasting backdrop for the introduction of Abraham.

NIMROD: "A MIGHTY ONE IN THE EARTH"

Nimrod and his kingdom are prototypes of the means by which Satan exercises his authority and power over the kingdom of the world. The man of the world is preeminently a user of people. He is typically interested in people, but his fundamental interest is self-interest. He takes pleasure in his friendships and does favors for his friends, but his friendships are essentially means of personal advancement. He sees his friends as subjects in his "kingdom." He may not consciously view them this way, but his actions and attitude will eventually reveal his perceptions.

To the extent, for example, that his friends help him in the fulfillment of his desires, to that extent they remain friends. When his friends' desires run counter to his, he either finds ways to subjugate them or looks for "better" friends. Nimrod is an example of the self-sufficient, self-centered man of the world. Having eaten of the Tree of the Knowledge of Good and Evil, he sees himself as "like God." As a god in his own perception, he will brook no rivals to his will.

Though in the course of life even the man of the world must realize his own inability and insufficiency, the spirit of the man of the world is the spirit of Nimrod. Given the opportunity, he will take his place among the gods.

ABRAHAM: "A PRINCE OF GOD"

In his early days, Abraham may well have been swept into the power orbit of Nimrod. On the assumption that like his contemporaries, Nimrod lived to be over four hundred years old, he would have been alive until Abraham was well over one hundred years old. Erech (Uruk), the southernmost city mentioned in Nimrod's primeval empire (Gen. 10:10–12), was just forty miles northwest of Ur. When Terah and his clan traveled north to Haran, they would have passed through the kingdom of Nimrod.

The story of Abraham emanates from a very brief and apparently incidental statement about his wife: "But Sarai was barren; she had no child" (Gen. 11:30). Had Sarai not been barren, the story of Abraham as we know it would not have taken place. Herein lies the dynamic difference between Nimrod, the mighty man of the world, and Abraham, the prince of God. Abraham's power base was a sense of personal weakness; Nimrod's power base lay in personal power and self-confidence.

Two hundred miles southeast of Baghdad, just west of the Euphrates River, lies the site of ancient Ur of the Chaldees. "My first impression was one of utter disappointment," wrote a recent traveler. "Ur was dusty and forlorn, with no discernible pulse. The only visual point of reference was the pyramid-like brick tower, or ziggurat, built in tribute to . . . the moon god, around 2100 BC."[2] Abraham (who lived from 2167–1992 BC) would have found it difficult to believe that his birthplace could ever sink into such dismal obscurity. In his day, Ur vibrated with life. Situated on the Euphrates River near the Persian Gulf, it was ideally located to take full advantage of the commercial traffic that flowed through that international intersection.[3]

Ur was also a renowned religious center. Dominating the city and providing its central focal point was ziggurat rising seventy-five feet into the sky. The tower consisted of four massive cubes stacked, it appeared, one on another. The black foundational block had sides one hundred twenty feet long. The upper stages were of red and blue brick. Each stage was graced, gardenlike, with trees. On the uppermost plateau was a holy place covered by a golden roof. In the silence of this holy place stood an image of Sin, the moon god. Here was a veritable mountain of worship—built fifteen centuries before Nebuchadnezzar erected his renowned "mountain of Media," the Hanging Gardens of Babylon. Terah and his family, including Abram, undoubtedly worshiped at this shrine.

---

[2] Tad Szulc, *National Geographic*, December 2001, 102.

[3] If we assume no gaps in the biblical chronologies of Genesis 5 and 11, the Flood would have taken place about 2500 BC and the Tower of Babel rebellion about a century later. Evidently, during the three centuries from the Tower of Babel to the time of Abram, Ur became prominent—and, at times, dominant—in southern Mesopotamia. About 2100 BC, Ur-Nammu established Ur's illustrious Third Dynasty, which lasted about one hundred years (2112–2004 BC).

The label to the narrative that we know as the story of Abraham is surprising: "The History of Terah." Why? Why not "The History of Abraham"? After all, Terah appears only as a very brief prelude (eight verses); and from that point on, Abraham dominates the narrative.

Perhaps the title is attached to Terah because his lineage plays an important part in the life of Abraham. Lot, Terah's grandson, travels with Abraham to Palestine and ultimately becomes the progenitor of the Moabites and Ammonites, Israel's inveterate enemies. Later, Abraham sends his servant to his relatives in Padan-aram to find a wife for his son Isaac. Still later, Abraham's grandson, Jacob, travels to this area to find a wife among Terah's descendants. But do these relationships require the title "The History of Terah"? The histories of Ishmael and Esau have their own titles, though the lives of these two are very much intertwined with the lives of Abraham and Isaac.

In fact, the title depicts the dynamics of the story. Though Abraham is the dominant character in the narrative, the entire story is "The History of Terah." It is the story of the response of members of the family of Terah to the redemptive revelation of God. The revelation came to Abraham; he was the divinely appointed messenger. But the entire family clearly knew that the true God had revealed Himself to a representative of their clan—and that this revelation carried with it a responsibility to respond.

How did they react to the revelation? At first Terah, perhaps moved with fear at the possibility of a curse on his family (his son had died suddenly, and his daughter-in-law Sarai was barren), responded in apparent obedience. "And Terah took Abram his son, and Lot the son of Haran his son's son, and Sarai his daughter in law, his son Abram's wife; and they went forth with them from Ur of the Chaldees, to go into the land of Canaan" (Gen. 11:31). It is Terah who takes the initiative, after the vision Abram has received, to travel to Canaan with those in his family who are willing to follow the divine message. (Nahor and Milcah did not go with them at this time.)

Though he left with the express purpose of going to Canaan, about halfway into the journey Terah made a fateful decision. Instead of continuing as a pilgrim toward Canaan, he chose instead to return to the idols of the past.

It would have taken Terah and his clan about a month to travel the four hundred miles from Ur to the great city of Mari. In another week or so, they would arrive at the juncture where the Balikh River, flowing from the north, joins the Euphrates. At that point, the natural route for Canaan would have led them to follow the established highway fifty miles northwest to the trade post city of Emar, then another fifty miles northwest to the prominent city of Aleppo. At Aleppo, they would have been about two hundred miles north of Damascus and about two hundred forty miles from the northern border of Canaan. Instead, Terah chose to turn north and follow the Balikh River valley sixty miles to Haran.

Strategically located on the main road connecting Asshur, Nineveh, Carchemish, and Aleppo, Haran was an important trading center throughout its history. It was located in the middle of a grassy steppe, well suited for grazing herds. Like Ur, it was well known as a prominent center for the worship of the moon god.[4] Apparently Terah, though he was caught up for a time in the vision of Abram, was unwilling to turn "to God from idols to serve the living and true God" (I Thess. 1:9b). Six centuries later, it was well known in Israel that Terah and his family "served other gods" in the land of Haran (Josh. 24:2).[5] He had left a strong and powerful city that was entrenched in the kingdom of the world, and his search for fulfillment had led him to another strong and powerful city in another part of the kingdom of the world. Like his prototype Cain, Terah was in fact "a fugitive and a vagabond in the earth"—restless to find fulfillment and security. And, like Cain, he settled for the false security of a new city in the kingdom of the world.

When Terah lost faith and chose to settle in Haran, his son Abram shared in his relapse. Then, when Terah died, the Redeemer graciously renewed His promise to Abram. The conditions for the blessings of the promise were, "Get thee out of thy country, and from thy kindred, and from thy father's house, unto a land that I will shew thee" (Gen. 12:1b).

---

[4] Haran continued to be a center of moon worship well into Christian times. King Nabonidus (555–539 BC), who, with his son Belshazzar, presided over the last days of the Babylonian Empire, was an avid devotee of the moon god. He boasted that he restored the ziggurat-shrine of Ur. His own mother served as a priestess in the temple to Sin at Haran and his daughter as a priestess in the temple at Ur.

[5] In the KJV, Josh. 24:2 reads, "And Joshua said unto all the people, Thus saith the Lord God of Israel, Your fathers dwelt on the other side of the flood in old time, even Terah, the father of Abraham, and the father of Nachor: and they served other gods." The word translated *flood* in this passage is the standard Hebrew word for river. The reference is clearly to the Euphrates River. It is also clear that Joshua is referring to the territory of Haran (Padan-aram) and not to Ur; for Ur was on the western side of the Euphrates, whereas Haran was on its "other side" (eastern side).

According to Acts 7:4, Abram left Haran for Palestine "when his father was dead." According to Genesis 12:4, Abram was 75 when he left Haran. Terah died at age 205 (Gen. 11:32). This means that Terah was 130 when Abram was born. The problem some see with this conclusion is that the biblical writers present the age of Abraham and Sarah as "impossible" obstacles to childbearing (Gen. 18:13; Rom. 4:19; Heb. 11:12). But this is a problem only if we ignore the original context into which Terah and his family are introduced. The chronology of Genesis 11:10–26 reveals that immediately after the Flood there was a sharp decline in longevity. Shem lived only 600 years, as compared with over 900 years for the pre-Deluge patriarchs. The next post-Deluge patriarchs listed lived an average of 445 years. Then beginning with Peleg, in whose days "the earth was divided," there is another sharp decline in longevity to an average of 212 years by the time of Terah. Evidently, by the time of Abraham, who lived to be 175, the infirmities of old age made it clear that it was "impossible" for him to father a child when he was close to 100.

It was another four hundred miles from Haran to Canaan—another separation from family, another four weeks of difficult and sometimes dangerous pilgrimage. But Abram obeyed this second call, journeyed to Canaan, and began passing through the land the Lord had led him to. If Abraham followed the Great Trunk Road from Damascus, he would have entered Palestine about ten miles north of the Sea of Galilee. About forty miles south, traveling west of Galilee then south again along the Jordan River, he would reach the important city of Bethshan. From Bethshan he would travel another thirty-five miles or so to Shechem, a major city on the Central Ridge Road of Palestine.

It was here at Shechem that the Lord confirmed the promise He had made that had uprooted Abram from Haran: "The Lord appeared unto Abram, and said, Unto thy seed will I give this land: and there builded he an altar unto the Lord, who appeared unto him" (Gen. 12:7). The blessing of this revelation came because Abram had chosen to "trust in the Lord, do good, and dwell in the land." By building an altar, Abram began to "cultivate faith."

It must have been in the glow of this revelation that he continued his survey of the land. When he came to Bethel some twenty miles south, he again built an altar and "called upon the name of the Lord." But then the unexpected happened. "There was a famine in the land." After his long journey, often through barren territory—a journey he had taken in response to the call and response of God—and after seeing the amazing fruitfulness of Canaan,[6] Abram would hardly have been prepared to face a famine.

THE PILGRIM'S REGRESS

It was after a time of rest and rejoicing at a pleasant river called "the river of the water of life" that Christian and his friend Hopeful found the narrow way getting rough and difficult. Then, a little before them on the left of the road, they saw a meadow called Bypath Meadow with a path leading along the fence of the road. It was a pleasant and easy path, compared to the one they had been following; and since it apparently led the same way, they decided to follow it. Christian and Hopeful soon found themselves in Doubting Castle, under the dreadful, tyrannical sway of its owner, Giant Despair.[7]

With the pilgrims Abram and Lot, also, it was after a time of basking in the beauty and riches of the Promised Land that the way turned hard for them. Their journey had been long and difficult, but now they had every reason to expect a turn for the better. Now they could settle down and begin to enjoy some of the fabled fruitfulness of the land. But instead of fruitfulness, they found famine—and with famine, the possibility of losing everything.

In the face of this emergency, Abram did what was natural. In many respects, his home in Mesopotamia was much like Egypt. As Egypt was the "gift of the Nile," Mesopotamia was largely the gift of the great rivers Tigris and Euphrates. The waters had been steadily running for centuries, and man needed only to channel them. Of course, famines occurred in these lands as well, but in general, man seemed to be more in control of his circumstances. He didn't find himself constantly looking toward the heavens. "For the land, whither thou goest in to possess it, is not as the land of Egypt, from whence ye came out, where thou sowedst thy seed, and wateredst it with thy foot, as a garden of herbs" (Deut. 11:10).

---

[6] In ancient times, one of the sages of Israel said, "If the Garden of Eden is in the Land of Israel—then its gate is at Bethshan." *Wycliffe Historical Geography*, 124.

[7] John Bunyan, *The Pilgrim's Progress* (New York: Books, Inc.), 105–8.

Therefore, as a native of a land much like Egypt, Abram would naturally continue his journey southward until he reached Egypt. He must have rationalized that his first calling was to take care of his family. He could not have doubted that God had called him to Canaan. The Lord had appeared to him in Ur, in Haran, and at Shechem. And he must not have doubted the greatness of the Lord Who had called him, for the inspired writer testifies that in Ur, Abram saw the Lord as the "God of glory" (Acts 7:2).

But for all that, the famine revealed areas of doubt in the Patriarch's life. In this time of darkness, he lost sight of God's sovereignty over every realm of life. He lost sight, in other words, of the very first revelation in the Bible: since God is the Creator and Sustainer of every realm of life, we must look to Him and Him alone for sustenance in the realm He ordains for us. The child of God never gains by stepping outside that realm. By dwelling in the land, as hard as it had become, Abraham would have continued cultivating faith. When he left the place God had ordained for him, he found his faith leaving also.

As he neared Egypt and witnessed both the sensual paganism and power of that land, Abram became more fearful for his safety.

> And it came to pass, when he was come near to enter into Egypt, that he said unto Sarai his wife, Behold now, I know that thou art a fair woman to look upon: therefore it shall come to pass, when the Egyptians shall see thee, that they shall say, This is his wife: and they will kill me, but they will save thee alive. Say, I pray thee, thou art my sister: that it may be well with me for thy sake; and my soul shall live because of thee (Gen. 12:11–13).

As a matter of fact, Abram had discussed this matter with his wife long before. Years later when he became entangled again in a web of deception, he offered as an apology to King Abimelech,

> I thought, Surely the fear of God is not in this place; and they will slay me for my wife's sake. And yet indeed she is my sister; she is the daughter of my father, but not the daughter of my mother; and she became my wife. And it came to pass, when God caused me to wander from my father's house, that I said unto her, This is thy kindness which thou shalt shew unto me; at every place whither we shall come, say of me, He is my brother (20:11–13).

Deceptiveness by policy tends to gather an aura of respectability, and in this case there was a ready-made rationale available. Abram could truthfully say she was his sister. Yet as truthful as those words might be, they conveyed a deceptive message. Now, apparently for the first time in his journeys, the Lord exposed this spirit of deceptiveness.

It wasn't long after he had arrived in Egypt that Abram found himself inextricably snared in the web of his own deceit. Somehow it seems not to have occurred to him that his claim that Sarai was merely his sister declared her eligible for marriage. It must not have occurred to him either that the king himself might claim her. "The princes also of Pharaoh saw her, and commended her before Pharaoh: and the woman was taken into Pharaoh's house." Now what could Abraham do but continue the façade he had begun? He received gifts from Pharaoh as if all were well.

It appeared that all was lost for Abram. The covenant promise the Lord had given him was that the nations of the earth would be blessed through his seed. But now that hope was gone. The inspired writer says nothing of the prayers of Abraham during this time. He focuses instead on the gracious work of the Lord: "And the Lord plagued Pharaoh and his house with great plagues because of Sarai Abram's wife" (12:17).

The Lord must have revealed the problem to Pharaoh also, for he summons Abram and rebukes him: "What is this that thou hast done unto me? why didst thou not tell me that she was thy wife? Why saidst thou, She is my sister? so I might have taken her to me to wife: now therefore behold thy wife, take her, and go thy way" (12:18b–19). These questions from a pagan king are the very questions Abram might have asked himself had not his fear taken over.

Pharaoh was evidently quite disgusted with Abram's deception, for he "commanded his men concerning him: and they sent him away, and his wife, and all that he had." In effect, he expelled Abram from the country.

CHAPTER THIRTEEN

KINGDOMS IN COUNTERPOINT

As the lives of Abraham and Nimrod were in counterpoint, so were the kingdoms they represented. Nimrod was the prototype of the mighty men (the *gibborim*) of the kingdom of the world. Abraham was the father of the faithful, the exemplar for the people of God's kingdom. God's covenant with Abraham was fundamentally a kingdom promise. It was the promise that ultimately the earthly kingdom of God would be established through his descendants.

THE PROMISED LAND IN GOD'S KINGDOM PLANS

When Abram arrived in Palestine, the Lord appeared to him and promised, "Unto thy seed will I give this land" (Gen. 12:7*b*). Then when the Patriarch and Lot separated, the Lord reaffirmed and enlarged His promise:

> Lift up now thine eyes, and look from the place where thou art northward, and southward, and eastward, and westward: for all the land which thou seest, to thee will I give it, and to thy seed for ever. And I will make thy seed as the dust of the earth: so that if a man can number the dust of the earth, then shall thy seed also be numbered. Arise, walk through the land in the length of it and in the breadth of it; for I will give it unto thee (13:14*b*–17).

The promise to Abram that his seed would inherit the land of Canaan was God's pledge of the ultimate fulfillment of His original commission for man. Mankind was to fill the earth, subdue it, and have dominion over it (Gen. 1:26–27). However, this commission presupposed—in fact, was conditioned on—man's recognition of God as his Sovereign.

When man rebelled against God, he renounced the sovereignty of God and accepted, instead, Satan's claim that man himself was sovereign—that his eating of the Tree of Knowledge would prepare him to assume his place as a god and reign over the earthly kingdom. Ironically, however, man's rejection of God as sovereign did not free him from subordination. He found himself instead subordinated to another king—his mentor in self-exaltation, "the prince of this world" (John 14:30).

In His temptation, our Lord left unchallenged Satan's statement that the power and glory of the kingdoms of the world "is delivered unto me; and to whomsoever I will I give it" (Luke 4:6*b*). Far from realizing his godhood and receiving his inheritance as lord of the earth as Satan had intimated, man found himself walking life's journey "according to the prince of the power of the air" (Eph. 2:2*b*). But the kingdom of the world, under the dominion of the prince of this world and those to whom he gives it, is destined to fail. The Promised Land represents God's pledge to His people that they will eventually inherit the earthly kingdom.

Consequently, for the Patriarchs and the people of Israel, the Promised Land became their "royal school." In accordance with God's original commission for man, they were to fill it, subdue it, and have dominion over it. In this land, they were to learn—and demonstrate to the world—the principles of reigning with God. Israel failed miserably in God's royal school. Under the old covenant, God's representative kingdom declined and eventually disintegrated. Ultimately, by the grace and power of the Lord working through the new covenant, this kingdom will succeed. Nevertheless, even under the old covenant, the principles of success are the same as those intimated in God's original commission for man. To the extent that, through the Redeemer, submits to God as his absolute Sovereign, to that extent he develops in the image of God, preparing to fulfill his destiny of reigning with Him.

A Pledge of Victory over the Kingdom of the World

Abram had to be abundantly conscious of the pervading power of the kingdom of the world. In his homeland of Shinar, he had lived in the shadow of Nimrod and his prototypical worldly empire. When he arrived in the Promised Land, he found that the Canaanites, a people dominated by the spirit and philosophy of the world, were in control.

He had been in Canaan perhaps not more than five years[1] when he again witnessed the extended shadow of Nimrod. In "the days of Amraphel king of Shinar," a confederacy of kings invaded the land that had been promised to Abraham (Gen. 14:1ff.). Moses sets the stage for the battle by orienting the reader first to the king of the land of Shinar, though the king of Elam, Chedorlaomer, was obviously the leader in the expedition and the sovereign who had subjugated the kingdoms now in rebellion (14:4–5). The base of power in the kingdom of the world had evidently shifted to the territory of ancient Persia,[2] but it was the same worldly kingdom. These circumstances set the stage for a war that has prophetic overtures. As Keil observes,

> We have here a prelude of the future assault of the worldly power upon the kingdom of God established in Canaan; and the importance of this event to sacred history consists in the fact, that the kings of the valley of Jordan and the surrounding country submitted to the worldly power, whilst Abram, on the contrary, with his home-born servants, smote the conquerors and rescued their booty—a prophetic sign that in the conflict with the power of the world the seed of Abram would not only not be subdued, but would be able to rescue from destruction those who appealed to it for aid.[3]

Evidently for commercial as well as strategic reasons, Chedorlaomer had previously secured the King's Highway in the Transjordan region. The

---

[1] Sometime after these events, when Abram took Hagar as his concubine, he had been in the land ten years (Gen. 16:3). We are assuming (somewhat arbitrarily) that the time from Abram's entrance into Palestine until his return from Egypt to Bethel was about two years. After his separation from Lot, Abram received a new revelation from the Lord that seemed to encourage him to "walk through the land in the length of it and in the breadth of it" (13:17). He then settled in Hebron and was there long enough to form a confederacy with certain Amorite clan leaders (13:18; 14:13, 24). These events may have taken another two or three years.

[2] According to ancient testimony, including that of Josephus (*Antiquities* 1.7.4), Elam, Chedorlaomer's kingdom, was in the territory of ancient Persia. The exact locations of the kingdoms of Arioch and Tidal are uncertain. Most scholars locate them in Mesopotamia.

[3] *The Pentateuch*, 1:202 (see chap. 3, n. 2).

King's Highway, extending some three hundred miles from Damascus to the Gulf of Aqaba, was the major north-south route through Transjordan. As the experience of Israel illustrates (Num. 20:17; 21:22), the countries through which this highway passed kept controlled access to the route, sometimes for security and sometimes for commercial reasons. When the kings of the vale of Siddim led a rebellion against their masters, therefore, Chedorlaomer and his allies came with a force sufficient to subjugate the whole territory.

Beginning in the north, east of the Sea of Galilee, and traveling south to the Gulf of Aqaba, they reclaimed the King's Highway by defeating in succession the Rephaim, the Zuzim, the Emim, and the Horites of Mount Seir.[4] From Elparan at the Gulf of Aqaba, the armies of the confederacy traveled another eighty miles or so northwest to the area of Kadesh-barnea where they subjugated "all the country of the Amalekites." Then, circling back northeastward to what is now the midpoint of the Dead Sea, they seized the oasis of Hazezon-tamar (Engedi, according to II Chron. 20:2) by defeating the Amorites of that region. From that point, on the western shore of the Dead Sea, the armies of the Mesopotamian kings traveled south about ten miles, where they met and defeated the five kings of the Valley of Siddim.[5]

Abram could not have been ignorant of these devastating wars, nor would he have been ignorant of the control the Mesopotamian powers had established over the territory of the King's Highway. But it was not until an escapee informed him of Lot's captivity that he took military action against the invaders. Abram did not yet own so much as a plot of

---

[4] The tribes defeated by the invading confederacy—a confederacy ultimately routed by Abram—makes this war all the more significant as a prophetic preview; for three of them (the Rephaims, Zuzims, and Emims) are identified in Scripture as giants (Deut. 2:10–11, 20–22; 3:11–13). The Zuzims were evidently the people the Ammonites called Zamzummims. Giants in Scripture can be viewed as the prototypical mighty men of the world. Though God used the agencies of the kingdom of the world, the destruction of these mighty men was the work of the Lord (Deut. 2:20–22).

[5] The words "the vale of Siddim, which is the salt sea" (Gen. 14:3b) seem to provide scriptural evidence for the commonly held view of scholars that in ancient times the Dead Sea extended south only as far as the Lisan peninsula. This peninsula, extending about nine miles across the ten-mile width of the sea, divides the sea into two basins. The larger northern basin reaches depths of thirteen hundred feet. By contrast, the southern basin fluctuates between only three and thirty feet; and at times when the sea reaches low levels, part of this basin lies exposed, "just as it possibly was during the biblical period." Barry J. Beitzel, *The Moody Atlas of Bible Lands* (Chicago: Moody, 1985), 40–41.

ground in the Promised Land.[6] Yet he launched into a precarious crusade against an army representing perhaps the most formidable combination of powers in the world of his day. Why? What motivated this man to such a noble—though apparently foolhardy—endeavor?

After all, Lot had made his own choice—a choice that had revealed a man dominated by shameless greed. When they had discussed their need to separate, Abram had magnanimously offered his nephew first choice of the land. As a younger subordinate in the clan, Lot should have insisted that his uncle choose first; but his covetous eyes overruled.

> And Lot lifted up his eyes, and beheld all the plain of Jordan, that it was well watered every where, before the Lord destroyed Sodom and Gomorrah, even as the garden of the Lord, like the land of Egypt, as thou comest unto Zoar. Then Lot chose him all the plain of Jordan; and Lot journeyed east: and they separated themselves the one from the other (Gen. 13:10–11).

Humanly speaking, no one could have blamed Abram had he simply shaken his head in sad resignation at his nephew's self-made trouble. However, the Lord was at work in behalf of both Abram and Lot. It was the Lord Who allowed a certain man—a man who knew Abram and Lot—to escape the slaughter (14:10, 13), and it was the Lord Who brought him as a messenger to Abram.

We should also recognize that the Lord's work of grace includes the (as yet) unwritten law of the kinsman-redeemer. In ancient times, the kinsman-redeemer, or kinsman-avenger, concept was universal. At the very dawn of history, Cain feared that "every one" in the extended family of his murdered brother would seek to slay him (Gen. 4:14–15). Vestiges of this ancient law exist to this day, particularly in isolated societies. In effect, the kinsman-avenger was a representative of God's system of social justice in the largely agrarian ancient world of no standing police forces.

In ancient societies, the responsibilities of the kinsman-redeemer were an integral part of the obligation of care for the family—that is, the obligation to provide for one's family included protecting and, if necessary, vindicating the honor and welfare of family members.

Learning of "his brother's" captivity therefore, was a call for Abram to assume the responsibilities of the kinsman-redeemer. This ancient and

---

[6] In fact, the inspired writer seems to call attention to this fact by calling the Patriarch (for the first time) *the Hebrew*—a term that, according to some scholars, literally means "the one from beyond or the immigrant." Klein, *Etymological Dictionary*, 62 (see chap. 3, n. 1).

honored custom may partially explain the readiness of the Patriarch's confederates (14:13) to join with him in this perilous venture. Their pact with Abram was undoubtedly a mutual defense agreement. Neither Abram nor his Amorite allies had been materially or physically harmed. The four kings had clearly accomplished their objectives with the securing of the King's Highway, and evidently they were content to return home with the spoils. But in the maltreatment of a brother, in those days, all heard a call for vengeance—not spiteful revenge, as we in our "enlightened times" spin the word, but vindication, the punishment of the guilty and the restoration of the innocent.

The fact that Abram had 318 "trained servants," practiced in warfare, speaks of the greatness of his household as well as of the violence of the times. The emphasis in the comment that these men were "born in his own house" is on the fact that they were loyal to their master—including, undoubtedly, their master's God (cf. Gen. 18:19; 24:2ff.). His pursuit of the enemy was long and arduous—probably close to one hundred fifty miles before he and his little army arrived at the enemy's camp in Dan of Gilead, east of the Sea of Galilee.[7]

As did Gideon many years later, Abram divided his small army into companies and attacked from different directions at night—undoubtedly to give the sated victors the impression that a huge army was attacking and threatening to surround them. The Mesopotamian soldiers panicked and fled toward Damascus. To insure a complete victory and to guard against the danger of a counterattack, Abram's army pursued the enemy another seventy miles to Hobah, north of Damascus.[8]

The victory was miraculously thorough. Abram and his army rescued not only Lot but "all the goods . . . and the women also, and the people." But as thorough as the victory was, it was not yet complete for Abram. As

---

[7] The town mentioned in Gen. 14:14 must not have been Laish, which the Danites conquered and named Dan (Judges 18:28–29). Aside from the fact that Laish was not renamed until years after the death of Moses, the situation of Dan-Laish, on the central source of the Jordan River, would hardly induce a fleeing army to retreat toward Damascus because of intervening rivers. The town of Gen. 14:14 must be the Dan of Deut. 34:1 (called Danjaan in II Sam. 24:6), on the northern border of Gilead, east of the southern end of the Sea of Galilee. Apparently, the victorious Mesopotamian army, after vanquishing the five kings in the Valley of Siddim, began their return by way of the King's Highway in Transjordan; and Abram, after crossing the Jordan north of the Dead Sea, followed the same trail. Keil, *The Pentateuch*, 1:206 (see chap. 3, n. 2); Leupold, *Genesis*, 459 (see chap. 6, n. 4).

[8] Apparently, Abram made it a point to keep the retreating army from taking refuge in Damascus. This city, situated on three major trade routes, may have been walled at this time and would have afforded the Mesopotamian armies an opportunity to regroup.

It is quite possible that Abram stopped at Salem (Jerusalem, Ps. 76:2) to consult with Melchizedek as he began his pursuit of the Mesopotamian kings. In ancient times, warriors always sought the blessing and guidance of a man of God before embarking on ventures of any consequence or danger. Undoubtedly, Abram, as well as his confederates, were well acquainted with this renowned priest-king; and their journey north would have taken them right past Salem where he reigned. Is it that unlikely that they would have stopped to seek God's counsel through him? This may be the time to which Abram refers when he says to the king of Sodom, "I have lift up mine hand unto the Lord, the most high God, the possessor of heaven and earth" (Gen. 14:22).

is often the case in victory, Abram faced an even greater trial—greater by virtue of its subtlety—before the victory would be truly won.

Undoubtedly all along the King's Highway, the once-vanquished people of Transjordan looked with mingled wonder and fear at Abram's army returning with the spoils of victory. The news of the victory preceded the triumphant warriors, and by the time they reached the vicinity of Jerusalem, a grand reception awaited them. The new king of Sodom had traveled some fifty miles to be a part of the ceremony and when Abram arrived was the first to go meet him. This, as it turned out, was Abram's greatest test.

At virtually the same time, Melchizedek, king of Salem, came with physical refreshments and spiritual blessing. "And he blessed him, and said, Blessed be Abram of the most high God, possessor of heaven and earth: and blessed be the most high God, which hath delivered thine enemies into thy hand" (Gen. 14:19b–20). In response to this blessing, Abram gave Melchizedek tithes of all the spoil—acknowledging his recognition and esteem for this "priest of the most high God" (Heb. 7:1–4).

The two kings presented to Abram two choices. The king of Sodom's proposition was an acknowledgment that the conqueror had the right to the spoils of the victory: "Give me the persons, and take the goods to thyself" (Gen. 14:21b). By the accepted laws of warfare, Abram might have become fabulously wealthy and powerful. The spoils of this victory would have included all that the Mesopotamian kings had gained from the entire Transjordan and the whole region south of the Dead Sea, seven great victories. The appeal to claim these riches may have been greatly intensified by the possibility—indeed, it would seem, the probability—of retribution from the four kings Abram had humiliated.

But to Abram, the revelation of God that came through Melchizedek was far more impressive than the riches he might have gained through his "rights." He began his pilgrimage looking "for a city which hath foundations, whose builder and maker is God" (Heb. 11:10)—looking for spiritual wealth and security. Abram had evidently taken a vow before he began his venture—a vow revealing that he was abundantly aware of the twofold peril he faced, the physical and the moral.

> And Abram said to the king of Sodom, I have lift up mine hand unto the Lord, the most high God, the possessor of heaven and earth, that I will not take from a thread even to a shoelatchet, and that I will not take any thing that is thine, lest thou shouldest say, I have made Abram rich (Gen. 14:22–23).

The impression Melchizedek made upon Abram must have been overwhelming. By receiving a blessing from Melchizedek and by giving him a tithe of all the spoil, Abram showed his recognition of and submission to this unique person as a priest of the true God (Heb. 7:1–7). By his use of Melchizedek's name for God, *El Elyon* ("God Most High"), "possessor of heaven and earth," Abram reveals that this great priest-king had enlarged his perception of the true God.

An enlarged perception of God: this is always the result when we respond to ventures of faith God ordains for us in His place of service.

CHAPTER FOURTEEN

"ABRAHAM BELIEVED GOD"

T HESE WORDS FROM ROMANS 4:3 reflect the central message of Abraham's life: "And he believed in the Lord; and he counted it to him for righteousness" (Gen. 15:6). Does this mark the beginning of Abraham's faith as a believer? Has all that precedes this been only prologue—a pilgrimage toward the light of true faith? The New Testament writers say otherwise. According to the writer of Hebrews, Abraham responded by faith when he was first called. "By faith Abraham, when he was called to go out into a place which he should after receive for an inheritance, obeyed; and he went out, not knowing whither he went" (11:8). And Paul testifies that Abraham responded to the gospel when he believed God's promise:

> And the scripture, foreseeing that God would justify the heathen through faith, preached before the gospel unto Abraham, saying, In thee shall all nations be blessed. So then they which be of faith are blessed with faithful Abraham (Gal. 3:8–9).

The words in Genesis, then, are words of confirmation and instruction. If we would ask, as Paul does in Romans, "On what basis was Abraham justified?" we must answer as Paul did, "Abraham believed God, and it was counted unto him for righteousness" (Rom. 4:3*b*).

But this day was more than simply a day of confirmation for Abram. It was a day that marked a new era in the Patriarch's life. He gained a new perception of God. Through his encounter with Melchizedek, he had seen the Lord as *El Elyon*, God Most High, possessor of heaven and earth. Now for the first time, in the inspired record, he addresses God as "Lord God" (*Adonai Yahweh*). He sees God as his Master (*Adonai*), the One Who is constantly and actively present in His covenant relationships with man (*Yahweh*).

The opening statement of Genesis 15 sets the stage for this momentous revelation: "After these things the word of the Lord came unto Abram in a vision, saying, Fear not, Abram: I am thy shield, and thy exceeding great reward." The words "after these things" refer to the events connected with Abram's conquest. They intimate that in the aftermath of his great victory, fear may have gripped the Patriarch concerning the possibility of retribution from the kings he had humiliated.

The Lord's words addressed real needs He saw in Abram's life. That God admonished Abram not to fear because He was his shield indicates that Abram was afraid—and particularly afraid of an attack in which he perceived himself as exposed to danger. The fact that God promised to be Abram's "exceeding great reward [*sakar*, 'wages']" suggests that the Patriarch's fears were related to the riches he might have had from his war spoils. With these riches, he might have hired more soldiers or even enlisted an army of mercenaries. The word the KJV translates *reward* is *sakar*, which in its basic idea denotes "engaging the services of a person in return for pay" (cf. II Sam. 10:6; II Kings 7:6; Ezek. 29:18–19).[1]

But how does this view of Abram's fears tie in with the context, particularly with the Patriarch's response to the Lord (Gen. 15:2–3)? "And Abram said, Lord God, what wilt thou give me, seeing I go childless, and the steward of my house is this Eliezer of Damascus? And Abram said, Behold, to me thou hast given no seed: and, lo, one born in my house is mine heir." According to Leupold, the rest of the chapter shows that "the fear of remaining childless is what Abram and the Lord alone refer to."[2] But in that case, why does God promise to be a shield for Abram? Were children the only means by which Abram could be shielded? He already had in his household an army of men trained for warfare, and he had con-

---

[1] *TWOT*, 2:878 (see chap. 3, n. 3).
[2] *Genesis*, 1:472 (see chap. 6, n. 4).

The significance of *Yahweh*, the special name of God generally depicted in the KJV as "LORD" or (in certain combinations) "GOD," is not easily captured in sound-bite expressions. The key passage in the revelation of this name is Exodus 3:13–15. In that passage, the Lord responds to Moses' question concerning His name with the words "I AM THAT I AM . . . Thus shalt thou say unto the children of Israel, I AM hath sent me unto you." Moses then, when he referred to God (in the third person) called Him *Yahweh*, or "HE IS." But what is the significance of the words "I AM THAT I AM" or "HE IS"? Bible scholars commonly interpret these expressions with words such as "He is the Self-Existent One"—meaning He is absolutely independent in His existence, not (as the Egyptian gods, for example) dependent on anyone or anything for life or sustenance. This is fine as far as it goes, but as Oehler has observed, the verb that is at the base of the name conveys not simply the idea of continuous existence "but that of *existence in motion*. . . . The form of the name . . . leads us to understand in it the existence of God, not as an existence at rest, but as one always becoming, always making itself known. . . . God is Jahve in as far as He has entered into an historical relation to mankind, and in particular to the chosen people Israel, and shows Himself continually in this historical relation as He who is. . . . While heathenism rests almost exclusively on the past revelations of its divinities, this name testifies . . . that the relation of God to the world is in a state of continual living activity." *Theology of the Old Testament* (repr., Minneapolis, MN: Klock & Klock, 1978), 95.

federates who were ready and willing to join with him in defense of potential enemies. And though it may be conceded that the expression "after these things" does not always strongly link the preceding with the following, the words do have some reference to the past. They at least invite the reader to review what has just happened as a possible prelude to the next episode in the story.

In fact, Abram's fear of retribution from the Mesopotamian kings has a dynamic relationship with his request: "What wilt thou give me, seeing I go childless, and the steward of my house is this Eliezer of Damascus? . . . Behold, to me thou hast given no seed: and, lo, one born in my house is mine heir." The fear of retaliation from the kings of the east was a real fear for Abram, but it was related to a deeper, more fundamental fear. Apparently, in the aftermath of his great victory, Abram found himself in the Slough of Despond over the possibility of God's promise ever being fulfilled through him. The power of the world was overwhelming. He was only one (cf. Ezek. 33:24). If they returned and obliterated his name from the earth, what of God's promise? What of the kingdom of God? What of the blessing to the world that was to come through One of his descendants? And even if these kings didn't return to avenge their defeat, all would still be lost if he had no heir. Was all that he had gained thus far to be transferred to his servant Eliezer, a man of Damascus? Was the promise of his seed inheriting this land now, after all, to be in the hands of a Syrian?

To Abram, this question was fundamental. He had begun his pilgrimage looking "for a city which hath foundations, whose builder and maker is God." It was on this vision that all his hopes and fears were based. If this—his place in the kingdom of God—were lost, all was lost. So "the word of the Lord came unto him, saying, This shall not be thine heir; but he that shall come forth out of thine own bowels shall be thine heir" (Gen. 15:4). The promised seed would not be transferred to another.

And the Lord "brought him forth abroad"—outside his tent—to broaden his perspective; and He said, "Look now toward heaven, and tell the stars, if thou be able to number them: and he said unto him, So shall thy seed be" (v. 5b). And it is in response to this enlarged perspective that Abram "believed in the Lord." "The biggest word in the chapter, one of the greatest in the Old Testament! Here is the first instance of the use of the word *believe* in the Scriptures." The construction suggests a settled attitude on the part of Abram.[3] In response to the enlarged esteem Abram had for the Lord, the Patriarch gained new value in the Lord's eyes—Who now saw him as righteous, conforming to His own spirit and character.

Though Abram is now supported by an enlarged faith in the Lord, his response to the Lord's promise of the land reveals something of the doubt he had at the beginning of the revelation: "Lord God, whereby shall I know that I shall inherit it?" (v. 8). He is asking God to give him renewed assurance, as He had done concerning an heir (vv. 4–5). The Lord responded by leading him into a covenant ceremony.

The ceremony followed ancient customs for the establishment of a covenant. God commanded Abram to take a heifer, a she-goat, a ram, a

---

[3] Ibid., 1:476–77.

turtledove, and a young pigeon—one of each type of animal suitable for sacrifice. He was to slay these animals, divide them (except for the birds), and lay the pieces opposite each other. Ordinarily, both parties making the covenant passed between the divided animals—signifying full acceptance of the covenant sealed by blood. In this case, God alone passed between the pieces, suggesting that He was establishing an unconditional covenant with Abram—a covenant whose fulfillment depended neither on the Patriarch nor on his seed.

As in a freewill offering, the sacrificial animals offered would represent the person giving them. The offerer would identify with the animal by placing his hand on its head (e.g., Lev. 1:3–4). Consequently, when he slew the animal, the offerer would be viewing himself as dying to his own desires and offering his life fully to God. Since God directed Abram to choose animals suitable for sacrifice, these must (in accordance with the context) represent Abram and his seed—as dying to their own purposes and being offered to fulfill the covenant purposes of God. The birds of prey, then, would represent the enemies of God and His people who seek to negate this covenant relationship and "eat" Israel, assimilating God's people into the kingdom of the world. Abram's driving the birds away would represent the fact that his faith in the promise God had given him would save Israel from such destruction (cf. Ps. 105:42).[4]

As the sun was going down, a deep sleep and terrifying darkness fell upon Abram (Gen. 15:12). As the words that follow indicate, this signified a time of great darkness and trouble for the people of Israel. They would be afflicted four hundred years in a strange land. But the Lord would judge the people who afflicted them and bring His people back to the Promised Land (vv. 13–16). Then, when the sun had fully gone down, Abram saw in the vision "a smoking furnace, and a burning lamp" pass between the pieces. This represented the Lord, the God of judgment and the God of light, ratifying the covenant and destroying its enemies (vv. 17–18; cf. v. 14).

This awesome revelation gave Abram not only a prophetic outline of the future of his seed but also an explanation for why he and his seed would not immediately inherit the land. It brought Abram, as a prophet, into the secret counsel of the Lord and made him an intimate "friend of God" (James 2:23).

---

[4] See Keil, *The Pentateuch*, 1:214ff. (see chap. 3, n. 2).

CHAPTER FIFTEEN

FRUSTRATION AND FULFILLMENT

VARIATIONS OF THE WORD *FRUSTRATE* appear only three times in the King James Version. In one of these passages, the word comes close to our English dictionary definition. In Ezra 4:5, the inspired writer informs us that the enemies of God's people "hired counsellors . . . to frustrate their purpose." According to the *American Heritage Dictionary*, the word means "to prevent from accomplishing a purpose or fulfilling a desire."

Somewhere in the connotative folds of the English word *frustrate* lurks the concept of deceptiveness. Our frustrations are connected, like Siamese twins, to our expectations. When our expectations are thwarted—when we are deceived by our expectations—frustration fills the void. As Solomon puts it, "Hope deferred maketh the heart sick" (Prov. 13:12). The next episode in the life of Abraham is a study in human frustration as well as in the divine overruling of man's follies that produces the frustrations of life. God, in His infinite wisdom and grace, often frustrates our highest desires in order to fulfill our deepest needs.

THE EARTHLY MAKING
OF FRUSTRATION

The opening sentence of this story presents two women who in nature, culture, and position epitomize frustrations in conflict. "Now Sarai Abram's wife bare him no children: and she had an handmaid, an Egyptian, whose name was Hagar" (Gen. 16:1). The name *Sarai* means "princess." *Hagar* means "to flee, escape."[1] Providentially, these names carry prophetic overtones for these women.

Hagar, we are told, is Sarai's "handmaid, an Egyptian." She was Sarai's personal handmaid, probably given to her while she was in Pharaoh's palace. When Pharaoh, having been warned by divine plagues (12:17), sent Sarai back to Abram, Hagar undoubtedly went with her.

Hagar's status as a handmaid to royalty suggests that she was a choice servant, the type who could "stand before the king" (see Dan. 1:5b). She was undoubtedly poised, intelligent, and beautiful, with the personal qualities Sarai and Abram would favor for a mother of their child.

But now this woman, accustomed to serving among the royalty of Egypt, is expelled with her mistress from the palace—and she finds herself entering a shepherd's tent! "Every shepherd is an abomination unto the Egyptians" (Gen. 46:34b; cf. 43:32). Is this woman she serves indeed a princess? She is the wife of a detestable shepherd![2]

HUMAN SOLUTIONS FOR FRUSTRATION

It is in this potentially explosive atmosphere that Sarai, frustrated after ten years of waiting, appeals to Abram, "Behold now, the Lord hath restrained me from bearing: I pray thee, go in unto my maid; it may be that I may obtain children by her" (16:2b). Like Abram in the previous chapter (15:2), she was searching for a human solution to a divinely imposed problem. The solution, in both cases, was acceptable according to

---

[1] Cf. the related Arabic-based word *Hegira*, representing the epochal flight of Muhammad from Mecca to Medina in AD 622.

[2] According to Herodotus, the Egyptians were divided into seven classes. The swine-herders were the most despised, but evidently all herdsmen were viewed as outcasts of society. He comments that swine-herders, even those of pure Egyptian blood, were the only people in the country who could never enter a temple. *Histories*, 148, 195 (see chap. 2, n. 1). Keil observes that on Egyptian monuments "shepherds are constantly depicted as lanky, withered, distorted, emaciated, and sometimes almost ghostly figures." *The Pentateuch*, 1:373 (see chap. 3, n. 2).

the customs of the day; but in neither case did the remedy accord with the promise they had received from the Lord. Sarai, no doubt aware of the Lord's promise to Abram ("He that shall come forth out of thine own bowels shall be thine heir"), must have rationalized that she was acting consistently with the promise. In this arrangement, her husband would be the father; and the Lord had confirmed His will by "restraining" her from bearing (16:2).

Abram, who had "believed in the Lord" concerning the promised seed (15:6), may well have seen that Sarai's proposal was inconsistent with God's word. But he "hearkened to the voice" of his anguished wife. He yielded to the emotional trauma of the moment. To do otherwise, he must have thought, would show insensitivity toward his wife's need. Little did he realize the distress his "sensitivity" would bring to his wife, to his family, and to his posterity.

The reaction of Hagar was predictable. She conceived, suggesting, particularly in those times, that God had favored her and cursed her mistress. "And when she saw that she had conceived, her mistress was despised in her eyes." What happened simply confirmed the feelings latent in her soul. Shepherds were from a caste whose lowly condition and uncleanness revealed that they were not favored by God (or the gods) and consequently should not be favored by decent society. She had likely held such feelings toward Abram as well, though being Sarai's handmaid would not have brought her into direct—and irritating—contact with the master of the household. She would naturally see the blessing of her conception as resulting from the favor God saw in her, not from His favor on the household in which she served.

Sarai appealed to Abram to correct the problem of her handmaid's insolence. Her words reveal something of the folly of human solutions to the frustrating problems that result from self-will. "My wrong be upon thee: I have given my maid into thy bosom; and when she saw that she had conceived, I was despised in her eyes: the Lord judge between me and thee" (16:5b). Her outburst "My wrong be upon thee" refers to the wrong done to her by her handmaid. The Hebrew word rendered *wrong* (*chamas*) here is commonly translated in the King James Version by words such as *violence* or *cruelty*. But in the Old Testament, the word "is used almost always in connection with sinful violence."[3] Sarai viewed the insolent attitude of Hagar as sinful cruelty—and even sinful violence, in the sense that her handmaid's actions brutally aggravated the pain of her heart (cf. Jer. 4:19).

The words that follow show something of the trauma Sarai had experienced in the cohabitation of her husband with her handmaid: "I have given my maid into thy bosom." These words speak of the intimacy that this surrogate arrangement necessarily produced. Sarai evidently had not counted on this. She undoubtedly envisioned herself rejoicing in the birth of her child and holding the baby in her arms. But her vision did not include the painful process by which her plan would be achieved nor enlighten her to the long-lasting consequences of the plan.

Having yielded, against his better judgment, to his wife's appeal concerning the surrogate arrangement, Abram now compounds the problem by evading her appeal for the discipline of Hagar. Sarai's words, wrought from her personal trauma, strongly urged her husband to assume the responsibility that was already his. To the oath "The wrong that has been done to me is upon thee—upon thy shoulders," she adds an idiomatic expression of potential censure ("The Lord judge between me and thee"). With this expression, Sarai is not only appealing to the Lord to confirm the justice of her request but also affirming that the Lord would fully agree with her appeal and would overrule any objections Abram might have concerning his responsibility.

Not only did Abram seem deaf to this appeal, but even the misplaced sensitivity he had showed toward Sarai's first appeal had all but disappeared. With apparent stoic silence, his wife had lived with the reproach of her barrenness all these years. Now, all the years of self-doubt and sensing God's disfavor had burst upon her through an insolent slave whom she had given the favor of intimate relations with her husband. She is in a state of frenzied anger and frustration, and it is at this point that Abram tells her, "Behold, thy maid is in thy hand; do to her as it pleaseth thee" (Gen. 16:6). Is it any wonder that Sarai "dealt hardly with her"?

---

[3] *TWOT*, 1:297 (see chap. 3, n. 3). Cf. Jer. 51:35 for the use of the same word in an expression similar to that of Gen. 16:5, "The violence done to me and to my flesh be upon Babylon."

THE DIVINE SOLUTION TO HUMAN FRUSTRATION

Evidently Sarai, in her anger, attempted to humble Hagar by giving her a severe beating.[4] Hagar, true to her name and possibly fearing for her life, "fled from her face" (cf. Gen. 35:7; Exod. 2:15). Her plan was evidently to escape to Egypt by way of the route, commonly used in those days, that leads from Hebron past Beersheba "in the way to Shur" (Gen. 16:7). She had traveled some eighty-five miles—probably three days—and was near the border of Egypt when "the angel of the Lord found her."[5]

The "angel of the Lord" in this passage is the Lord Himself (cf. v. 13), a preincarnate appearance of the Messiah. Here is an example of the marvelous grace of God. The Lord had promised Abram, "In thee shall all families of the earth be blessed" (Gen. 12:3b). The circumstances, from all vantage points, seemed hardly conducive to divine blessing. But the Savior intervened to begin His covenant work of grace in behalf of the seed of the child Hagar was carrying.

The Savior's first exhortation to Hagar was "Return to thy mistress, and submit thyself under her hands" (Gen. 16:9b). With the expression "Submit thyself under her hands," the Lord touched a sensitive nerve with Hagar. The word translated *submit* is the same word (*anah*) that depicts the humiliating discipline she had received from Sarai (v. 6)—only the call, in this case, is to voluntarily humble herself and submit to the mistress she had so recently despised.

In His tender grace, the Lord did not present this requirement to Hagar in the first heat of her angry flight. He waited three days for her anger to abate and her wounds to heal somewhat, and it was "by a fountain of water" (v. 7) that He spoke to her. He had waited patiently—until her energy had been spent and she had been refreshed by spring water—

---

[4] The Hebrew word *anah*, translated "dealt hardly," here has the primary meaning of "forcing submission by afflicting, browbeating, or inflicting pain upon." The word is closely associated with the concept of humiliation. In the KJV, *anah* is very often translated "afflict," quite often "humble." See *TWOT*, 2:682.

[5] Moses locates Beer-lahai-roi (16:14) "between Kadesh and Bered." Though scholars are not certain about the identity of Bered, they commonly locate Kadesh (Kadesh-barnea) about fifty miles south of Beersheba, which is about thirty miles south of Hebron. Wadi el-Arish ("the brook of Egypt"), in the vicinity of Kadesh-barnea, was viewed as the border of Egypt.

before He touched with His words the sensitive wounds she had been nurturing.

The promise that follows the condition must have been overwhelming to her. "I will multiply thy seed exceedingly, that it shall not be numbered for multitude" (v. 10). As she neared the border of Egypt, her mind must have been flooded with fearful thoughts: "Will my child survive? How will I provide for him? Will I again become a slave? Will he spend his life as a slave?" And now she hears the Lord saying, "I will multiply your seed until it becomes an innumerable multitude."

The next word from the divine Messenger is as awesome in its tenderness and condescension as the other had been in its greatness. "And the angel of the Lord said unto her, Behold, thou art with child, and shalt bear a son, and shalt call his name Ishmael; because the Lord hath heard thy affliction" (v. 11). The son you are carrying will, by his name, be a living memorial of the affliction (*anah*, the same word as in vv. 6 and 9) you have borne. No, he will be infinitely more than that. He will remind you that the Lord actually cares about your affliction, that He has heard your anguished cries.

Now after all this—the tenderness, the care, the wonder of His grace bestowed—how could the Savior say what comes next? "And he will be a wild man [literally, a wild donkey of a man]; his hand will be against every man, and every man's hand against him; and he shall dwell in the presence of all his brethren" (v. 12). What mother wants to hear such words as these: "Your child will be wild, fighting everybody and anybody and being fought by anybody and everybody"?

The message is a word of reality in an atmosphere of ecstasy. By it the divine Messenger brings Hagar's soaring spirit back to the real world— the world of conflict and trouble in which she lives. On the one hand, the Messenger tells Hagar, your son will be free. On the other hand, in his freedom he will be constantly fighting with his fellow man.

The expression "wild donkey of a man" would not have had then the same derogatory connotations it has in our time. The poetic description of Job 39:5–8 suggests the spirit in which the prophecy of Genesis 16:12 should be taken.

Who hath sent out the wild ass free? or who hath loosed the bands of the wild ass? Whose house I have made the wilderness, and the barren land his dwellings. He scorneth the multitude of the city, neither regardeth he the crying of the driver. The range of the mountains is his pasture, and he searcheth after every green thing.

These are words describing the freedom of the wild donkey.

In contrast with you, the Lord says to Hagar, your son and his descendants will be as free as you are now in this boundless wilderness. He will not flee, as you have, from those who would restrain him. He will be a fighter, often at war with his fellow man. But he will maintain his independence "in the presence of [literally "against the face of"] all his brethren."[6]

Hagar must have seen something of her own spirit in this characterization. To this extent, she was receiving an admonition—wise, fatherly, counsel concerning the care and discipline of her child. The Scriptures speak of man being born "like a wild ass's colt" (Job 11:12). By nature, every child has the potential of becoming a "wild donkey of a man"— untamed, undisciplined, and consequently unprepared to live successfully in the world. Hagar, recognizing that these were to be the characteristics of her son, had first to deal with her own nature. She had to return to her mistress and humbly submit to her authority (Gen. 16:9). If she did this voluntarily, in spirit as well as in body, she could have a salutary influence on her son and descendants (cf. 18:19).

But there is another side to the message of Genesis 16:12. To bring Hagar back to reality, the divine Messenger had to disabuse her of some of the thoughts she must have entertained concerning the child she was carrying. This child would not be the heir Sarai and Abram had been promised. It would not be through him that all the families of the earth would be blessed. God would abundantly bless and multiply his seed, but the promised Messiah was not to come through him.

The next words reveal the overwhelming effect the revelation had on Hagar: "And she called the name of the Lord that spake unto her, Thou God seest me: for she said, Have I also here looked after him that seeth me?" A new name given to the Lord represents a new, or enlarged, perception of God. In this case, the introductory characterization of the Lord

---

[6] What is translated "in the presence of" (al pani, "against the face of") is an idiomatic expression for "east of" (e.g., in Gen. 25:18 "before Egypt" is literally "against the face of," or east of Egypt). However, as Keil observes, "the geographical notice of the dwelling-place of the Ishmaelites hardly exhausts the force of the expression, which also indicated that Ishmael would maintain an independent standing before (in the presence of) all the descendants of Abraham." *The Pentateuch*, 1:220.

as "the One speaking to her" tells us about the impression Hagar had of this encounter with the Angel of the Lord—an impression that led her to name Him *El Roi*, "the God Who sees." She was overwhelmed at the thought that God actually took notice of her—that her needs caught the attention of the Almighty, and that He was willing to communicate with her about them and make provision for them.

The word *see* (*raah*), in this context, has the connotation (as it often does in Hebrew, as well as in other languages) of "taking special interest in and providing for" (e.g., Gen. 22:8, 14; 39:23; Exod. 4:31). Hagar's expression is in the form of a direct address, "Thou (art) *El Roi*." She is basking in seeing His presence, His concern, and her own freedom to communicate with Him about her needs (cf. v. 8). Hagar's explanation of the name she gave to the Lord is an emphatic question: "Have I also here looked after him that seeth me?" The expression *looked after*, in this context, has the connotation of "looking expectantly" to Him (cf. Exod. 33:8; Ezek. 29:16). She had discovered the glorious truth that the Lord looked upon her with such concern and pity that she could in turn look to Him, confidently expecting Him to meet her needs.

It is on the basis of Hagar's experience here that the well where God met with her was hereafter memorialized with the name "Beer-lahai-roi," the "Well of the Living One Who Sees" (Gen. 16:14). The Patriarch himself may have named it this, but the name reflects the testimony of Hagar as she related her glorious experience of meeting with the Angel of the Lord. She recognizes now that He looks with active compassion upon the needs even of slaves, but she also perceives that He is the Living One. This God, in contrast to the gods of Egypt and the gods of the Canaanites, is alive. He is aware of what is happening on earth, and He reacts to the needs and desires of the people He created.

Was this the day of Hagar's salvation? It may well have been. Just about a decade before this, when she was a servant in the Egyptian court, she must have been a worshiper of the gods of Egypt. Given the pride of the Egyptians in matters of religion, their disdain for shepherds, and the circumstances that led to the expulsion of Abram and Sarai from Egypt, it is unlikely that Hagar would have been easily converted to the worship of the God of her master and mistress. Furthermore, the intolerable pride she showed toward Sarai when she conceived suggests that she viewed her conception as a confirmation of her spiritual and social superiority.

Nevertheless, the Lord had evidently begun His work of grace in Hagar long before this climactic day. In spite of the circumstances of Abram's expulsion from Egypt, Hagar must have been impressed with the fact that the Lord of Abram had "plagued Pharaoh and his house with great plagues because of Sarai" (12:17). In this, Abram's God had demonstrated His superiority to the gods of the great king himself. And she must have been impressed with the "impossible" victory Abram achieved over the kings of Mesopotamia—through his God *El Elyon*, God Most High, possessor of heaven and earth. Then she may have listened with reverent wonder as Abram told Sarai of his awesome vision of *Adonai Yahweh*, in which the Lord told him of things to come and made a firm covenant with him for the land in which he dwelt.

But to Hagar, all of this may well have been but the work of another god, a god of another people and culture—a god of shepherds who worked mysteriously and powerfully in behalf of a favored few of these people, but not a god of the Egyptians and certainly not likely to favor slaves. But these thoughts, raging as they had been within her, must have vanished quickly when "the angel of the Lord found her." This may indeed have been the day of Hagar's salvation. It is evident, whatever the case, that she told Sarai and Abram of her experience. Abram called the son she bare "Ishmael," as the Lord had told her.

CHAPTER SIXTEEN

NEW HORIZONS

THE WELL-KNOWN PRAYER OF JABEZ suggests the Lord's modus operandi with His people. "Oh that thou wouldest bless me indeed, and enlarge my coast, and that thine hand might be with me, and that thou wouldest keep me from evil, that it may not grieve me!" (I Chron. 4:10b). From the beginning, God's plan was that man would be constantly enlarging his borders. God's first commission for man, the command that lies at the foundation of man's ultimate fulfillment in life, was "Fill the earth, subdue it, and have dominion over it." By this means, man was to be constantly enlarging his knowledge of God in preparation for his destiny to reign with Him.

AN ENLARGED PERCEPTION OF GOD

With the words "I am the Almighty God [*El Shaddai*]; walk before me, and be thou perfect. And I will make my covenant between me and thee, and will multiply thee exceedingly" (Gen. 17:1b–2), God is enlarging Abram's horizons. It had been thirteen years since the birth of Ishmael, and twenty-four years had passed since he had entered Canaan on the promise that he would become a great nation through which all the families of the earth would be blessed. Thus far he had received nothing, and his hopes had diminished as the infirmities of age had increased.

The Lord revealed Himself as *El Shaddai* to restore power to Abram's waning faith. As he had to Hagar almost fourteen years before, the Lord came to Abram in visible form as well as spoke to him. This twofold manifestation increased the sense of the reality of the revelation, and it also set the stage for the reception of God's message by producing reverence in Abram (see v. 3).

The name *El Shaddai* added a new dimension to Abram's concept of the power of God. *Shaddai* depicts God as the Almighty, able to overpower any combination of circumstances that appear to obstruct the accomplishment of His will.[1] This manifestation of the Lord as *El Shaddai* was to be the characteristic revelation of God to the Patriarchs (Exod. 6:3; cf. Gen. 28:3; 35:11; 43:14; 48:3; 49:25).

A CALL FOR REDEDICATION AS A SERVANT

The Lord's admonishment "Walk before me, and be thou perfect" is a call for Abram to rededicate himself as a wholehearted servant of the Almighty. The expression "Walk before me" is an idiomatic way of saying "Be my servant" or (more precisely) "Be readily at hand for me as a servant" (I Sam. 2:35; II Chron. 6:14; cf. also Ps. 105:6, 42, where Abraham is called "his servant"). The root idea in the word translated *perfect* (*tamim*) is "complete, whole, or sound." In this context the word may allude to the problem Abram had fourteen years before, when he "hearkened to the voice" of his wife rather than to the voice of the Lord. Temporarily, he became the servant of another; he was not wholly walking before the Lord.

The covenant had been formally established with Abram fourteen years before (Gen. 15:18). But at this critical time in his life, Abram needed strong confirmation from the Lord that the covenant was still in effect—that his rashness and weakness had not annulled it. Consequently, the Lord declares, "I will make [give] my covenant between me and thee, and will multiply thee exceedingly." The wording of Genesis 15:18 is more literally "The Lord cut [*karath*] a covenant." This is the expression the inspired

---

[1] The translation of *Shaddai*, as a divine designation, by *Almighty* or a comparable word goes back to ancient times. E.g., the LXX often translates *Shaddai* as *pantokrator*, "all-powerful." The etymology of the word is not clear.

writers commonly use for the formal establishment of a covenant—evidently referring to the ceremonial cutting of the animals.[2]

NEW NAMES—ENLARGED POTENTIAL

Now the Lord is graciously reaffirming His covenant with Abram, sealing it by changing the names of Abram and Sarai and by establishing the sign of circumcision. In ancient times, when names were more than mere designations, a change of name signified a change of status and a new era in the person's life. By this change of names, then, the Lord was telling Abram and Sarai that they were entering a new era in their lives. From now on they were to live in the light of the enlarged destiny that their new names depicted. *Abram*, "Exalted father," is now to be *Abraham*, "Father of many nations" (cf. vv. 5–6). *Sarai*, "Princely" or "Like a princess," from now on will be *Sarah*, "Princess."

Here is a marvelous illustration of "Where sin abounded, grace did much more abound!" It may well have seemed to Abram and Sarai that the God they had so offended by their unbelief would annul the covenant or, at best, greatly restrict its blessings. But in spite of their sin, God enlarges the vision of their blessings. The natural human (or should we say carnal) question is "Did the sin of Abram and Sarai cause grace to abound?" In the words of Paul, "Perish such a thought!" (cf. Rom. 6:1–2).[3] From the beginning, the Lord had promised that in Abram all the families of the earth would be blessed (Gen. 12:1–3). This enlarged vision of the future was, in effect, God's assurance that His original promise had not diminished. Abram could not have justly seen this gracious promise as somehow erasing, or even diminishing, the sinfulness of his choice on that fateful day. If he saw clearly on this new day, he had instead an enlarged perception of God.

A SYMBOL OF SECURE
COVENANT BLESSINGS

Since the covenant promise to Abraham had a distinct and emphatic relationship to his lineage, the Lord ordained that the sign of the covenant

---

[2] The expression "I will give my covenant" (Gen. 17:2) "signifies, not to make a covenant, but to give, to put, i.e. to realize, to set in operation the things promised in the covenant." Keil, *Pentateuch*, 1:223 (see chap. 3, n. 2).

[3] The idiomatic expression translated "God forbid" (*me genoito*) in Rom. 6:2 could be more literally rendered "Let it not become!" or (in our idiom) "Perish the thought!"

be circumcision, a special reference to reproduction (Gen. 17:10–14). And since the promise included all the families of the earth, the rite of circumcision was not limited to the lineal descendants of Abraham. All in his household, including foreigners, were to be circumcised (vv. 12–13). The suggestion in this commandment is that in the future, all who come under the influence of Israel are to be brought into a covenant relationship with the Lord. As we know from later revelation, this does not mean that all who were circumcised were to be viewed as believers. Obedience to the rite of circumcision was supposed to be an avowal of faith in the covenant promises of the Lord, particularly those concerning the Messiah. But as the New Testament writers emphatically emphasize, the rite did not bring a person into a saving relationship with the Lord (e.g., Rom. 4:8–14).[4]

SHALL SARAH . . . BEAR A CHILD?

The focus in the first half of the chapter has been wholly upon Abraham. *El Shaddai* has called him to rededication, has reaffirmed and enlarged the covenant promise by changing his name from Abram to Abraham, and has established circumcision as a sign of the covenant promise.

It might have crossed Abraham's mind that God was now going to bypass Sarai in His program to fulfill His covenant. The excursion from the path the two of them had taken fourteen years before was begun at Sarai's suggestion. Even in his weakness in yielding to her suggestion, Abram may well have continued believing God's promise (cf. Gen. 15:2–6 with Rom. 4:18–22).[5] But what of Sarai? Had her unbelief disinherited her from the special blessings of the sacred promise?

If such thoughts crossed Abraham's mind, *El Shaddai* interrupted them wonderfully with these words, "As for Sarai thy wife, thou shalt not call her name Sarai, but Sarah shall her name be. And I will bless her, and give thee a son also of her: yea, I will bless her, and she shall be a mother

---

[4] This is not simply a New Testament revelation. In the Old Testament, the inspired writers repeatedly heap words of condemnation, including reprobation, upon Israelites who conscientiously kept the Levitical rituals (e.g., I Sam. 8:7–8; Isa. 1:10–21; 65:2–5). On the other hand, godly men such as David reveal an understanding that ritual without true faith has no saving power (e.g., Ps. 51:5–19).

[5] His sin, in that case, would be comparable to that of Adam. The Scriptures tell us that Adam was not deceived, as Eve was (I Tim. 2:14). It was not Satan's deception concerning God and His word that led Adam into sin. It was his desire for his wife. So it may have been with Abraham: it was his desire to please his wife, not unbelief, that led him astray.

of nations; kings of people shall be of her" (Gen. 17:15b–16). In response, Abraham, in an ecstasy of joy, "fell upon his face, and laughed, and
said in his heart, Shall a child be born unto him that is an hundred years
old? and shall Sarah, that is ninety years old, bear?"

Was it an ecstasy of joy? Wasn't it, rather, an outburst of unbelief? Was
not Abraham expressing in his heart the same inward doubt for which
the Lord later rebuked Sarah (18:12–15)? But there is a striking, though
often overlooked, difference between the two responses. The fact that
at the beginning of the revelation Abraham "fell on his face" before God
makes this action of awe-filled reverence all the more remarkable. After
the initial revelation of God, Abraham had evidently stood before the
Lord (perhaps at God's bidding, cf. Dan. 8:17–18; 10:8–11) as a servant
would stand to receive instructions. However, when this word concerning
Sarah came, Abraham was so overwhelmed that he again fell on his face
before the Lord.[6] The difference between his attitude toward the promise
and that of Sarah's was in their perspective of the One Who uttered the
promise.

What then is the meaning of Abraham's outburst, "O that Ishmael
might live before thee!" Evidently, Abraham feared that the glorious
promise that the covenant would be fulfilled through Isaac would bring
a curse on Ishmael. Since he was the product of unbelief and spiritual
weakness, how could he be blessed? As the Lord, thirteen years before,
had to disabuse Hagar of the thought that her son was heir of the promises of the covenant (16:12), now He must relieve Abraham of the misconception that the glorious blessing of Isaac allowed for no blessing on
Ishmael.

After reaffirming that the "everlasting covenant" would come through
Sarah's son, the Lord responds to Abraham's appeal. "And as for Ishmael,
I have heard thee: behold, I have blessed him, and will make him fruitful,
and will multiply him exceedingly; twelve princes shall he beget, and I
will make him a great nation" (Gen. 17:20).

Perhaps with a play upon the name *Ishmael*, the Lord declares to
Abraham, "I have heard thee." What had He heard? "O that Ishmael

---

[6] Cf. the responses of Martha and Mary to the Lord concerning the death of Lazarus. Their words
were the same: "Lord, if thou hadst been here, my brother had not died" (John 11:21, 32). But John
tells us that "when Mary was come where Jesus was, and saw him, she fell down at his feet" before
she spoke to him. The difference between the two was profound—not in their words, but in their
perception and attitude.

might live before thee!" Was this a prayer only for the material and numerical blessing of Ishmael? Most interpreters seem to assume this, but it is difficult for me to see how Abraham could have been thinking only of material blessings—all the more so when his prayer included the words "before thee." This was a prayer for the spiritual, as well as the material, blessing of Ishmael and his descendants.

To many, the characterization of Ishmael in Genesis 16:12 opposes the idea that Abraham's prayer included a spiritual blessing: "And he will be a wild man; his hand will be against every man, and every man's hand against him." Furthermore, the history of the Arab nations—which includes the violent propagation of the Muslim religion—seems to verify the notion that these people are a spiritual curse to mankind rather than a blessing.[7] But the same type of objections could be raised concerning the Hebrew people. The inspired writers repeatedly label them as a "stiff-necked people"—obstinate, hardhearted, and rebellious (e.g., Exod. 32:9; Deut. 9:6; Ps. 78:8; Isa. 48:4). Though they have been highly favored as the chosen people, they could also be cited as the source of much that has been a spiritual curse in the world. Nevertheless, God will ultimately fulfill His promise to make Israel a blessing in the earth (Isa. 43:21; 44:1–5, 23; 49:3; Rom. 11:12, 15). If we believe that God will fulfill His sacred promise concerning Israel, why should we not believe that He will fulfill His promise to Abraham concerning Ishmael?

---

[7] In general, the term *Arab* refers to the peoples who live in Arabia, the peninsula between the Red Sea and the Persian Gulf. According to Gen. 25:18, the Ishmaelites dwelt "from Havilah unto Shur, that is before [east of] Egypt, . . . toward [in the direction of] Assyria." According to Josephus (*Antiquities* 1.12.4), this covered the whole territory of the Arabian peninsula from the Euphrates to the Red Sea. However, it is clear both from Scripture (e.g., Gen. 25:1–6) and from history that there was a good deal of ethnic mixture among the Arab peoples.

Chapter Seventeen

"Some Have Entertained Angels Unawares"

"**B**E NOT FORGETFUL TO ENTERTAIN strangers: for thereby some have entertained angels unawares" (Heb. 13:2). The writer of Hebrews may well have had Abraham and Lot in mind when he wrote these words. The exhortation of the inspired writer has interesting connotations. The expression *entertain strangers*, one word in the Greek, literally means "to love strangers." The word *entertained* is also derived from the word for *stranger*. These root concepts suggest that true hospitality is rooted in a person's love for mankind—which in turn is rooted in God's love for mankind (Deut. 10:17–19).

Not long after the Lord had revealed Himself to Abraham as El Shaddai (see Gen. 17:1; 18:14; 21:5), He appeared to him again "by the oaks of Mamre, while he was sitting at the tent door in the heat of the day" (18:1*b*, NASB). He revealed Himself this time in the form of a man in the company of two "men." From Abraham's vantage point, the travelers had approached silently and undetected. When he looked up, suddenly there they were, standing a short distance away.

The story that follows reveals that the Lord had a twofold purpose for this revelation: (1) to establish Sarah's faith that she would indeed bear a son, and (2) to reveal to Abraham the judgment that was to come on Sodom and Gomorrah.

THE MESSAGE TO SARAH

Sarah had not yet recovered from the clouds of doubt that had entered her soul some fourteen years before; yet she was to be the "mother of the faithful," a pattern and example for believers through the ages (I Pet. 3:6; Gal. 4.31). Consequently, the first half of Genesis 18 focuses on Sarah, though she discreetly attempts to stay "behind the scenes."

Preparation for the Message

It was Abraham's hospitality—his love for mankind—that opened the door for God to manifest Himself. When he saw the three men,

> he ran to meet them from the tent door, and bowed himself toward the ground, and said, My Lord, if now I have found favour in thy sight, pass not away, I pray thee, from thy servant: let a little water, I pray you, be fetched, and wash your feet, and rest yourselves under the tree: and I will fetch a morsel of bread, and comfort ye your hearts; after that ye shall pass on: for therefore are ye come to your servant (Gen. 18:2b–5).

In his twenty-five years in the land of Canaan, this could not have been the first time Abraham extended such hospitality. Hebron, where he now resided, was on the Central Ridge Road, a major route in Palestine. Connected in the north with international roadways, the Central Ridge Road led south through Shechem, Bethel, Jerusalem, Hebron, Beersheba, and ultimately to On (Heliopolis), the seat of the worship of the sun god in Egypt. Situated about halfway between Jerusalem and Beersheba, Hebron would have been a natural stopping place for travelers.

It would have been quite natural, therefore, for Abraham on this occasion to extend this hospitality "unawares"—oblivious to the fact that he was opening his home and life not only to angels but to his Lord. "In true oriental fashion" we modern westerners tend to say when we describe Abraham's seemingly obsequious attitude toward his visitors. By such words we soften cultural shock—so much so, unfortunately, that we glide smoothly over the message in the Patriarch's attitude. This "oriental fashion" was born of a spirit of respect for others. By his actions and attitude, Abraham was testifying, "As a servant of the Lord, I am a servant to my fellow man. I am here to help you in any way I can."

So Abraham begins by bowing "himself to the ground" before them. Then he addresses the one who seems to be the leader, "My lord,[1] if now I have found favor in your sight, please do not pass your servant by" (v. 3, NASB)—or, "Don't let me miss this opportunity of serving you." What Abraham says next could be called the patriarchal equivalent of the old southern expression, "Come over for a bite to eat."

Please let a little water be brought and wash your feet, and rest yourselves under the tree; and I will bring a piece of bread that you may refresh yourselves; after that you may go on, since you have visited your servant (vv. 4–5, NASB).

When the visitors agree to stay, Abraham hurries to the tent and instructs Sarah, "Make ready quickly three measures of fine meal, knead it, and make cakes upon the hearth" (v. 6). A measure (*seah*) would be the equivalent of 374 cubic inches[2]—over five quarts of fine flour for the bread of each man! Then Abraham "ran unto the herd, and fetcht a calf tender and good, and gave it unto a young man; and he hasted to dress it" (v. 7). When all was prepared, he set the meal before them and stood by them—as a servant would—while they ate.

The Message for Sarah

The question "Where is Sarah thy wife?" was designed, no doubt, to get Sarah's attention. And—no surprise—it did get her attention. The writer tells us that Sarah "was listening at the tent door" (v. 10*b*, NASB) when the Lord spoke the next words. "I will certainly return unto thee according to the time of life; and, lo, Sarah thy wife shall have a son."

In a sense, the words of the narrator that follow blend into the thought patterns of Sarah. "Now Abraham and Sarah were old and well stricken in age; and it ceased to be with Sarah after the manner of women." For many years such thoughts had clashed in Sarah's mind with the promise Abraham had received. They had found expression fourteen years before in the words "the Lord hath restrained me from bearing" (16:2). If she

---

[1] In the culture of biblical times, both *adon* and *kurios*, the Hebrew and Greek words commonly translated *lord*, were often used as terms of respect with reference to men. E.g., Sarah uses *adon* of her husband (18:12) and Abraham's servant repeatedly uses this word of his master (ch. 24). The Masoretes, the medieval Jewish scholars who superimposed vowel markings to the Hebrew words of Scripture, interpreted *adon* (by special markings) in 18:3 as a reference to the Lord. However, the context in the early part of the story demonstrates otherwise. If Abraham had known that this was the Lord and two angels, he would never have offered them food.

[2] Keil, *The Pentateuch*, 1:228 (see chap. 3, n. 2).

was to bear a child, why had the Lord not rejuvenated her—and why had He not done so with her husband? Long before, Abraham had grappled with this twofold "impossibility," and against the backdrop of the stars of heaven, he had "believed in the Lord."

> And being not weak in faith, he considered not his own body now dead, when he was about an hundred years old, neither yet the deadness of Sara's womb: he staggered not at the promise of God through unbelief; but was strong in faith, giving glory to God; . . . being fully persuaded that, what he had promised, he was able also to perform (Rom. 4:19–21).

But Sarah, standing at the tent door behind this mysterious Messenger, "laughed within herself, saying, After I am waxed old shall I have pleasure, my lord being old also?" The message of rebuke for Sarah was addressed to Abraham:

> And the Lord said unto Abraham, Wherefore did Sarah laugh, saying, Shall I of a surety bear a child, which am old? Is any thing too hard for the Lord? At the time appointed I will return unto thee, according to the time of life, and Sarah shall have a son (Gen. 18:13–14).

Did Abraham share somewhat in Sarah's unbelief? Had the promise that had glowed those years before with the glory of God now faded? Or did he by his silence concerning the promise share in the responsibility for Sarah's doubt? Had he been intimidated into silence by Sarah's apparent unbelief?

Abraham and Sarah both must have been electrified by the words they heard from their Guest; now they could have no doubt that this was a divine Messenger speaking. But Sarah was more than electrified. She was terrified. This Man, this God, had read and repeated the very words of her heart—words so offensive to a godly and sensitive woman that she could not bear their shame, could not believe she had actually said them. Bowing and trembling before the Lord, she expelled the last lie of her heart. "I laughed not." And the Lord, rising from the table with His angelic servants, squelched this last deceit with the words "Nay; but thou didst laugh."

THE MESSAGE TO ABRAHAM

As the men rose from the table, they looked toward Sodom—toward the southeast, away from the usual route that led southwestward to Beersheba. A secondary road led from Hebron southeastward to Arad, which lay about fifteen miles west of the ancient valley of Siddim. It was perhaps down this road that Abraham "went with them to bring them on the way."[3] What a picture this is—the terrestrial and the heavenly walking together! By now Abraham knew that he was in the company of the Lord and His angels; yet, sensing they were on an earthly mission, he conducted them, as he would earthly travelers, toward their destination.

The next words reveal something of the purpose of divine revelation.

And the Lord said, Shall I hide from Abraham that thing which I do; seeing that Abraham shall surely become a great and mighty nation, and all the nations of the earth shall be blessed in him? For I know him, that he will command his children and his household after him, and they shall keep the way of the Lord, to do justice and judgment; that the Lord may bring upon Abraham that which he hath spoken of him (vv. 17–19).

Divine revelation comes "that the man of God may be perfect [specifically adapted for his task], throughly furnished unto all good works" (II Tim. 3:17; cf. II Pet. 1:3). Abraham—as all of us—needed a revelation of God's judgment, set against the backdrop of loved ones in danger of judgment. Without such a revelation, he would not rightly "command his children and his household after him" so that they would "keep the way of the Lord"; and consequently, he would not fulfill God's purpose for him.

So the Lord reveals to Abraham the imminent threat of judgment that Sodom and Gomorrah lay under.

And the Lord said, Because the cry of Sodom and Gomorrah is great, and because their sin is very grievous; I will go down now, and see whether they have done altogether according to the cry of it, which is come unto me; and if not, I will know (Gen. 18:20–21).

The cry of Sodom and Gomorrah is the indignant cry for justice and judgment that ascends to heaven because of sin (cf. Gen. 4:10). There is a sense in which the entire universe, created for God's glory, "groaneth and travaileth in pain together" (Rom. 8:22) because of the sin that violates the holy nature of the Creator. The words "I will go down now, and see," in anthropomorphic language, picture the Judge of the universe as actively and intelligently responding to the outcry of sin.

---

[3] According to tradition, Abraham went with them several miles across the mountains eastward to a place Jerome called *Caphar Barucha*, where through a deep ravine the Dead Sea comes into view Leupold, *Genesis*, 1:544 (see chap. 6, n. 4).

At these words (Gen. 18:20–21), the angels turned and descended toward Sodom, "but Abraham stood yet before the Lord." He had seen God as *El Elyon*, the Most High; as *El Shaddai*, the all-powerful One; and as *Elohim Yahweh*, the Creator Who is an ever-present help in time of need. Now he sees Him as the Judge of the universe.

It is on this basis—that God is the righteous Judge of all the earth (v. 25)—that Abraham begins his intercession for the wicked city of Sodom. His first appeal is, "Wilt thou also destroy the righteous with the wicked?" He doesn't deny that Sodom is wicked, nor does he deny the greatness of its wickedness. His appeal is for the righteous who would perish with the city if the city were destroyed.

It goes without saying that Abraham was thinking of Lot and his family and, perhaps, of those he assumed Lot had influenced. The Lord's willingness to listen and respond to Abraham's pleas encourages him to make six successive requests, each time asking for more mercy to be shown. When at last he makes his final petition, "Peradventure ten shall be found there," he must surely have been able to picture in his mind ten people in the household of Lot—family members, sons-in-law, servants—whom he thought to be righteous.

What some might call Abraham's bargaining with God is actually true prayer. The greatness and holiness of God naturally arouses in sinful man a fear of approaching and communicating with Him. Even on the human level, we are naturally reluctant to communicate freely with those we perceive to be great. It is only when we find a "great one" approachable and willing to listen that we begin to lose our reluctance to speak. As the angels went on their way toward Sodom, Abraham found that the Lord was willing to stand and listen to him. Encouraged by this willingness, he "drew near" to the Lord and made his first request. As he drew near to God, he found that God drew near to him (James 4:8) by listening and granting his timid petition. At each step, he grew bolder with his requests while at the same time becoming more and more conscious of his own unworthiness (Ps. 116:1–6).

And what compelled Abraham to so intercede for such a wicked place? "He was led to intercede in this way . . . by the love which springs from consciousness that one's own preservation and rescue are due to compassionate grace alone; love, too, which cannot conceive of the guilt of others as too great for salvation to be possible."[4]

And though this love focused quite naturally on those he knew in Sodom—Lot and his household—yet his prayer comprehended, in its potential power, the whole valley of Siddim; for Abraham's initial prayer was "If there are fifty righteous within the city (of Sodom), will You destroy the place [the whole region]?" The Lord's reply was "If I find in Sodom fifty righteous, I will spare all the place for their sakes."

---

[4] Keil, *The Pentateuch*, 1:231.

Chapter Eighteen

"God Remembered Abraham, and Sent Lot Out"

I T MUST NOT HAVE SEEMED to Abraham that God remembered him when He destroyed the cities of the plain (Gen. 19:29). Abraham had risen early that morning and had hurried to the spot where he had stood before the Lord. The day before, he had left that place confident that the Lord had granted his petition to spare the cities of the valley of Siddim. Surely there were ten righteous people in Sodom! But what he saw that fateful morning must have sickened and terrified him. "And he looked toward Sodom and Gomorrah, and toward all the land of the plain, and beheld, and, lo, the smoke of the country went up as the smoke of a furnace" (v. 28). Little could he have known—nor would he know for years to come—that God had indeed remembered him, though he had been sadly mistaken about the number of righteous people in the city where Lot had chosen to dwell.

The Rescue of Lot and the Judgment of Sodom

The angels arrived in Sodom in the evening. They had left Hebron in the early afternoon. The forty-mile trip would have taken almost two days for ordinary travelers, but these travelers were not ordinary. Their arrival at the gates of Sodom in early evening was by design. They had a twofold mission. They were to stay in Sodom that night to witness the cause of the heinous, cacophonous outcry that had so vexed their King—and they were to rescue Lot and his family from the city's impending doom.

When the visitors arrived at Sodom, Lot was sitting in the gate, suggesting that he was actively involved as an elder—comparable to a government official—in the social, commercial, and judicial affairs of the city.[1] He must have gained considerable prestige among the elders of the city when, some twenty years before, he was the instrument of their rescue through his uncle Abraham. Belonging to the family of an illustrious hero, particularly in the culture of that day, would have automatically elevated his standing in the community. As a man of some status, then, Lot was "dwelling among" the Sodomites (II Pet. 2:8) when the emissaries arrived.

To be sure, as Peter informs us, he was "vexed" ("oppressed, distressed") by the licentious and lawless conduct of the people; and on occasion, he admonished them concerning their deeds (Gen. 19:9). Nevertheless, the vexation and torment he felt in his soul concerning the pandemic depravity he witnessed in Sodom did not prevent him from approving marriage ties for his daughters with men of this city—men who evidently shared in the haughty and disdainful attitude of the Sodomites toward the Judge of mankind (19:14).

How had all this happened to a man the Scriptures call "righteous"? Abraham, Lot's spiritual mentor, had chosen to leave the stability and security of a great city and become a tent-dwelling sojourner because "he looked for a city which hath foundations, whose builder and maker is God" (Heb. 11:10)—he looked for reality and fulfillment in another kingdom. Evidently, some time before he separated from his uncle, Lot had become disenchanted with the pilgrim life he had shared with him. Perhaps the attraction of Egypt had remained with him as he traveled with Abraham back to Bethel. When the time of separation came, his willingness to violate propriety and take advantage of his uncle's magnanimity (Gen. 13:10–11) reveals that his heart had already drifted from the divine promise he had shared with the Patriarch.

---

[1] In a sense, what the forum was to the Romans and the agora to the Greeks, the city gate was in the ancient East. It was the place where the elders of the city customarily gathered to transact business and settle disputes (Gen. 34:20; Deut. 21:19; Ruth 4:1; Prov. 31:23).

And immediately after the separation, Lot showed his aversion to the pilgrim life of his uncle by his choice to dwell "in the cities" of the Jordan valley. The inspired writer shows the inclination of Lot's heart during this time with the observation that he "pitched his tent toward Sodom" (13:12b). As he began his separate existence, Lot would have been a good fifty miles north of Sodom—for he had traveled east from Bethel (13:11), which would bring him into the Jordan valley about ten miles north of the Dead Sea. But to his covetous eyes, the lure of that distant city was too great to resist.

When he saw the strangers, he rose, bowed humbly before them, and offered to lodge them in his home for the night. When they declined the offer, "he pressed upon them greatly." Undoubtedly, Lot was moved by a spirit of hospitality and, perhaps, by an uneasy fear for the welfare of these innocent travelers if they remained in the open during the night.

Nevertheless, it is difficult not to see the contrast between the hospitality of Abraham and that of his nephew Lot. The narrator seems to go overboard in his description of Abraham's generosity: three measures (close to seventeen quarts!) of fine meal for bread cakes, a choice calf "which he had dressed" for the meal, plus the "extras"—butter (curds) and milk. Though he presents Lot as hospitable, the inspired writer describes no such flourishes of generosity with him. It is interesting, also, that the narrator says nothing about the involvement of Lot's wife and daughters in preparation of the meal.

It was yet early in the evening, before the travelers lay down, that Lot and his guests heard raucous calls of the rabble of Sodom who had surrounded the house. And what a rabble it was! By definition, rabble consists of the lowest or coarsest class of people; but this crowd had people from every quarter of the city. Old and young, rich and poor together were screaming, "Where are the men which came in to thee this night? bring them out unto us, that we may know them" (19:5b). What is the cause of such an irrational outburst of passion? With the pandemic availability of consensual sex in Sodom, why were these people so intent on "knowing" these visitors?

At the root of all sin is an innate hatred in unregenerate man for God and His people. "If ye were of the world, the world would love his own: but because ye are not of the world, but I have chosen you out of the world, therefore the world hateth you" (John 15:19; cf. Ps. 37:12; Prov. 29:27). This hatred God restricts and suppresses in various ways; in law-abiding and enlightened societies, it may even lie dormant and unnoticed for a time. Nevertheless, whether dormant or overt, there is a seething rage within the heathen against the Lord and against His Messiah—waiting only for direction and opportunity to break the bands of divine restrictions (Ps. 2:1–3).

Such is the restlessness of the wicked man that he is, in his own diabolical way, evangelistic about his "gospel"—inordinately anxious to win converts and make them "twofold more" children of hell than himself (Matt. 23:15). "For they sleep not, except they have done mischief; and their sleep is taken away, unless they cause some to fall" (Prov. 4:16; cf. Rom. 1:32).

In his portrayal of the progressive degeneration of heathen society (Rom. 1:21–32), Paul presents homosexuality as the second stage in God's judicial abandonment of willful sinners to their sin. In the first stage, "God . . . gave them up to uncleanness through the lusts of their own hearts" (v. 24)—that is, God gave them over to the sensuality that flows naturally from an idolatrous material view of God (v. 23).[2] In the second state, that of the Sodomites, "God gave them up unto vile affections," so that both men and women became so perverted against nature that they "burned in their lust one toward another; men with men working that which is unseemly" (v. 27b). In the first stage, God abandoned willful sinners to their lusts (epithumia), active, evil longings. In the second stage, God gave them over to vile affections (pathos), "the diseased condition out of which the lusts spring."[3] In the third stage, God abandoned willful sinners, such as the Sodomites, to a reprobate mind—a mind so marred and benumbed by sin that it becomes capable of justifying the most outrageous actions against propriety (v. 28).

Having arrived, then, at this final stage of depravity, the Sodomites could brook no argument against their plans, nor could they feel the restraint either of shame or propriety. Lot tried to reason with them and, in a shameful way, tried to shame them. When he offered his daughters to this vicious crowd, he surely must have rationalized—with a mind now intoxicated with the atmosphere of Sodom—that the thought of defiling the virgin daughters of a respected elder in their city would shock them

---

[2] "To abandon voluntarily the true idea of God is to fall necessarily under the empire of material nature, with all its dominant instincts and desires." H. P. Liddon, Explanatory Analysis of St. Paul's Epistle to the Romans (Grand Rapids: Zondervan, 1961), 29.

[3] Marvin R. Vincent, Word Studies in the New Testament (Grand Rapids: Eerdmans, 1946), 3:19.

into shame. He found otherwise; instead of being shamed they rushed madly at him screaming, "Stand back. . . . This one came in merely to sojourn, and he is constantly judging: now will we deal worse with you, than with them. And they were pressing hard upon the man Lot, crowding near to break the door down" (Gen. 19:9).[4]

The angels, now revealing their true nature, pulled Lot into the house and afflicted the entire mob, "both small and great," with blindness—"so that they wearied themselves to find the door" (vv. 10–11). These last words are an omen of the Sodomites' impending doom. Though they were miraculously judged with blindness, they stubbornly persisted in trying to find the door until they finally became exasperated and gave up.[5]

At the warning of the angels, "Lot went out and spoke to his sons-in-law, who were to marry his daughters, and said, 'Up, get out of this place, for the Lord will destroy the city.' But he appeared to his sons-in-law to be jesting" (v. 14 NASB).[6] The fact that their father-in-law appeared to be joking when he spoke of God's judgment says as much about his spiritual state as it does about that of his sons-in-law. However the conduct of the Sodomites had distressed Lot in the past, and whatever admonitions he

---

[4] Personal translation, comparable to that of Keil, Leupold, and some modern translations. The Hebrew syntax depicts the Sodomites as scornfully and angrily accusing Lot of constantly judging them without being even a citizen of the town.

[5] Keil and several others suggest that this was a "mental blindness, in which the eye sees, but does not see the right object." The Hebrew word for blindness in this passage is used only two other times in the Old Testament, both in II Kings 6:18. The word (*sanwer*) means *to blind or to dazzle*, connoting (some say) *sudden blindness*. Keil bases his interpretation, not on the meaning of the word itself, but on the circumstances in these two passages. Though this interpretation provides a reasonable explanation for the actions of the Sodomites, it seems to me that it neutralizes the literary purpose of the description. The words "both small and great" and "they wearied themselves to find the door" form the climax of the narrator's description of the persistent and pandemic depravity of the Sodomites. Keil, *The Pentateuch*, 1:233 (see chap. 3, n. 2); Klein, *Etymological Dictionary*, 451 (see chap. 3, n. 1); *TWOT*, 2:629 (see chap. 3, n. 3).

[6] The KJV follows the Septuagint in assuming that the sons-in-law had already married Lot's daughters. The Hebrew word translated *married* is, more literally, *taking* or *were taking* (*loqeche*, an active participle). In accordance with ancient customs, the term son-in-law would be used during the betrothal period. The rendering *had taken* or *had married* would be more naturally expressed by the Hebrew Qal perfect than by an active participle—as, e.g., Num. 12:1 where Miriam and Aaron complained that Moses "had married an Ethiopian woman." Some interpreters say that the wording of Gen. 19:15 ("Arise, take thy wife, and thy two daughters, *which are here*") favors the LXX translation. But, as Keil points out, the expression *which are here* refers to Lot's wife and two daughters who were in the house in distinction from the bridegrooms who, in a sense, also belonged to the family. *The Pentateuch*, 1:234. Notice, also, that the inspired writer speaks of the appeal to and response of only the sons-in-law—a circumstance supporting the idea that they were not yet living with Lot's daughters. It is difficult to believe that Lot would not have appealed directly to his married daughters had they been there.

had made, he evidently had not—at least in the eyes of his sons-in-law—taken God very seriously himself.

Lot's obtuse hesitancy about leaving Sodom, even at the urging of the messengers of judgment, is both astounding and predictable. It may have been that his wife and daughters were tearfully urging him to wait a little longer for the sons-in-law, but the heart of his problem was a problem of the heart. He had grown insensitive to spiritual realities by degrees, and now his benumbed spirit was incapable of responding quickly to the angels' urgent appeals. The words of Hosea apply to Lot: "Whoredom and wine and new wine take away the heart" (Hosea 4:11). Though he had maintained a degree of righteousness in his standing with God, he had lived on the level of the sensual in his relationship with men.

At last, with the ominous signs of dawn beginning to appear (Gen. 19:15), the angels seized the hands of Lot, his wife, and daughters, "the Lord being merciful unto him," drew them out of the city, and urgently warned, "Escape for thy life; look not behind thee, neither stay thou in all the plain; escape to the mountain, lest thou be consumed" (vv. 16–17). But even now, a sense of the impending judgment having at last gripped his soul, Lot turns from the counsel of the heavenly messengers to his own darkened understanding for a solution. It is now too late, he argues, to reach the mountains before the judgment falls. Can he not find refuge, instead, in this nearby little city?

> Oh, no, my lords! . . . I cannot escape to the mountains, for the disaster will overtake me and I will die; now behold, this town is near enough to flee to, and it is small. Please, let me escape there (is it not small?) that my life may be saved (vv. 18–20, NASB).

Notwithstanding Lot's acknowledgment of the angels' mercy in saving him, this request was presumptuous to the point of insolence. The "little city," Zoar, in which he wished to take refuge was in the valley of Siddim that was marked for judgment (19:17). The king of Zoar was one of the confederates with the king of Sodom in the battle against the kings of Mesopotamia (14:2). Lot's argument with the angels, remarkably, was "Is not this city a little one?"—as if to say, the sins of this town must be relatively small when compared with the sins of the great city of Sodom. Therefore, couldn't this little town be exempted from the judgment?

Zoar must have been not less than five miles from Sodom, which means it would have taken Lot and his daughters at least two hours to reach it. The dawn had just begun to break when the angels pulled Lot

How much further was it to the mountains? Not that far, evidently. Zoar has generally been located at the southeastern point of the Dead Sea, at the foot of the mountains of Moab.

About AD 1100, crusaders marching eastward around the south end of the Dead Sea came to Zoar (called sometimes Segor or Zoghar), at which point "they began to enter the eastern mountains." Edward Robinson, *Biblical Researches in Palestine* (Boston: Crocker & Brewster, 1874), 2:518. Later references in the Bible to Zoar (Deut. 34:3; Isa. 15:5; Jer. 48:34) are consistent with the view of Robinson and many others that Zoar was on the border of Moab. The same may be said concerning references in later history (e.g., Josephus, Eusebius, and Jerome). In general, Moab is situated on a high plateau or tableland, averaging about two thousand feet above sea level. North of the Lisan Peninsula, the mountains of Moab often form a veritable wall on the east coast of the Dead Sea. The cliffs begin to recede, leaving a narrow beach-like plain, for the last ten miles south of the Lisan Peninsula. Richard E. Baney, *Search for Sodom and Gomorrah* (Kansas City: CAM Press, 1963), 160.

Lot may have had another compelling motive (other than the fear he would not have time to reach the mountains) for wanting to find refuge in a city rather than in the mountains. It appears that by the time he separated from Abraham, Lot had developed an aversion to the pilgrim life and a penchant for "city life" (Gen. 13:12*b*—"And Lot dwelled in the cities of the plain, and pitched his tent toward Sodom").

out of the city. Now, as he and his daughters entered Zoar, the sun had risen, and Sodom's business and pleasure had fully begun: "They did eat, they drank, they bought, they sold, they planted, they builded" (Luke 17:28), oblivious to the possibility of judgment. "But the same day that Lot went out of Sodom it rained fire and brimstone from heaven, and destroyed them all" (Luke 17:29).

With the falling of judgment on Sodom and Gomorrah, the Lord, before Whom Abraham had stood, made His appearance again. "Then the Lord rained upon Sodom and upon Gomorrah brimstone and fire from the Lord out of heaven; and he overthrew those cities, and all the plain, and all the inhabitants of the cities, and that which grew upon the ground" (Gen. 19:24–25). The remarkable combination "The Lord rained

... brimstone and fire from the Lord" reveals two members of the Trinity: God the Son, Who had appeared before Abraham to announce the judgment, and God the Father, Who now administers the judgment.

"REMEMBER LOT'S WIFE"

How far was Lot's wife from Zoar when the fire and brimstone fell from heaven? Disregarding the angel's warning, she "looked back from behind him, and ... became a pillar of salt" (v. 26). The wording indicates that she was lingering behind her husband and daughters. Why? The warning, centuries later, of the Savior and Judge Who had called the fire and brimstone down on the Valley of Siddim, gives the answer to that question:

> In that day, he which shall be upon the housetop, and his stuff in the house, let him not come down to take it away: and he that is in the field, let him likewise not return back. Remember Lot's wife. Whosoever shall seek to save his life shall lose it; and whosoever shall lose his life shall preserve it (Luke 17:31–33).

Lot's wife put a high priority on the "stuff in the house" and on the life she had left in Sodom. In seeking to save that life, she lost it.

THE LEGACY OF LOT

It was only after he witnessed the fury of God's judgment that Lot's mind and heart cleared enough to allow him to see the wisdom of the angels' heavenly perspective. After he saw the raining of "brimstone and fire," Lot "went up out of Zoar, and dwelt in the mountain, and his two daughters with him; for he feared to dwell in Zoar" (Gen. 19:24, 30). What did he fear in Zoar? He must have feared that God's judgment would soon fall on it as it had fallen on the other cities of the plain. Its people were a part of the society of the valley of Siddim and had undoubtedly sought business and pleasure in nearby Sodom. Lot, who had been vexed with the filthy lives of the Sodomites, must have seen the same sins in Zoar; for rarely do hardened sinners benefit from witnessing judgment. "Who knowing the judgment of God, that they which commit such things are worthy of death, not only do the same, but have pleasure in them that do them" (Rom. 1:32; cf. 2:4–5; Rev. 9:20–21). Even in his spiritual dullness, Lot now had a new perspective on the judgment of God.

It must have been with considerable reluctance that Lot's daughters went with him from Zoar to the mountains of Moab. They must have wondered at the fear they saw in their father's eyes—to them more of a phobia than a reasonable fear. Perhaps, after the announcement of his intention to move to the mountains, they thought at first that he was jesting (as their fiancés had thought that fateful evening). But they soon found he was serious—almost to the point of hysteria, in their minds. They must have protested the move. What chance would they have for a new life in the mountains? What chance for marriage and a family? But their father was determined, and they had no choice. How could they, pampered as they had been in Sodom, exist alone in Zoar? Their only hope for a new future was with their father. They would indulge him for a while—until he got over his phobias. Then, with their father, they would find a new city and a new life.

But what they found in their new home was shocking and unbearably shameful. They became cave-dwellers, living as brute savages (Job 30:5–6) in one of the limestone caves that abound in that area.[7] All hope for family, all hope for a name, all hope for a legacy was now gone. What could they do? In this case, desperate times apparently called for diabolically desperate measures. On successive nights, they would get their father drunk, and each sister would lie—would commit incest—with her father. Incest is a form of fornication that even the heathen are ashamed to discuss (I Cor. 5:1)—"one of those few crimes that all cultures agreed were terrible."[8] Yet somehow, against the backdrop of an outraged humanity, they found a way to justify this crime. God, it seems, had given "them over to a reprobate mind."

What was the elder sister thinking when she reasoned, "Our father is old"? How did that fact elevate or ennoble her proposal? Was she thinking, "He will soon die, and this will end all opportunity for us to be given in marriage"? And what about the second plank in her rationale: "And there is not a man in the earth to come in unto us after the manner of all the earth"? Her view of the world—and of God—had evidently become

---

[7] "At Petra in Arabia the mountain-sides are honeycombed with caves, the dens of early troglodytes and Horites, the pre-Semitic people of Edom. Cave dwellers may still be found in Palestine, Transjordania, and Petra." J. McKee Adams, *Biblical Backgrounds* (Nashville: Broadman, 1955), 478.

[8] Craig S. Keener, *Bible Background Commentary* (Downers Grove, IL: InterVarsity, 1993), 462.

so atrophied that it now conformed to her present cave-dwelling circumstances.

Their father, so recently bereaved and despondent over the cataclysmic changes in his fortunes, was an easy prey for their scheme. On successive nights, they were able to get him so drunk that when each sister lay with her father, "he perceived not when she lay down, nor when she arose." But what happened later when he found that his daughters were pregnant? Did he recoil in disgust at the actions of his daughters? Did he condemn himself?

The inspired writer draws a veil of silence over this part of Lot's life, but the last picture we have of him tells us much about the inevitable result of his pitching his tent toward Sodom those years ago. Lying by himself in a drunken stupor, Lot is totally oblivious to the part he has played in the degeneration of his daughters. Sadly, the words of Alexander Pope have poignant application to Lot—and to all who have lost the capacity to be shocked by sin:

> Vice is a monster of so frightful mien,
> As to be hated, needs but to be seen;
> Yet seen too *oft*, familiar with her Face,
> We first endure, then pity, then embrace.[9]

And what of Lot's legacy? In naming her son *Moab* ("of his father"), the older sister shamelessly announced her incest. The younger sister obscured the sin somewhat by naming her child, the progenitor of the Ammonites, *Benammi* ("son of my people").

Lot was a believer in the true God. He undoubtedly came to that belief, on the testimony of his uncle Abraham, while he was living with his family in Ur of the Chaldees. With his grandfather, Terah, Lot joined Abraham on his pilgrim journey. When his grandfather died in Haran, he chose, in contrast to his uncle Nahor, to leave the city of the moon god and search with Abraham for "a city which hath foundations, whose builder and maker is God." Even during the years of his entanglement in Sodom, he maintained—however imperfectly—his allegiance to God, for his soul was vexed at the wickedness he saw.

So he must have taught his family of the true God, and even his daughters must have professed some allegiance to Him. But Lot's legacy for his

---

[9] Alexander Pope, *An Essay on Man*, in *Eighteenth-Century English Literature* (Harcourt Brace Jovanovich, 1969), 642.

family was a twisted view of God. His offer to sacrifice his daughters to the passions of the Sodomites reveals a fatally impaired perception of God. The image of God that reflected in his soul was evidently of a God willing to sacrifice eternal principle on the altar of propriety. Likewise, his insane confidence that he knew better than the angels of the Lord how he could best be saved from impending judgment suggests that he had developed the habit of eating from the Tree of Knowledge—exalting his own judgment over that of God.

Expedient self-centeredness inevitably warps a man's view of God. Though made in the image of God, the egocentric man seeks to conform God to his own image. The inexorable law for those who make their own gods is "They that make them are like unto them" (Ps. 115:8). As Lot became increasingly self-centered and self-indulgent, he began to view God as he viewed himself—as a Being of supreme self-interest. God became to him what others were to him—a means by which his personal desires would be fulfilled. Lot's attitude toward Abraham when they separated provides an ominous illustration of his deteriorating view of God. Abraham, the friend of God and Lot's spiritual mentor, became to him simply a means by which he would gain the best land and (so he thought) the best future. Abraham's trust in God and gracious generosity became to Lot, not examples to emulate, but tools to use.

It was out of this philosophy that the Moabites and the Ammonites developed their perception of God. The Moabites called their god *Chemosh* ("subduer"). The Ammonite name for this god was *Molech* ("king").[10] These descendants of Lot, the Moabites and the Ammonites, may well have been monotheists in a polytheistic society throughout much of their history; for they are consistently identified in Scripture with this one god. But their view of God was warped. The god they worshiped was a god made in their own image: self-centered, self-seeking, and consequently a tyrant—an autocratic king who demanded the sacrifice of his subjects' most precious possessions, their children (II Kings 3:26–27; Jer. 19:5; Ezek. 16:20–21).

---

[10] According to I Kings 11:7, Solomon built an high place both for Chemosh and for Molech. This suggests that different images, and possibly different ceremonies, were used in the worship of these gods. Nevertheless, it is probable that titles such as *Chemosh*, *Molech*, and *Baal* were simply different names for one god worshiped in various ways in different countries. In Judges 11:24, Jephthah refers to Chemosh (generally called the god of the Moabites) as the god of the Ammonites—suggesting that the names could be interchanged. The prophet Jeremiah (32:35) associates Baal and Molech together. In meaning, the names *Chemosh* ("subduer"), *Molech* ("king"), and *Baal* ("lord") are similar.

How could it possibly be that Lot, whom the Bible calls "righteous" (II Pet. 2:7–8), left a legacy of child sacrifice? As impossible as it may seem, the roots of that legacy appeared in Lot's own home when, on that fateful night, he cried to the Sodomites, "I have two daughters which have not known man; let me, I pray you, bring them out unto you, and do ye to them as is good in your eyes" (Gen. 19:8).

And how could it be that Lot's legacy included a curse—unique in the Old Testament—upon the people he fathered? "An Ammonite or Moabite shall not enter into the congregation of the Lord; even to their tenth generation shall they not enter into the congregation of the Lord for ever" (Deut. 23:3). The roots of this legacy appeared in Lot himself. When Lot separated from his uncle Abraham, as congenial as the division appeared outwardly, it was in reality much more than that to Lot. For on that day when Lot began moving his flocks and his family, he also began distancing himself spiritually—from Abraham, the man of God, and from the people of God. No wonder, then, that the people Lot fathered, following his pattern, drifted further into spiritual darkness. What started in him as a congenial separation for business purposes became, in his descendants, a spirit of antagonism and even enmity.

CHAPTER NINETEEN

THE PILGRIM'S SECOND REGRESS

DID ABRAHAM EVER SEE LOT again? Probably not. Eventually, perhaps years later, the news would reach him that, in fact, Lot had escaped. But from his vantage point on the mountains of Hebron all he could see was smoke ascending "as the smoke of a furnace" from the whole valley of Siddim. God had remembered him and had sent his angels to rescue Lot and his family, but Abraham had no way of knowing that. His prayers, it appeared, had been futile.

But even against this smoking furnace of judgment, God's promise to Abraham and Sarah must have been shining now with a new radiance. The day before the judgment, the Lord had promised, "I will surely return to you at this time next year; and behold, Sarah your wife shall have a son" (Gen. 18:10, NASB). The judgment should not have dimmed but enhanced the promise of new life. In fact, the revelation of the judgment was given to Abraham to shed new and needed life on the importance of his fatherhood (18:19).

It was in the light of both judgment and promise, then, that Abraham began a new pilgrimage from the mountains of Hebron to the lowlands of the south (the Negev). The narrator tells us that he "journeyed ... toward the south country, and dwelled between Kadesh and Shur, and sojourned in Gerar" (20:1). This period of migration, which included traveling not less than one hundred fifty miles and sojourning in various places before settling in Gerar, may well have involved close to two months—two of the twelve months before the promised child was to be born. This suggests that the time for Sarah's conception might have been only a few weeks away.

Nevertheless, at this critical time, with the fulfillment of the long-awaited promise on the horizon, Abraham—and Sarah—experienced another lapse in faith. "And Abraham said of Sarah his wife, She is my sister: and Abimelech king of Gerar sent, and took Sarah" (Gen. 20:2).[1] But God graciously intervened. He appeared to Abimelech in a dream with an ominous message: "Behold, thou art but a dead man, for the woman which thou hast taken; for she is a man's wife."

When Abimelech awoke from this dream he was understandably seized both with fear and indignation. He summoned first his servants, who were terrified by the revelation (v. 8); then he summoned Abraham, who rationalized concerning his deceptiveness. As too often happens in the experience of God's people, the believer was more blinded by his penchant for pious rationalization than the unbeliever was by his unregenerate heart.

Abimelech's rebuke of Abraham, which was evidently in the presence of the king's servants (as the use of plurals suggests), is very instructive.

> What hast thou done unto us? and what have I offended [literally, sinned against] thee, that thou hast brought on me and on my kingdom a great sin? thou hast done deeds unto me that ought not to be done. . . . What sawest thou, that thou hast done this thing? (20:9*b*–10).

To the latter question, Abraham responded, "Because I thought, Surely the fear of God is not in this place; and they will slay me for my wife's sake" (v.11). On this count, the Patriarch's perception, in contrast to that of Abimelech, was crystal clear (in his dream, Abimelech had naively called his people "a righteous nation"). But in his next breath, Abraham reverted to his standard alibi.

---

[1] Some people have a problem with the fact that Abimelech desired to take her as his wife even though she was close to ninety years old. We must remember that Sarah was destined to live another thirty-seven years (Gen. 23:1) and that God had performed a vitalizing work in her body to prepare her for childbearing. Furthermore, Abimelech may have had "political" reasons for wanting Sarah as his wife. The Philistines had not yet been established as the dominant power in Palestine, and Abimelech must have seen in Abraham a powerful and potentially valuable ally (cf. 21:22–34).

And yet indeed she is my sister; she is the daughter of my father, but not the daughter of my mother; and she became my wife. And it came to pass, when God caused me to wander from my father's house, that I said unto her, This is thy kindness which thou shalt shew unto me; at every place whither we shall come, say of me, He is my brother (vv. 12–13).

Abimelech, however, couldn't digest such subtle sophistry. Still burdened by the greatness of his sin and by his fear of judgment, and now recognizing Abraham as a prophet of God (v. 7), he loaded the Patriarch with gifts, restored his wife, and gave him the liberty to dwell where he wished in his realm (vv. 14–15).

But Abimelech's fear and his heightened sensitivity about the sin of adultery carried him even further. In the process of restoring Sarah, this pagan king issued a rebuke worthy of a prophet of God. A literal, somewhat expanded, rendering of his admonishment to Sarah would be, "Lo, I have given a thousand pieces of silver to your brother. Lo, it is to you a covering for the eyes to all those with you; and by all you are being reasoned with" (v. 16).

There is a fine bit of irony in the king's reference to Sarah's husband as "your brother." Terrified at the thought of committing adultery in violation of the laws of the holy God he had just encountered, Abimelech saw through the rationalization Abraham and Sarah had attempted to foist upon him. Then, with forceful delicacy, he explains the purpose of the great sum of money he gave to her "brother."[2] It was to serve as a veil, he said, to cover the eyes of "all those with Sarah"—servants in her retinue who would justly look upon her actions as shameful.

The king's final statement, "by all you are being reasoned with," must have struck with disconcerting devastation at the rationalization that had deluded Sarah and Abraham. The expression translated *reasoned* is the same word (and grammatical form) Isaiah uses of the Lord's message to Israel, "Come now, and let us reason together, saith the Lord: though your sins be as scarlet, they shall be as white as snow; though they be red like crimson, they shall be as wool" (Isa. 1:18; cf. Job 23:7). Both the basic meaning of the word and the context of the passages in which it appears have judicial overtones. It pictures the presentation of arguments in a court of law. In effect, Abimelech is saying, "All—the host of witnesses

---

[2] Considering that a common assessment of a slave's value seems to have been thirty silver shekels (Exod. 21:32; Matt. 26:15), Abimelech's gift of a thousand shekels must have been viewed as enormous.

to which I have alluded—are reasoning with you, on an infinitely higher level than the feeble reasoning that led you to the threshold of adultery, that your actions were shameful." Sadly, it is often the case that relatively unenlightened pagans can see sin more clearly than believers who have allowed self-interest to becloud their minds (I Cor. 5:1).

It seems a strange twist in events that the one whose deceptiveness had nearly brought this pagan king to tragedy should be the means of his healing and restoration, but "Abraham prayed unto God: and God healed Abimelech, and his wife, and his maidservants; and they bare children. For the Lord had fast closed up all the wombs of the house of Abimelech, because of Sarah Abraham's wife" (Gen. 20:17–18). In his revelation to Abimelech, God had warned him, "Now therefore restore the man his wife; for he is a prophet, and he shall pray for thee, and thou shalt live" (v. 7). Evidently, the king's life and welfare depended not only on his restoring Sarah but on Abraham's prayers. Though Abraham had been weak in his faith, he still was a prophet of God—and consequently an instrument of healing and restoration.

The designations for God in these two verses are significant. Abraham prays in behalf of this pagan king to *Elohim*, the more universal designation for God—the Creator of the universe and the true God of all its inhabitants; and it is *Elohim* who heals Abimelech and his household. But it is *Yahweh*, the covenant God of Abraham and his seed, Who "had fast closed up all the wombs of the house of Abimelech, because of Sarah Abraham's wife." The faithful Lord, in His mercy, jealously protected the mother of the covenant child.

CHAPTER TWENTY

AN ANCHOR FOR THE SOUL

T HE HOPE OF THE COMING kingdom lies in the covenant promise. To inherit the promises of God, the writer of Hebrews tells us, two things are required: faith and patience. "That ye be not slothful, but followers of them who through faith and patience inherit the promises" (Heb. 6:12). His primary example of these qualities is Abraham. And by what means did Abraham, though (like Elijah) "subject to like passions as we are," develop such qualities? Abraham's faith and perseverance were grounded in the promise of God—in God's word—and ultimately, in God Himself. "For when God made promise to Abraham, because he could swear by no greater, he sware by himself, saying, Surely blessing I will bless thee, and multiplying I will multiply thee" (Heb. 6:13–14). That God "sware by himself" means that He vowed on the basis of His nature—Who He is—to fulfill His promise.

To the wavering Hebrew Christians, the inspired writer adds these remarkable words,

> Wherein God, willing more abundantly to shew unto the heirs of promise the immutability of his counsel, confirmed it by an oath: that by two immutable things, in which it was impossible for God to lie, we might have a strong consolation, who have fled for refuge to lay hold upon the hope set before

us: which hope we have as an anchor of the soul, both sure and stedfast." (6:17–19).

The "two immutable things" in the passage are God's promise and His oath. If it is inconceivable that God's promise should fail, it is all the more so that His promise sealed with an oath should fail. God, recognizing man's frailty, gave both that we might be strongly encouraged to lay hold of the hope He has set before us—which hope provides a sure and steadfast anchor for the soul. The word *hope* in the Bible doesn't have the connotations of doubt that our English word has. Both the Old and the New Testament words for *hope* denote the concept of eager, often joyful, anticipation.[1]

It was the Lord Who used providentially ordained circumstances to expose the weaknesses in the faith and patience of Abraham and Sarah. He did this so that He might strengthen the anchor of their souls. In Genesis 21, the Lord again strengthens this anchor by a joyful fulfillment (vv. 1–7), a painful separation (vv. 8–21), and a covenant with a pagan king (vv. 22–34).

A Promise Fulfilled

The announcement of the birth of Isaac puts strong emphasis on the fact that the birth came just as the Lord had promised and just at the time He had promised:

And the Lord visited Sarah *as he had said*, and the Lord did unto Sarah *as he had spoken*. For Sarah conceived, and bare Abraham a son in his old age, *at the set time of which God had spoken to him*" (21:1–2, emphasis added).

It is as if the inspired writer is making sure we recognize that this fulfillment is a prototype for the fulfillment of the promised Messiah.

The Messiah Himself testified, "Abraham rejoiced to see my day: and he saw it, and was glad" (John 8:56). Our Lord was undoubtedly alluding to the birth of Isaac. When Isaac was born, Abraham was ecstatic with joy;[2] but as jubilant as he must have been at this miraculous birth,

---

[1] The root of the Hebrew word (*qavah*) means "to wait or to look for with eager expectation." *TWOT*, 2:791 (see chap. 3, n. 3). The Greek word (*elpis*) generally translated *hope* in the New Testament most frequently describes "the happy anticipation of good." W. E. Vine, *An Expository Dictionary of New Testament Words* (London: Oliphants, Ltd., 1953), 2:232.

[2] The word translated *rejoiced* (*agalliao*) in John 8:56 means "to exult, rejoice exceedingly, be exceeding glad."

the spirit of prophecy carried him infinitely beyond the child he saw that day. He saw in Isaac God's pledge to fulfill the promise that in his seed all the families of the earth would be blessed—a promise that would be fulfilled ultimately through the Messiah. "These all died in faith, not having received the promises, but having seen them afar off, and were persuaded of them, and embraced them, and confessed that they were strangers and pilgrims on the earth" (Hebrews 11:13).

In accordance with the Lord's command (Gen. 17:19), Abraham named this promised son *Isaac* (*Yitzchaq*, "he is laughing"). The occasion of this command had been the renewal of the Lord's covenant promise to Abraham, thirteen years after his spiritual lapse in the matter of Hagar and Ishmael. At that time, Abraham may have thought that his lapse had broken the covenant and forfeited its blessings. So when the Lord appeared to him with the glorious news that His covenant was still in effect and that Sarah herself (Abraham's partner in the lapse) would bear the heir of the promise, he fell on his face and laughed (*yitzchaq*) in an ecstasy of joy.

As Keil well observes, this name was given to the child

> to indicate the nature of his birth and existence. For as [Abraham's] laughing sprang from the contrast between the idea and the reality; so through a miracle of grace the birth of Isaac gave effect to this contrast between the promise of God and the pledge of its fulfillment on the one hand, and the incapacity of Abraham for begetting children, and of Sarah for bearing them, on the other; and through this name, Isaac was designated as the fruit of omnipotent grace working against and above the forces of nature.[3]

The name also is prophetically appropriate for its representation of the dark side of the Lord's covenant promises. Before she conceived, Sarah had laughed in unbelief at the thought of such a miracle; and even after the miracle, Ishmael laughed in mockery (Gen. 18:12; 21:9).[4] The name *Isaac*, then, represented two diametrically opposed reactions to the Messianic prophecies: the humble and joyful embracing of the promise, or unbelief—itself a form of mockery. For Sarah, and for multitudes of others who have yielded to the "natural" impulse to distrust God's Word, God's grace turned the laughter of unbelief into the laughter of ecstatic joy in the new life received (21:5).

---

[3] *The Pentateuch*, 1:243 (see chap. 3, n. 2).

[4] In both cases a form of the word *yitzchaq* is used.

A Painful Separation

"And the child grew, and was weaned: and Abraham made a great feast the same day that Isaac was weaned. And Sarah saw the son of Hagar the Egyptian, which she had born unto Abraham, mocking" (21:8–9). In ancient times it was common for a child to be nursed at least until he was three years old.[5] Ishmael, then, must have been about seventeen years old at the time of this great feast.

The Expulsion of Hagar and Ishmael

The emphasis of the inspired writer here is striking; and by means of this emphasis we can enter somewhat into Sarah's feelings as she observed the incident that was to determine the circumstances of the destiny of Ishmael and his descendants. She saw Ishmael not as Abraham's son, as he is referred to elsewhere (e.g., Gen. 17:23, 25; 25:9, 12), but as "the son of Hagar the Egyptian, which she had born unto Abraham." When she saw this boy mocking her son on this special occasion, the old feelings of antagonism between her and her handmaid evidently returned with a vengeance.

Seventeen years before, the Angel of the Lord had admonished Hagar to return to her mistress and submit—humble herself—"under her hands" (16:9). The word translated *submit* in that passage is the same basic word the inspired writer uses to describe how Sarah "dealt hardly" with her servant (16:6; cf. 16:11). Hagar would have to humble herself, because after her servant's insubordination, Sarah would feel it necessary to assert her own authority.

Now, seventeen years later, Sarah saw Ishmael mocking her son, the heir of the promise; and the memory of that painful encounter years ago revived. Hagar had assumed on that occasion that since God had favored her (rather than her mistress) with a child of her master, this child—her child—would be the heir.

Did she still entertain such thoughts? Wasn't the attitude of her son a reflection of her own attitude? Certainly, she must have been indoctrinating

---

[5] II Macc. 7:27; cf. I Sam 1:22–28, where Hannah waits until the child Samuel was weaned before taking him to be left to serve at the tabernacle. Though there were dedicated women serving at the tabernacle and temple (Exod. 38:8; I Sam. 2:22; Luke 2:36–37), it seems likely that the child would have been not less than four or five years old at this time. Cf. the comments of John Peter Lange on Genesis 21:8. *Commentary on the Holy Scriptures: Genesis.* John Peter Lange, ed. (1868; repr. Grand Rapids: Zondervan, 1960), 1:457.

him all these years that he was the real, the rightful, heir. After all, he was older than Isaac—old enough, in fact, to be married and receive his inheritance. And the thought must have occurred to Sarah, "What if my husband dies before I do? What chance would Isaac have then?" Such questions, such thoughts, such poignant emotions must have been swirling within when her word erupted before Abraham, "Cast out this bondwoman and her son: for the son of this bondwoman shall not be heir with my son, even with Isaac" (v. 10b).

What a shock this must have been to Abraham! "And the thing was very grievous in Abraham's sight"—grievous because of his natural attachment to his son, and grievous also because of Hagar (vv. 11–12). Naturally it was painful for him to think of this long-time family servant being expelled from the family and having to fend for herself. But judging from the Lord's response to the Patriarch's grief (v. 13), Abraham's chief concern for Hagar was a concern he also shared. Expulsion from the family meant dashing any dreams for this beloved child's success. Abraham had undoubtedly envisioned this special handmaid and her son living harmoniously in the family, agreeing amicably that Ishmael's inheritance would be secondary, that the birthright belonged to Isaac.

But the spirit of Hagar and her son clashed fiercely with Abraham's irenic dream. For all these years, Ishmael had been the heir apparent. Should he now simply step aside and let this little infant disinherit him? His feisty spirit (Gen. 16:12), a copy of his mother's, wouldn't allow this. He would fight for his rights—or what he perceived to be his rights; and as a seventeen-year-old, fighting took the form of mockery. The mocking, evidently, was not simply a one-time action. The Hebrew word, a participle, suggests continual action—perhaps throughout the feast.[6] In fact, in the words of the apostle Paul, Ishmael "persecuted" Isaac (Gal. 4:29). Whatever the case, in Sarah's perception, Ishmael was a threat to her son's inheritance: "The son of this bondwoman shall not be heir with my son, even with Isaac" (Gen. 21:10b).

As grievous as all this was in Abraham's sight, Sarah's perception (however ignoble her thoughts may have been) was consistent with God's plan for the two sons:

---

[6] "We have rendered [the Hebrew word], 'was (always) mocking'—the 'always' to cover the frequentative participle." Leupold, Genesis, 2:599 (see chap. 6, n. 4).

And God said unto Abraham, Let it not be grievous in thy sight because of the lad, and because of thy bondwoman; in all that Sarah hath said unto thee, hearken unto her voice; for in Isaac shall thy seed be called. And also of the son of the bondwoman will I make a nation, because he is thy seed (vv. 12–13).

The Preservation of Hagar and Ishmael

Abraham was living at Beersheba at this time, and he prepared Hagar and Ishmael for the trip further south—perhaps to Egypt—by supplying them with water and bread.[7] Seventeen years before, when Hagar fled from her masters, she had traveled toward Egypt on one of the well-known caravan trails. On that occasion, though her journey began in Hebron (a full day's walk north of Beersheba), she evidently had no problem with supplies; for the Angel of the Lord found her by the fountain at Beer-lahai-roi (another two day's walk southwest of Beersheba). This time, however, Hagar and Ishmael "wandered in the wilderness of Beersheba" until their water was exhausted and Ishmael was near death. Why? What happened that made them lose their way?

Hagar was evidently distraught at this sudden turn in her fortunes. Furthermore, she may have been fearful of traveling on the caravan trail where she and her son might have been taken by a band of traders and sold into slavery. She evidently had in mind finding an oasis in the wilderness near Beersheba where she would be relatively safe. Abraham, as a wealthy and powerful "prince" (Gen. 23:6), would have been well known by Bedouin tribal leaders in the area. Perhaps Hagar hoped to link with one of these friends of her former master through the marriage of her son.

But above all, there was a providential reason Hagar lost her way in the wilderness. It was through a desperate time of crisis that she had first met the Angel of the Lord. Now she needed another crisis. She needed to learn anew the lesson she had learned at Beer-lahai-roi—that God is indeed the living One Who sees and responds to the needs of His people. And her son, whose name depicted God's willingness to hear those in need, needed to experience the message of Beer-lahai-roi.

Resigned now to her fate, Hagar "cast the child under one of the shrubs," sat down a good way off so that she would not see the agony of

---

[7] The word *bread* is no doubt used representatively here, as it often is (e.g., Gen. 3:19; 18:5; 28:20; Matt. 6:11), for food in general. In fact, considering Abraham's generous and benevolent character, he would probably supply Hagar with money (or valuables that could be used as money) as well. Furthermore, he would be very concerned that his beloved son be established well in his new life. Cf. Gen. 25:6.

his last moments, "lift up her voice, and wept" (v. 15–16). And while she was lifting up her voice and weeping—in loud, agonizing lamentation—God was compassionately listening to the feeble cries of her son. Was he uttering prayers or simply crying out in agony? It is impossible to say with certainty. The key message in the passage is that "God heard [*yishma*]"—as He had heard seventeen years before and as He memorialized in the name Ishmael, *Yishmael* (Gen. 16:11). God brought Hagar and Ishmael to this crisis to show them anew His love for them and their need to depend wholly on Him.

And God continued His preserving work in behalf of Hagar and Ishmael. "And God was with the lad; and he grew, and dwelt in the wilderness, and became an archer" (21:20). His mother returned to her roots and took him a wife out of Egypt, and "he dwelt in the wilderness of Paran."

Largely on the basis of the wording in the KJV, some have imagined that the account of Hagar and Ishmael in Genesis 21:14–18 presents chronological circumstances that are inconsistent with other references relating to Ishmael. In these verses, they say, Ishmael appears to be an infant, though the general narrative would require that at this time he must have been a boy in his teens. However, these objectors overlook or misconstrue key elements of the narrative. The word translated *child* (*yeled*) was used both of infants and of young men (cf. Gen. 21:17, where Ishmael is called a lad, *naar*). The same Hebrew word is used, for example, of Joseph when he was seventeen years old (Gen. 42:22). The word is also used of the young contemporaries of King Rehoboam whom he favored as his counselors (I Kings 12:8)—men who must have been in their thirties or early forties (I Kings 14:21). Likewise, the assumption that the words "she cast the child under one of the shrubs" (v. 15) and the command "lift up the lad, and hold [*chazaq*, "grasp, support"] him in thine hand" (v. 18) must refer to an infant is invalid. Compare Matthew 15:30, where people brought lame and otherwise afflicted adults "and cast them down at Jesus' feet," and Genesis 19:16, where "the men laid hold [*chazaq*] of Lot, his wife, and daughters to take them out of the city. Some have seen problems, also, with the fact that the young man Ishmael is at the point of death from thirst, whereas his mother appears to be relatively strong. But comparative instances appear often in history where young men (who may have considerable "brute strength") are not as able to endure deprivation as well as older men and women.

A Covenant Confirming God's Promise

Inherent in God's covenant blessing was the promise that through Abraham's seed "all the nations of the earth shall be blessed" (Gen. 18:18; cf. 22:18). This blessedness also suggested a certain prominence—and perhaps even dominance—among the nations, an inheritance later prophecies would confirm and enlarge (Gen. 27:29; Pss. 2:8–9; 72:8; Isa. 2:2–3; 9:7; Dan. 2:44–45; 7:18).

Over twenty years before, the Lord had given Abraham—and the citizens of the kingdom of this world—a sign of things to come through the miraculous defeat of the kings of Mesopotamia. Now, through a pagan Philistine king, He gave the Patriarch another confirmation of the ultimate completion of His covenant promise.

A year or so before, when he migrated to the area of Gerar in southern Philistia, Abraham thought, "Surely the fear of God is not in this place" (Gen. 20:11*b*). He had seen godless behavior elsewhere in Canaan— enough so that he determined not to take a wife for Isaac from there (24:3; cf. 15:16)—but he must have seen something in Philistia that really disturbed him. Notably, Abraham's journey to Philistia took place not long after he had witnessed the judgment of Sodom and Gomorrah, and he may well have seen things in Gerar that reminded him of the wickedness of the cities of the plain.

Now, remarkably, Abimelech, the Philistine king of Gerar, comes with the commanding general of his armies to Abraham and testifies, "God is with thee in all that thou doest" (21:22*b*). The fact that Abimelech brings Phichol, his commanding general, with him suggests that the king is concerned about Abraham's growing power—so much so that he perceives that Abraham's descendants will eventually gain control of Palestine.

How did this pagan king come to such a perceptive conclusion? Whence this wisdom? The fear of the Lord is the beginning of wisdom, even to unbelievers. In Abimelech's case, the fear of God seized him suddenly at night in a dream (20:3). In this terrifying atmosphere, with the threat of death hanging over him, he had been informed that Abraham was a man of God who, in a sense, already had power over him; for this prophet's prayers would make the difference between life and death in his household (20:7, 17).

By this time, furthermore, the reason for Abraham's original journey from Mesopotamia may well have been common knowledge. Abraham would have told his story often when his neighbors inquired about his God; with the fear of Abraham's God fresh on his mind, Abimelech probably inquired further of the Patriarch's experience with God and his knowledge of how best to worship Him.

He would have known, therefore, that God had promised the land of Canaan to Abraham and his descendants. No doubt he had also heard the amazing promise that through this man's seed all nations of the earth would be blessed. For a time, Abimelech may have regarded these promises with an unbeliever's natural skepticism—until news came of Isaac's miraculous birth. The news of this birth must have traveled far and wide in southern Canaan and Philistia; and when it reached the king's court in Gerar, it must have struck anew the chords of fear for the God of Abraham. It was "at that time" (21:22b) that the king came to the home of the Patriarch declaring, "God is with thee in all that thou doest."

No wonder, then, that Abimelech proposed that a covenant be established: "Now therefore swear unto me here by God that thou wilt not deal falsely with me, nor with my son, nor with my son's son: but according to the kindness that I have done unto thee, thou shalt do unto me, and to the land wherein thou hast sojourned" (21:23). But since Abimelech proposed to establish the covenant on honesty and kindness, Abraham called to his attention an obstacle that if left uncorrected would demolish the covenant at the outset: the king's servants had violently taken away a well from Abraham. The king pleaded that he had not been aware of this and that Abraham himself had said nothing of it previously. He then restored the well and, by the ceremonial reception of seven ewe lambs, confirmed that the well belonged to Abraham and his descendants. The name *Beersheba*, "well-of-the-seven-oath," memorialized the seven-lamb ceremony.[8]

---

[8] The Hebrew words for the number seven (*sheba*) and for the action of swearing or taking an oath (*shaba*) are from the same root. According to Brown, Driver, and Briggs, the Hebrew word for *swear* (*shava*), literally rendered, would probably be "to seven oneself or bind oneself by seven things." *The New Brown-Driver-Briggs-Gesenius Hebrew and English Lexicon* (Peabody, MA: Hendrickson, 1979), 989a. The Bible, as well as in other ancient literature, suggests the number seven had symbolic connotations of sacredness—probably because of the special use of this number in divine revelation (e.g., seven days of Creation, the Sabbath, etc.). Herodotus refers to the use of seven stones in the sacred oaths of the Arabs. *Histories* 3.8.

The value of this covenant was more in what it symbolized than in the goodwill it brought. Abraham was undoubtedly discerning enough to recognize that the sinfulness of the Philistines would soon neutralize the covenant. After all, the king himself, however noble his intentions were, had been ignorant of his servants' violent actions. And what of future generations? Isaac would one day find the Philistines oblivious to this covenant of peace (Gen. 26:15–21), and these people were destined to be the inveterate enemies of the seed of Abraham. But the covenant was nevertheless a pledge of God's marvelous promise to Abraham: the kingdom of God, which was to be established through his seed, would ultimately prevail.

CHAPTER TWENTY-ONE

"TAKE NOW THY SON, THINE ONLY SON"

YEARS BEFORE, ABRAHAM HAD REJOICED to see the day of the Messiah in the miraculous birth of his son Isaac (John 8:56). Now he hears a command from heaven that could not have brought rejoicing—but one that would bring an even more profound joy through an infinitely higher perspective of the Messiah.

> And it came to pass after these things, that God did tempt Abraham, and said unto him, Abraham: and he said, Behold, here I am. And he said, Take now thy son, thine only son Isaac, whom thou lovest, and get thee into the land of Moriah; and offer him there for a burnt offering upon one of the mountains which I will tell thee of (Gen. 22:1–2).

How much time does the expression "after these things" cover? The Hebrew language and culture commonly used this formula to depict a new stage in the events of a narrative—a stage that provided a significant development in the story. The formula did not in itself indicate close chronological sequence to the preceding events.

The major events of the preceding chapter (Gen. 21:1–33) took place about the time of the birth of Isaac. Then, the writer says, "Abraham sojourned in the Philistines' land many days" (v. 34). How many years are represented in these "many days"? Did Isaac grow to manhood during this time? Josephus suggests that he did; with some confidence, the

Jewish historian asserts that Isaac was twenty-five when Abraham was commanded to sacrifice him.[1] But the inspired writer gives us no hint of his age, and we must conclude from this silence that his age is of no real importance in the story.

The ordeal of Abraham was supremely a spiritual test—a means of proving and developing his relationship with the Lord. The issue with Abraham was much greater even than his willingness to yield to the Lord his beloved son Isaac—he had already gone through the agonizing trial of expelling from his home another beloved son, Ishmael. Infinitely beyond the issue of the loss of a son was his relationship with the Lord—his faith in the coming Messiah. Therefore, this crisis concerned the eternal issues of personal salvation and the saving work of the Lord throughout the earth. For from the beginning, the promise had been that all the families of the earth would be blessed in Abraham's Seed, the Messiah Whose day Abraham had rejoiced to see (John 8:56).

The central question Abraham had to face in this ordeal was, Is the word of God reliable? Can I indeed trust God to do what He promised He would do? Or are there times when it is better for me to rely on my own understanding? This has been the foundational issue for mankind ever since the Garden of Eden. Should I eat of the Tree of Knowledge—thereby declaring my right and power to govern my life as I choose? Or should I hope, instead, in the Tree of Life—acknowledging that I depend wholly on God for life and all that goes with it, including knowledge?

So Abraham had to reconcile seemingly contradictory commands: "Believe the promise that in Isaac shall the promised seed come, but slay Isaac, the son of the promise." The writer of Hebrews tells us:

> By faith Abraham, when he was tried, offered up Isaac: and he that had received the promises offered up his only begotten son, of whom it was said, That in Isaac shall thy seed be called: accounting that God was able to raise him up, even from the dead; from whence also he received him in a figure (Heb. 11:17–19).

The focus of Abraham's mind was on God's integrity and power to fulfill His promise. He had settled this issue, in fact, years before. When he heard the Lord promise that He would give life—the life of a new-born child—through his "dead body" and through that of Sarah's,

---

[1] *Antiquities* 1.13.2. Luther, with equal confidence, says Isaac was twenty-one at the time. *Commentary on Genesis*, 2:8.

being not weak in faith, he considered not his own body now dead, when he was about an hundred years old, neither yet the deadness of Sarah's womb: he staggered not at the promise of God through unbelief; but was strong in faith, giving glory to God; and being fully persuaded that, what he had promised, he was able also to perform (Rom. 4:19–21).

It is difficult to imagine the emotions that flooded Abraham's soul, and the thoughts that clamored within, when he heard these words from God. Were they actually words from God? That would be the first and most natural thought mere mortals would have in the face of such a command. But to Abraham the message was crystal clear. He never questioned its reality or its source. By direct address that elicited an oral response ("Abraham!" . . . "Behold, here I am"), God impressed upon the Patriarch the reality of this divine communication.

The command (literally rendered) is vibrant with emotion: "Abraham, I am asking you to take your son, your only one, whom you love, Isaac . . . and offer him . . . as a burnt offering."[2] These words convey to Abraham that God fully understood what He was asking of him. They reveal God's concern for the Patriarch.

There is an inherent danger in debating with others about clear commands of God—and all the more so if those commands involve personal sacrifice (see Gal. 1:15–17). Sooner or later the heart will enlist the mind in its cause, and would-be counselors who have not felt the emotional impact of the revelation will offer guidance that may be little more than human rationalization. "When thine eye is single," says the Wisdom of God, "thy whole body also is full of light." But, He warns, if your eye is evil—if you have double vision, seeking the things of God and the things of the world at the same time—you may find that the "light" in you is actually darkness (Luke 11:34–35).

Intuitively, Abraham knew this; and he evidently told Isaac—and Sarah—only the essence of the revelation: "God has commanded me to travel with Isaac to the land of Moriah for a special sacrifice." Since the revelation called for Isaac to go as well, Sarah would immediately see that this sacrifice must somehow relate to the covenant inheritance of her son; and the fact that the land of Moriah was in the territory of Melchizedek,

---

[2] The Hebrew word (*na*, translated "now" in the KJV) here rendered "I am asking you" could be translated "I pray you" or "I entreat you." This word adds softness and warmth to a command that could otherwise sound cold and harsh.

the priest of the Most High God, would add a special significance to the journey.

Abraham rose early the next morning and made full preparation for the sacrifice—even to the point of choosing and cutting the wood for the sacrificial fire. This was to be a time of worship, and there would be no unseemly searching for wood on the day of sacrifice. The journey itself was part of the trial. It would occupy two full days and part of a third.[3] This would give Abraham time to think about his decision. It would be no rash act. Though consecration doesn't require full understanding of God's call, it is never thoughtless nor even primarily emotional. With careful thought it counts the cost—though it doesn't concentrate on the cost (see Luke 14:28–33).

On the third day, "Abraham lifted up his eyes, and saw the place afar off" (Gen. 22:4). He would be about two miles north of Bethlehem, three miles south of Jerusalem (or "Salem," at that time).[4] The statement that he saw "the place" suggests that by this time the Lord had told Abraham which of the mountains in "the land of Moriah" would be the place of his sacrifice. It was to be on the mountain north of Salem. The Patriarch probably knew this area well. He had lived for a time near Bethel, twelve miles north; and for a number of years at Hebron, about a day's journey south. Salem was at the juncture of important caravan roads which ran southward from Shechem through Beersheba to Egypt and westward from the King's Highway in Transjordan to the Mediterranean coast.

Abraham's command to his servants to wait while he and Isaac went to worship would not have seemed strange to them. The special revelation to their master and the long trip made it obvious that this was a very special occasion. Furthermore, the ascent on which Salem and Mount Moriah stood, the domain of the illustrious priest-king, Melchizedek, must have been viewed as holy ground. It was natural that the priest of the family and the heir apparent should approach this place of worship alone. It was natural also that they not take the donkey—though it was bearing the wood for his sacrifice—with them to this holy place.

---

[3] From Beersheba to Jerusalem is about fifty airline miles. According to Edward Robinson, the trip on foot took over twenty hours. *Palestine*, vol. 3, app. 66–67 (see box in chap. 18).

[4] A traveler coming from Beersheba could not see Mount Moriah until he was about three miles from Jerusalem. *Wycliffe Historical Geography*, 160. The small hamlet of Bethlehem (called Ephrath, Gen. 35:16, 19) was situated as a potential caravan stop on the well-traveled Central Ridge Road leading from Shechem in the north through Beersheba to Egypt.

In Genesis, the burnt offering is mentioned only seven times (8:20; six times in this chapter). Later in the divine record (Lev. 1–7), the inspired writer presents the requirements for five types of offerings that serve as the basis of the sacrificial system of the covenant nation. These five sacrifices present a five-fold portrayal of the sacrificial work of the Redeemer (see chap. 8). They also can be applied, secondarily, to the believer (Rom. 12:1; Matt. 16:24; I John 4:17). Since divine revelation was given long before written revelation came through Moses, we may reasonably assume that the significance of the offerings in Genesis is consistent with that in the later written revelation. Of course, the written revelation of the Pentateuch, including Genesis, was not given until the time of Moses (c. 1445 BC). It would be natural, therefore, for the Jews to interpret the offerings in Genesis in the light of the revelation they had received through Moses.

Remember that in the Mosaic law, the burnt offering (Lev. 1; 6:8–13) was the only offering to consume the entire animal (except for its skin) on the altar. By laying his hands on the head of the animal (Lev. 1:4–5), the offerer identified himself with the animal, as if saying, "I am dying to myself and giving myself wholly to God." In freely offering his beloved son, Abraham illustrates not only the consecration of the believer but also the love of the Father—Who willingly and fully gave His only begotten Son.

It must have been with a silent sense of reverence that the servants watched their master, as the presiding priest, take the wood for the burnt offering and lay it upon the shoulders of his son Isaac. But they could not have sensed in that dark hour the wonder of divinely wrought faith in his commonplace instructions for them to "abide ye here with the ass; and I and the lad will go yonder and worship, and come again to you" (v. 5b).

"And he took the fire in his hand, and a knife; and they went"—and the inspired writer adds, significantly—"both of them together" (v. 6b). They were one in spirit, the sacrifice and the worshiper. But how fully did Abraham know they were one in spirit? Something of Isaac's spiritual nature must have been apparent as he was growing up, but he had never really been tested—and Abraham knew only too well that even what appears to be vibrant faith may collapse in the face of life-threatening trials. A veteran of many trials, he knew by experience that God is faithful— that, if necessary, He would raise his son from the dead in order to fulfill His promise—but could he make Isaac understand this?

They must have walked in silence for quite some time before Isaac asked, "Where is the lamb?" The form of the question and response suggests this. The words of the inspired writer are not those describing intermittent conversation. The interjection "My father" and the response "Here am I, my son" signify a break in silence—for Abraham a sudden interruption in the reverie of anguished thought.

This dramatic interchange may also suggest where they were when the question was asked. Isaac's question should not convey the idea that it suddenly occurred to him that they had forgotten to bring a sacrificial lamb. In fact, the general practice for worshipers traveling a great distance to a sacred place would be to purchase the sacrificial animal somewhere near the destination. Isaac must have expected his father to purchase a lamb in Salem, but his father (understandably, on this occasion) chose not to go through the city.

In keeping with the prophetic significance of this occasion, the Lord very likely guided the Patriarch to walk along the Kidron Valley, east of the city. Then, having bypassed the southern and eastern gates of the old city of Salem, just as the Mount of Olives began to appear on the right, he and Isaac would begin making their ascent north of the city walls toward Mount Moriah. The name *Moriah* means "the Lord sees"—He sees the need and provides for it.[5]

Now, as they began to walk up the mountain and away from the city, Isaac would have reason to ask about the provision of a lamb. Literally rendered, his father's answer turns his focus on God as the ever-faithful provider and includes a play on the name of the mountain they are climbing: "Elohim will be seeing to the lamb for the burnt offering, my son." These words, cryptic and mysterious, are nevertheless strangely satisfying to Isaac. The inspired writer again signifies the oneness of spirit of the priest and the sacrifice as they walk toward the holy place. "So they went both of them together" (v. 8).

The eastern ridge of what later became Jerusalem slopes upward from south to north so that the northern part of Mount Moriah, the place

---

[5] In English as well, "I see" can mean "I understand" with the connotation "I will take care of it." After God intervened and provided a ram as a substitute for Isaac, Abraham named the place *Jehovah-jireh*—a term that was afterwards explained to mean "In the mount of the Lord it shall be seen [provided]" (22:14; cf. the NASB translation). The inspired writer uses the same basic expression referring to Hagar's flight from Sarai. He tells us that Hagar called the Lord Who met with her and provided for her "God (Who) Sees Me" (*El Roi*) and the well at which God spoke with her was called Beer-lahai-roi, "The Well of the Living One Who Sees" (Gen. 16:13–14).

of the sacrifice and the place where the temple was to be built, was two hundred fifty feet higher than the southeastern hill on which Salem was located.[6] The climb from the Kidron Valley to the place of sacrifice would probably not take more than twenty minutes. So it was soon after Isaac had asked his question about the sacrifice that "they came to the place which God had told him of; and Abraham built an altar there, and laid the wood in order, and bound Isaac his son, and laid him on the altar upon the wood" (v. 9). We sense a spirit of reverent reticence in the inspired writer's description—all the more so as we reach these climactic moments. With the words "they came to the place which God had told him of," he tells us that we are now on holy ground. "And Abraham built an altar there and laid the wood in order"—*there* on that sacred spot, he emphasizes, and the wood was arranged *in order*, in careful observance of sacrificial propriety (cf. Lev. 1:7).

When did he tell Isaac that he was to be the sacrifice? A veil of silence covers this tremulous conversation—tremulous in spite of Abraham's unwavering faith.[7] The whole account, his every action, testifies that he was governed throughout by the integrity of God's word and by His power to fulfill His promise, "accounting that God was able to raise him up, even from the dead" (Heb. 11:19). Abraham must have told his son of his faith that God would certainly raise him from the dead and fulfill His promise. But however strong his faith was, he must have had some apprehension about his son's faith. How would he face the prospect of death? And even beyond the prospect of death, Isaac had to face the prospect that, after death, his body would be destroyed in the fires of the burnt offering. Would God—could God—resurrect him from these ashes?

---

[6] The eastern ridge on which Salem and Mount Moriah were located measured from north to south a little more than one-half mile. It was bounded on the east by the Kidron valley and on the west by the Tyropoeon ("Cheese-makers") valley. Salem (later the City of David) occupied the southern end of this ridge. It extended, north to south, about five hundred yards and encompassed about ten acres. From the northern wall of Salem to Moriah, where the temple would be built, was another five hundred yards or so. Eventually the city of Jerusalem, having expanded considerably to the west and north, would encompass about three hundred acres.

[7] Why do we have nothing in the account about Isaac's response to the thought of yielding himself to the sacrificial knife? This question is tied to the purpose of divine revelation. In every aspect of the divine revelation God selects the material in accordance with His message. In this case, the inspired writer tells us at the beginning of the story that God's revelation to Abraham was designed to test him. Concerning the sacrifice of the Son of God, it is wonderfully true that the Son gave Himself (Gal. 1:4; 2:20). But the ultimate message in this story is that "God so loved . . . that he gave his only begotten Son" (John 3:16).

In our translation, only a comma—representing in ordinary language only a slight pause—separates the preparation of the altar and wood from the binding of the sacrifice. But it may have been here that the father communicated to the son the true meaning of faith—and the true meaning of sacrifice. Then, having prepared the altar, having laid the wood in order, and having led his son into the deepest secrets of the blood sacrifice—the paradoxical mystery of the promise of life through death—Abraham "bound Isaac his son, and laid him on the altar upon the wood. And [he] stretched forth his hand, and took the knife to slay his son" (Gen. 22:9b–10).

Was Isaac a willing sacrifice? The twice-repeated statement "they went both of them together" (vv. 6, 8) leads us to believe that he was one in spirit with his father—and with his father's God—throughout. Why then was it necessary for Abraham to bind him? The sacredness of the sacrificial act demanded this. Just as the altar must be built with care and the wood laid in order, so the sacrifice must be bound—lest traumatic movement in the throes of death mar the message of the sacrifice. This was a holy sacrifice—the most sacred Abraham had ever offered—and he would not have dared to violate any aspect of the ritual. And in fulfilling this sacred ceremony, he prepared also for the prophetic fulfillment of the Antitype (Matt. 27:2).

If we follow the developing narrative in the light of its ultimate fulfillment (as I think we should), it was early afternoon by the time the preparations were finished for the sacrifice. It must have been in the morning of the third day, perhaps mid-morning, that Abraham, three miles from Mount Moriah, "lifted up his eyes, and saw the place afar off." It would have taken another three hours or so for him to reach the place of sacrifice and begin the preparations. In the time of our Lord, the evening sacrifice was ordinarily slain about 2:30 in the afternoon and offered about 3:30. At the Passover, the lamb was slain an hour earlier.[8] By ancient tradition, a sacrifice was always offered facing the sun.[9]

Abraham, then, would have been facing west when he reached out to take the knife to slay his son. And the ram that climbed Mount Moriah that day would have come silently behind him from the east—driven by a mysterious inward compulsion up the steep sides of the Kidron ravine,

---

[8] Edersheim, *The Temple*, 222 (see chap. 8, n. 5).

[9] Ibid., 161, footnote.

directly across from the Mount of Olives where the Lamb of God would one day begin a similar, yet different, journey.

At this fateful moment, the call came from heaven from the angel of the Lord, "Abraham, Abraham . . . lay not thine hand upon the lad, neither do thou any thing unto him: for now I know that thou fearest God, seeing thou hast not withheld thy son, thine only son from me" (Gen. 21:11b–12). The heavenly voice may have come from behind Abraham; for he evidently turned as he "lifted up his eyes, and looked, and behold behind him a ram caught in a thicket by his horns." As an invisible Hand had driven the ram up the mountain, so, providentially, that Hand moved him toward a thicket and with infinite care entangled his horns—and only his horns. Otherwise his body might have been cut and thus disqualified as an offering. It was a ram, a male sheep; for the burnt offering required a male sacrifice.

So as the voice from heaven drew Abraham's eyes to the substitute offering, he released his son from the cords that bound him and from the altar on which he had laid him—receiving him, the writer of Hebrews tells us, as "from the dead" (Heb. 11:19). Then "Abraham went and took the ram, and offered him up for a burnt offering in the stead of his son" (Gen. 22:13). And as he and his son worshiped, he saw anew that they were on ground made holy by the presence of the Lord Who sees and provides. So he gave that holy place a name, a name by which it was to be known for centuries to come: "Jehovah-jireh: as it is said to this day, In the mount of the Lord it shall be seen" (v. 14).

Full consecration brings yet fuller revelation. "If . . . thine eye be single, thy whole body shall be full of light" (Matt. 6:22b). And the angel of the Lord calls again out of heaven,

> By myself have I sworn, saith the Lord, for because thou hast done this thing, and hast not withheld thy son, thine only son: That in blessing I will bless thee, and in multiplying I will multiply thy seed as the stars of the heaven, and as the sand which is upon the sea shore; and thy seed shall possess the gate of his enemies; and in thy seed shall all the nations of the earth be blessed; because thou hast obeyed my voice (Gen. 21:16b–18).

The remarkable thing about this promise is that it includes an oath— a binding pledge from the God of truth Himself. Fundamentally, oaths, pledges, and written contracts speak of an inherent weakness in those making them. Ideally, honest men should not need written contracts or formal pledges in their dealings with one another; but in the real world, men who appear to be honest have often proven otherwise. When God makes a pledge, as he does here with Abraham, it is wholly a matter of grace, in concession to man's weakness.

The writer of Hebrews, commenting on this passage, says that "when God made promise to Abraham, because he could swear by no greater, he sware by himself." And He did this because He was

> willing more abundantly to shew unto the heirs of promise the immutability of his counsel . . . that by two immutable things [the promise and the oath], in which it was impossible for God to lie, we might have a strong consolation . . . to lay hold upon the hope set before us (Heb. 6:13, 17–18).

CHAPTER TWENTY-TWO

THE LEGACY OF ABRAHAM

HIS SUPREME ACT OF CONSECRATION brought Abraham a new revelation of the Lord. He saw Him now as Jehovah-jireh, the Lord Who sees and provides—not simply for man's daily needs, but for the needs of his soul. All that follows in Abraham's life and legacy flows from this revelation of the Lord of the covenant.

Strange as it may seem, it was in the glow of this revelation of the Lord as Jehovah-jireh that Abraham buried his wife Sarah (Gen. 23:1–20). Even in this devastating loss, the purchase of property in the Promised Land confirmed the promise of Jehovah-jireh. Over sixty years before, Abraham had been "called to go out into a place which he should after receive for an inheritance." He had obeyed the call, but all this time he had "sojourned in the land of promise, as in a strange country" (Heb. 11:8–9). Now for the first time he owned property in the land of his inheritance.

True, it was only a small field—and a field containing the grave of his wife and fellow heir, at that; and it was infinitely far removed from the place he had been looking for, "a city which hath foundations, whose builder and maker is God" (Heb. 11:10). But however small and insignificant this field must have seemed, it was nevertheless a pledge—a sure guarantee that God Himself would establish an everlasting kingdom in this land.

So it was after burying Sarah that Abraham began to prepare for the "godly seed" that was to come through Isaac for the fulfillment of the covenant promise.

"THAT HE MIGHT SEEK A GODLY SEED"

Shall I hide from Abraham that thing which I do; seeing that Abraham shall surely become a great and mighty nation, and all the nations of the earth shall be blessed in him? For I know him, that he will command his children and his household after him, and they shall keep the way of the Lord, to do justice and judgment; that the Lord may bring upon Abraham that which he hath spoken of him (Gen. 18:17b–19).

These words, spoken at another crisis in Abraham's life, reveal that "a godly seed" (Mal. 2:15) will be instrumental in the fulfillment of the covenant promise. Whether or not Abraham heard these words at the time the Lord spoke them, he nevertheless knew that obedience to the covenant was part of its fulfillment.[1]

Upon his return from Mount Moriah with Isaac, Abraham received news that at that moment in his life must have seemed supremely significant. On Mount Moriah, he had received his son back "in a figure" as one raised from the dead (Heb. 11:19). The news he received of his brother Nahor's family must have resonated in his soul as a sign of God's providential preparation of a wife—and fellow heir of the promise—for the son he had just received anew (Gen. 22:20–24). Now, three years after he buried his wife Sarah (cf. 23:1 with 25:20), Abraham sensed that the time had come to find a wife for Isaac.

The entire focus of the beautiful story that follows is on the gracious work of Jehovah-jireh to provide a godly seed for the fulfillment of His covenant. This was in Abraham's heart from the beginning. The inspired writer describes him as now "old, advanced in age" (24:1, NASB). He was not decrepit, as the wording of the King James Version ("well stricken in age") implies. He was destined to live another thirty-five years, take

---

[1] Here again we have one of the grand paradoxes of Scripture. The fulfillment of the Abrahamic Covenant is certain (Heb. 6:13–18); yet in some way, its fulfillment depends on man's obedience to it. Ultimately, God will fulfill His covenant through a godly seed in Israel—operating through the perfect obedience, and perfect sacrifice, of the Son of Man.

another wife, and have six children by her (25:1–2).[2] Rather, because he was advanced in age, he recognized that he needed to ensure the full inheritance of his son. As he looked about and reviewed his life, he was reminded that "the Lord had blessed Abraham in all things"—fulfilling His covenant promise (Gen. 12:2). It remained now for him to claim the final blessing, the promised seed.

The precautions Abraham took to ensure that his son would marry the right person were extraordinary. The eldest servant he called for the task must have been Eliezer of Damascus, the man he had once thought of as a potential heir (15:2–3). He had been in the service of Abraham now for some sixty-five years, the trusted steward of his household, "ruling over all that he had." As the story reveals, he was also a deeply devout man, one in spirit with Abraham.

The pledge the Patriarch requests of Eliezer speaks of the supreme importance of his mission.

> Put, I pray thee, thy hand under my thigh: and I will make thee swear by the Lord, the God of heaven, and the God of the earth, that thou shalt not take a wife unto my son of the daughters of the Canaanites, among whom I dwell: but thou shalt go unto my country, and to my kindred, and take a wife unto my son Isaac" (24:2b–4).

It also reveals that Abraham thought he might die before Eliezer accomplished his mission. The Lord had chosen to take Sarah, who was ten years younger than he. What reason did he have to believe that he would see the day of his son's wedding—or the seed God had promised? As it turned out, he was destined to live until the fifteenth year of his grandsons, Jacob and Esau.

---

[2] Keil holds that Abraham took Keturah as his concubine (Gen. 25:6; I Chron. 1:32) before Sarah died. He sees the fact that Abraham sent the sons of his concubines away during his lifetime as a problem. He argues that at the time of Abraham's death, the youngest sons of Keturah would be no more than twenty-five or thirty years old—too young for them to be sent from their father's house. "In those days," he says, "marriages were not generally contracted before the fortieth year." But as Keil himself acknowledges, this "difficulty . . . is not decisive." *The Pentateuch*, 1:261–262 (see chap. 3, n. 2). Is Keil's generalization concerning the common age of marriage in those days true? Though Isaac and Esau were forty years old when they married (Gen. 25:20; 26:34), we know that it became quite common in the ancient world for girls to be given in marriage between the ages of twelve and fourteen. When Shechem inquired through his father about marrying Dinah, Jacob's daughter would not have been over sixteen years old.

Keil acknowledges also that the fact that Keturah was a concubine is no valid argument favoring his position. It is natural to suppose that Abraham would not want to give another wife the same status as Sarah, the mother of the promised seed. Keturah may have been one of his servants and therefore would have the status of a concubine.

Eliezer was to solemnize his oath by putting his hand under his master's thigh, or loins. This symbolic act, which must have been commonly practiced in ancient times (see Gen. 47:29), had special reference to the descendants of the one requiring the pledge (cf. the use of the same Hebrew word in Gen. 46:26; Exod. 1:5; and Judges 8:30). In effect, the pledge was "I swear by all that is most precious in your life: your legacy to your children and descendants." It is virtually impossible for the modern mind to conceive of the solemnity of such a pledge in ancient times. To the ancients, success or failure in life depended on a person's legacy—on the number and prominence of his descendants and on the nobility of the name they inherited. For Abraham, however, this solemn pledge had more significance than his contemporaries could possibly have seen. Abraham saw—and no doubt Eliezer did as well—that the promised Seed, the Messiah, was destined to come from him.[3]

Abraham requires that Eliezer swear by the Lord, the God of the covenant, because this is a matter that pertains to the kingdom of God. But he expands this covenant designation to include "the God of heaven, and the God of the earth"; for the kingdom of God is to include all the nations of the earth, and it is to be the kingdom of heaven as well.

Abraham's desire for a godly seed demanded that he exclude the daughters of the Canaanites from consideration. From his years of living among them (Gen. 24:3), Abraham knew that they were a godless people (13:13; 20:11); and he knew by divine revelation that they would continue degenerating until judgment overtook them (15:16–21).[4] But he must also have known of Noah's prophetic curse on the Canaanites and of the Lord's special blessing on Shem (Gen. 9:25–27). Furthermore, Abraham would have been well aware of the rebellion of the Hamite Nimrod and of the revolt at the tower of Babel, which, according to ancient tradition, was instigated and led by Nimrod.[5] He had every reason, therefore, to make the stipulation "But thou shalt go unto my country, and to my kindred, and take a wife unto my son Isaac" (24:4).

---

[3] Even some orthodox interpreters seem reluctant to attribute to the Patriarchs much more than an obscure notion of a coming Messiah. Yet the promise of the coming Savior has its roots in the very dawn of history (Gen. 3:15).

[4] Abraham is undoubtedly using the term *Canaanite* in a generic sense to represent the various nations in the Promised Land. Likewise the Lord uses the term *Amorites*, a dominant people in Canaan at that time, as a representative designation for ten nations that will eventually be disinherited by Israel (Gen. 15:16, 19–21).

[5] Josephus, *Antiquities* 1.4.2.

In response, the wise servant seeks his master's will concerning possible obstacles he might face in accomplishing his mission. "Peradventure the woman will not be willing to follow me unto this land: must I needs bring thy son again unto the land from whence thou camest?" He recognizes that getting a woman to leave her family and travel into virtually another world to establish a home among strangers will not be easy. Since he would have known that Canaan was the Promised Land, he undoubtedly is thinking of Isaac staying only a short time in Haran to meet his future bride and her family. To this possibility—even to the thought of a temporary visit—Abraham responds with a stern "Beware thou that thou bring not my son thither again."

This is so important that he repeats the warning. He tells Eliezer, in effect, "If the woman absolutely refuses to come, you are released from my oath; only don't take my son to Haran." But between these two warnings, he appeals to his servant to have faith in the Lord of the covenant Who has so abundantly demonstrated His faithfulness for all these years. "The Lord God of heaven, which took me from my father's house, and from the land of my kindred, and which spake unto me, and that sware unto me, saying, Unto thy seed will I give this land; he shall send his angel before thee, and thou shalt take a wife unto my son from thence." Eliezer, now understanding his mission, and recognizing that only by faith in the Lord will his mission be accomplished, puts his hand under his master's thigh and pledges his fidelity (v. 9).

Having received his commission, the servant took ten camels, loaded with provisions for the trip and with gifts for the bride and her family. Here the inspired writer tells us again that this man was the steward in charge of all that his master owned, a reminder of the vital importance of this mission. As the Patriarch had entrusted his entire estate to this gifted and faithful servant, he now put in Eliezer's hands the welfare and future of his son—and much more; for the earthly progress of the kingdom of God was now in the hands of this servant. Eliezer must have realized this. At every move, he appeals to the Lord, the covenant God of his master; and at each stage of his progress, he radiates the spirit of grateful worship.

The five-hundred-mile trip from Beersheba to Haran would take three or four weeks.[6] The plan Eliezer followed when he and his entourage ar-

---

[6] Sarah died in Hebron (23:2). Evidently, not long after her death Abraham moved to Beersheba (24:62, 67).

rived in Haran is a beautiful illustration of the harmony between man and God when they walk together. His overall objective is simply to find God's will concerning the mission with which he had been entrusted— what is the Lord's judgment concerning a wife for his master's son?[7] Nevertheless, he assumed throughout that it was his responsibility to use his judgment in the search. "Commit thy works unto the Lord," declares the wisdom of God, "and thy thoughts shall be established" (Prov. 16:3b).

Thus, when he approached the city, "he made his camels to kneel down without the city by a well of water at the time of the evening, even the time that women go out to draw water" (Gen. 24:11). He settled at the well at a time he knew the women of the town would be coming. Then, in his heart (v. 45), he made his appeal to the Lord.

> O Lord God of my master Abraham, I pray thee, send me good speed this day, and shew kindness unto my master Abraham. Behold, I stand here by the well of water; and the daughters of the men of the city come out to draw water: and let it come to pass, that the damsel to whom I shall say, Let down thy pitcher, I pray thee, that I may drink; and she shall say, Drink, and I will give thy camels drink also: let the same be she that thou hast appointed for thy servant Isaac; and thereby shall I know that thou hast shewed kindness unto my master" (vv. 12–14).

Before he had finished this prayer, Rebekah came with her pitcher on her shoulder and went immediately down the steps to the well. In his prayer, Eliezer had established a spirit of self-sacrificing kindness as the primary quality he sought. Would the woman not only fulfill his request for a drink (a common and expected courtesy) but offer to draw water for his camels also? This well, as was typical of the wells of the East in that day, was evidently in a gully, which would require Rebekah to go down and up steps each time she drew water (v. 16). This man had ten camels, and he had servants with him (v. 32). It would have been quite easy for Rebekah to assume that the man's servants would take care of him. Her offer, therefore, revealed a rare quality of character. "Rebekah's address to the servant will be given you in the exact idiom by the first gentle Rebekah you ask water from; but I have never found any young lady so generous as this fair daughter of Bethuel."[8]

---

[7] The word translated "appointed" in v. 14 (yakach) denotes "to judge, decide."

[8] Thomson, *The Land and Book* (Grand Rapids: Baker, 1955), 592.

But he evidently had another criterion in mind. He assumed it was his prerogative and responsibility to choose which woman to ask, so he chose one who was very beautiful. Was this a lapse into human carnality? Not really. In his prayer, his focus was upon the inward qualities of character this woman must have. He said nothing in his prayer about beauty. Nevertheless, he was seeking a wife for his master's son; and, of course, he wanted to please both his master and Isaac. Furthermore, there was a sense in which the outward beauty of the woman would be to him an indication that God had providentially prepared her for Isaac. After all, the Messiah—the King—was to come from her line.[9]

As remarkable as Rebekah's magnanimous response was, Eliezer seems to have remained reverently cautious. His commission was to find a wife among Abraham's kindred (v. 4), and he did not yet know the identity of this generous woman. Nevertheless, he was caught up in wonder of the possibility that God had graciously heard his prayer. He watched her intently and thoughtfully as time and again she went down and up the steps of the well until, at last, the camels ceased drinking.

It appears that with each pitcher Rebekah emptied into the trough, Eliezer's confidence increased; for when she was finished, he presented her with a golden nose ring and two golden bracelets—gifts of enormous value—before he knew whose daughter she was. When Rebekah identified herself as the granddaughter of Nahor, Abraham's brother,[10] Eliezer "bowed down his head, and worshipped the Lord. And he said, Blessed be the Lord God of my master Abraham, who hath not left destitute my master of his mercy and his truth: I being in the way, the Lord led me to the house of my master's brethren" (Gen. 24:26–27).

The man is so filled with wonder at the thought of God's mercy and direction that he publicly bows and audibly worships the Lord—in fact, he chooses this method, rather than direct communication, to inform

---

[9] Human kings were to come from this line as well. In ancient times, there were physical characteristics that people generally expected of a king. It is remarkable how little the Bible says (in contrast with virtually all other literature) about the physical characteristics of its subjects. When the inspired writers do describe physical characteristics, there is always a contextual reason for it. In the cases of Saul, David, and Esther, for example, their physical qualities were evidence of God's providential preparation of them for the positions they were to fill.

[10] It is noteworthy that Rebekah specifically identifies her grandmother as Milcah (cf. Gen. 11:29; 22:20). This distinguishes her from the children of Nahor's concubine (22:24). Had she been the daughter of a concubine, she would likely have had the status of a slave and perhaps would not have been viewed (legally) as a true relative of Abraham.

The fact that the inspired account mentions that the nose ring (not "earring," as in the KJV) and bracelets were of gold and specifies their weight tells us that they were of great value. An Old Testament shekel was about 0.4 of an ounce. On this basis, if we assume a value of $550 per ounce (a recent market price), the nose ring would be worth about $110 and the bracelets (assuming both together weighed 10 shekels) would be worth close to $2200. However, as impressive as these amounts are, we still have no idea of their relative value in that culture at that time. Perhaps the best we can do in this regard is to think in terms of the days a common laborer would have to work to earn the roughly $2300 these two gifts would cost. Evidently, a day's wage in New Testament times was one denarius (Matt. 20:2); and though this era is about two thousand years later, we will use this wage as our standard. The Roman denarius was a silver coin weighing .1371 of an ounce. In a recent market price, silver was valued at $10 an ounce. On this basis, a denarius earned for a day's wage would be worth about $1.35. This means that if a laborer worked three hundred days a year, he would have to work over five years to earn the value of the gifts Eliezer gave to Rebekah!

Rebekah that he has been sent by her grandfather's brother, Abraham. Rebekah, of course overwhelmed and ecstatic at this news, immediately runs to "her mother's house" (the women's quarters of the family house) and tells all that had happened, including Eliezer's song of praise.

Rebekah's brother, Laban, rushes to see his sister and get the word firsthand, and he is struck first by the elegant and expensive jewelry she is wearing. She then repeats her story to him, and he, knowing that the man she has met must have at his disposal immense wealth, runs to meet him. Taking up the words he has heard from Rebekah, he presents his invitation, "Come in, thou blessed of the Lord; wherefore standest thou without? for I have prepared the house, and room for the camels" (v. 31). We can almost see the glitter of gold in Laban's eyes as he says these words (cf. v. 30; 31:7, 41). Undoubtedly, his blessing in the name of Yahweh was based on what he had heard from Rebekah.[11]

---

[11] Being polytheistic (Gen. 31:30–34; Josh. 24:15, NASB), Laban could pronounce a blessing in the name of Yahweh as a matter of courtesy and respect for the god of another territory. However, knowing what we know about Laban, it seems more likely that his major objective was to impress this important man. In all probability, Laban surmised that Eliezer's mission was to find a wife for Abraham's son. Why else would Abraham send his chief servant, laden with expensive gifts, on a five-hundred-mile journey to the home of his relatives? Laban, whose family was probably not wealthy (Gen. 30:30), wanted to make sure he and his family did not miss this golden opportunity.

Eliezer, however, was so intent on fulfilling his mission that he refused to eat until he had explained his commission (v. 33). This was not the usual way of doing business in that culture. Customarily, all present would have spent a considerable amount of time eating, inquiring about each other's health and families, and sharing anecdotes—all with outward aplomb and inward excitement; for everyone would suspect the purpose of this visiting delegation.

So whatever cultural shock Eliezer may have produced, we can almost hear a collective sigh of relief in the words of his host, "Say on." Eliezer then gives a vivid account of his commission, of the Lord's blessing on his master's household, and of the marvelous way in which the Lord led him to Rebekah. The story of Yahweh's call of Abraham from Ur of Chaldees would certainly have been a part of Bethuel's family tradition. Through Terah, the entire clan had been influenced by this call, though only Abraham fully followed the Lord and owned Him as the one true God of the universe. Eliezer's emphasis throughout—without the slightest trace of apology or deference to the gods of his hosts—is on this one true God of glory. "And now," he concludes, "if ye will deal kindly and truly with my master, tell me: and if not, tell me; that I may turn to the right hand, or to the left" (v. 49).

In behalf of his master, he asks for a response characterized by both mercy and truth. "Deal kindly with my master," he says, "and deal with him in accordance with the evidence you have heard." Even with their obscure view of God, Laban and Bethuel are compelled by the evidence to answer, "The thing proceedeth from the Lord: we cannot speak unto thee bad or good" (v. 50).[12] Eliezer is again overwhelmed at the goodness of the Lord in fulfilling his request—so much so that right there, in the midst of this all-important conference, he worshiped the Lord, "bowing himself to the earth."

The celebration that followed would be expected on such an occasion. They must have celebrated late into the night. It was already evening when Eliezer first met Rebekah; and they would have lingered, oriental-style, over the meal—even more so as the gifts were given and received. If

---

[12] Laban's very active part in the negotiations is consistent with ancient customs (cf. Gen. 34:11, 25; Judges 21:22; II Sam. 13:22). As the full brother of Rebekah, he would be expected to assume the responsibility for her welfare. This was particularly important in a polygamous society, in which a father might show favor or disfavor toward his children according to his regard or disregard for their mothers.

the servant's introductory gifts to Rebekah at the well were exquisite and invaluable, we can only imagine what his betrothal gifts were like.

Ordinarily a celebration of this type would last several days—and all the more so in this case, where people have come from a great distance, and especially since the arrangements call for the daughter to move to a distant place and probably never see her family again. It must have come as a shock, and almost as an affront, therefore, when Eliezer the very next morning asked to be sent away. To the natural objections of Rebekah's mother and brother, the servant again appealed to the work of the Lord. In effect, he was saying, "The Lord Himself by His blessing has revealed His timing in this matter." He must also have thought of the possibility that his master might not live much longer.[13]

It may well have been after an extended discussion that Laban and his mother yielded on the condition that Rebekah herself make the decision whether to leave that day. Rebekah, no doubt aware of the conversation and sensitive now to the marvelous work of the Lord through this godly servant, consented to go with him. The family's parting blessing on Rebekah, though given by the self-seeking Laban (the spokesman for the household), was an echo of the Lord's covenant blessing on the seed of Abraham: "Thou art our sister, be thou the mother of thousands of millions, and let thy seed possess the gate of those which hate them" (v. 60).

THE FULFILLMENT

A few delicate touches bring this beautiful story to a fitting consummation. "And Isaac came from the way of the well Lahai-roi; for he dwelt in the south country" (v. 62). What is the significance of this bit of information? This story is designed to reveal the Lord's gracious work in providing a "godly seed" (Mal. 2:15) to fulfill His promise to Abraham. It is in connection with this objective that the writer tells us that Isaac had just returned from a trip to Beer-lahai-roi, the well at which the Lord revealed

---

[13] Abraham himself must have had this thought in mind when he commissioned his servant. His wife, ten years younger than he, had died three years before. It was with this possibility in mind, no doubt, that Eliezer asked whether he should take Isaac to Haran if the woman refused to follow him. Had he assuredly known that Abraham would be alive when he returned, such a question would be unnecessary, for he simply could have asked his master what to do. Likewise, Abraham's warning against taking Isaac there contemplates the same possibility of his not being alive when Eliezer returned.

Himself to Hagar as the "Living One Who Sees and Provides" (Gen. 16:13–14).

Isaac must have heard the story of Beer-lahai-roi often from his father, and eventually he so identified with its message that he evidently made pilgrimages to this sacred place from time to time.[14] This place would have all the more significance to Isaac because at his sacrifice on Mount Moriah he had, as Hagar, seen God as the Living One Who Sees and Provides; for the names *Moriah* and *Jehovah-jireh* (22:2, 14) both include the concept of seeing or providing depicted in the name *Beer-lahai-roi* (in three forms of the word *raah*, "to see, provide"). To Isaac, therefore, the message of Beer-lahai-roi must have been integrally tied to the gracious redemptive work of the promised Messiah.

The fact that the inspired writer connects Isaac's return from Beer-lahai-roi with his going out into the field to meditate suggests that he was absorbed in his meditation with the message of that sacred place—and, by extension, with the message of Mount Moriah. Of course he knew that his father's servant would be coming soon with his bride, but the combination of thoughts here suggests that he would see in her much more than a companion and mother of his children. He would see in her the love of the Living One Who Sees and Provides.

Then, with his veiled bride before him, the servant "told Isaac all things that he had done"—gave a detailed and reverent account of the Lord's guidance and provision that must have echoed in Isaac the words of Rebekah's family, "The thing proceedeth from the Lord." "And Isaac brought her into his mother Sarah's tent, and took Rebekah, and she became his wife; and he loved her: and Isaac was comforted after his mother's death." This closing comment is more than just a beautiful account of the consummation of the marriage. It tells us that Rebekah did indeed continue the legacy of Abraham and Sarah—that God had chosen her, as He had Sarah, to bear the promised seed that would link the nations of the world to the Messiah.

---

[14] The writer's comment "for he dwelt in the south country" (24:62) tells us that Isaac was near enough to make such trips (not that he was now living apart from his father, a circumstance that v. 67 rules against). Three years before, when Abraham buried Sarah, the clan had been living at Hebron. This notice tells us that they had now moved back to the south country, probably with Beersheba as their central base. Beersheba is a two-day journey (fifty-five miles) from Beer-lahai-roi, but the writer's use of the more general term "south country" (*Negev*) suggests that grazing the flocks might have periodically brought them closer to this special oasis.

ABRAHAM'S LEGACY IN THE EAST

The closing years of Abraham's life seem anticlimactic—almost to the point of tarnishing some of the luster of this man's walk of faith. What are we to make of the statement "Then again Abraham took a wife, and her name was Keturah"? And what are we to make of the fact that this woman bore Abraham six sons who, with their descendants, settled in "the east country"? How does all this tie in with the eternal covenant the Lord established through Abraham? How do these events develop the story of Abraham as the father of all who believe and as the prototype of the prince of God, the man who is destined to reign with God?

Does Keturah represent a lapse in Abraham's life? She was, the inspired writers tell us, a concubine (Gen. 25:6: I Chron. 1:32)—a woman, often a servant, who did not have the inheritance rights of a wife. Was she, as some interpreters say (e.g., Keil), taken as a concubine while Sarah was still alive?

We should notice first that the inspired writers do not even broach the possibility of wrongdoing concerning the marriage. Secondly, if we read the text just as it stands the most natural interpretation would be that Abraham married Keturah after Sarah died. The expression translated "then again" (*asaph*, literally "he added") is a Hebrew idiom commonly depicting a sequential event (e.g., Gen. 4:2, 12; 8:10, 12; 18:29; 38:5). Third, the entire story of Abraham indicates that he was committed in spirit to monogamy—so much so that he took Hagar only at the urging of his wife.

> Since the patriarch's body at 100 years was practically dead, it is almost certain that his marriage with Keturah took place after the renewal of his powers; and it is easier to suppose that his physical vigour remained for some years after Sarah's death than that, with his former experience of concubinage, and his parental joy in the birth of Isaac, he should add a second wife while Sarah lived.[15]

What, then, is the significance of this addendum to Abraham's life? In His covenant promise to the Patriarch, the Lord not only declared that He would bless Abraham and give the Promised Land to his seed; but He promised also that through him and His seed "all families of the earth" would be blessed. One writer suggests that all the promises of

---

[15] *The Pulpit Commentary* (Grand Rapids: Eerdmans, 1961), 1:313.

the Abrahamic Covenant could be arranged under two main headings he calls "the top and bottom line" of the covenant promise.[16] The *top line* focuses on Israel and the Promised Land. The *bottom line* of the covenant promise gives the ultimate purpose for the Abrahamic Covenant: to reach all nations. In reality, the covenant was narrowed to the line of Abraham in order that it might be broadened to reach the entire world.

But what of these six sons of Abraham by Keturah? In what way did their relationship with Abraham affect their spiritual destiny? We must start, I think, with the biblical revelation of Genesis 18:17–19.

> And the Lord said, Shall I hide from Abraham that thing which I do; seeing that Abraham shall surely become a great and mighty nation, and all the nations of the earth shall be blessed in him? For I know him, that he will command his children and his household after him, and they shall keep the way of the Lord, to do justice and judgment; that the Lord may bring upon Abraham that which he hath spoken of him.

This passage cannot be limited to Isaac and Ishmael. It is by virtue of Abraham's relationship with the Lord that he will "command his children and his household after him." It must therefore apply to all his children and "his household," which would include all under his authority, including his servants.

But in light of the history of the "children of the east" (identified often under the generic term *Arabs*), can we really say that they were taught in the way of the Lord? We could ask the same question concerning Israel—or, for that matter, concerning the entire human race. Of the Jews, favored as they were, Paul declared, "But after thy hardness and impenitent heart treasurest up unto thyself wrath against the day of wrath and revelation of the righteous judgment of God"; and of the Gentiles, the same inspired writer declares that they "knew God" yet chose not to glorify Him as God (Rom. 2:5; 1:21).

Whatever the response of men may be, the fundamental message of the Abrahamic Covenant is that God's redemptive plan is designed to reach all people. Abraham's giving gifts to his children by Keturah and sending them to live in the east was perfectly consistent with the covenant promise, for the covenant called for the preservation of the messianic seed through Isaac—without which there would be no salvation for the nations.

---

[16] Richardson, *Eternity in Their Hearts*, 153–66 (see chap. 2, n. 5).

LIFE: THE SUPREME LEGACY

Emerson once said, "There is properly no history, only biography." History is the story of people. Bible history is the story of God's working in and through people to fulfill their royal destiny. The inspired biography of Abraham, "the father of us all" (Rom. 4:16), is the prototypical story of the believer's pilgrimage toward the royal city.

Two symbols mark Abraham's life: a tent and an altar. The tent represented his calling as a stranger and pilgrim in a land he would one day inherit. The altar testified of his faith in God, Who had called him to this inheritance (Heb. 11:13). The tent gave meaning to the altar and the altar to the tent. Had there been no tent, the altar he built at each new home would have represented only the religious ritual of an empty soul. Had there been no altar, the tent would have been no more than a dreary reminder of the wanderings of an unsatisfied soul. It was the fires of the altar that warmed the pilgrim's tent with the radiance of life. And it was those fires that forged crowns for the pilgrim in the tent who "looked for a city which hath foundations, whose builder and maker is God" (Heb. 11:10).

Abraham died in faith, looking joyfully toward the heavenly city of God. But some fourteen hundred years later, a young man who had followed his father Abraham's path of faith found himself tearfully looking back at the scattered rubble of the earthly city of God. As Daniel walked in chains toward the city of Nimrod that Abraham had passed in the first glow of his pilgrim journey, surely the exiled psalmist's words would have echoed in his aching heart: "How shall we sing the Lord's song in a strange land?" (Ps. 137:4).

But Daniel did learn to sing the Lord's song in that strange land. Beyond and above the walls of Babylon, he saw the city and kingdom his father Abraham had looked for. In visions born of the darkest of nights, Daniel saw in panorama the fall of the kingdom of the world, the victory of the kingdom of God—and the coronation of the King of kings and His heirs.

PART FOUR

THE FINAL WAR

And there was war in heaven . . .

And there was war in heaven: Michael and his angels fought against the dragon; and the dragon fought and his angels, and prevailed not; neither was their place found any more in heaven. And the great dragon was cast out, that old serpent, called the Devil, and Satan, which deceiveth the whole world: he was cast out into the earth, and his angels were cast out with him. And I heard a loud voice saying in heaven, Now is come salvation, and strength, and the kingdom of our God, and the power of his Christ: for the accuser of our brethren is cast down, which accused them before our God day and night. And they overcame him by the blood of the Lamb, and by the word of their testimony; and they loved not their lives unto the death.

Revelation 12:7–11

THE WORDS OF REVELATION 12:7–11 are set against a paradoxical backdrop. John, the writer, is on the Isle of Patmos as a prisoner of Rome. He is writing to seven feeble enclaves in Rome's vast empire—little beleaguered camps of "foreigners" who serve another King and look for another kingdom. What an unlikely scenario for an announcement of victory!

These chapters reveal the final victory of the kingdom of God over the kingdom of the world, and, as a consequence of that victory, the ultimate fulfillment of God's purpose for man. God's revelation of this final victory was not given simply to comfort the people of God. It was given to make them conquerors in their earthly warfare.

Overcoming is one of the major themes of the book of Revelation. Again and again the inspired writer admonishes the saints to conquer in their earthly battles. Of the twenty-eight times the word *nikao*, "conquer," appears in the New Testament, fifteen are in this final book.

Our victory is assured because the Lamb of God has prevailed to conquer sin and to open the seals of judgment against His enemies (Rev. 5:5–6), and because this same Lamb is King of kings, the supreme Sovereign of the universe (Rev. 17:14). The certainty of final victory is the way kingdom saints achieve the interim victories of this life.

CHAPTER TWENTY-THREE

A PROPHETIC PROFILE OF THE KINGDOM OF THE WORLD

DANIEL WAS PROBABLY NOT MORE than fifteen years old when he was taken to Babylon, along with other promising young men of the nobility of Judah, to be prepared for service in King Nebuchadnezzar's court.[1] He was destined to live into the reign of Cyrus, king of Persia. He witnessed both the rise and the fall of the golden city, the capital and prototype of the kingdom of the world. But Daniel also "had understanding in all visions and dreams"; and as a prophet, he saw far beyond the earthly city in which he served. From his vantage point in the royal courts of world empires, God gave him in two remarkable visions a panoramic profile of the kingdom of the world. He received the first of these prophetic visions (Dan. 2) while he was still in his teens, having just completed his three-year training period. The second (Dan. 7) came over fifty years later, when he was close to seventy.

As a young teenager, Daniel was taken captive by the kingdom of the world. Even as a spiritually sensitive young man, he could not help but feel the power and influence of this diabolical kingdom on his soul. The philosophy and spirit of Babylon pervaded everything and, it seemed,

---

[1] According to Plato (*Alcibiades* 1:121), the education of Persian youths for the king's service began at fourteen years; and according to Xenophon (*Cyropaedia* 1:2), at seventeen these young men were capable of entering the service of the king. The Babylonian system was likely similar.

Nebuchadnezzar was appointed king September 7, 605 BC, after the death of his father in August. Daniel and his friends were taken captive when Jerusalem fell to the Babylonians in the summer of 605 BC. Their three-year training period probably began in September of 605 BC. According to Daniel 2:1, Nebuchadnezzar's dream came in the second year of his reign. At first glance, it would appear from this that Daniel had not yet finished his training period when he was called to interpret the king's dream. However, in accordance with a custom commonly followed in ancient times, a new king's accession year was viewed as belonging to his predecessor and the first year of his reign would be reckoned as beginning the year following the year he assumed the throne. This would mean that Nebuchadnezzar's first regnal year would be from 604 to 603 BC and his second regnal year from 603 to 602 BC. Finegan's *Handbook of Biblical Chronology*, 252–53, has a good discussion of the dates of Nebuchadnezzar's accession and reign.

In 602 BC, then, Daniel and his friends would have just completed their three-year training period. A comparison of Daniel 1:17–20 and 2:48 supports the interpretation that Daniel had completed his training before he interpreted the king's dream. The four friends were examined and approved by the king at the end of their training program (1:17–20). Immediately after the prophet had interpreted his dream, "then the king made Daniel a great man, and gave him many great gifts, and made him ruler over the whole province of Babylon, and chief of the governors over all the wise men of Babylon." Daniel then requested that his three friends also be given places of leadership (2:48–49)—all of which indicates that the four had completed their training by this time.

everybody—including many who professed to be children of God. Nevertheless, not everything he saw in Babylon was blatantly wicked. He must have seen much in his education that was good and valuable, and he certainly experienced kindness and congeniality from his captors. And he would have heard some lofty ideals expressed, some appreciation for justice and even some reverential regard for spiritual things.

We are also living in "Babylon" and witnessing daily the same things Daniel experienced. So how do we sort things out? How do we live in the world without being of the world? We begin by getting our perspective in line with God's. As with Nebuchadnezzar, the magicians and wise men of this world can't help us with that problem—but Daniel can. His two visions give us an overview of the battlefield and the perspective we need to win the war. In these visions, the prophet seeks to align our perspective with God's as to the nature and doom of the kingdom of the world. In its nature it is one kingdom, though it appears in the world in different forms. Nevertheless, as powerful and all-consuming as this kingdom seems, its doom is sealed. The heavenly King will demolish it and replace it with His own kingdom.

In the process of these two revelations, Daniel presents a fine irony similar to another prophet's response to the impudent disavowal of God's authority by the kings of the earth: "He that sitteth in the heavens shall laugh: the Lord shall have them in derision" (Ps. 2:4). In the first vision, Daniel sees (through the dream of an earthly king) the kingdom of the world as the reign of an ideal, awesome man (Dan. 2:31–40). In the second, he sees (through a direct revelation from God) the kingdom of the world as the reign of degenerate men of bestial, brutish nature. However, in the destruction of this kingdom, he sees the "ideal man" destroyed—not, as you would expect, by the regal Ancient of Days Himself—but by a "mere" stone. On the other hand, in the second vision Daniel sees the brutish beast destroyed—not, as you would expect, by a stone, but by the Ancient of Days, Who then commissions the Son of Man to reign as King of kings (7:9–14).

THE NATURE OF THE KINGDOM OF THE WORLD

One Kingdom in Different Forms

When I first came across the marvelous prophecy imbedded in Nebuchadnezzar's dream, I was absolutely fascinated by it. Here was Daniel, in 600 or so BC, telling the king about the nature and characteristics of world empires (Babylon, Persia, Greece, and Rome) for centuries to come. Empires that we had to learn about from musty old history tomes, Daniel saw in a dream before they ever came into existence! But in my fascination with all this, I missed an essential part of the message of the vision. The great and awesome statue Nebuchadnezzar saw in his dream, though it represented the kingdoms of many centuries to come, was *one* statue. It stood as one; and when it fell, it all fell together.

This tells us something about the nature of the kingdom of the world. Though it may exist on the earth in different forms in various ages, it is nevertheless one kingdom. It has, whatever form it may take, one ruling prince and one ruling philosophy. Its ruling prince is the Devil himself. Its ruling philosophy is that man, by means of the Tree of Knowledge, may reign as a god in his own right. If he will but submit himself to the prince of this world, he will ultimately come into his full inheritance. Its ruling impulses are the lust of the flesh, the lust of the eyes, and the pride of life.

True, the four beasts of chapter 7 are not presented as one in Daniel's prophecy; but we must remember that this prophecy is obviously meant to complement and augment the earlier prophecy—and we should read it in that light. By not identifying the final beast with a known animal and by describing it as having ten horns that represented different kingdoms, Daniel hints that it was a composite creature. And John in the book of Revelation confirms this suggestion, adding that the dragon gave this creature its power, its throne, and great authority (Rev. 13:1–2).

Guided by a Religious Educational System

Not long after Daniel's time, a Babylonian astronomer named Naburimannu (c. 500 BC) calculated the length of the year to be 365 days, 6 hours, 15 minutes, and 41 seconds. He overshot the mark by only 26 minutes and 55 seconds (a deviation of .005 percent from the calculations of modern scientists)![2] The educational system of Babylonia was second to none in the ancient world. But inextricably intertwined with a demanding system of painstaking and precise scholarship was a curious mixture of a "multitude" of sorceries and a "great abundance" of enchantments (Isa. 47:9).

Places of worship in Babylon included fifty-three temples of the great gods, fifty-five chapels to Marduk, three hundred chapels for the earthly deities, six hundred for the heavenly deities, and nearly four hundred altars to various gods.[3] In one of the temples of the great gods, according to Herodotus, there was "a great sitting figure of Bel, all of gold on a golden throne, supported on a base of gold, with a golden table standing beside it." He said he was told by the Chaldeans that it had taken more than twenty-two tons of gold to make all this.[4]

Scholarly superstition? Is there such a thing? Was there such a thing? Indeed there was in Babylon. When the priestly sages of Chaldea were

---

[2] John C. Whitcomb, *Daniel* (Chicago: Moody, 1985), 36–37.

[3] *The World's Last Mysteries* (Pleasantville, NY: Reader's Digest Association, 1978), 176.

[4] *The Histories*, 114 (see chap. 2, n. 1).

called upon to interpret omens, signs, or dreams, they didn't just conjure up answers from visceral impulses. They turned instead to their scribal archives—reference manuals where scholars of their caste had painstakingly recorded long lists of earthly and unearthly phenomena with appropriate interpretations. Yes, they were intensely religious and superstitious; but at the same time, they were curious and careful observers—and thus masters of the preeminent qualification of the scientist.

Not much has changed, has it? Modern Babylon also practices scholarly superstition. One of the dictionary definitions of *religion* is "a cause, a principle, or an activity pursued with zeal or conscientious devotion." The educational system of modern Babylon is all of the above. It has its own high priests, prophets, and evangelists; its own rituals and mantras. It even posts its own lists of sacred and profane words and expressions.

In the drama of Daniel, the wise men of Babylon have two functions: they enter and they exit. When they are summoned by the king to solve a problem, they enter with pride, pomp, and circumstance; then, having duly pondered the king's problem, they leave it with him and hastily exit. When it comes to solving the real problems of life, the wise men of modern Babylon follow the same pattern.

Characterized as the Reign of Idolized Man

So terrifying was the dream Nebuchadnezzar saw that fateful night that "his sleep brake from him"—he was startled into sleeplessness. "Thou, O king, sawest," said Daniel later, "and behold a great image. This great image, whose brightness was excellent, stood before thee; and the form thereof was terrible" (Dan. 2:1, 31). In his dream the king saw an immense giant standing before him, radiating an almost-blinding light. It was terrifying to look at—as if it had the power to spring to life and lunge at him.

For all this, it was the representation of a man that stood before him. This suggests to us another key characteristic of the kingdom of the world—it is a man-centered kingdom. Satan first appealed to man with the promise "ye shall be as gods," and the goal of his subjects ever since has been to reign as gods, independent of their Creator and God.

The history of mankind is largely a record of man's frustrating attempts to reach this goal. Having rejected the divine revelation that God alone is his Creator and Sustainer, he has rejected also the divinely ordained means by which he may fulfill his destiny to reign with God, which is humble submission to Him and His will.

In accordance with man's nature as a social creature in a structured society, his search for fulfillment has become a search for the ideal man—a "messiah"—who will lead the rest of mankind to the utopian fulfillment for which they are destined. From the dawn of history, one mighty man after another has pushed his way through the mass of people to claim this place. In a startling moment of truth, Paul-Henri Spaak, the first chairman of the United Nations' General Assembly, once expressed the cry of the unregenerate heart for such a messiah:

> We do not want another committee; we have too many already. What we want is a man of sufficient stature to hold the allegiance of all the people and to lift us out of the economic morass into which we are sinking. Send us such a man, and be he god or devil, we will receive him.[5]

The fact that the world would welcome such a man has been settled beyond dispute by the blunt testimony of history, to say nothing of the infallible testimony of Scripture.

Characterized as Brutish in Nature

The parallel revelation of Daniel 7 characterizes these same kingdoms as brute beasts. The ideal man of the kingdom of the world—the mighty one who is to lead his people to Utopia—is in fact brutish at heart.

Here we have the revelation of a tragic irony in the history of mankind. At Satan's invitation, man began his quest for deification at the base of the Tree of Knowledge. Yet those who were preeminent in gaining apparent mastery over life and their fellow man, repeatedly proved to be little more than beasts at heart.

Alexander the Great is a case in point. Highly intelligent, educated under Aristotle, he was a product of the best in Greek education and culture. And he had many redeeming qualities through which he won the admiration, love, and loyalty of his troops and subjects. In warfare, he was persistent, brave, and self-sacrificing. In victory, he was often incredibly magnanimous with the vanquished. In Persia, he saw himself as commissioned by the gods to be the harmonizer and reconciler of the world.[6]

---

[5] Peter Lalonde, *One World Under Anti-Christ* (Eugene, OR: Harvest House, 1991), 267.

[6] At a banquet in Persia for nine thousand distinguished guests, Alexander "prayed for partnership in the empire and for unity and concord . . . in a joint commonwealth where all peoples were to be partners rather than subjects—a prayer that marks a revolution in human thought." Charles Alexander Robinson, Jr., *Ancient History* (London: Macmillan, 1967), 347.

Yet Alexander proved to be fundamentally brutish in his nature. He was just twenty-six years old when he became master of the empire that had belonged to Persia. From all appearances at this time he was master of himself as well. He rarely drank, never overate, and was temperate, moderate, and judicious in his conduct. But though the animal within had been tamed and cultured, it was there nonetheless; it awaited only its opportunity for expression.

In fact, brutishness was at the wellspring of Alexander's nature; he had eaten heartily at the Tree of Knowledge and had fully accepted the proposition that he was destined to be "as God." He claimed he was a descendant of the deified Hercules; when he reached the pinnacle of his power, he began to demand more and more recognition of his deification. Then, as if to confirm his deification in his own mind, he began to indulge in the luxuries and pleasures he imagined were the domain of the gods. He provided himself with a harem of three hundred sixty young women. He spent whole nights in drunkenness, dissipation, and vice. Under questionable circumstances, he executed his most able general, the aged Parmenio, a man Alexander's father had called his "only general." Later, in a drunken rage, Alexander murdered another renowned general, his foster brother Clitus.

In short, Alexander the Great was little more than a highly efficient murderer. His whole life was dedicated to one grand objective: his own glory. The fact that he was an inspiring leader and a military genius served only to multiply his crimes and to leave in his trail a legacy of murderous imitators. The psalmist reveals the divine assessment of such people.

> Their inward thought is, that their houses shall continue for ever, and their dwelling places to all generations; they call their lands after their own names. Nevertheless man being in honour abideth not: he is like the beasts that perish. This their way is their folly: yet their posterity approve their sayings" (Ps. 49:11–13).

"Yet their posterity approve" well summarizes how the citizens of the world's kingdom view men like of Alexander the Great. Not only do they condone the words and deeds of such heroes; they take pleasure in them and accept them fully as their own.[7] Here we have a strange dichotomy in the thinking of the typical man of the world. On the one hand, he decries

---

[7] The Hebrew word translated *approve* in this passage (*ratsah*) means "to be pleased with, be favorable to, accept favorably."

injustice, murder, and oppression; on the other, he has the remarkable ability to overlook—or even sanctify—such vices in his heroes.

If you wonder if this is indeed so—that man fundamentally contradicts his own professed standards—look at the attitude of the ancients toward their gods. The gods of the ancient world indulged promiscuously in all the vices known to man. Yet the men of the world—including intelligent, cultured men—respected, worshiped, and even aspired to emulate them. But aren't we in the modern world beyond such pagan worship? Are we? Just as ancient Rome did, we have our pantheon of gods. We simply call them by different names and worship them with different rituals.

How could this be? Because unregenerate man is fundamentally brutish in nature. Nevertheless, this brutish nature is housed in the body of a creature made in the image of God and designed to reign with God. Consequently, the man of the world is not simply a dichotomy: he is a dichotomy in the process of self-destructing, enmeshed in an internal battle with insurgents—a war he is destined to lose. His search for internal unity is governed by the ultimatum that he must be sovereign. But his creation and well-being hang on realizing that God is sovereign.

The Doom of the Kingdom of the World

A Kingdom Standing on Feet of Clay

Thou sawest till that a stone was cut out without hands, which smote the image upon his feet that were of iron and clay, and brake them to pieces. Then was the iron, the clay, the brass, the silver, and the gold, broken to pieces together, and became like the chaff of the summer threshingfloors; and the wind carried them away, that no place was found for them: and the stone that smote the image became a great mountain, and filled the whole earth (Dan. 2:34–35).

I knew a businessman who had an interesting method of assessing employment potential. He studied applicants' shoes. He reasoned that a person who kept his shoes in good order would probably be reliable and conscientious as an employee. This businessman was a cut above the average. Most of us are not inclined to see footwear as an important tool for assessing strength of character.

I dare say that Nebuchadnezzar was like most of us in this regard. When, in his dream, he saw that statue, he must have scarcely paid any attention to the feet—at least until he saw the stone roll upon them. Undoubtedly, he was overwhelmed by the brightness, the splendor, the fearfulness of the image; and until he saw otherwise, he would never have imagined that this magnificent statue had a fatal flaw—a flaw by which the whole image would be crushed to fine dust and disappear from the earth. For the feet of this marvelous image were "part of iron, and part of clay."

In his interpretation of the dream, Daniel spends more time describing the feet than any other part of the statue. This tells us something of the importance of this feature to the message.

> And whereas thou sawest the feet and toes, part of potters' clay, and part of iron, the kingdom shall be divided; but there shall be in it of the strength of the iron, forasmuch as thou sawest the iron mixed with miry clay. And as the toes of the feet were part of iron, and part of clay, so the kingdom shall be partly strong, and partly broken. And whereas thou sawest iron mixed with miry clay, they shall mingle themselves with the seed of men: but they shall not cleave one to another, even as iron is not mixed with clay (vv. 41–43).

The feet and toes represent the kingdom of the world (appearing in the form of the revived Roman Empire) in the last days, for it is in the days of "these kings" (represented by the ten toes) that "the God of heaven set up a kingdom, which shall never be destroyed" (v. 44). In these last days, God will abundantly demonstrate to the world the fatal weakness of the world system, the kingdom of the Devil.

And what is this fatal weakness? It is the weakness that inevitably comes when man chooses to eat from the Tree of Knowledge rather than the Tree of Life; for this choice is both a declaration of independence from God and an assumption of godhood. And what happens when you have a kingdom of would-be gods? Look at Israel during the period of the judges. "In those days there was no king in Israel: every man did that which was right in his own eyes" (Judges 21:25).

When people lose sight of, or blatantly reject, the sovereignty of God, every man does that which is right in his own eyes—each mortal microcosm becoming a law and judge to himself. The starry-eyed promoters of the world's kingdom would have us hear bells of freedom and songs of harmony in this system, but history has proven this score stubbornly dissonant. The rule is that the strongest takes all, giving only to those who will radiate his glory and promote his security. Everyone else must be content with dreams.

The image of Nebuchadnezzar's vision provides a vivid illustration of the development and inevitable doom of this kingdom. As history progresses, the kingdom of the world declines in unity while increasing in power. The silver kingdom of Persia is inferior to golden Babylon in unity; but as silver is stronger than gold, so Persia is stronger in brute strength than Babylon. And so it is with each succeeding kingdom.

The declining unity of mankind became obvious first at the Tower of Babel. As men lost a sense of inner unity, they found it necessary to create an outward symbol and source of unity. And so it has been throughout history. As the inner sense of unity has declined in the kingdom of the world, kings and potentates have resorted more and more to external unifying structures supported by brute strength. So by the time we get to Rome, we find iron that "breaketh in pieces and subdueth all things." And the degeneration continues until the last days when the iron, no longer solidly consistent, is bridged together with brittle terra cotta.[8]

So the kingdom of the world is doomed because it stands on a faulty foundation—the foundation of independence from God, a foundation of man's sovereignty as opposed to the reality of God's, a foundation that inevitably leads to disunity in the human race.

A King and Kingdom Destined for Judgment

The Antichrist's Rise to Power

And the ten horns out of this kingdom are ten kings that shall arise: and another shall rise after them; and he shall be diverse from the first, and he shall subdue three kings (Dan. 7:24)

And the king shall do according to his will; and he shall exalt himself, and magnify himself above every god, and shall speak marvellous things against the God of gods, and shall prosper (Dan. 11:36).

Alexander the Great, a prototypical hero of the world, appears in the Bible as a horn on a goat; and the Antichrist, the last hope of the kingdom of Satan, appears first as a "little horn" on a beast. This little horn, representing one of the ten kings in the final bestial form of the Roman Empire, is said to have "eyes like the eyes of man, and a mouth speaking

---

[8] The word translated *clay* (*chasaph*) refers to potter's clay (2:41) and, by extension, to tile or terra cotta. Such material was often used in ancient architecture. Undoubtedly, the feet of the statue appeared to be as strong as the legs. See John F. Walvoord, *Daniel: The Key to Prophetic Revelation* (Chicago: Moody, 1971), 69–70.

great things" (Dan. 7:8). Eyes in ancient symbolism represent intelligence and insight (cf. Gen. 3:5; Ezek. 1:18). The mouth, of course, shows the power to communicate; but in this case the emphasis is on "great things" spoken against the Most High (Dan. 7:25).

Taken together, the symbols depict the Antichrist as a highly intelligent person who speaks with persuasive power against the King of kings. He will evidently have the intelligence and insight to solve, or appear to solve, many of the great problems that have plagued mankind. In this context, his speaking great things against the Lord cannot simply be promiscuous and thoughtless blasphemy, as is generally the case with the profane.

In the symbolism, his power of communication is tied to his intelligence. As so many antichrists have done throughout history, he will provide what appears to be a supremely intelligent rationale for breaking the bands and casting aside the cords that bind people to God. Only, in contrast to those of the past, this man's proposals will seem irrefutable to the masses. He will convince them that they no longer need to fear God—they no longer need Him. In the eyes of the people, he will set God aside and provide a better alternative.[9]

The New Age Movement may well be preparing the way, then, for the success of the Antichrist. New Age philosophy says that all that is, is God (pantheism); and that man, who is a part of all that is, is divine. Man's problems, therefore, all flow from the fact that he is not fully conscious of his divinity. New Agers would agree that Jesus Christ is divine, but they would add that He is not more divine than anyone else. Jesus of Nazareth, they say, simply realized and demonstrated His divine potential more fully than others. By following His example of self-realization, all people could realize their divine potential. Unfortunately, however, followers of Jesus deviously created a cult that made Him alone one with God and therefore an object of worship.[10]

According to this scheme, the world leader of the future will correct this age-old misconception. He will fully realize and demonstrate his godhood and will lead others into the same "truth." His plan to set God

---

[9] According to Keil, the Aramaic word translated *against* (*tsad*) in v. 25 includes the meaning "at the side of" and denotes that the Antichrist will use language by which he would set God aside in order to present himself as God (II Thess. 2:4). *Biblical Commentary on the Old Testament: Daniel* (Eerdmans, 1959), 241.

[10] For an excellent discussion of this heresy, see Elliot Miller, *A Crash Course on the New Age Movement* (Grand Rapids: Baker, 1989).

aside will include a program to "wear out the saints of the most High, and ... to change times and laws."

The strategy of "wearing out" God's people reveals something of the genius of the Antichrist. Though he will not be averse to bloodshed, he will realize, as intelligent conquerors always have, that he must deal with people of faith more subtly. Open confrontation generally solidifies resistance, and brutal persecution often produces heroic determination.

Wearing down the enemy is quite another matter. This strategy helped Rome become master of the ancient world. In her life-and-death struggle with Carthage, Rome appeared for a time to be on the verge of losing all. After crossing the Alps in 218 BC, the renowned general Hannibal devastated Roman armies in victory after victory. By the spring of 217 BC, after stunning victories at Trebia River and Lake Trasimenes, Hannibal was the undisputed master of the land; and Rome seemed defenseless and on the verge of collapse. But rather than sue for peace, as Hannibal might have expected, the Romans took the drastic action of appointing a dictator to reorganize and lead their armies.

Quintus Fabius Maximus, a Roman of the old school, would eventually earn the derogatory nickname *Cunctator*, "the delayer," because of his guerrilla tactic of harassing and undermining the enemy rather than directly confronting him. But the strategy of Fabius led, though in painfully slow stages, to Hannibal's withdrawal from Italy and the final destruction of Carthage. Fabius knew that for all of Hannibal's ingenious power, he and his army were largely isolated on foreign soil. Notwithstanding his consistent resounding victories (in fifteen years in Italy, he never lost a battle), his army was slowly diminishing in manpower; and the sea passages by which Carthage could replenish his forces were steadily being constricted by the Roman navy.

The Satanic strategy of wearing down God's people is comparable in many ways to the strategy of the Roman Cunctator. The losses sustained by the people of God in this process are so gradual that they are almost imperceptible. After his initial great victories, Hannibal at first seemed able to go where he pleased when he pleased; but as a matter of fact, Fabius followed him wherever he went, blocking the way through certain mountain passages, harassing his troops when they foraged for food and when they got careless and indulgent, and intimidating those who might be inclined to help the Carthaginians. And so it is with the wearing-down process of Christians. Even as they glory in their liberty and supposed gains, imperceptibly they become weaker and weaker.

A One-Term Potentate

"And he shall . . . think to change times and laws: and they shall be given into his hand until a time and times and the dividing of time" (Dan. 7:25).

In America, a president who stays in office for only one term is commonly viewed as something of a failure. The Antichrist will share this fate—only more so. The expression "a time and times and the dividing of time" denotes three and one-half years (cf. Dan. 12:7; Rev. 11:2–3; 12:14; 13:5). Though the Antichrist will attempt to change times and laws, he will find that his times are in the hands of Another.

After the Antichrist's furious and intensive term in which the people of God are "given into his hand," the situation will be dramatically reversed. "The judgment shall sit." Ominous words! And in his vision, Daniel witnesses a correspondingly ominous scene.

> As I looked,
>   thrones were placed,
>   and the Ancient of days took his seat;
> his clothing was white as snow,
>   and the hair of his head like pure wool;
> his throne was fiery flames;
>   its wheels were burning fire.
> A stream of fire issued
>   and came out from before him;
> a thousand thousands served him,
>   and ten thousand times ten thousand stood before him;
> the court sat in judgment,
>   and the books were opened (Dan. 7:9–10, ESV).

How often have earthly seats of authority and courts of law been scorned and frustrated! After many years, the story is still vivid in my mind of the vicious rape and abuse of a beautiful young woman. She later identified the offenders, and they were arrested and eventually brought to court. But the criminals had influential friends; and the judge, bribed and intimidated, pronounced them innocent. The enraged parents and their abused daughter, scarred now for life by her experience, could only watch helplessly as these perverts walked out of the courtroom, full of gloating mockery.

Not so with this throne in the last days. The throne itself is of "fiery flames," utterly intolerant of any corruption; and from it "a stream of fire" issues, signifying that its decrees are irresistible. And countless myriads of servants stand before it, ready to enforce the decrees and desires of its Occupant.

The presiding Judge is the Ancient of Days, a title depicting the antiquity of His reign. In stark contrast to the short-lived, troubled tenure of the would-be king of kings, the reign of the true King has been from everlasting. And as David had long ago prophesied (Ps. 2), the heir to the throne so coveted by the mighty of the earth was long ago appointed.

> I saw in the night visions, and, behold, one like the Son of man came with the clouds of heaven, and came to the Ancient of days, and they brought him near before him. And there was given him dominion, and glory, and a kingdom, that all people, nations, and languages, should serve him: his dominion is an everlasting dominion, which shall not pass away, and his kingdom that which shall not be destroyed (Dan. 7:13–14).

So overwhelming was this vision that Daniel was left with great anxiety of spirit, confessing "the visions of my head alarmed me" (7:15, ESV). Therefore, he asked "the truth of all this" (v. 16). So many dynamic, fearful scenes had passed before him that he found himself unable to digest their message. His request was for a clear, concise summary of the significance of the whole vision. The angel, true to Daniel's request, summarizes the whole vision in these few words: "These great beasts, which are four, are four kings, which shall arise out of the earth. But the saints of the most High shall take the kingdom, and possess the kingdom for ever, even for ever and ever" (vv. 17–18).

This is a remarkable summary. There are so many dynamic scenes in this prophecy that it would be very easy for an interpreter to see another central message than the one the angel gives in these verses. It might appear, for example, that the central message might focus on the fourth beast—the rise, power, and doom of the Antichrist. Or, the focus might be on the Ancient of Days and His judgment. Or it might be on the appointed Heir, the Son of Man Who comes "with the clouds of heaven" to receive His long-awaited inheritance of "an everlasting dominion . . . a kingdom . . . which shall never be destroyed" (vv. 13–14).

But the message of this vision is that the saints of the Most High shall take the kingdom and possess it for ever and ever. In this message is a beautiful irony. These were the very saints who had been given into the hand of the beast to be worn down, abused, degraded, and slain at his will. Now they have come into their own. They—not the mighty of the world—have fulfilled their destiny to be "like God" and to reign with Him.

CHAPTER TWENTY-FOUR

JACOB'S TROUBLE AND ISRAEL'S TRIUMPH

DANIEL'S SEVENTY SEPTETS

The ninth chapter of Daniel has been called the "backbone" of biblical prophecy because in it "we have the indispensable chronological key to all New Testament prophecy."[1] As remarkable as it is, however, this revelation was not given to the people of God as simply a chronological key to prophetic Scripture. The Bible, we must continually remind ourselves, is predominantly about God. This prophecy tells us that in the great war between the two kingdoms, our Commander in Chief is in sovereign control of the appointed times of His people.

Years before (in 551 BC), God had revealed to Daniel that He controls the appointed times of the enemies of God's people (Dan. 8). Now that Babylon has fallen to Persia, He shows Daniel, through two striking revelations (9:1–27, in 538 BC, and 10:1–12:13, in 535 BC), His sovereign plan for His people in the war. In chapter nine, the Lord reveals His program for Israel in outline form; in chapters ten through twelve, He delineates some of the details of His program so that His soldiers may accomplish His divine purpose in their warfare. In chapter nine, the revelation of Scripture sets the stage for this prophecy (vv. 1–2), the

---

[1] Alva J. McClain, *Daniel's Prophecy of the Seventy Weeks* (Grand Rapids: Zondervan, 1940), 5–6.

supplication of Daniel reveals its focus (vv. 3–23), and the revelation of the seventy septets shows God's program for His people (vv. 24–27).

THE REVELATION OF SCRIPTURE (DAN. 9:1–2)

In the first year of Darius the son of Ahasuerus, of the seed of the Medes, which was made king over the realm of the Chaldeans; in the first year of his reign I Daniel understood by books the number of the years, whereof the word of the Lord came to Jeremiah the prophet, that he would accomplish seventy years in the desolations of Jerusalem.

Passages from these books of Jeremiah triggered in Daniel a latent hope that led ultimately to one of the greatest revelations of prophecy in the Bible. How did Daniel interpret these passages? Given his understanding of the times, what did he expect from the promises he read? In order to understand this important prophecy, we must first understand the light (the revelation) Daniel received from it. This will involve understanding the cultural and theological context in which he received it.

The first year of Darius the Mede (538–537 BC) was a momentous year for Daniel.[2] He was now in his eighties, and his reputation in Babylon had followed him into Medo-Persia. Darius had appointed him as one of the chief rulers in the kingdom and was so impressed with him that he was thinking about making him prime minister of the realm. This resulted in a vicious power struggle (Dan. 6) that turned out to be a battle between the kingdom of light and the kingdom of darkness. This struggle, in which God intervened in behalf of His kingdom, provides a backdrop for the momentous revelation of chapter nine, which took place in the same year.[3]

After Daniel's miraculous deliverance from the den of lions, Darius made a decree that enhanced Daniel's reputation—and enlarged the knowledge of his God—far and wide. It may have been these events that resulted in Daniel's receiving scrolls written through the impulse of the Spirit by his mentor of long ago, the prophet Jeremiah. We can only

---

[2] For a good discussion of conservative theories concerning the identity of Darius the Mede, see Stephen R. Miller, Daniel: The New American Commentary (Nashville: Broadman & Holman, 1994), 18:171–77. Miller seems to favor the view that Darius the Mede is another name for Cyrus.

[3] The events of chapter 6 evidently took place during the transition of governments, not long after the fall of Babylon. Historical documents reveal that, as a general rule, Cyrus allowed the former

imagine Daniel's excitement and awe as he read that scroll. But when he gets about halfway through the scroll, his eyes are suddenly riveted on the words "seventy years," and his excitement turns to ecstasy.

And this whole land shall be a desolation, and an astonishment; and these nations shall serve the king of Babylon seventy years. And it shall come to pass, when seventy years are accomplished, that I will punish the king of Babylon, and that nation, saith the Lord, for their iniquity, and the land of the Chaldeans, and will make it perpetual desolations. And I will bring upon that land all my words which I have pronounced against it, even all that is written in this book, which Jeremiah hath prophesied against all the nations (Jer. 25:11–13).

Daniel had been in captivity sixty-seven years (605–538 BC). How would he have interpreted this prophecy? He might have reasoned that the fall of Babylon he had witnessed was the first stage of its fulfillment. God had not yet made the land of the Chaldeans "perpetual desolations." Whatever the case, he must have thrilled at the thought that God had ordained not only the captivity but also the years of the captivity.

After a time of rejoicing and wonder, Daniel reads further; and not long after, he is electrified as he reads these words:

For thus saith the Lord, That after seventy years be accomplished at Babylon I will visit you, and perform my good word toward you, in causing you to return to this place. For I know the thoughts that I think toward you, saith the Lord, thoughts of peace, and not of evil, to give you an expected end. Then shall ye call upon me, and ye shall go and pray unto me, and I will hearken unto you. And ye shall seek me, and find me, when ye shall search for me with all your heart. And I will be found of you, saith the Lord: and I will turn away your captivity, and I will gather you from all the nations, and from all the places whither I have driven you, saith the Lord; and I will bring you again into the place whence I caused you to be carried away captive (Jer. 29:10–14).

government officials to continue in their positions. Nevertheless, there must have been ambitious office-seekers and power brokers among the foreign conquerors who would have been relatively ignorant of Daniel's character and renown. This would be the best time, and perhaps the only time, such people would have the temerity (and ignorance) to attempt a coup of this type. Daniel may possibly be alluding to the publication throughout the empire of his deliverance from the lions' den (6:25–27) in his supplication when he says, "And now, O Lord our God, that hast brought thy people forth out of the land of Egypt with a mighty hand, and hast gotten thee renown, as at this day" (9:15). The expression "as at this day" may refer to this great deliverance by which the name of the God of Israel was magnified throughout the nations. Jeremiah (32:20) and Nehemiah (9:10) use the same expression, but both of them had also seen God intervene in behalf of Israel as Daniel had.

Not only is the full punishment of Babylon at hand, but the return of Israel from captivity is as well. Some forty years before, Daniel's contemporary, Ezekiel, had prophesied that the nation Israel would be re-united and "raised from the dead" (Ezek. 37:1–14). The "desolations" of Jerusalem are to be brought to an end! After another time of rejoicing and wonder, Daniel reads on; and just about a "page" later, he comes across these words:

> For, lo, the days come, saith the Lord, that I will bring again the captivity of my people Israel and Judah, saith the Lord: and I will cause them to return to the land that I gave to their fathers, and they shall possess it. And these are the words that the Lord spake concerning Israel and concerning Judah. For thus saith the Lord; We have heard a voice of trembling, of fear, and not of peace. Ask ye now, and see whether a man doth travail with child? wherefore do I see every man with his hands on his loins, as a woman in travail, and all faces are turned into paleness? Alas! for that day is great, so that none is like it: it is even the time of Jacob's trouble; but he shall be saved out of it. For it shall come to pass in that day, saith the Lord of hosts, that I will break his yoke from off thy neck, and will burst thy bonds, and strangers shall no more serve themselves of him: but they shall serve the Lord their God, and David their king, whom I will raise up unto them (Jer. 30:3–9).

These words add another dimension to the thoughts that have been forming in Daniel's mind. The return, restoration, and reign of Israel will be preceded by "the time of Jacob's trouble." Daniel must have been well aware that his people would need more chastisement before they would be brought to repentance. To his friend Ezekiel, the Lord had warned that the Israelites were "a rebellious nation," obstinate and hardhearted, hostile and even dangerous, like thorns and scorpions (Ezek. 2:3–6).

Nevertheless, the revelation that his beloved people would go through a time of trouble such as never had been in history burdened him greatly— so much so that his last recorded questions had to do with this tribulation time (Dan. 12:6–8). This burden stirred him to prayer and fasting on his people's behalf.

As Daniel began his vigil, another thought may have entered his mind. At Mount Sinai, the Lord had instructed the people that, once they had possession of Palestine, they were to give the land a sabbatical rest every seventh year (Lev. 25:2–6). This was to be a matter of faith for the people of God; for Moses anticipates the questions that could trouble the people as they sought to obey this law ("And if ye shall say, What shall we eat the seventh year? behold, we shall not sow, nor gather in our increase"), and he responds by reminding them that the Lord will provide for them and will add blessings to them for their obedience (Lev. 25:20–22).

Later, the Lord warns the people that if they refuse to trust Him and obey His ordinances, He would allow their enemies to conquer them and He would remove them from the Promised Land, scattering them among the heathen. Then, He said, "shall the land enjoy her sabbaths, as long as it lieth desolate, and ye be in your enemies' land; even then shall the land rest, and enjoy her sabbaths. As long as it lieth desolate it shall rest; because it did not rest in your sabbaths, when ye dwelt upon it" (Lev. 26:31–35). The writer of Chronicles implies that the captivity lasted seventy years because of Israel's violation of the sabbatical year. He says that the fall of Jerusalem and the Exile happened "to fulfil the word of the Lord by the mouth of Jeremiah, until the land had enjoyed her sabbaths: for as long as she lay desolate she kept sabbath, to fulfil threescore and ten years" (II Chron. 36:21).

The author of Chronicles may have lived decades after Daniel.[4] Nevertheless, the warnings in Leviticus would have led Daniel naturally to the same conclusion. The Chronicles passage implies that there had been widespread neglect of the sabbatical year in Israel for 490 years—since about the time of Saul (1050–1010 BC).

His heart now aflame with renewed hope through the prophetic promises of Jeremiah, Daniel begins his supplication for Israel. But though hope has been kindled anew, Daniel's mind must have been swirling. The people of Israel would soon be restored to the Promised Land, but the restoration would somehow involve a great time of tribulation: "Jacob's Trouble."

And what would Daniel see as the dynamics involved in the restoration of his people? Some of the passages he would have read in Jeremiah would imply that not long after the restoration of Israel, the millennial kingdom would be established (see Jer. 24:6–7; 32:37–41; 33:7–9, 14–16). On the other hand, his own visions indicated that thus far only one of the four kingdoms to rule over the earth had passed away. Medo-Persia had just begun its reign; Greece was to come next, then Rome; and

---

[4] Genealogical information in Chronicles (e.g., I Chron. 3:19–21) indicates that these books were probably not written before the time of Ezra, who served during the reign of Artaxerxes, 465–424 BC (Ezra 7:1)—almost eighty years after Daniel's vision of the seventy weeks.

it was to be in the days of ten kings in the fourth kingdom that Messiah was to come and establish His universal kingdom (Dan. 2:40–45; 7:7–14, 19–27).

So how would Daniel put all this together? Probably, his prototype for Israel's golden age would have been the time of the reigns of David and Solomon. During his entire reign, David battled the kingdom of the world, and it was not until the days of Solomon that peace and prosperity were finally established. Yet even then, there were other powerful kingdoms in the world.

This picture of the kingdoms of David and Solomon would likely provide the paradigm through which Daniel would envision Israel's coming restoration. Given his circumstances and this setting, he would likely envision a restoration, first, under the control of the Medo-Persians. He knows from Jeremiah's prophecy that in the process of restoration, Israel will endure a terrible time of trouble; but, eventually, the prophecies say, peace and prosperity will be established. Yet for a time, as it was in the days of Solomon, Israel will coexist with other powerful kingdoms in the earth—until the Messiah comes and establishes His universal kingdom.

But "in the multitude of [his] thoughts within" him, the uppermost must have been the need he felt for his people to repent of their sins. And so, he said, "I set my face unto the Lord God, to seek by prayer and supplications, with fasting, and sackcloth, and ashes."

THE SUPPLICATION OF DANIEL (DAN. 9:3–23)

As a young teenager being led into captivity, Daniel undoubtedly meditated again and again on Solomon's prayer at the dedication of the temple. In that prayer, Solomon envisions a time like the one Daniel and his friends were experiencing—a time when Israel through its sinfulness would be conquered by her enemies and carried away captive to a foreign land. Ponder the conclusion to his prayer (I Kings 8:46–53):

> If they sin against thee, (for there is no man that sinneth not,) and thou be angry with them, and deliver them to the enemy, so that they carry them away captives unto the land of the enemy, far or near; yet if they shall bethink themselves in the land whither they were carried captives, and repent, and make supplication unto thee in the land of them that carried them captives, saying, We have sinned, and have done perversely, we have committed wick-

edness; and so return unto thee with all their heart, and with all their soul, in the land of their enemies, which led them away captive, and pray unto thee toward their land, which thou gavest unto their fathers, the city which thou hast chosen, and the house which I have built for thy name: then hear thou their prayer and their supplication in heaven thy dwelling place, and maintain their cause, and forgive thy people that have sinned against thee, and all their transgressions wherein they have transgressed against thee, and give them compassion before them who carried them captive, that they may have compassion on them: for they be thy people, and thine inheritance, which thou broughtest forth out of Egypt, from the midst of the furnace of iron: that thine eyes may be open unto the supplication of thy servant, and unto the supplication of thy people Israel, to hearken unto them in all that they call for unto thee. For thou didst separate them from among all the people of the earth, to be thine inheritance, as thou spakest by the hand of Moses thy servant, when thou broughtest our fathers out of Egypt, O Lord God.

For nearly seventy years, Daniel had followed the master plan of this prayer—kneeling three times a day, facing Jerusalem, praying for himself and his people in the land of captivity. His prayers, we're told, included giving thanks to God, even when the threat of death loomed overhead (Dan. 6:10); but they must have focused largely on Solomon's central petitions for the covenant people and for the fulfillment of their ordained purpose in God's plan. Solomon's prayer included an acknowledgment of sin, a call for repentance, a petition for favor from their enemies, and a hope for deliverance from the "iron furnace" of captivity, as they had been delivered from Egypt.

Now, with the scrolls of Jeremiah's prophecy before him, Daniel's prayers are much the same as they had been throughout the ten septets of his captivity—but with a new fervency and a new hope. He begins his supplication with the infinite greatness and faithfulness of the God of the covenant: "O Lord, the great and dreadful God, keeping the covenant and mercy to them that love him, and to them that keep his commandments" (Dan. 9:4).

He then acknowledges, "We have sinned," and we haven't listened to Your prophets, and as You warned us, You have driven us into foreign lands of captivity. All that has come upon us has fulfilled Your Word; but now, for Your own name's sake, fulfill also Your promises concerning Your people, Your city Jerusalem, and Your holy temple mountain.

THE REVELATION OF GOD'S PROGRAM FOR ISRAEL (DAN. 9:24–27)

Three Keys to Interpretation: Context, Context, Context

As we begin to look at this important prophecy in more detail, we need to remind ourselves that the key to the interpretation of any Scripture, including prophecy, is context. Quite often we hear Bible scholars speak of this prophecy as "controversial." Much of the controversy—at least among Bible believers—would disappear if we paid closer attention to the context.

Thus far, the context has informed us that Daniel's prayer focuses entirely on Israel, specifically on Jerusalem and the temple mountain. We should remember that the central sign of God's covenant relationship with Israel was the manifestation of His presence in their midst (Exod. 33:14–16; Deut. 12:5; Joel 3:17; Isa. 12:6; cf. Isa. 7:14). The temple mount was the central focus of Daniel's prayer, then, because he saw in the restoration of the temple the sign of God's covenant with Israel being renewed. Daniel's friend Ezekiel has seen in a vision the glory of the Lord's presence removed, first from the temple sanctuary (Ezek. 10:3–4, 18–19) and then from the city (11:23). Later the glory of the Lord's presence had returned to the future temple of restored and regenerated Israel (43:2–5). As Daniel prayed, he was undoubtedly hoping that Ezekiel's prophetic vision was soon to be fulfilled.

The Context of the Answer to Daniel's Prayer

About the time of the evening sacrifice (about 3 p.m.), while Daniel was yet praying, the angel Gabriel arrived with the announcement that God had sent him to help His beloved child understand a profound message He had for him. Gabriel's arrival while Daniel was in the process of praying for Israel and for the holy mountain of God (Dan. 9:20–21) reveals that Gabriel's message was in direct response to Daniel's prayers—that the central subject of the message is the people of Israel and the temple mount.

By his discovery in the prophecy of Jeremiah that the captivity would last seventy years, Daniel had been encouraged to believe that the restoration and ultimate reign of Israel was in the process of being fulfilled. Was he right? Gabriel responds with a message of good news and bad news. Yes, Daniel, God is preparing to fulfill His covenant promises to Israel.

He is going to forgive their sins, bring in everlasting righteousness, and once again anoint the most holy place of the temple with His presence. That's the good news. But there is bad news also. The restoration and re-generation of Israel is going to take a lot longer than your hopes have led you to believe.

The 70-year exile was the result of a 490-year "testing period" that Israel had failed through widespread violation of the Lord's sabbatical years. Now, Gabriel announces, since Israel has failed her first test, she will have to have another:

> Seventy weeks are determined upon thy people and upon thy holy city, to fin-ish the transgression, and to make an end of sins, and to make reconciliation for iniquity, and to bring in everlasting righteousness, and to seal up the vision and prophecy, and to anoint the most Holy (v. 24).[5]

The Objectives of the Seventy Septets (Dan. 9:24)

Through this seventy-septet training period, God will fulfill the two basic requests of Daniel's prayer: (1) He will reconcile Israel to Himself; and (2) He will establish His eternal kingdom on earth through mani-festing His Presence in the most holy place of the temple mount. Gabriel uses three parallel statements to express these objectives, each statement focusing on what will be accomplished in Israel.[6]

The statements "to finish the transgression" and "to make an end of sins" refer to the continual failure of Israel that Daniel had been confessing. Jeremiah's promise concerning the seventy-year captivity included the provision "And ye shall seek me, and find me, when ye shall search for me with all your heart" (Jer. 29:13). The Lord said that though she knew full

---

[5] A more literal rendition of the Hebrew would be "Seventy sevens [or septets] are determined." Since the Jews had a septet of years as well as a septet of days, the reader or listener would have to interpret the term by the context. In this case, the context makes it clear that the reference is to seventy septets of years.

[6] Down through the centuries, especially when postmillennialism and amillennialism have dominated Christian thinking, Christian interpreters have been hard pressed to resist viewing this passage entirely from a New Testament perspective. From this perspective, it seems natural to interpret the reconciliation of v. 24 as being Christ's work of reconciliation in behalf of the world. But the context simply does not allow this interpretation. It is true that Christ died for the sins of the whole world, but the issue in this passage is when Israel will respond to the atoning work of Christ and God will accomplish His prophesied work of reconciliation in them. This of course is the issue in any conversion. It is a settled Scriptural fact that Christ completed His work of reconciliation in behalf of the whole world. The issue is when—if ever—sinners will respond to this atoning work so they can be reconciled to God. For New Testament examples of the general work of reconciliation and its specific application, see II Corinthians 5:19–20 and Colossians 1:20–21.

well His judgment on Israel, "Judah hath not turned unto me with her whole heart, but feignedly, saith the Lord" (Jer. 3:10; cf. Isa. 58:1–2). And Hosea lamented, "Your goodness is as a morning cloud, and as the early dew it goeth away" (Hosea 6:4).

Repeatedly throughout her history, Israel "repented" of her sins and amended her ways; but in each case her righteousness was short-lived (Judges 2:18–19; Pss. 78:34–37; 106:12–13). Is there any hope for such a people as this? Jeremiah said, Yes, there is hope for you, but in the distant future:

> Behold, the days come, saith the Lord, that I will make a new covenant with the house of Israel, and with the house of Judah: not according to the covenant that I made with their fathers in the day that I took them by the hand to bring them out of the land of Egypt; which my covenant they brake, although I was an husband unto them, saith the Lord: But this shall be the covenant that I will make with the house of Israel; after those days, saith the Lord, I will put my law in their inward parts, and write it in their hearts; and will be their God, and they shall be my people (Jer. 31:31–33).

And it is the distant future that Gabriel points Daniel to as well. It will take seventy septets for God to complete His work of finishing Israel's transgression, of making an end of her sins, and of making reconciliation for her iniquity.

The determination of the seventy septets for the reconciliation of Israel applies to the establishment of the eternal kingdom as well. Gabriel announces the accomplishment of this work with three counterpart statements to the descriptions of reconciliation. When Israel ends her inveterate rebellion, the Lord will begin His gracious work of bringing in everlasting righteousness. When the Lord makes an end of sins, He will then be able to seal up vision and prophecy as no longer necessary for Israel. Finally, the atoning work of reconciliation will prepare the most holy place on the temple mount for the Lord to dwell in the midst of Israel.[7]

The Focal Points of the Prophecy (Dan. 9:25–27)

Having presented the general purpose and objectives of the seventy septets (v. 24), Gabriel now reveals salient details of this 490-year period

---

[7] In the Hebrew, the expression translated "most Holy" in the KJV (*qodesh qadashim*) "occurs, either with or without the article, thirty-nine times in the Old Testament, always in reference to the Tabernacle or Temple or to the holy articles used in them." Leon Wood, *A Commentary on Daniel* (Grand Rapids: Zondervan, 1990), 250.

(vv. 25–27). The initial revelation that Daniel received through Jeremiah's prophecy was that the Lord "would accomplish seventy years in the desolations of Jerusalem" (v. 2). It is quite natural, then, to find that Jerusalem, in its desolate condition, becomes a focal point both of Daniel's prayer and of the revelation that comes through Gabriel. Daniel refers to Jerusalem and its desolate condition six times in his prayer; in answering it, Gabriel mentions the city three times and the desolations connected with it four times.

The response Daniel received was not all he had hoped for. In his prayer, Daniel repeatedly appeals to God to forgive and reconcile his people so that the desolation of Jerusalem would come to an end and the Lord's presence would once again be manifest there. His hope was clearly that God would begin fulfilling these requests soon. But in His answer, the Lord said, in effect, "Daniel, your beloved city, Jerusalem, is destined for trouble, heartache, and desolations for many years to come. Yes, Jerusalem will be rebuilt—but in troubled times. And yes, the Messiah will come to Jerusalem—but she will reject Him; and the city, including its holy temple, will again be destroyed. Even after this, more desolations will come—until the last days."

We could say, then, that the message of the prophecy develops in three stages: (1) there will be trials at the rebuilt city of Jerusalem for sixty-nine septets as the nation awaits the Messiah (v. 25); (2) however, after that period, the Messiah will be cut off from His inheritance and the city will be destroyed (v. 26); (3) in the final septet, the seventieth, another prince will make a firm covenant with the nation; and in the latter half of that period, he will establish the abomination of desolation in Jerusalem (v. 27).

Trials in Jerusalem (v. 25)

The words "Know therefore and understand" reveal the importance of the description of the seventy septets. These words tell us that Daniel and his people needed to understand, not only that God would in His time fulfill His promises to Israel, but that a long process of discipline would necessary in God's training program.

God's schooling program for Israel will come in three stages.[8] First there will be seven septets, then sixty-two; and finally, in the last days,

---

[8] The analogy of an educational program is quite appropriate. After dealing with the providential work of God among mankind, Elihu asks the rhetorical question, "Who teacheth like him?" (Job 36:22). God is constantly teaching—revealing Himself—to mankind by every available means in

the seventieth septet will be fulfilled. Gabriel announces the beginning of the period with the words "from the going forth of the commandment to restore and to build Jerusalem." In 445 BC, Artaxerxes I Longimanus issued this commandment (Neh. 2:1–8).

Several passages indicate that Daniel's seventy septets are based on lunar years (twelve lunar months of thirty days each) of 360 days rather than on solar years. Twice Daniel was told that the persecution of his people by the Antichrist would last for "a time, times, and an half" (7:25; cf. 12:7). A comparison of other passages in his prophecy suggests that Daniel understood this expression as representing three and one-half years (e.g., 4:16, 23, 25, 32; 12:11, 12), half of Nebuchadnezzar's seven-year trial and half of the seventieth septet of Gabriel's message (9:27). The book of Revelation confirms this suggestion and specifies the length of this period as 1,260 days (11:2–3; 12:6, 14; 13:5), half of the number of days in seven lunar years.

The Rejection of the Messiah and the Destruction of Jerusalem (v. 26)

As the prophecy unfolds, we can envision Daniel's hope soaring when he hears the words "unto the Messiah the Prince." The thought must have flashed in his mind, "Now, at last, after all the troubles my people will endure, the Messiah will intervene and will bring in the kingdom." But the very next sentence dashes Daniel's hopes again. *After* the sixty-ninth septet (not "in the seventieth septet," as we might expect, since the septets appear to be consecutive), the Messiah will be "cut off," the city and sanctuary will be destroyed, war will come, and desolations are decreed.

The passage calls for "the people of the prince that shall come" to destroy Jerusalem; the wording of this statement is striking. Ordinarily in ancient times, credit for the destruction of a city went to the king who had conquered it. In this case, the credit went to the people of "a prince [or ruler] that shall come." Daniel knew from previous revelations that a king would come who would persecute Israel, and he knew this king would be associated with the fourth kingdom in the last days (Dan. 7:8, 11, 24–26; 11:36–45). This destruction came at the hands of the

---

the universe. This passage reveals that He has a specific "structured" program for His people. The rebuilding of Jerusalem, the trials the Jews endured then and afterward, the birth and ministry of the Messiah, all were a part of God's 69-septet training program for them. Their final exam, the seventieth septet, is yet to come. Yet even during this "recess" period, God is still dealing with His ancient people; in bringing Gentiles to Himself, He is provoking His covenant people to jealousy to "save some of them" (Rom. 11:14; cf. Rom. 10:19; Deut. 32:21).

Romans in AD 70, almost forty years after the Messiah was cut off; but Daniel, from his perspective, could not have seen such a break in the seventy septets.

The Covenant with Hell and the Abomination of Desolation (v. 27)

Daniel would have been familiar with Isaiah's words, "We have made a covenant with death, and with hell are we at agreement" (28:15). In that context, Isaiah is condemning profligate Israel for trusting in Egypt rather than the Lord as a defense against Assyria. In principle, however, the covenant the prince makes with Israel in the last days is the same.

As he listened to the words of Gabriel, Daniel would have undoubtedly seen this "prince that shall come" as in direct conflict with the Messiah. (In New Testament terms, he would have seen him as antichrist.) He probably would have seen him as causing the Messiah to be cut off and as bringing about the destruction of the city in the process. Now he hears these words:

> And he will make a firm covenant with the many for one week, but in the middle of the week he will put a stop to sacrifice and grain offering; and on the wing of abominations will come one who makes desolate, even until a complete destruction, one that is decreed, is poured out on the one who makes desolate (Dan. 9:27, NASB).

Daniel was painfully aware of Israel's history of forming alliances with wicked kings for peace and security. Now he sees this king, this antichrist, making an alliance with "the many"—the majority—in Israel in the last days. As it was in Isaiah's day and in Jeremiah's time, so it will be in the last days—only a remnant will oppose such alliances.

The Antichrist by this time will have as his power base the revived Roman Empire, but the prophecy of Daniel reveals that his rise to power may be largely through diplomatic skills and deception. Antiochus Epiphanes, the prototype of the Antichrist, "shall come in peaceably, and obtain the kingdom by flatteries" (Dan. 11:21). This firm covenant with Israel is such a move—a pact of peace and protection for Israel, but an opportunity for control and expansion for the Antichrist.

For many centuries Jerusalem, the "City of Peace," has known very little peace. As Daniel prophesied, the return of the exiles, the rebuilding of the temple, and the restoration and fortification of the city have not brought peace. Instead, "troublous times"—years of anguish and distress—have come. "We looked for peace, but no good came; and for a time of

Daniel 9:25 calls for a commandment "to restore and to build Jerusalem." The word translated *restore* (*shuv*) indicates that the city will be returned to a state comparable to its condition before its destruction. The word translated *build* (*banah*) denotes the process of constructing and enlarging that was necessary before the city could truly be called "restored." Together these words indicate that the commandment includes the authorization to rebuild the walls—so that the city will be a safe, viable place for business and worship. This commandment could not be fulfilled simply by people building homes in the vicinity of old Jerusalem. The inspired writer assumes, and history verifies, that it would be the restored, fortified city that would be conquered by the people (the Romans) of the prince that will come (Dan. 9:26); and Nehemiah's request presupposes the rebuilding of the walls (Neh. 2:1–18). Only the decree of 445 BC fully meets these criteria.

Various interpreters have advocated four decrees as the starting point of the seventy septets: (1) the decree of Cyrus in 538 BC (II Chron. 36:22–23; Ezra 1:1–4) specifically authorized only the building of a "house at Jerusalem" for the Lord; (2) the decree of Darius in 519 BC (Ezra 6:1–12) confirmed the decree of Cyrus; (3) the decree of the seventh year of Artaxerxes I Longimanus, 458 BC (Ezra 7:1–26), authorized Ezra to set in order and improve the service of the temple; (4) the decree of the twentieth year of Artaxerxes I, 445 BC (Neh. 2:1–8), authorized the restoration and building of the city. A study of the passages relating to the first three of these decrees will show that they all focus on the temple rather than on the restoration and building of the city.

The fifty thousand people or so who returned to Jerusalem to build the temple required a certain amount of "building the city" for dwelling places. Consequently, passages relating to the first three decrees may include references to building the city in this sense. But only the fourth decree authorizes the restoration of the fortified city. We must remember that in these times, authorization to rebuild a fortified city like Jerusalem was risky at best. A fortified city could hold out against a vastly superior army for months and even years—and Jerusalem had a reputation for repeatedly rebelling against its conquerors.

Starting in 445 BC, Daniel's seventy septets are then presented according to the lunar year of 360 days rather than the solar of 365 days. We know from Daniel 9:25–26 that the first sixty-nine septets bring us to the time of the Messiah, and that after the sixty-ninth septet, He will be "cut off." Scholars commonly say that the crucifixion of Christ took place in AD 30–33. The temptation is to go first to the Persian decrees concerning Jerusalem and to accept the one that best agrees with this time period; but this approach violates the expository method. Faithful exposition demands that we go first to the passage itself. Only the decree of 445/444 BC fulfills the wording of the prophecy ("the commandment to restore and to build Jerusalem," v. 25). Also, various passages in Daniel and Revelation tell us that at least the seventieth septet is presented in terms of a lunar year of 360 days. (More precisely, a lunar month averages 29½ (29.530588) days, making a lunar year 354 days; but the common practice was to ascribe 30 days to a month, 360 to a lunar year.)

Daniel and the people of Israel would have been well aware of the solar year of about 365 days, which modern astronomers calculate as 365.24219879 days. By the eighth century BC, two centuries before Daniel's time, Babylonian astronomers had devised a nineteen-year cycle with seven interpolated months that differed only 0.086403 of a day (2 hours, 4 minutes, 25.22 seconds) from the modern calculation.

Furthermore, before the time of Abraham, ancient Egyptians used phenomena relating to the disappearance and rise of the star Sirius (the Dog Star) to gauge the time of the Nile's annual flood. The length of the year from one rising of Sirius to the next was very close to the length of the solar year (only twelve minutes shorter). The people of Israel, who lived in Egypt for over four centuries, would have been well aware of these phenomena.

We would naturally expect people in the largely agricultural societies of ancient times to take special note of the changing seasons, of the two equinoxes when day and night are of equal length, etc. Consequently, we must assume that adjustments to the calendar were made in Palestine as they were in other ancient lands—probably by inserting an additional month every two or three years—to realign their lunar system to the solar year. For a good discussion of the reckoning of time in the ancient world, see Jack Finegan, *Handbook of Biblical Chronology*, 6–39 (See chap. 10, n. 4).

So if Daniel was familiar with the solar year, why did the Lord reveal the seventy septets in terms of the lunar year? This question has its roots in God's mysterious purposes and may never be answered satisfactorily. However, in our search for an answer, one of the first questions we should ask is,

"What message is the prophecy communicating?" According to v. 24, God ordained the septets to fulfill two great promises to Israel: their redemption from sin and their reign in the millennial kingdom. They were a sinful people because they had repeatedly violated the Lord's ordinances, which were designed to enable His people to know Him and to worship Him. The ordinances for Israel's worship were based on lunar cycles, and the septets are presented in lunar terms.

The major purpose of the prophecy was not to tell readers how long it would be before the Messiah came. It does delineate a remarkable timeline that tells us that only Jesus of Nazareth could be the Messiah. Even if we allow for some uncertainty as to the exact time of the Crucifixion, the prophecy informs us in no uncertain terms that only one Personality in all history fulfills its requirements. Nevertheless, as marvelous as this revelation is, it is secondary to the central message of the prophecy.

health, and behold trouble!" (Jer. 8:15; cf. Isa. 48:22; 57:21; Jer. 6:14; Ezek. 13:16).

And why have Jerusalem's inhabitants had no peace? Because they "cut off" the One Who came to offer them peace:

O Jerusalem, Jerusalem, thou that killest the prophets, and stonest them which are sent unto thee, how often would I have gathered thy children together, even as a hen gathereth her chickens under her wings, and ye would not! Behold, your house is left unto you desolate. For I say unto you, Ye shall not see me henceforth, till ye shall say, Blessed is he that cometh in the name of the Lord (Matt. 23:37–39).

Yet if you asked a Jew today why he refuses to recognize Jesus of Nazareth as the Messiah, he would likely answer, "Because he brought no peace." And just as the Lord warned them, "I am come in my Father's name, and ye receive me not: if another shall come in his own name, him ye will receive" (John 5:43), the time will come when a "messiah" will present himself to beleaguered Israel as its savior and peacemaker, and him they will receive.

Today seven million or so Israelis reside on a tiny sliver of land not much larger than the state of Massachusetts. Crowded around this tiny nation to the north, east, south, and southwest are predominantly Muslim countries with a combined population of about 350 million;

and virtually all of these countries are openly hostile to Israel. Is it any wonder, then, that when this charismatic leader, with the backing of the Roman Empire, offers peace and security to Israel, "the many"—the vast majority of the people—will receive his covenant with joy? Undoubtedly, he will be hailed and regaled as the messiah the nation (and the world) has been looking for.

The expression "firm covenant" is significant and appropriate for the times depicted. Agreements between nations are historically little more than instruments for strategic maneuvering. The Hebrew word translated "firm" (in the NASB) is, more literally, "strengthened." Its root word conveys the idea of overcoming or prevailing against opposition. The term therefore suggests a covenant on terms that overcome all the inherent suspicions and antagonism that have been brewing in the Middle East for centuries. Evidently, the agreement will not only be accepted enthusiastically in Israel but be honored by the Arab nations as well—perhaps providing economic advantages for all concerned.

Nevertheless, after being hailed as the messiah of the new world, this prince will find it convenient to break his covenant with Israel "in the middle of the week," halfway through the seventieth septet. Momentous events are destined for the middle of that septet. There will be "war in heaven," and Satan will be cast to the earth, where he will furiously persecute Israel (Rev. 12:7–17). It may be about this time that the hordes of Gog and Magog invade Palestine and are destroyed (Ezek. 38–39). And—most significant for the promotion of Satan's kingdom—it is evidently at this time that the Antichrist will be slain and miraculously resurrected.

This event, the resurrection of the Antichrist, will cause "all the world" to wonder and to worship him and Satan his master (Rev. 13:3–4). It will then be a relatively easy matter for him to stop the sacrifice in the temple, establish himself in the temple of God, and "reveal" his deity (II Thess. 2:4).

These events trigger the time of "Jacob's trouble," the Great Tribulation. The Lord Himself tells us this.

> When ye therefore shall see the abomination of desolation, spoken of by Daniel the prophet, stand in the holy place, (whoso readeth, let him understand:) Then let them which be in Judæa flee into the mountains . . . for then shall be great tribulation, such as was not since the beginning of the world to this time, no, nor ever shall be (Matt. 24:15–16, 21).

Though the abomination of desolation is spoken of also in connection with Antiochus Epiphanes (Dan. 8:13; 11:31), our Lord's reference here is obviously to the end times (Dan. 9:27); for He informs us that this great tribulation will take place just before His Second Coming (Matt. 24:29–31; cf. Dan. 12:11).

Nevertheless, the abomination of desolation under Antiochus Epiphanes illustrates the type of thing that will take place under the Antichrist. On December 25, 167 BC, Antiochus stopped the daily sacrifices, put an image of Zeus in the temple, and offered a pig on the altar.[9] The word translated *abominations* (*shiqquwts*) "is always used in connection with idolatrous practices, either referring to the idols themselves as being abhorrent and detestable in God's sight, or to something associated with the idolatrous ritual" (e.g., I Kings 11:5, 7; II Chron. 15:8; Jer. 16:18; Ezek. 7:20).[10] The word translated *desolate* (*shamem*) depicts something shocking that leaves a person stunned or appalled. Therefore, the expression "abomination of desolation" would depict a display of idolatry so outrageous that it leaves believers in a state of shock.

The Antichrist, having been miraculously raised from the dead, will immediately assume the prerogatives of deity (II Thess. 2:4; cf. Dan. 11:45). A great miracle-working false prophet will make a lifelike image of him and compel all to worship both the image and the Antichrist himself (Rev. 13:11–17; 14:9, 11; 16:2; 19:20; 20:4). Evidently, both the Antichrist himself and his image will be in the temple at times as objects of worship.[11]

Gabriel's message presents the Antichrist as coming in "on the wing of abominations." In Hebrew, the word translated *wing* (*kanaph*) is sometimes used figuratively to represent the extremity of something (e.g., the skirts of a garment or the ends of the earth). Thus the expression "wing

---

[9] The writer of I Maccabees (1:54) uses the expression "an abomination of desolation" to depict the desecration of the temple by the image of Zeus.

[10] *TWOT*, 2:955 (see chap. 3, n. 3).

[11] Hiebert has observed that in the reference to the abomination of desolation in Mark 13:14, the word *standing* (*estekota*) is a masculine participle, although the noun *abomination* (*bdelugma*) is neuter. "The fact that Mark deliberately, though ungrammatically, used the masculine points to the fact that he regarded the abomination as personal." *Mark: A Portrait of the Servant* (Chicago: Moody, 1974), 324. On the other hand, the parallel passage in Matthew (24:15) has *standing* (*estos*) in the neuter, agreeing with the neuter *abomination* (*bdelugma*). The Mark passage suggests that when the Antichrist himself is in the temple, he is viewed as the abomination of desolation (a man who has become an idol to the people). The Matthew passage indicates that the image of the Antichrist is also the abomination of desolation.

of abominations" (particularly with *abominations* in the plural) suggests that the Antichrist represents the ultimate in outrageous idolatry. And as he represents the ultimate in wickedness, he is destined for the ultimate in poetic justice. Complete destruction is decreed for him, a judgment "poured out on the one who makes desolate" (Dan. 9:27, NASB).

CHAPTER TWENTY-FIVE

BEHIND ENEMY LINES

THE BOOK OF REVELATION IS the grand finale of the Bible. It brings to a glorious culmination the story of God's covenant kingdom. The message of this final revelation

fills every passage of the Old Testament with life . . . makes the whole of Scripture harmonious and complete, crowning and perfecting and bringing it home to us with universal application as altogether divine. Without it the Scriptures themselves were as a house without a roof.[1]

John's use of the Old Testament in the Apocalypse is remarkable and unique. In the 404 verses in Revelation, there are 348 significant allusions to the Old Testament.[2] Yet, in contrast to other New Testament books,

---

[1] Isaac Williams, cited by Edward M. Panosian, "The Pulpit of Patmos," *Biblical Viewpoint* (November, 1982), 122.

[2] See Merrill C. Tenney, *Interpreting Revelation* (Grand Rapids: Eerdmans, 1973), 101–16, for a helpful discussion of the Old Testament background of Revelation. Tenney (p. 102) distinguishes between a citation, a quotation, and an allusion as follows: "A citation is a fairly exact reproduction of the words of the original text, accompanied by a statement of the fact that they are being quoted and by an identification of the source. A quotation is a general reproduction of the original text, sufficiently close to give the meaning of its thought and to establish unquestionably the passage from which it is taken. . . . An allusion consists of one or more words which by their peculiar character and general content are traceable to a known body of text, but which do not constitute a complete reproduction of any part of it." He acknowledges that the statistics he gives may vary among commentators. Henry Barclay Swete, for example, in his commentary *The Apocalypse of St. John* (1908; repr., Grand Rapids: Eerdmans, n.d.), says that out of 404 verses, 278 refer to the Old Testament.

there is not a single direct citation in the book from the Old Testament. It is as if the inspired writer has gathered the various strands of the Old Testament and formed them into this culminating message.

Genesis announces man's divine destiny to reign with God; Revelation gloriously fulfills it. In Genesis, the Serpent first attacks the newly founded kingdom of God; in Revelation, the Dragon is soundly defeated and doomed. In Genesis, the way to the Tree of Life is guarded by cherubim and a flaming sword, lest unregenerate men eat from it and be doomed in their sinful state. In Revelation, the Tree of Life at last fulfills its purpose by offering its fruit freely and abundantly to the citizens of the kingdom.

As a story in itself and as the final volume of a greater story, the book of Revelation describes the dramatic fulfillment of the divine purpose through Christ, the High Priest, final Prophet, and glorious King. John lays the foundation for the development of the story of Revelation with a prologue (1:1–8) and with a revelation to the people of God of the King in His threefold office (1:9–3:22). He then reveals to the beleaguered citizens of the kingdom the divine council of war in heaven and the King's cataclysmic attack on the kingdom of the world (4:1–16:21). Then comes the long-awaited fall of the kingdom of the world (17:1–21:8) and the glorious establishment of the eternal kingdom (21:9–22:5). Finally, in his epilogue, John reminds the reader of the truthfulness and timeliness of this revelation (22:6–21).

THE PROLOGUE (REV. 1:1–8)

As is the case often in literature, the prologue to the Apocalypse sets the stage and the mood for the revelation that follows, establishing the perspective necessary for understanding the book. The opening verses tell us that this is a preeminent revelation important enough to merit a special blessing for its effectual exposition and reception (vv. 1–3). The churches are the target audience of the revelation (v. 1:4a); and the message is to be received in the favor and peace granted by the triune God— Who is coming, as He promised, to judge the nations and to complete all that He began at Creation (vv. 4b–8).

The Importance of This Revelation (Rev. 1:1–3)

The very first word in this prophecy, "revelation" (*apokalupsis*), suggests its importance. By using the word *apokalupsis* without the article, John is emphasizing the quality of the revelation. The book constitutes a unique and distinct unveiling, or manifestation. The Messenger of this revelation is Jesus Christ Himself.[3] It is a revelation "of Jesus Christ, which God gave unto him, to shew unto his servants things which must shortly come to pass." In ancient times, the rank of the messenger spoke symbolically of the importance and nature of the message. A message containing bad news would come through a low-ranking servant, a good message by a man of higher rank (II Sam. 18:19–20, 27; I Kings 1:42). Likewise, the more important or urgent the message, the more honorable the messenger who conveyed it (Num. 22:15). This revelation is so important and so urgent that God has chosen as its Messenger none other than His own Son. Furthermore, the nature and character of the Messenger reveal that this prophecy is preeminently a message of good news for the people of God.

The unique blessing of this prophecy also testifies of its importance. "Blessed is he that readeth, and they that hear the words of this prophecy, and keep those things which are written therein" (Rev. 1:3). The Lord pronounces a special blessing on the preacher who carefully reads and explains the words of this book to his congregation, as well as on those who carefully listen to these words and seek to obey them. This blessing is designed to encourage the preacher to do what he might be inclined not to do. The first recipients of this prophecy might well have felt (as many modern readers do) that the book contained too many mysteries, too many judgments, and too much symbolism to be a blessing. But this

---

Revelation 1:3 is commonly taken to mean that a special blessing is pronounced on anyone who conscientiously reads the book; but people in ancient times would not have understood this to be the meaning of the inspired writer. John refers to the one reading in the singular ("he that readeth") and to the hearers in the plural ("they that hear"). In the early church, the presiding elder read and explained the Word (cf. Neh. 8:8), and the people in the congregation had the responsibility of carefully listening to the exposition and obeying its message. Very few Christians would have possessed copies of the Word, and many would not have been able to read.

---

[3] Interpreters have often observed that the words "of Jesus Christ" could be taken to mean "a revelation about Jesus Christ" or "a revelation by Jesus Christ." As attractive as the first interpretation is, John makes it clear by the words "which God gave unto him" that it is the latter idea he had in mind.

unique beatitude tells us that God intended for the message of Revelation to be distributed widely, studied carefully, and obeyed earnestly.

The Recipients of the Revelation (Rev. 1:4–8)

John announces that this prophecy—the entire book—is addressed to "the seven churches which are in Asia" (v. 4). He later makes it clear that the seven churches represent all the churches of God throughout the ages.[4] As the dramatic story of the Apocalypse unfolds, it is easy to lose sight of this vitally important fact—that the entire prophecy is addressed to the churches.

Furthermore, the verses that follow confirm the idea established in verse 3: this prophecy is designed to do more than inform the saints of things to come. The writer follows his address line with a benediction of grace and peace from the triune God (vv. 4b–6), but his blessing is not simply the repetition of a standard Christian greeting. To each member of the Trinity he ascribes attributes consistent with the message of his prophecy.

God is the eternal Father "which is, and which was, and which is to come" (v. 4b). He is also the "Alpha and Omega, the beginning and the ending . . . the Almighty" (v. 8). The Creator of Genesis must be recognized also as Fulfiller of all. The Spirit he describes as "the seven Spirits . . . before his throne" (v. 4c). Seven, in this case, speaks of the comprehensive work of the Holy Spirit (cf. Isa. 11:2; Zech. 4:2, 6, 10; Rev. 3:1; 4:5; 5:6). The ascription "before throne" signifies that the multifaceted work of the Spirit fulfills the purpose of the Sovereign God of the throne.

The Son of God John sees as Prophet, Priest, and King. As Prophet, He is "the faithful witness." As Priest, He is "the first begotten of the dead" Who "loved us, and washed us from our sins in his own blood." As King, He is "the prince"—the supreme Ruler (*archon*)—of the kings of the earth, presiding over the destinies of the nations.

And now the prophet sees this King of kings anew, coming soon to assume His lordship over the earth:

---

[4] The Roman province of Asia covered the western half of Asia Minor, modern Turkey. Of course, there were other churches in this territory, including Colossae (just six miles from Laodicea), and there were other churches beyond this province John could have addressed. His choice of the number seven (representing completeness) and his repeated use of the expression "He that hath an ear, let him hear what the Spirit saith unto the churches" indicate that these seven churches represented the entire church of God throughout the ages.

Behold, he cometh with clouds; and every eye shall see him, and they also which pierced him: and all kindreds of the earth shall wail because of him. Even so, Amen. I am Alpha and Omega, the beginning and the ending, saith the Lord, which is, and which was, and which is to come, the Almighty (vv. 7–8).

The words of the eternal Father ("I am Alpha and Omega," v. 8) attached to this announcement indicate that Christ's coming as King and Judge fulfills the eternal purpose of the Father. God's purpose for creating man will be fulfilled ultimately through the work of the Son as Priest, Prophet, and King; for the Son is one with the Father (John 10:30).

THE REVELATION OF THE KING TO HIS PEOPLE (REV. 1:9–3:22)

The Greek armies of the fourth century BC, though often greatly outnumbered, fought with such daring fierceness and skill that in less than a decade they were masters of the civilized world. What inspired them? How do we account for their success? For the answer to that question, we have but to look at one man, Alexander the Great. By his actions, his attitude, his brilliance, and his skill he became to his followers the visible prototype of the ideal man of war. He was always at the forefront of the battle, impervious, it seemed, to danger or fear, supremely confident of his destiny as a conqueror.

For the Christian soldier, the Commander in Chief is *El Shaddai* Himself—a Man of War, all-wise and all-powerful, destined to conquer the world and rule over the nations. It remains only for his soldiers to recognize Him for what He is.

The Vision of the Glorified Christ

Christ gives John a vision that sets the stage for all that is to follow. The opening and closing scenes of this vision suggest its overriding message for the churches. John, in the Spirit on the Lord's Day, hears a great voice "as of a trumpet" proclaiming, "I am Alpha and Omega, the first and the last" (v. 11). In his prologue, he ascribed these same words to God the Father as the eternal First Cause and Conclusion of all. Now he hears the Son, one with the Father, identifying Himself fully with His Father's eternal purpose and program.

At the conclusion of the vision, the prophet was so overwhelmed by the One he had previously known only as the Son of Man that he "fell at his feet as dead." The vision of the glorious Priest-King had left him terrified and lifeless. When, at the beginning of the vision, John turned to see the One Who spoke with "a great voice, as the sound of a trumpet," the first thing he saw was "seven golden candlesticks," representing the churches; and then he saw "in the midst of the seven candlesticks one like unto the Son of Man." This wording tells us that focus of the vision is on the churches, the people of God.

He recognizes that the One he sees is like the Son of Man he knew on earth, yet not like the gentle Shepherd he remembered. Now He is a fear-inspiring judge: "his eyes were as a flame of fire; and his feet like unto fine brass, as if they burned in a furnace; and his voice as the sound of many waters." From His mouth, it seemed, there were no soothing messages for the church; His words were the cutting words of judgment. In his prologue, at the thought of the Lord coming to judge the nations, John said, "Even so, Amen" (v. 7); but these are God's people the King is dealing with, not the heathen nations. Is there any hope for the churches? Will God's people also perish in the holy presence of their royal Judge?

To these unspoken questions the Lord responds, "Fear not; I am the first and the last: I am he that liveth, and was dead; and, behold, I am alive for evermore, Amen; and have the keys of hell and of death" (vv. 17b–18). Then the Lord again commands John to write; but note this time the added word *therefore*: "*Therefore* write the things which you have seen, and the things which are, and the things which shall take place after these things" (v. 19, NASB, emphasis added). This word takes on special significance in the context of John's reaction to the vision he has just seen. It points to the reason for the Lord's "Fear not." It tells John and the churches that though the Son of Man is among them as their High Priest, King, and Judge, they need not fear; He is the First and the Last, the conqueror of death and the Author of Life.

These ascriptions tell the people of God that whatever corrective judgment may be necessary, He will ultimately fulfill His divine purpose for them. However feeble they may feel, however sinful they may recognize themselves to be, the King will ultimately bring them to final redemption.

These words provide the necessary foundation and the necessary perspective for the people of God to profit from the message of the book of Revelation. No sensitive person can view vivid scenes of judgment without becoming more and more conscious of his own standing before the thrice-holy Judge of the universe. When Isaiah saw (as John did) the Lord high and lifted up, he cried, "Woe is me! for I am undone; because I am a man of unclean lips, and I dwell in the midst of a people of unclean lips: for mine eyes have seen the King, the Lord of hosts" (Isa. 6:5). And the Lord responded to him, as He did centuries later to John, by cleansing him through His eternal sacrifice, then fulfilling His purpose in him.

The Messages to the Churches

It had been over sixty years since John, as a fiery young "son of thunder" (Mark 3:17), had first heard Jesus's discourse on the parables of the kingdom. As with the other disciples, his concept of the coming kingdom of God was fundamentally scriptural in principle but grievously flawed in perception. John had thought, as most of his contemporaries did, that the appearance of the Messiah on earth signified the imminent inauguration of His universal kingdom. Consequently, he was looking for a throne, a realm over which to reign, and an expanding and prosperous kingdom.

In fact, so enamored was John with the thought of reigning with Christ that he and his brother enlisted the aid of their mother to solicit their Master for special thrones next to His (Matt. 20:20–23; Mark 10:35–40). It was through this philosophical filter that John and the other disciples heard the parables of the kingdom (Matt. 13). In effect, Jesus warned His disciples that the kingdom program would not develop as they expected. They would find a mixed reception to the kingdom message, not continuous growth, expansion, and glory. The kingdom would come to include many tares, and some professed kingdom saints would ultimately be cast into "the furnace of fire," where they would suffer eternal damnation (Matt. 13:42, 50). Just as the disciples were unable to comprehend our Lord's announcements of His impending crucifixion, so they found it difficult to grasp heaven's kingdom program.

Now, some sixty years later, John has finally digested the Lord's message for the kingdom saints. From his prison on Patmos, he sees the churches as they really are. As the Lord had warned decades before, the churches are mixed and will be so until the end of the age. In fact, it could well be that, just like an individual Christian, a church might go through several stages of spiritual strength and weakness in its lifetime. John had undoubtedly witnessed such stages in some of these churches. Likely he had seen the saints at Ephesus in the glow of their first love; to his un-speakable grief, he had lived to see that glow disappear.[5]

What part then do the churches have in this warfare for dominion over the earth? Far from winning their earthly battle, it appears that the king-dom saints are barely holding their own. At this point the people of God have suffered immense losses in perspective and spirit by losing sight of a vitally important principle of warfare. Success in Christian warfare is gov-erned entirely by our Commander's objectives.

Just before our Commander in Chief departed for His heavenly throne, He gave the kingdom saints of the church age their assignment. This Great Commission revealed His objectives for their strategically important units. They are to be witnesses to the uttermost parts of the earth—to shine as lights in the midst of the world's encroaching darkness (Phil. 2:15). The commission for these battalions said nothing about hav-ing dominion or taking control of the earth. In fact, their Commander, in so many words, told His followers to set aside for now all thoughts of an earthly reign and to concentrate on their assignment (Acts 1:6–8). On one occasion, Pyrrhus (319–272 BC), king of Epirus (known today mainly for his costly victories over the Romans), convinced an entire hos-tile army to renounce their allegiance to his antagonist and come over to his standard. The objective of the church-age battalions is comparable to what Pyrrhus did—to convince the enemies of their King to abandon the kingdom of darkness and become citizen-soldiers of the kingdom of light.

For the church, if their objectives in the warfare are clear, the temporary dominance of the kingdom of darkness is no longer an issue. Church saints, for example, have no need to bolster the illusion of Christianity's earthly progress by surveying statistics of how many people claim to have had a "born-again experience." As with Paul, their objective is to provide beacons of light throughout the kingdom of darkness. Their one fear should be not their failure to dominate in the world but their failure to shine clearly.

As it turns out, this is the key issue in the Lord's messages to the seven churches. Each of the churches is a part of the Lord's lampstand. Each

---

[5] Though John was in Jerusalem at least until about AD 51 (Gal. 2:1, 9), various ancient writers say he lived in Ephesus for a number of years and that he died and was buried there during Trajan's reign (AD 98–117). According to Irenaeus (c. 130–c. 202), all the elders in the province of Asia associated with John and testified that he taught them. *Eusebius: The Church History*, Paul L. Maier, ed. (Grand Rapids: Kregel, 1999), 110.

has a commission to provide light in the place of its assignment, and each has the potential of losing that light. In the midst of a crooked and perverse generation, in the midst of the contrary winds of the kingdom of darkness, how can they best make sure that "the light of the glorious gospel of Christ" shines in their assigned place?

The introduction to each of the letters gives the answer to that question. The address line to each church contains a descriptive statement about Christ, most of which are taken from John's vision of Christ in Revelation 1, and each of which calls attention to some attribute of Christ that the church addressed particularly needed. These leading statements suggest that in each case the preeminent need of that church was directly related to that aspect of the person of Jesus Christ. Just as good physical health demands balanced nourishment, good spiritual health demands a balanced perspective of Christ.

The governing principle of the messages to the churches, then, is this: the spiritual health of the churches (and of "he that hath an ear" within the churches) is directly proportional to the accuracy of their perception of Christ. The believer's means of strength and ultimate victory is fundamentally the same as it has been from man's original commission in the Garden of Eden. He must recognize and respect his Lord as absolutely sovereign over every realm of life. The method by which he maintains this attitude is to contemplate the Person of his Lord. Just as John saw the Commander in Chief in His various attributes, so must each soldier in the battle.

As God is Lord over every realm of life, He deploys His soldiers throughout these realms for the ultimate conquest of all. Each realm has its own obstacles to overcome and its own peculiar enemies. Each realm is the property of *El Shaddai*, but in each case the citizen of the kingdom of light finds a "Canaanite" occupying the territory, determined to claim it as his own.

The warfare of each battalion differs according to the nature of the terrain in the assigned territory. In some cases, the preeminent battle is against an enemy within the camp (e.g., Ephesus). In others, the battle is openly confrontational and bloody (e.g., Smyrna). In virtually every case, there is an internal spiritual battle to be won before the battle against the enemy can succeed. Relatively early in their history, the ancient Romans developed the attitude that they were destined to rule the world. This attitude gave the Roman soldier the determination of an overcomer. In the course of their military history, the Romans suffered many defeats—some so devastating that their enemies marveled they didn't sue for peace. But even in their darkest hours, the Romans regarded no defeat as final.

The kingdom of God will certainly rule the world. That is settled and sure. It remains only for the child of God to fully realize his destiny to reign with God. He does this by focusing his attention on the One Who is leading him toward the fulfillment of that destiny:

Thou hast put all things in subjection under his feet. For in that he put all in subjection under him, he left nothing that is not put under him. But now we see not yet all things put under him. But we see Jesus, who was made a little lower than the angels for the suffering of death, crowned with glory and honour; that he by the grace of God should taste death for every man (Heb. 2:8–9).

CHAPTER TWENTY-SIX

THE COUNCIL OF WAR IN HEAVEN

"**L**ORD, HOW LONG SHALL THE wicked, how long shall the wicked triumph?" (Ps. 94:3). Almost since the beginning of time, this has been the cry of the godly. By faith, the people of God know that eventually the final judgment will come and the people of God will triumph. But why is it taking so long? And why in the face of the enemy's arrogance and blasphemy is God not taking action? "Why withdrawest thou thy hand, even thy right hand? pluck it out of thy bosom," the Psalmist cried (74:11).

John must have had such thoughts often in his long life. But now at last, from his prison on Patmos, he sees a door standing open in heaven, hears the trumpetlike voice of the Lord calling him upward, and finds himself in the throne room of the Almighty.

Though John was to see things no man had ever seen, he would nevertheless have been familiar with the earthly equivalent of this heavenly scene. It was a council of war. In ancient times such a council generally preceded a declaration of war. Subordinate kings would meet with the supreme monarch, taking their places on thrones befitting their status in the realm. Evidence would then be presented of the need for "justice" (vengeance) against a nation that had in some way violated the rights of the supreme king and his subjects. Then a call would be sounded for a worthy and able man who could lead the armies of the king and execute judgment upon the offenders. The ceremony would also include sacrifices and an appeal to the gods to support and vindicate the "righteous cause" of the supreme king.

Now John witnesses the proclamation of this timeless principle: the throne of the eternal kingdom belongs to the triune God, for He is the Creator and Redeemer.

If the book of Revelation is the "Throne Book" of the Bible, then these two chapters are the "Throne Room." The Greek word generally translated *throne* (sometimes *seat*) appears sixty-one times in the New Testament. Forty-six of those times are in the book of Revelation, and eighteen are in chapters four and five. This council of war unfolds in two dramatic scenes: the convocation for judgment (ch. 4) and the commissioning of the Lamb to execute judgment (ch. 5). These two chapters prepare the way for all that is to follow. They could well be viewed as containing in a nutshell the entire message of the Apocalypse.

THE CONVOCATION FOR JUDGMENT (REV. 4)

Though virtually every line of this chapter is weighted with significance, two features have special significance for the culmination of the message of the Bible. These two features are the elders seated on twenty-four thrones and the four "beasts" (cherubim) who served "round about the throne."

The Enthroned Elders

The first thing John sees is a throne—as it turns out, the throne of the King of kings. Then he looks around and sees twenty-four other thrones. Seated on each is an elder wearing white raiment and a crown of gold. The crowns are victors' crowns (*stephanos*), and the white robes symbolize the purity by which victory was gained.

The word *elder* in Scripture could simply depict an older person, but in contexts such as this, it denotes a leader or representative of the people. Here the elders evidently represent the people of God reigning with the King of kings and participating in His judgment of the kingdom of the world. Six centuries before, the prophet Daniel had witnessed the same scene and, as John did, also saw that the saints would reign with their King.

> As I looked,
>> thrones were placed,
>> and the Ancient of days took his seat;
> his clothing was white as snow,
>> and the hair of his head like pure wool;
> his throne was fiery flames;
>> its wheels were burning fire.
> A stream of fire issued
>> and came out from before him;
> a thousand thousands served him,
>> and ten thousand times ten thousand stood before him;
> the court sat in judgment
>> and the books were opened....

As for me, Daniel, my spirit within me was anxious, and the visions of my head alarmed me. I approached one of those who stood there and asked him the truth concerning all this. So he told me and made known to me the interpretation of the things. These four great beasts are four kings who shall arise out of the earth. But the saints of the Most High shall receive the kingdom and possess the kingdom forever, forever and forever (Dan. 7:9–10, 15–18, ESV).

The Cherubim

The attributes of the creatures the KJV translators call "beasts" (e.g. Rev. 4:6–9) reveal that they should be identified with the cherubim of

The fact that Daniel witnessed virtually the same scene indicates that the elders in John's vision represent all of God's people, not just the church-age saints. The nature of the book of Revelation suggests this also. As the conclusion of the written revelation of God, this book tells the story of the culmination of the work of God from the beginning of time. From the beginning, God intended for His work to be universal, as evidenced by the promises of the Abrahamic Covenant that Abraham's seed would bless all the families of the earth. This concept of the universal culmination of the plan of God is suggested also in the fact that the twelve gates of the walls of New Jerusalem were inscribed with the names of the twelve tribes of Israel, and the twelve foundations with the names of the twelve apostles.

the Old Testament. What is the nature of these creatures, and what is the message conveyed through them?

Names of the Cherubim

Unfortunately, the etymology of the designation *cherubim* is obscure, and every effort to trace the word's origin has been futile. According to C. F. Keil, "All the derivations that have been proposed from the Hebrew or any other Semitic dialect cannot make the slightest pretensions to probability."[1] However, both the prophet Ezekiel and the apostle John repeatedly call these creatures "living ones." In fact, Ezekiel's first impression of these marvelous beings is captured in this expression (1:5), and he continued to use the term even after he realized they were cherubim (10:17).

In the book of Revelation, where John refers to the cherubim no less than twenty times, he always calls them *living ones* (*zoa*), never *cherubim*. E. W. Hengstenberg suggests that the designation *living ones* as used in Ezekiel and Revelation becomes a proper name and, as such, epitomizes the nature of the creatures.[2] Evidently both Ezekiel and John connected the cherubim in some way with the concept of life.

Descriptions of the Cherubim

The descriptions of the cherubim in Ezekiel and Revelation, where the creatures are described in symbolic form, confirm the interpretation that they represent the concept of life.[3] Ezekiel depicts them, in the first place, as having "the likeness of a man" (1:5). That is, in general they had a human form and "are to be conceived as presenting the appearance of a human body in all points not otherwise specified in the following narrative."[4] Thus they symbolize the highest form of created life.

But they could not be depicted simply as human beings without losing their more general significance. Accordingly, they are described as having four faces: the face of a man, the face of a lion, the face of an ox, and the

---

[1] *Biblical Commentary on the Prophecies of Ezekiel* (Grand Rapids: Eerdmans, 1959), 1:39. For a more detailed discussion of the cherubim, see my article "The Cherubim," *Biblical Viewpoint* (November, 1976): 124–32.

[2] *The Prophecies of the Prophet Ezekiel Elucidated* (Edinburgh: T & T Clark, 1874), 508.

[3] Because of the highly symbolical nature of the descriptions of the cherubim, a number of interpreters view them as nothing more than symbolical expression of divine truth. However, Gen. 3:24 represents them as real beings. The nature of these spiritual beings may be presented to the human eye in various symbolical forms; but the symbols in every case would have to point back to the real creatures they represent.

[4] Keil, *Ezekiel*, 1:22.

face of an eagle. These creatures represent the noblest forms of the classes of animal life distinguished in the Bible. These classes, as presented in the accounts of the creation and the Flood (Gen. 1:24–30; 7:21–23), are man, domestic animals, wild animals, fowl, fish, and "creeping things."

Of these, only the first four are represented in the cherubim of Ezekiel and Revelation. Fish and creeping things are omitted because they would destroy the significance of the symbol. Both of these classes are by their natural characteristics and habitats associated with lower forms of life, and reptiles in Scripture also represent curse, sin, and death.

According to some interpreters (e.g., Hengstenberg), this symbolization of life must be limited to earthly life, representing the fact that God created all earthly life. However, the inspired writers also represent the living creatures as having wings—a well-known symbol of the supernatural. Furthermore, Ezekiel describes them as gleaming "like burning coals of fire" (1:13). In speed of movement they were like lightning, dashing to and fro (Ezek. 1:14). It is difficult to see how the prophet could see all this and not think of extraterrestrial as well as terrestrial life. In fact, it is difficult to see how a godly prophet-priest could think of life itself without associating it in some way with the supernatural.

In Eden. This concept of the cherubim as representing life in its highest form agrees with references to these creatures throughout the Bible. In the first reference, Genesis 3:24, the cherubim together with a flaming sword are stationed at the east end of the garden of Eden "to keep the way of the tree of life." Here the cherubim are introduced into written revelation as representatives of divine life, standing, as God Himself does, diametrically opposed to death in any form. This account, in the opening pages of written revelation, sets the stage for the later revelation about these creatures.

In the tabernacle and temple. In Exodus, where the living creatures are first associated with the throne of God in the tabernacle, God commanded Moses to make a golden cherub for each end of the mercy seat. These cherubs, He emphasized, were to rise from the mercy seat.[5] They were not merely to be placed on or attached to the mercy seat; they were to be made of the same gold and were to rise from it as an integral part of

---

[5] The Hebrew preposition for *from* or *out of* (*min*) is used six times in two verses (Exod. 25:18–19) to describe the fact that the cherubim were to be formed rising from the mercy seat (the *capporeth*) "so as to form one whole with the *capporeth* itself, and be inseparable from it." Keil, *The Pentateuch*, 2:168.

it (Exod. 25:18–19). As they rose from the mercy seat, they were to have their wings spread upward so their wings covered the mercy seat. Finally, they were to be formed facing one another, looking toward the mercy seat (Exod. 25:20).

The word translated "mercy seat" is *capporeth*, from *caphar*, "to cover." This word is used consistently in Scripture to represent the figurative covering of sin or making atonement. On the Day of Atonement, the sacrificial blood was sprinkled on and in front of the mercy seat (Lev. 16:14–15). According to Leviticus 17:11, blood represents life. Consequently, shed blood would represent life poured out, or the sacrificial death. The mercy seat, then, would symbolize the sacrificial death; but at the same time, the cherubim would represent the new life which springs from the atoning death.

Furthermore, the wings of the cherubim were to cover or screen the mercy seat (Exod. 25:20). The statement "the cherubim shall stretch forth their wings on high" would be quite adequate to portray the creatures as flying or perhaps standing in adoration. But the passage makes it very clear that the purpose for spreading forth their wings was to shield the mercy seat. In fact, so prominent is this feature that the priest-prophet Ezekiel, with obvious reference to the temple cherubim, twice calls the king of Tyre the "covering cherub" (28:14, 16). The writer of Hebrews likewise emphasizes this feature when he describes the cherubim as "overshadowing" (*kataskiazonta*) the mercy seat (Heb. 9:5, NASB).

The symbolism in the form and position of the cherubim could not be, as is often claimed, that of guardianship of the throne of God, or of the divine Presence, or of the ark of the covenant. If they are guards, why are they facing one another? The most natural posture for guards would be facing away from the throne, as if ready to ward off intruders. And with their wings spread over their heads, from whom would they be shielding the throne? For since the Shekinah Presence was above the cherubim,[6] it would have been more appropriate, had the symbolism been that of

---

[6] The statement that the Lord was to appear "between the two cherubims" (Exod. 25:22) certainly should not be construed to suggest the idea that the Shekinah Presence was compressed between the narrow circle of the cherubim's wings. The references to the cloud of glory "filling" the sanctuary (e.g., Exod. 40:34–35; I Kings 8:10), together with the concept of the cherubim themselves as the chariot throne of God (Ps. 18:10–11; I Chron. 28:18; Ezek. 1:5–28), indicate that the manifestation of the Lord was above both the mercy seat and the cherubim.

guarding, for the cherubim to have their wings spread in front and behind the mercy seat.

Furthermore, the whole concept of guarding the throne of the Lord is inappropriate. It is incongruous to think of the omnipotent God being guarded. Royal guards in Bible times represented the fact that kings were subject to death, were fearful of death, and were incapable by themselves of standing against the threat of death. Guards, therefore, symbolized the king's weakness rather than his strength. On the other hand, Jehovah, throughout the Bible—and particularly when shown on His throne—is depicted as unassailable because of His own majesty and power. The inspired writers picture Him as having armies and servants, for these speak of the king's loyal followers who exist because of Him and are strong only by virtue of His leadership; but He is never pictured as having guards.

The wings of the cherubim, then, far from guarding, simply cover the mercy seat where the blood was sprinkled. And since their wings are spread over their heads, rather than in front and behind, they represent the idea that the living God is to be associated with life (the cherubim) rather than death (the shed blood).

The whole mercy seat, therefore, forms a beautiful picture of atonement. The shed blood, representing the atoning death, was sprinkled on the mercy seat; and as a result, life (in the form of the cherubim) springs up. The cherubim then, with wings overshadowing the representation of death, gaze steadfastly at the shed blood as the source of divine life.

This view is consistent not only with the nature of God but also with the nature of the Atonement. For in the revelation of the plan of Redemption, the atoning death, as vital as it is, constantly gives way to the redeeming life: "It is Christ that died, yea rather, that is risen again, who is even at the right hand of God, who also maketh intercession for us" (Rom. 8:34).

In the book of Revelation. The representation of the cherubim in the Apocalypse also confirms the view that they are symbols of life and intimately associated with the Atonement. In this final revelation, the cherubim are constantly designated as "living ones" (*zoa*). And, just as in the tabernacle and temple, they are associated with the *capporeth* (mercy-seat) throne.

John first sees the cherubim "in the midst of the throne" and around it (Rev. 4:6). Interpreters commonly explain this description as an unusual way of saying that the cherubim were around the throne. But there is nothing in the context that forbids taking the words just as they stand: John sees the living creatures as if they are merged with the throne.

He first sees twenty-four elders around the throne, then flashes of lightning coming from the throne, accompanied by thunderings and voices. Then, as he looks more intently at the throne, he sees the living creatures, not merely around the throne (as the elders had been), but in its midst (Rev. 4:4–6).

In addition to being in harmony with the immediate context, this interpretation has the advantage also of being in harmony with the image of the *capporeth* throne of the tabernacle and temple. The throne in Revelation is related to the *capporeth* throne of the temple is intimated several times in the book. For example, John beholds not only the temple cherubim in the midst of the throne, but also a Lamb "as it had been slain" (5:6). Here is the climactic revelation of the mercy seat: the representation of the atoning death merged, and submerged, in the representation of divine life. In another connection from the throne of Revelation to the *capporeth* throne of the temple, the living creatures are constantly associated in this book with the twenty-four elders (4:4–6, 9–10; 5:6, 8, 11–14; 7:11; 14:3; 19:4), who are representatives of the redeemed.

The association of the cherubim with judgment (Rev. 6:1–7; 15:7; Ezek. 10) is consistent with their nature as supreme manifestations of life. As representatives of the living God, the cherubim would by nature oppose sin and sinners, harbingers of death. The concluding words of Revelation 15:7 illustrate this principle: "And one of the four beasts gave unto the seven angels seven golden vials full of the wrath of God, *who liveth for ever and ever*" (emphasis added).

But the cherubim are not "death angels"—dispensing the judgments of death—for that would be opposed to their natures and signification. In Revelation 6:1–7 the cherubim announce the judgment to John, but they do not execute it. In Revelation 15:7 a cherub gives the seven bowls of wrath to seven angels, but he himself does not pour them out. In Ezekiel 10:7 a cherub takes fire from within and gives it, for execution, to the man clothed in linen. Even in Genesis 3:24 the flaming sword is not in the hands of the cherubim but distinct from them.

From the Foundation to the Capstone

So how does all this develop the story of the Bible? This last book of the Bible is the culmination of the foundational principles established in the first. The first revelation of God in the Bible is that He is the Creator and Sustainer of all life and all that relates to life. When sin and death entered, He revealed Himself also as the Redeemer of fallen life. Now in this convocation that sets the stage for the grand culmination of His creative and redemptive work, the call for judgment sounds forth antiphonally from the living ones and the redeemed to the One sitting on the throne, "who liveth for ever and ever" (Rev. 4:9–11).

COMMISSIONING OF THE LAMB FOR JUDGMENT (REV. 5)

In ancient Rome, as in other ancient societies, commanders of the army were appointed year by year. In the early days of the Roman Republic, the Assembly annually elected two consuls (magistrates) with equal power. During a time of war, the two consuls alternated day by day as commanders of the army. In a time of emergency, however, the Senate could approve a dictator who for the duration of the emergency would put the state under martial law and rule over the citizens and army with absolute power.

In his vision of the heavenly Council of War, the prophet sees a development take place comparable to these ancient customs. The King of kings is preparing to declare war on those who have occupied and misused the earthly territory He created. Upon His right hand is a seven-sealed list of grievances—extended, ominously, to both sides of the scroll—against the inhabitants of the earth. At His bidding, a mighty angel heralds, "Who is worthy to open the book, and to loose the seals thereof?" And all—in heaven, on earth, and under the earth—shrink from the thought of opening this scroll.

At this, John "wept much"—burst into tears and kept weeping. Why? Because he knew this scroll was important. He undoubtedly remembered the words of Scripture in which the Lord said, "Go thy way, Daniel: for the words are closed up and sealed till the time of the end" (Dan. 12:9); and he must have been sickened with grief at the thought that perhaps his hope might also be deferred (Prov. 13:12).

What is the significance of this fear-inspiring scroll? It could be called "The Last Will and Testament of the King of Kings." It contains the final steps in the execution of God's plan for the implementation and inheri-

Ancient Roman law required that a will be sealed seven times. Ordinarily a scribe wrote on only one side of a papyrus scroll. Not only would a scroll written on both sides lose privacy, it would be particularly inconvenient for the recipient—requiring him to rewind it. Furthermore, writing on the reverse side of a scroll was more difficult. Ancient papyrus writing material was composed of two layers, with the fibers of the top piece running horizontally and those of the bottom perpendicularly. Thus a scribe using the reverse side of a scroll would have to write "across the grain" and therefore would use this expedient only in the case of demanding circumstances. For more information on these topics, see James Hastings, ed., *A Dictionary of the Bible* (New York: Charles Scribner's Sons, 1911), 4:944–56; Alan F. Johnson, *Revelation: Expositor's Bible Commentary*, Frank E. Gaebelein, gen. ed. (Grand Rapids: Zondervan, 1981), 13:465–66; Ethelbert Stauffer, *Christ and the Caesars* (London: S.C.M. Press, 1955), 182–83.

tance of His eternal kingdom. Christ, the Messiah, is the sole Executor of this divine will. Now at last the decree that David saw was to be fulfilled:

I will declare the decree: the Lord hath said unto me, Thou art my Son; this day have I begotten thee. Ask of me, and I shall give thee the heathen for thine inheritance, and the uttermost parts of the earth for thy possession. Thou shalt break them with a rod of iron; thou shalt dash them in pieces like a potter's vessel. Be wise now therefore, O ye kings: be instructed, ye judges of the earth. Serve the Lord with fear, and rejoice with trembling. Kiss the Son, lest he be angry, and ye perish from the way, when his wrath is kindled but a little. Blessed are all they that put their trust in him (Ps. 2:7–12).

And one of the elders, one of the representatives of the redeemed saints, silenced John's lamentation with, "Weep not: behold, the Lion of the tribe of Juda, the Root of David, hath prevailed to open the book, and to loose the seven seals thereof" (Rev. 5:5). In effect, the elder declared, "There is no need now for weeping. The scroll need no longer remain sealed. Our long-awaited Messiah has come and He has conquered death and sin. Therefore He is worthy as the Redeemer to open the seals."

"Behold the Lion, the lineal King"—references to prophecies John knew well (Gen. 49:9–10; Isa. 11:1); but when he looked, he saw, as it were, the whole prophetic picture of the Messiah in a scene wonderfully appropriate, yet never before depicted. "And I beheld, and, lo, in the midst of the throne and of the four beasts, and in the midst of the elders, stood a Lamb as it had been slain, having seven horns and seven eyes, which are the seven Spirits of God sent forth into all the earth" (Rev. 5:6).

When he had first looked at the throne, he saw One sitting on it Who appeared "like a jasper and a sardine stone" (Rev. 4:2–3). Later he was to see the holy Jerusalem descending from heaven, "having the glory of God: and her light was like unto a stone most precious, even like a jasper stone, clear as crystal" (21:11). Some five or ten years before, John had written, "God is light" (I John 1:5). Here he sees Him in the brilliant radiance of precious stones.

But now as he looks again, he sees, as if superimposed on the throne, a Lamb, which though it had been slain, was standing—alive, almighty, and all-seeing. The whole of John's heavenly vision has been in a temple setting. He has seen "the Lord . . . in his holy temple, the Lord's throne . . . in heaven: his eyes behold, his eyelids try, the children of men" (Ps. 11:4; Rev. 4:5; 5:6). The cherubim, the white-robed elders (royal priests of God, Rev. 1:6; 5:10; Exod. 19:6), and even the precious stones he saw at the throne may well have reminded the prophet of our High Priest (Exod. 28:4, 17–21).

Then he sees this Lamb come and take the scroll that was on the hand of the One sitting on the throne—which produces ecstatic song and praise in heaven. Why this ecstasy? That is easy for anyone to understand who has experienced the sickening feeling John had when it appeared his hope had been once again deferred. Gathered in this one action of the Savior are all the hopes of fallen creation—every creature in heaven, and on earth, and under the earth, and in the sea (Rev. 5:13).

All creation, Paul tells us, "groaneth and travaileth in pain together." Likewise, we who have the first fruits of the Spirit "groan within our-selves"; and even the Spirit of God "maketh intercession for us with groanings which cannot be uttered" (Rom. 8:22–26). And why this groaning? All are waiting for the "adoption . . . the redemption of our body"—waiting, that is, for the final fulfillment of God's plan. The song of praise began because, by taking the scroll, the Savior displayed His willingness and ability to do just that.

CHAPTER TWENTY-SEVEN

THE DEATH THROES OF THE DRAGON, PART I

> Therefore rejoice, ye heavens, and ye that dwell in them. Woe to the inhabiters of the earth and of the sea! for the devil is come down unto you, having great wrath, because he knoweth that he hath but a short time (Rev. 12:12).

FOR THE PROUD, THERE IS no wrath so great as that which comes with the realization of impending defeat. The words above announce the beginning of the Great Tribulation, three and one-half years before the glorious return of Christ. Satan knew at this time that he had "but a short time" left. But had he known before this that his days were numbered? I am inclined to think so. The Bible speaks of wicked sinners who "knowing the judgment of God, that they which commit such things are worthy of death, not only do the same, but have pleasure in them that do them" (Rom. 1:32). Surely, then, the father of these sinners knows his day of reckoning is inevitable. There is a certain insane optimism that sinners seek to cultivate; but as criminals often testify when their judgment time comes, deep down they know they are courting disaster. So it must be with Satan.

Whatever the case, we will better understand the last stages of the war between the Dragon and the Lamb if we can get an overview of its development. We will begin with the seventieth septet, seven years before the Second Coming of Christ.

THE ESTABLISHMENT OF THE NEW ROMAN EMPIRE

The world has never really gotten over the loss of the old Roman Empire. For all its bloodshed, tyranny, and corruption, it provided for its subjects a certain sense of power and security, which the people of the world will gladly overlook nearly any evil to gain.

The Roman Empire revived mankind's Tower-of-Babel dream for a world government that would establish a man-centered utopian kingdom of peace and prosperity. Both the old Roman Empire and the revived Roman Empire, then, are part of a bigger dream—a step toward man's dominion over the earth through his self-made deification. This bigger goal has been a central platform in man's agenda ever since the Tower of Babel.

It didn't take long after the fall of the old Roman Empire for a "new" Roman empire to be established. On Christmas Day AD 800, Pope Leo III crowned Charlemagne, the king of the Franks, as emperor at Rome. This "Holy Roman Empire," which Charlemagne claimed was the successor to that of the Caesars, lasted in some form until 1806, when Napoleon dictated its dissolution.

Though the union of European states under the Holy Roman Empire proved ineffectual, the idea of such a union remained alive. In 1634 the Duke of Sully, France, published *The Grand Design*, containing proposals

The Council of Europe used a poster of the Tower of Babel as a symbol of their efforts to build a unified Europe. In contrast to Bruegel's famous painting of the Tower's construction disrupted and its builders frustrated, this poster depicts the work progressing successfully and the workers proceeding confidently and in harmony. The motto on the poster provides a human solution for the Lord's corrective of confounding their language: "Europe: Many Tongues, One Voice." Above the tower is a circle of stars representing the nations of the European Community. In what appears to be conscious defiance of biblical truth, the stars are upside-down pentagrams, a well-known occult and satanic symbol. For a picture of this poster, see William F. Jasper, *Global Tyranny Step by Step* (Appleton, WI: Western Islands Publishers, 1992), 255.

for a federation of European states governed by a senate of sixty-six members. At the Hague Congress in 1948, Winston Churchill said, "After this long passage of years, we are all servants of *The Grand Design*."[1] In 1930, Aristide Briand, a co-recipient of the Nobel Peace Prize, presented proposals through the French government for a European federation of states with a central body to deal with questions of mutual welfare.[2]

In 1957, six European countries (Belgium, France, Holland, Italy, Luxembourg, and West Germany) signed treaties in Rome establishing the European Economic Community (the Common Market) and the European Atomic Energy Community (EURATOM). In 1967 these organizations merged, creating the European Community (EC).

Nineteen ninety-three was a benchmark year for the European federation. In that year, the Treaty on European Union, signed in 1991 at Maastricht, Netherlands, was ratified and put into effect—providing for the economic union of 345 million people in twelve nations. The European Union (EU) created the euro to replace the national currencies of its member countries. By 2002, this goal had largely been accomplished. The EU introduced euro currency notes and coins that replaced the national currencies of participating countries (though Denmark rejected the euro and Britain and Sweden decided not to adopt it immediately).

THE RISE OF THE ANTICHRIST
(THE FIRST SEAL)

Evidently, by the time the seventieth septet arrives, the Antichrist will have established himself as ruler of the revived Roman Empire. At the beginning of this period he establishes his "firm covenant" with Israel, guaranteeing peace for them for the first time in centuries (Dan. 9:27). This is a time of conquest and expansion for this charismatic world leader—largely, it seems, with very little bloodshed; for he is pictured in John's Patmos vision as going forth "conquering, and to conquer" (Rev. 6:2).

---

[1] Frederick A. Tatford, *Five Minutes to Midnight* (Ft. Washington, PA: Christian Literature Crusade, 1971), 63.

[2] Ibid.

THE REBUILT TEMPLE AT
JERUSALEM BECOMES CENTRAL

For centuries devout, Jews have prayed three times a day, "May it be Thy will that the Temple be speedily rebuilt in our days."[3] For nineteen centuries, even the most pious must have wondered if the memorized prayer ever got above the ceiling. The Six-Day War changed everything. On June 7, 1967, Jewish soldiers entered the Old City, and at 9:50 a.m. they reached the Temple Mount.

True, the Mosque of Omar still sat unperturbed and defiant on the Temple Mount where it had been for almost thirteen centuries. Jewish soldiers, even in the euphoria of this historic occasion, dared not disturb this Muslim holy place. Nevertheless, in Jewish minds everywhere, pious and not so pious, the hope was born anew of a temple in Jerusalem that would symbolize the rebirth of the nation and unify its people.

On June 30, 1967, *Time* magazine published an article entitled "Should the Temple Be Rebuilt?" The author of that article reported that at a recent rededication of the main Jewish synagogue in the Jewish quarter of Old Jerusalem, the officiating rabbi declared, "As the city has been reunited in our lifetime, so will the rebuilding of the Temple be accomplished in our lifetime."[4]

In 1989, Israel's Ministry of Religious Affairs hosted a Conference of Temple Research. At that conference, the booklet *Treasures of the Temple* expressed the longing and expectations of the Jews concerning a rebuilt temple:

> The dream of rebuilding the Temple spans 50 generations of Jews, five continents and innumerable seas and oceans . . . we will soon be able to rebuild the Temple on its holy mountain in Jerusalem, ushering in an era of peace and understanding, love and kindness.[5]

Bloodshed, brinkmanship, and sword-rattling have done nothing to slacken the pace of these plans. Consider this list of evidence portending things to come:

> Two Talmudic schools are training nearly two hundred descendants of Levi in the details of temple service.

---

[3] Hal Lindsey, *The Final Battle* (Palos Verdes, CA: Western Front, 1995), 104.

[4] H. L. Willmington, *The King is Coming* (Wheaton, IL: Tyndale, 1988), 137–139.

[5] Charles H. Dyer, *World News and Bible Prophecy* (Wheaton, IL: Tyndale, 1993), 75–76.

Thirty-eight special vessels required for animal sacrifices in the temple have already been recreated.

Uniforms for the high priest and attending priests have been prepared according to the specifications of the Torah—even to the point of using hand-spun flax.

Hundreds of ancient musical instruments for Temple worship have been crafted.

Diligent search has been made to find pure red heifer cattle so that the requirements for cleansing of the priests for Temple service (Num. 19:1–10) may be fulfilled.

How the Mosque of Omar will be removed no one knows—except God. But that there will be a temple in Jerusalem during the Tribulation period is a settled biblical fact (e.g. Matt. 24:15ff.; II Thess. 2:4).[6]

BABYLON BECOMES AN IMPORTANT RELIGIOUS CENTER

Nimrod and his followers had visions of grandeur. "Come," they said, "let us build ourselves a city and a tower with its top in the heavens, and let us make a name for ourselves" (Gen. 11:4, ESV). Many centuries later, Nebuchadnezzar, king and hero of the golden city that boasted Nimrod as its founder, had similar visions of grandeur. Even after Daniel's ominous prophecy of his downfall, he yet boasted, "Is not this great Babylon, that I have built for the house of the kingdom by the might of my power, and for the honour of my majesty?" (Dan. 4:30).

Many more centuries bring us into modern times, and still the ancient visions of Nimrod and Nebuchadnezzar haven't died, though they turned quixotic in a would-be hero named Saddam Hussein.

Saddam Hussein was born April 28, 1937, sixteen years after the British created the kingdom of Iraq. He was raised in an atmosphere of violence and confusion by an uncle, an Iraqi army officer and a crusader for Arab unity. According to reports, Saddam committed his first murder while he was yet in his teens. When he was 19, he joined the socialist Baath Party, who advocated an Arab renaissance under the banner "One

[6] Hal Lindsey, *Planet Earth—2000 A.D.* (Palos Verdes, CA: Western Front, 1994), 156–57.

Arab nation, one immortal message!" It was largely through this group that he came to power as president-dictator of Iraq in July 1979.

Intoxicated by his newfound power, Saddam began to see himself as a second Nebuchadnezzar. As his mentor and prototype had done, he decided he would build great Babylon. Restoration of the ancient city had begun as early as 1978, but Saddam had loftier visions than a restored archaeological site.

He decided that the new Babylon would look as nearly like the ancient golden city as possible. According to former Babylon governor Arif Gita Suheil, Saddam "signed an open check to reconstruct the ancient city and revive the marvelous shape it had . . . more than 20 centuries ago."[7] By 1990, under Hussein's heavy-handed leadership, workers had reconstructed the Southern Palace of Nebuchadnezzar, the Procession Street, a Greek theater, and many temples; and had built a half-scale model of the Ishtar Gate.[8]

> When King Nebuchadnezzar ran things around here some 2,500 years ago, he left clear instructions for the future kings of Babylon that are finally being carried out. Writing in cuneiform script on tablets of clay, the royal scribes urged their master's successors to repair and rebuild his temples and palaces. Today, in a gesture rich in political significance, President Saddam Hussein, Iraq's strong-armed ruler, is sparing no effort to obey that now-distant command.[9]

Will Babylon Really be Rebuilt in Iraq?

As I write this, Saddam Hussein is languishing in prison, his dreams of grandeur contorted by contemptuous reality. Will his dreams of Babylon perish also?

Many Bible scholars are convinced that ancient Babylon perished never to rise again, that prophecies such as Isaiah 13:19–22 have been literally fulfilled:

> And Babylon, the glory of kingdoms, the beauty of the Chaldees' excellency, shall be as when God overthrew Sodom and Gomorrah. It shall never be

---

[7] Subhy Haddad, "Babylon Is Being Rebuilt to Lure Tourists and Build Iraqi Morals," *Philadelphia Inquirer*, October 10, 1986, quoted in Charles H. Dyer, *The Rise of Babylon* (Wheaton, IL: Tyndale, 1991), 32.

[8] Dyer, *Rise of Babylon*, 27.

[9] Paul Lewis, "Nebuchadnezzar's Revenge: Iraq Flexes Its Muscles by Building Babylon," *San Francisco Chronicle*, April 30, 1989, quoted in Dyer, *Rise of Babylon*, 25.

inhabited, neither shall it be dwelt in from generation to generation: neither shall the Arabian pitch tent there; neither shall the shepherds make their fold there. But wild beasts of the desert shall lie there; and their houses shall be full of doleful creatures; and owls shall dwell there, and satyrs shall dance there. And the wild beasts of the islands shall cry in their desolate houses, and dragons in their pleasant palaces: and her time is near to come, and her days shall not be prolonged.

But have the prophecies against Babylon literally been fulfilled? Isaiah's prophecy calls for Babylon *never* to be inhabited—not from generation to generation, not even temporarily by Bedouins or shepherds. As a matter of fact, the site of ancient Babylon has been continuously inhabited from the time of its fall in 539 BC to modern times.

Babylon remained as a prominent city for over two hundred years after its fall. Alexander had great plans for the city as the capitol of his new empire. In 325 BC, the city willingly opened its gates to him and his advancing troops; but two years later the angel of death cut his plans short. The city began to decline in prestige after Seleucus I Nicator (r. 312–281 BC), who had previously taken the title "King of Babylon," built a new capital, Seleucia, on the Tigris River. Nevertheless, it continued to be inhabited and for some time was even viewed as a religious center.

Josephus mentions "great numbers of Jews" in Babylon about the time of the New Testament.[10] In the twelfth century, a Jew called Benjamin of Tudela traveling through the region of Babylon reported that ten thousand Jews lived in the village of Al Hillah, six miles from Babylon, and that the Jews attended the Synagogue of Daniel in Babylon, one mile from the ruins of Nebuchadnezzar's temple.[11]

In the late nineteenth century, the German archaeologist Robert Koldewey identified four Arab villages on the site of ancient Babylon. He found that the natives in the region had for decades been mining and selling the excellent kiln bricks from the buildings of the city—and that this quarry had certainly been in use in the Parthian days of occupation (from about 140 BC).[12]

This rather mundane fact about the bricks of Babylon being mined for use elsewhere is immensely significant; according to Jeremiah, at the final

---

[10] *Antiquities of the Jews* 15.2.2 and 18.9.1.

[11] M. N. Adler, "Benjamin of Tudela, Itinerary of," *Jewish Quarterly Review* 17 (1905): 514–30, quoted in Dyer, *Rise of Babylon*, 128.

[12] Dyer, *Rise of Babylon*, 177.

destruction of Babylon "they shall not take of thee a stone for a corner, nor a stone for foundations; but thou shalt be desolate for ever, saith the Lord" (Jer. 51:26).

Babylon's Final Judgment Yet to Come

Of Babylon's final judgment, Isaiah warned, "Howl ye; for the day of the Lord is at hand; it shall come as a destruction from the Almighty" (13:6). The "day of the Lord" is an expression used repeatedly by the prophets to depict the events of the last days, the days beginning with the Tribulation. In contrast to Babylon's fall to the Persians, this judgment will be complete and sudden "as when God overthrew Sodom and Gomorrah" (Isa. 13:19).

Among those who responded to the decree of Cyrus, king of Persia, to return to Jerusalem and build the house of the Lord of Hosts were the prophets Haggai and Zechariah. The decree was issued in Cyrus's first year as emperor, 539 BC. About fifty thousand Jewish exiles in Babylonia, caught up in the ecstasy of this amazing proclamation from a pagan king, left their homes and journeyed to Jerusalem to be a part of this historic occasion: the rebuilding of the temple of the Lord.

They made rapid progress at first. By 536 BC, they were celebrating the completed foundation. But then opposition began to intensify. Their enemies hired "counselors" to lobby against them in the courts of the palaces of Persia. Finally, under both external and internal pressures, the returned exiles decided that perhaps it wasn't God's will after all to complete the noble work they had begun. Under the well-worn umbrella of this rationalization, the work languished for a number of years.

Then in the second year of Darius (519 BC), God moved the prophets Haggai and Zechariah to preach the people back to work. The prophecies of both of these men of God reveal two grand objectives: (1) to complete this second temple so that the covenant nation might have new life as part of God's kingdom, and (2) to impress anew upon the people of God that their work was connected with God's eternal plan—that they were involved in a work that reached into the last days and into eternity.

It is in connection with this second objective that Zechariah's prophecy concerning Babylonia, the prototype of the kingdom of the world, has special significance. To his sublime vision of the building of the house of the Lord, God adds a different kind of vision—a vision of a house built for wickedness.

Then the angel that talked with me went forth, and said unto me, Lift up now thine eyes, and see what is this that goeth forth. And I said, What is it? And he said, This is an ephah that goeth forth. He said moreover, This is their resemblance through all the earth. And, behold, there was lifted up a talent of lead: and this is a woman that sitteth in the midst of the ephah. And he said, This is wickedness. And he cast it into the midst of the ephah; and he cast the weight of lead upon the mouth thereof. Then lifted I up mine eyes, and looked, and, behold, there came out two women, and the wind was in their wings; for they had wings like the wings of a stork: and they lifted up the ephah between the earth and the heaven. Then said I to the angel that talked with me, Whither do these bear the ephah? And he said unto me, To build it an house in the land of Shinar: and it shall be established, and set there upon her own base (Zech. 5:5–11).

Here is wickedness, personified in a woman, being confined and transported in a measuring basket to the land of Shinar, Babylonia. In Babylonia, the angel tells Zechariah, a house is to be built for wickedness to dwell in.

The prophet is speaking here of the last days. In Zechariah's day, Babylon was a conquered city under the Persian Empire. Zechariah, as he does repeatedly in his prophecy, is looking into the distant future. In that day, he says, wickedness will again be concentrated and intensified in this ancient capital and prototype of the kingdom of the world. The city where man's organized rebellion against God began will be established again—and in God's providence will meet its final doom.

THE CALLING AND MINISTRY OF SPECIAL WITNESSES

As Satan establishes his world leader in the early days of the seventieth septet, El Shaddai is making His countermove. He first decrees that none of the seal judgments fall until He has sealed His chosen witnesses of Israel (Rev. 7:1–3), 12,000 from each of Israel's tribes. Though the kingdom of darkness appears to be dominating the world as never before, these 144,000 witnesses prove that God is still accomplishing His redemptive purposes on earth.

The Firstfruits of Israel

These 144,000 witnesses are sealed for the same duration that the two witnesses of Jerusalem are sealed: until "they shall have finished their testimony" (Rev. 11:7; cf. John 8:20), for they are destined for martyrdom (Rev. 14:1–3).[13] John describes them as "the firstfruits unto God and to the Lamb" (14:4). This suggests that they are the first converts of the great harvest of Israel that is to come by the end of the seventieth septet (cf. Rom. 16:5; I Cor. 16:15). Their witness is evidently "to the Jew first," as Paul's was. Undoubtedly, though, they proclaimed the Gospel to all who would hear, for they "follow the Lamb whithersoever he goeth" (Rev. 14:4).

The Rise and Ministry of the Two Witnesses of Jerusalem

Near the beginning of the seventieth septet, God raises up and empowers two phenomenal witnesses in Jerusalem (Rev. 11:3–13). They may be two of the 144,000, or they may be instrumental in the conversion of these witnesses from the twelve tribes. Whatever the case, their mission is the same as that of the tribal witnesses; but their mission field is Jerusalem and the Jews.

Before these prophets are called, the prisoner John has just been commissioned anew as a prophet to the nations (10:8–11). Now the angel gives him a reed and commands him to measure the inner court of the temple but not to measure the outer court, "for it is given unto the Gentiles: and the holy city shall they tread under foot forty and two months" (11:1–2).[14]

The inner court in this picture would represent the more serious worshipers in Israel. And as the outer court by New Testament times had become largely a marketplace for greedy religious leaders, it would represent the people of Israel who had no heart for God. Those in the outer court, then, would represent the "many" (Dan. 9:27) in the nation who welcome the peace covenant of the Antichrist, as well as the two-thirds of the nation who will ultimately be slaughtered in God's purging process (Zech. 13:8–9).

It is in this context of impending judgment on Israel that the two prophets begin their ministry. Their message is the same as that of John the Baptist, "Repent ye: for the kingdom of heaven is at hand" (Matt. 3:2). Like Daniel (9:3), they are girded with sackcloth as a sign of the sin-

---

[13] The Mount Zion of Rev. 14 must be a reference to heaven, as in Heb. 12:22. The entire scene is in the context of heaven (14:2–3).

[14] The word translated *temple* (*naos*) in 11:1–2 generally refers to the inner court where only true Israelites could enter (Matt. 23:35; 27:5) or to the holy place in the temple building where only priests could enter (Luke 1:9, 21; Matt. 23:17).

The domination of Jerusalem for forty-two months (Rev. 11:1–2) clearly refers to the last half of the seventieth septet, the Great Tribulation. Nevertheless, events at the end of the seven-year tribulation indicate that the 1260-day ministry of the two prophets will be in the first half of this period. In His Olivet Discourse, the Lord told His disciples that "immediately after the tribulation" the Son of Man will return to earth (Matt. 24:29-30). Also, we are told in Zechariah that Jerusalem will be besieged by the armies of the world (in the battle of Armageddon) in the latter part of the Great Tribulation, that the nation will be converted at this time (Rev. 12:11-13:9), and that Christ's coming will culminate the battle (14:1-9). On the other hand, the two witnesses minister 1260 days and are slain by the Beast who ascended out of the bottomless pit. And after the world rejoices over their exposed corpses for three days, they are called to heaven in full view of their enemies. Then a great earthquake destroys one-tenth of the city, kills seven thousand people, and causes the remnant to give glory to God (11:7-13). If the ministry of the two witnesses were in the latter half of the Tribulation, this would mean that the world would be rejoicing and exchanging gifts for three days during the battle of Armageddon, and the resurrection of the witnesses would come (presumably) just before the Lord's return.

fulness of the people and of their need for repentance. Their message will not reach the hearts of most in the nation, but God will use them to plant the seed of truth in the hearts of many. Ultimately that seed will bear abundant fruit in the conversion of the purged nation.

But who are these two prophets? In my view, there has been much too much unfruitful speculation about this question. The only "identification" John receives is this: "These are the two olive trees, and the two candlesticks standing before the God of the earth" (Rev. 11:4). This refers to two men the Lord used as key instruments in building the second temple: Joshua the high priest and Zerubbabel the appointed ruler of the returned exiles (Zech. 4:14). So these two prophets will be key instruments, as Joshua and Zerubbabel were, in restoring Israel as the covenant nation.[15]

---

[15] It is noteworthy in this connection that Haggai and Zechariah, whom God used to arouse Israel to complete the rebuilding the temple in Zerubbabel's day, both speak also of the final temple of the Lord in the latter days (e.g., Hag. 2:6–9; Zech. 6:12–13; 14:16–21).

Our best approach is to leave these two prophets anonymous, as the Bible does. Of Enoch, a popular candidate for one of these prophetic offices, the writer of Hebrews says, "By faith Enoch was translated that he should not see death; and was not found, because God had translated him: for before his translation he had this testimony, that he pleased God." (Heb. 11:5). This verse should make us more comfortable with anonymous prophets. Three times in the passage the writer mentions the concept of *translation* (*metatithemi*), and he declares that this happened to Enoch "that he should not see death." If we take the passage just as it reads, we should remove Enoch from our candidate list. If we look at the principle involved, we should throw our list away. Once a person has been translated into immortality, he cannot be again made subject to death.

THE HARVEST IN THE NATIONS

Following his vision of the sealing of the 144,000, John declares, "After this I beheld, and, lo, a great multitude, which no man could number, of all nations, and kindreds, and people, and tongues, stood before the throne, and before the Lamb, clothed with white robes, and palms in their hands."

Most of these believers from all nations will likely be the fruit, directly or indirectly, of the 144,000—won to Christ during the first half of the seventieth septet, though they are destined for martyrdom during the second half of the septet.

The fact that there is a multitude "no man could number" speaks of the power of Christ to "draw all men" to Himself even during times of greatest opposition. During the Tribulation, the restraining and convicting influence of the Holy Spirit will greatly decrease when the Rapture removes the saints He indwells. Furthermore, through Satanic power the Antichrist will deceive the world with signs and "lying wonders" (II Thess. 2:7–12). Nevertheless, the saving power of Christ is such that countless multitudes will be saved during this time, even in the face of persecution and death. No wonder these redeemed saints make heaven ring with their cry, "Salvation to our God which sitteth upon the throne, and unto the Lamb!" (Rev. 7:10).

WAR (THE SECOND SEAL)

"For when they shall say, Peace and safety; then sudden destruction cometh upon them, as travail upon a woman with child; and they shall not escape." Though the Day of the Lord will come at the Rapture "as a thief in the night," at first it will not appear to be an ominous time to the people of the world. In fact, various Scripture passages indicate that there will be a sense of euphoria and promises of peace in the world before the storms of tribulation break (Ezek. 38:14; I Thess. 5:2–3; cf. Matt. 24:38; Luke 17:28–29). When the Lamb opened the first judgment seal of the seventieth septet, John heard "as it were the noise of thunder" (Rev. 6:1). The distant sound of thunder forebodes a coming storm, but only those who are carefully watching the times will hear this thunderclap. Even as I write, in the aftermath of the war with Iraq, with violence and terrorism escalating throughout the world, pacifism is viewed everywhere as the only true elixir of life, the one-stop store to cure all the world's ills.

In the euphoria that generally surrounds a charismatic world leader, many, especially in the Middle East, will undoubtedly be hailing a new *Pax Romana* for the world. But such euphoria quickly degenerates into wistful thinking and idle dreams. After the usual eulogies concerning the peace, safety, and unity the Antichrist is bringing to the world, the world will awaken again to the stark reality of war. Peace is gone, and people who last night were speaking ecstatically about love and brotherhood are now killing each other.

CHAPTER TWENTY-EIGHT

THE DEATH THROES OF THE DRAGON, PART II

SATAN IS CAST OUT OF HEAVEN

IN HIS BEST-SELLING AUTOBIOGRAPHY, Lee Iacocca acknowledged that he enjoyed the perks he had as president of Ford Motor Company. As president of Ford (1970–1978), second in rank only to Henry Ford II, he was drawing close to one million in salary; and the executives at Ford in those days lived like royalty, with "white-coated waiters . . . on call throughout the day." The executive dining room, no ordinary cafeteria, had special fish delicacies flown over from England daily. The finest fruits were always available, whatever the season—plus fancy chocolates at tables graced by exotic flowers. For all of this, each executive paid a grand total of $2.00. One day, some of them got into a discussion about how much these lunches cost the company. They ran a study and found that each meal cost $104![1]

Eventually (according to Iacocca) Henry Ford II became concerned that Iacocca's rising popularity and power threatened to overshadow his own, and he decided to fire him. But rather than fire him directly, he decided on a course of step-by-step humiliation designed to anger him into resignation. He would reduce his status in the company first to the num-

---

[1] *Iacocca* (New York: Bantam, 1986). 127, 101–2.

ber three man, then to number four and so on. If Iacocca resigned, there would be no need to explain why the company was firing its president after two of the best years in its history.[2]

On an infinitely higher level and for an infinitely purer reason, the supreme Sovereign of the universe has chosen a course of step-by-step humiliation for the highest executive in the kingdom of darkness. In the dementia that comes from nurturing pride, Lucifer once saw himself as just five steps from the throne of the Most High:

> For thou hast said in thine heart, I will ascend into heaven, I will exalt my throne above the stars of God: I will sit also upon the mount of the congregation, in the sides of the north: I will ascend above the heights of the clouds; I will be like the most High (Isa. 14:13–14).

Contrary to the popular caricature of Satan, he does not have a forked tail, wear a red suit, and stoke the fires of hell. Strange as it may seem, much of the pervasive jocular attitude about Satan (unfortunately common even among Christians) is contrary to the Bible. Even after the rebellion of Lucifer, God chose, as part of His plan for mankind, to allow him to remain a "prince," a high-ranking dignitary in the heavenly realms (Luke 4:5–7; John 14:30; cf. Job 1–2). His rank is so high that even "Michael the archangel, when contending with the devil he disputed about the body of Moses, durst not bring against him a railing accusation, but said, The Lord rebuke thee" (Jude 9).

But in God's time, Satan will be cast down from his lofty place. That time begins in the last days, at the midpoint of the seventieth septet of Daniel's prophecy, halfway through the Tribulation.

> And there was war in heaven: Michael and his angels fought against the dragon; and the dragon fought and his angels, and prevailed not; neither was their place found any more in heaven. And the great dragon was cast out, that old serpent, called the Devil, and Satan, which deceiveth the whole world: he was cast out into the earth, and his angels were cast out with him.... Therefore rejoice, ye heavens, and ye that dwell in them. Woe to the inhabiters of the earth and of the sea! for the devil is come down unto you, having great wrath, because he knoweth that he hath but a short time (Rev. 12:7–9, 12).

John gives us little room to speculate about the time of Satan's expulsion from heaven; knowing his time is short, the Dragon begins an intense persecution of the "woman" (Israel) that lasts "for a time, and times,

---

[2] Ibid., 130–34.

and half a time"—"a thousand two hundred and threescore days" (Rev. 12:6, 14; cf. 13:5).

So for Satan, this is the beginning of the end. But for the people of God, and for the nation Israel, it may not seem that way. Here begins "the time of Jacob's trouble" (Jer. 30:7; cf. Dan. 12:1), the Great Tribulation.

THE INVASION OF PALESTINE BY THE CONFEDERACY OF GOG

Much of the war of the second seal judgment may well take place in the Middle East. The "feet of clay" on the colossus of Daniel's vision depict, among other things, the weakness of humanity that will ultimately bring down the kingdom of darkness. And because of this human weakness, there will be insubordination, intrigues, jealousies, power plays, and wars in the world of the Antichrist.

It takes no stretch in imagination to see the stage being set for the conflict between Russia and her confederates and the federation of Europe.

For years now Russia has been cultivating alliances with Muslim nations, trading arms and technical expertise for much-needed cash to strongly Islamic nations such as Iran. Given the current milieu in the Middle East, there seems to be no question that in the event of another Arab-Israeli war, Russia would side with the Islamic nations.[3]

Likewise, it is not hard even now to see the potential for conflict between the European Union and the Russian-Muslim bloc of nations. At the beginning of the seventieth septet, when the leader of the European federation reaches a covenant agreement with Israel, the potential for conflict will take on a new intensity. Such an agreement would be tantamount to making Israel an affiliate of the European Union and would virtually guarantee her continuance as a nation—a situation totally incompatible with inveterate Islamic vows.

It is in this context that the dictator of Russia, guided by a strong providential Hand, makes his fateful move to overthrow Israel (Ezek. 38:4). His move will bring him into direct conflict with the new Roman emperor, the Antichrist. "And at the time of the end shall the king of the south push at him: and the king of the north shall come against him like a whirlwind, with chariots, and with horsemen, and with many ships; and

---

[3] Hal Lindsey, *Planet Earth—2000 A.D.* (Palos Verdes, CA: Western Front, 1994), 185–202.

Three times in Ezekiel 38 and 39 the armies of Magog are said to come from "the uttermost parts of the north" (38:6, 15; 39:2, ESV; cf. the NASB, "remote/remotest parts" and NIV, "far north"). The word translated *uttermost* "refers to the backside or farthest part of anything." *TWOT*, 1:408 (see chap. 3, n. 3). These passages reveal that we should look beyond the Fertile Crescent enemies of Israel (e.g., Syria, Assyria, and Babylon) for Magog. The "remotest parts of the north" from Israel would be Russia. (Moscow is due north of Jerusalem.) According to Josephus (*Antiquities* 1.6.1), the Magogites (descendants of Magog) were the people the Greeks called "Scythians." The Scythians at one time "held sway over an area embracing most of modern-day Ukraine and the plains of southern Russia." Mike Edwards, "Searching for the Scythians," *National Geographic*, September 1996, 61. Wilhelm Gesenius (1786–1842), an outspoken rationalist but one of the preeminent pioneers in Hebrew linguistics, held that the people of Ezekiel 38:2 were located in the territory associated with modern Russia.

Russia's confederates that are named include Persia, Ethiopia, Libya, Gomer, and Togarmah (Ezek. 38:5–6). Persia, all agree, is modern Iran. Ethiopia (Hebrew: *Cush*) and Libya (Hebrew: *Put*) are both in North Africa, perhaps roughly the same areas as modern Ethiopia and Libya. Gomer has generally been identified with the Cimmerians, located first in the region of the Black and Caspian Seas, with branches spreading later into north Germany. Togarmah is one of the names for Armenia.

he shall enter into the countries, and shall overflow and pass over" (Dan. 11:40). This description suggests a coordinated attack, with the first move coming from the south, North Africa, and the major invasion from the hordes of the far north.

But this is not simply an attack against the Antichrist or against the apparently vulnerable little nation of Israel. It is an attack against the Lord Himself. At the very inception of the Abrahamic Covenant, the Lord promised, "I will bless them that bless thee, and curse him that curseth thee" (Gen. 12:3). Repeatedly and emphatically the Lord has enlarged on this promise and warning in His written revelation. "For I, saith the Lord, will be unto her a wall of fire round about, and will be the glory in the midst of her. . . . He that toucheth you toucheth the apple of his eye" (Zech. 2:5, 8).

To Israel, the Lord's promise of blessing and protection was based on the nation's response to Him: "But if thou shalt indeed obey his voice, and do all that I speak; then I will be an enemy unto thine enemies, and an adversary unto thine adversaries" (Exod. 23:22). Nevertheless, God's eternal plan to bring salvation to the world through Israel included His jealous protection of His covenant nation, even when they were under His disciplinary judgment.

> For thy violence against thy brother Jacob shame shall cover thee, and thou shalt be cut off for ever. . . . For thus saith the Lord God; Because thou hast clapped thine hands, and stamped with the feet, and rejoiced in heart with all thy despite against the land of Israel; behold, therefore I will stretch out mine hand upon thee, and will deliver thee for a spoil to the heathen; and I will cut thee off from the people, and I will cause thee to perish out of the countries: I will destroy thee; and thou shalt know that I am the Lord (Obad. 1:10; Ezek. 25:6–7).

Even when the founding fathers of Israel strayed from the Lord and grievously violated His word, He jealously guarded His people and held their enemies accountable for their attitude toward them (e.g., Gen. 12:17; 20:2–7; 31:20–24; 35:1–5). And so it has been with Israel throughout history. God has fulfilled His warnings that He would use other nations for disciplinary judgments on Israel, but at the same time He has always held the nations accountable that He used as tools of these judgments.

The Time of the Invasion

Ezekiel is quite specific about the time of this invasion.

> After many days thou shalt be visited: in the latter years thou shalt come into the land that is brought back from the sword, and is gathered out of many people, against the mountains of Israel, which have been always waste: but is brought forth out of the nations, and they shall dwell safely all of them (Ezek. 38:8).

The prophecy, from Ezekiel's standpoint, is to be fulfilled in the distant future, "in the latter years"—the time of the Messianic fulfillment of the kingdom promises. The prophet further specifies that the invasion will occur after the Jews have been gathered from the nations of the world to return to their land, and "all of them" are dwelling safely in it.

The requirement that "all" Israel—that is, the vast majority of the nation—be living in Palestine still awaits fulfillment; and their "dwelling safely" in the land will evidently not take place until the Antichrist makes his covenant with them at the beginning of the seventieth septet.

The Significance of the Invasion as a Revelation of God

Ezekiel hints that in that day Jewish students of the Bible may recognize this invasion as the fulfillment of ancient prophecies.

> Thus saith the Lord God; Art thou he of whom I have spoken in old time by my servants the prophets of Israel, which prophesied in those days many years that I would bring thee against them? (38:17).

Whatever the case, the invasion will provide a compelling occasion for the Lord to reveal Himself as the God of judgment and as the Lord and Redeemer of Israel.

> And it shall come to pass at the same time when Gog shall come against the land of Israel, saith the Lord God, that my fury shall come up in my face. For in my jealousy and in the fire of my wrath have I spoken, Surely in that day there shall be a great shaking in the land of Israel; so that the fishes of the sea, and the fowls of the heaven, and the beasts of the field, and all creeping things that creep upon the earth, and all the men that are upon the face of the earth, shall shake at my presence, and the mountains shall be thrown down, and the steep places shall fall, and every wall shall fall to the ground. And I will call for a sword against him throughout all my mountains, saith the Lord God: every man's sword shall be against his brother. And I will plead against him with pestilence and with blood; and I will rain upon him, and upon his bands, and upon the many people that are with him, an overflowing rain, and great hailstones, fire, and brimstone. Thus will I magnify myself, and sanctify myself; and I will be known in the eyes of many nations, and they shall know that I am the Lord (38:18–23; cf. 39:6–7, 21–23, 28).

The Significance of the Invasion to the Kingdom of the World

Though countless multitudes throughout the world will be spiritually awakened through the Lord's judgment and the ministry of His witnesses (Rev. 7:9–17), many more will respond with increased resistance and antagonism—another testimony to the fact that the real problem with man is not the clarity of God's revelation but the sinful stubbornness of the human heart. As the Egyptians did in the days of the Exodus, and as people in general have done on a daily basis did throughout history, the children of the world in the last days will ignore and even denigrate the revelation of God through His marvelous works.

THE ANTICHRIST ASSUMES CONTROL
OF THE HOLY LAND

Israel, now in a protectorate relationship with the new Roman Empire, is at the mercy of the new Roman Emperor. Because of his "firm covenant" with Israel, the invasion of the Russian horde was an attack on him and the powers over which he presided (Dan. 11:40). Therefore "he shall enter . . . into the glorious land"; and with his enemies already decimated and bewildered by the Lord's actions against them (Ezek. 38:19–22), he shall destroy the remnants of the invading armies, gain control over Israel, and take possession of Egypt and her North African allies (Dan. 11:41–42).

But while he is consolidating his possessions in North Africa, he hears alarming rumors "out of the east and out of the north." Infuriated that even after his overwhelming victories he still has enemies who challenge his authority, he lashes out "with great fury to destroy, and utterly to make away many" (Dan. 11:43–44). We are not told who these enemies are, but the general context suggests a couple of possibilities.

According to Ezekiel's prophecy, the miraculous intervention of the Lord against the Russian onslaught will cause many in Israel to recognize Him as their Lord and Redeemer (Ezek. 38:7, 22–23). It seems likely that these people would renounce any allegiance they may have with the Antichrist and begin looking for Another, the true Messiah. So some of the news that alarms the new Roman Empire may be stories of conspiracy and rebellion. This would be similar to when Antiochus Epiphanes, in a comparable circumstance, returned from Egypt in great fury to destroy and defile Jerusalem (Dan. 11:30–35).

Does all of this undermine the power and popularity of this new world leader? Not at all. The world needs him more than ever now. After all, it wasn't his principles that caused the wars; it was the violation of his principles and leadership. If we can just eliminate the troublemakers—the Christians and other backward people who refuse to cooperate—all will be well. And so, at the instigation of the Antichrist, the uncooperative are hunted down and eliminated (Rev. 6:9–11).

A Phenomenal Earthquake
Awakens Many to Judgment

But then an event occurs that, in spite of all the propaganda to the contrary, awakens some to reality: an earthquake of such magnitude that the entire atmosphere changes. The sun turns black, the moon turns blood red, the heavens seem to be disappearing, and cataclysmic eruptions shake the entire earth. Now even great men of the earth, world leaders, cry out in terror that the Day of the Lord has come. And the claims of Christ, the Lamb of God—the call for redemption so recently rejected and ridiculed—will now appear as harbingers of judgment to those who cry to the mountains and rocks, "Fall on us, and hide us from the face of him that sitteth on the throne, and from the wrath of the Lamb" (Rev. 6:12–17).

Some eight centuries before John's vision on Patmos, Isaiah had warned the unbelievers of Judah and Jerusalem that, in the last days, the Lord would arise "to shake terribly the earth."

> Enter into the rock, and hide thee in the dust, for fear of the Lord and for the glory of his majesty. The lofty looks of man shall be humbled, and the haughtiness of men shall be bowed down, and the Lord alone shall be exalted in that day. For the day of the Lord of hosts shall be upon every one that is proud and lofty, and upon every one that is lifted up; and he shall be brought low.... And they shall go into the holes of the rocks, and into the caves of the earth, for fear of the Lord, and for the glory of his majesty, when he ariseth to shake terribly the earth. In that day a man shall cast his idols of silver, and his idols of gold, which they made each one for himself to worship, to the moles and to the bats; to go into the clefts of the rocks, and into the tops of the ragged rocks, for fear of the Lord, and for the glory of his majesty, when he ariseth to shake terribly the earth (Isa. 2:10–12, 19–21).

Now the prophet of Patmos sees Isaiah's vision being fulfilled before his eyes. Up to this point, he has seen judgments originating largely in human actions. Now he sees the Lord Himself taking direct action; and it seems as if His wrath, kindled and intensified by the appeal of the martyred witnesses (Rev. 6:9–11), now explodes. For when the Lamb opens the sixth seal, the prophet witnesses "a great earthquake"—greater than anyone on earth has ever seen. Even the sun is darkened and the moon turns blood red; and there is a terrifying shower of meteorites.[4]

On August 27, 1883, one of the most violent eruptions in recorded history took place on the volcanic island of Krakatoa (Krakatau), now a part of the Indonesian Islands. The eruption was heard as far as three thousand miles away, and the shock was felt nine thousand miles away in California. Volcanic dust rose into the air and formed with clouds, eventually spreading over much of the world, dramatically affecting the weather and producing vivid sunrises and sunsets. But this eruption, yet to come, will move "every mountain and island . . . out of their places." And the atmospheric changes will be so dynamic that the heavens will seem to be disappearing, "as a scroll when it is rolled together" (v. 14; cf. Isa. 34:4).

With the shaking and disappearance of all that seemed so stable, man's ability to rationalize vanishes also. Then

> the kings of the earth, and the great men, and the rich men, and the chief captains, and the mighty men, and every bondman, and every free man, hid themselves in the dens and in the rocks of the mountains; and said to the mountains and rocks, Fall on us, and hide us from the face of him that sitteth on the throne, and from the wrath of the Lamb: for the great day of his wrath is come; and who shall be able to stand? (Rev. 6:15–17).

Perhaps the most striking thing about this description is its revelation of man's latent knowledge of God. John depicts seven types of men who beg in unison, in a moment of terrifying truth, to be hidden from the Sovereign on the throne and from the Redeemer, the Lamb of God—yet these are men who would under ordinary circumstances (and all the more so in the midst of the preceding turmoil) greatly differ from one another.

People everywhere are awakening to the reality that the day of God's long-awaited and long-denied judgment has begun. And why the focus here on both the throne and the Lamb? Because here is the twofold issue of life that has been before man from the beginning. On the first page of the Bible, God revealed Himself as the sovereign Creator and Sustainer of all life. Then when death entered the world at the fall of man, the Lord revealed Himself as the Redeemer of man, the restorer of divine life. Now

---

[4] "There has not been a really impressive meteor shower for some time, but on November 13, 1833, eyewitnesses testified that hundreds of meteors could be seen simultaneously. People actually fell to their knees and begged God for mercy!" Stewart Custer, *From Patmos to Paradise* (Greenville, SC: BJU Press, 2004), 81.

at the end of time, the dual issue of life comes back into focus: the sovereign God and the rejected Lamb now appear before mankind as Judge and Executor of the earthly kingdom.

But for most of mankind it is indeed only a moment of truth. When unregenerate men escape impending judgment, the vast majority of them simply return to their default position. Their repentance, their resolutions, "as the early dew" (Hosea 6:4) disappear. "Because sentence against an evil work is not executed speedily, therefore the heart of the sons of men is fully set in them to do evil" (Eccles. 8:11). "Who knowing the judgment of God, that they which commit such things are worthy of death, not only do the same, but have pleasure in them that do them" (Rom. 1:32). Furthermore, the man on the white horse, the Antichrist, will provide them an alternative which accords more with their natural inclinations.

THE ANTICHRIST SLAIN AND RESTORED TO LIFE

The powers in the Middle East could not long tolerate the sovereign presence of the Antichrist in their territory, and they mobilized for war. Just after he solidifies his hold on Palestine, "tidings out of the east and out of the north shall trouble him: therefore he shall go forth with great fury to destroy, and utterly to make away many" (Dan. 11:44).

It may well be that it was at this time, during his furious attack on his enemies, that he was slain "by a sword" (Rev. 13:14). The writer's use of the word *sword* here indicates that his death was violent and sudden; and John's language declares forcefully that he actually died. He did not just appear to die; for after he had received the stroke of death, all the world "wondered"—marveled—at him; and they worshiped him who had died and lived again (Rev. 13:3, 12, 14).

I remember many years ago reading excerpts from a book that trumpeted the progress and achievements of science. In his last chapter, the author listed some areas he confidently expected the scientific community to master in the future. One of the problems he predicted scientists would overcome was the problem of death. In the last days, when the Antichrist rises from the dead, it will appear to the people of the world that man has at last arrived, that he has attained the godhood he has been seeking since the Garden of Eden.

It was the Dragon who gave authority to the Beast (the Antichrist) and who gave him life (Rev. 13:4; cf.13:15). But how could this be? Isn't God alone the author of life? In fact, God alone is the Creator of everything. He alone chooses when a man, or even a sparrow, lives or dies. He "is before all things, and by him all things consist" (Col. 1:17). But He has chosen also to delegate power—even in some cases to those antagonistic to Him—for accomplishing His plan in the earth.

So now, with the Antichrist having apparently achieved mankind's hope for immortality, people all over the world are bowing before him, crying as they bow, "He died for us and through him we will achieve life and immortality."

With the world at his feet, the Antichrist now openly reviles the God of heaven and declares war on His people.

> And he opened his mouth in blasphemy against God, to blaspheme his name, and his tabernacle, and them that dwell in heaven. And it was given unto him to make war with the saints, and to overcome them: and power was given him over all kindreds, and tongues, and nations (Rev. 13:6–7).

The expression "he opened his mouth" seems to be an idiomatic expression for the beginning of an extended speech (e.g., Matt. 5:2; Acts 8:35; 10:34). These two verses may be a synopsis of the "inaugural" speech of the Antichrist. Whatever the case, they express his spirit and philosophy and they portend ominous things to come during his administration.

The word translated *blasphemy* refers to slanderous and reproachful speech. The word *against* is, more literally, *toward*. This suggests that John envisioned the Antichrist lifting his head toward God in heaven and challenging Him with reproachful speech. It is surprising to read that he not only blasphemed the name, or nature, of God, but he also spoke against "his tabernacle, and them that dwell in heaven." What is the significance of this?

I envision the Antichrist as speaking scornfully of God and His saints in heaven, calling them aloof and distant. In contrast, he pictures himself as an "emmanuel," a god with the people and of the people—interested and concerned about their needs.

When I was young, even people of the world had difficulty imagining anyone speaking so blatantly against God; but the New Age philosophy has changed all that. The notion that everyone is a potential "Christ," that the person we know as Jesus of Nazareth simply discovered the secret of his godhood some two thousand years ago—that the Person Christians believe to be the Creator of the universe is simply another being Who discovered the secret of his godhood—is of course just a modern version of the satanic lie that men and women by eating of the Tree of Knowledge can be "as God." This philosophy, popularized again by New Age doctrine, is pervasive in the world today. And when the Antichrist takes the stage, he will give ominous direction to the latent beliefs of mankind.

With the people thus prepared, the Antichrist enters the Holy of Holies in the temple and "reveals" that he "is God" (II Thess. 2:4; cf. Dan. 11:45). Empowered by the Dragon, he launches a concerted attack on the two witnesses in Jerusalem who have for three and one-half years been a scourge to the people of the world—and he is successful. At least he appears for a time to succeed; but in the midst of euphoric celebration, the Lord restores life to these dead prophets, makes them stand on their feet, and causes them to ascend into heaven in the sight of their enemies.

Then, as a grand climax, "the same hour was there a great earthquake, and the tenth part of the city fell, and in the earthquake were slain of men seven thousand"—possibly dignitaries gathered for this special celebration of the victory of the Antichrist over these "enemies of the people."[5] "And the remnant were affrighted, and gave glory to the God of heaven" (Rev. 11:7–13).

A GREAT FALSE PROPHET ARISES IN PALESTINE

With the rise of the False Prophet, the satanic trinity is complete. The Dragon is the counterpart to the Father; the Beast is the false Messiah, the antagonist of the Son; and the False Prophet promotes the person

---

[5] More literally, the expression is "slain of *names* of men seven thousand." According to A. T. Robertson, the use of *names* (*onomata*) here is comparable to that in Rev. 3:4 and Acts 1:15. *Word Pictures in the New Testament* (Nashville: Broadman, 1930). On the other hand, the Old Testament writers quite often use the word *name* (*shem*), much as it is used in many cultures, to represent fame or renown (e.g., Gen. 6:4; 11:4; Num. 16:2; Ezek. 16:14–15; Dan. 9:15; I Kings 4:31; I Chron. 14:17). Whatever the case, the scene John depicts in Rev. 11:8–11 indicates that a public celebration was going on, with the attention of the world focused on Jerusalem. It seems likely that by satellite TV "they of the people and kindreds and tongues and nations shall see their dead bodies three days and an half, and shall not suffer their dead bodies to be put in graves." And it would be passing strange if the Antichrist did not take maximum advantage of the PR potential of this occasion with appropriate "gloating ceremonies."

and work of the would-be redeemer of the world, the Antichrist—a feeble counterpart to the Holy Spirit Who promotes the Person and work of the true Messiah.

To the people of the world generally, and to many renegade Jews, this prophet will seem to be another Elijah. John envisions him as "coming up out of the earth" (possibly Palestine) and he says "he had two horns like a lamb, and he spake as a dragon" (Rev. 13:11*b*). That is, he had the demeanor and bearing of a benevolent prophet, but his message was satanic.

And this prophet, like Elijah, has the power to work miracles. "And he doeth great wonders, so that he maketh fire come down from heaven on the earth in the sight of men" (v. 13) to deceive the people of the earth. His ultimate miracle was the creation of a marvelous image of the Antichrist and then to give to that image the appearance and attributes of life. "And he had power to give life, that the image of the beast should both speak, and cause that as many as would not worship the image of the beast should be killed" (v. 15).

Furthermore, as if he were a prophet of old, this man insists on absolute and public commitment to the Antichrist.

> And he causeth all, both small and great, rich and poor, free and bond, to receive a mark in their right hand, or in their foreheads: and that no man might buy or sell, save he that had the mark, or the name of the beast, or the number of his name (vv. 16–17).

And so, as in Old Testament times, a false prophet will relieve people of the confining doctrines of the Bible and will enable them to fit comfortably in a world dominated by the lust of the flesh, the lust of the eyes, and the pride of life.

Does the Bible support the idea that the Antichrist will be a Jew? Repeatedly, ancient Jewish writers refer to the Messiah as "the Son of David." This appellation is based on the covenant the Lord established with David. The Lord promised him that the Messiah, the King Who will reign on earth, would be of his seed (II Sam. 7:12–13; Isa. 9:7; Jer. 23:5). In the Gospels, all classes of people, including Gentiles, referred to Christ as "the Son of David" (e.g., Matt. 9:27; 12:23; 15:22; 21:9; 22:42). The people of Israel in New Testament times expected the Messiah to be a Jew of David's lineage, and they were ready to reject anyone who did not meet these expectations (John 7:41–42, 50–52).

Though the Jews often misinterpreted the Scriptures, their expectations of the Messiah were based on the Old Testament prophecies. On more than one occasion, Jesus challenged them concerning their perception of these prophecies (e.g., Matt. 22:42–46; John 5:39–40); but neither He nor the apostles ever questioned their acceptance of the Old Testament Scriptures that the Messiah would be a Jew and could only be a Jew.

Jesus prophesied that the Jews, after rejecting Him as the Messiah, would in the future accept false messiahs—antichrists (e.g., John 5:43; Matt. 24:5, 24), and history testifies that this is exactly what has happened. Josephus speaks of a certain Theudas (not the Theudas of Acts 5:36) who, some fifteen years after our Lord's crucifixion, "persuaded a great part of the people to . . . follow him to the river Jordan; for he told them . . . he would . . . divide the river." *Antiquities* 20.5.1. In AD 132, Simon bar Kokhba led a disastrous revolt again the Roman Emperor Hadrian. Rabbi Akiba ben Joseph, renowned as one of the founders of rabbinic Judaism, hailed Bar Kokhba ("Son of the Star," Num. 24:17) as a messiah.

To this day unbelieving Jews use Scripture (as well as liberal reasoning) to repudiate the idea that Jesus is their Messiah. The authors of the popular and widely endorsed website "Jews for Judaism" refer to over forty Scripture passages in their response to Christian claims regarding the Messiah.

But isn't it true that the vast majority of Jews today are religious liberals who don't believe that the Old Testament is divinely inspired and authoritative? Why would they not accept a Gentile messiah? A survey published in 1993 by the prestigious Guttman Institute of Applied Social Research revealed some surprising results concerning Israeli religious practices and beliefs. Sixty-three percent said that they believe completely that there is a

God and another 24 percent said they were not sure, leaving 13 percent who professed to be atheists. Fifty-five percent said they believe completely that the Torah (the Law) was given to Moses on Mount Sinai, and another 31 percent said they were not sure. Fifty percent said they believed completely that the Jews were the chosen people, and only 20 percent said they did not believe this. As to the coming of the Messiah, 39 percent said they believed completely and another 29 percent said they were not sure.

Perhaps even more telling were the responses of Israeli Jews concerning their religious practices. A startling 98 percent said they have the *mezuzah* (a container of Scripture passages attached to door frames in conformity with Jewish law and as a sign of faith) at their front doors. Seventy-eight percent said they always participated in the Passover feast, and only 5 percent said they never did. Seventy percent said they always fasted on Yom Kippur (the Day of Atonement) and another 11 percent said they sometimes did. A complete report of this survey is available at the web site of the Jerusalem Center for Public Affairs (www.jcpa.org/dje/articles2/howrelisr.htm).

But whatever their religious beliefs may be, the dynamics of Jewish nationalism and traditionalism make it virtually impossible for the nation of Israel to accept the leadership and control of a Gentile messiah. When the United Nations approved the creation of the nation Israel in 1948, "the Zionists . . . were mostly non-religious or even anti-religious." Nevertheless, they "invoked the aid of Judaism. They had no alternative. Without Judaism, without the idea of the Jews as a people united by faith, Zionism was nothing, just a cranky sect. They invoked the Bible too." And "just as Zionists used Judaism to create their state, so some pious Jews believed the Zionist national spirit could be exploited to bring Jews back to Judaism." Paul Johnson, *A History of the Jews* (New York: Harper & Row, 1988), 547.

But what about a Jew being the leader of the revived Roman Empire? There is both biblical and historical precedence for Jews leading non-Jewish governments. Joseph became prime minister of Egypt, second only to Pharaoh, even though the Egyptians viewed people of his shepherd class as an "abomination" (Gen. 43:32; 46:34). In the nineteenth century, the Rothschilds had considerable influence in governments on the European continent and in Great Britain, and one member of this family held office in the British Parliament. Later, Benjamin Disraeli served as prime minister of Great Britain. Two of the chief architects of Bolshevik Communism, Karl Marx and Leon Trotsky, were Jewish—though, ironically, both were fiercely anti-Semitic.

CHAPTER TWENTY-NINE

THE DEATH THROES OF THE DRAGON, PART III

THE SURPRISING SMELL OF WAR

SOME PEOPLE HAVE ALLERGIES TRIGGERED by the beautiful aroma of flowers, and to some insects the sweet fragrance of perfume is the smell of death. In his vision of the opening of the seventh seal (Rev. 8:1–5), John sees in the temple of heaven an angel offering incense on the golden altar before the throne of God. To the King, the aroma of the incense, representing the prayers of His beloved children, is beautiful; but to the people on earth, it is the smell of war and death.

John the Apostle, in his younger days, must have heard the story often of the miraculous birth of John the Baptist; but since then, thoughts of that momentous event must have seldom entered his mind—until now. For now in his vision John finds himself witnessing in the heavenly temple one of the most dramatic of the temple ceremonies, the offering of incense.

The offering of incense was the grand climax of the daily sin offering. When the sin offering was slain, the priest took some of the blood and put it on the horns of the altar of incense in the Holy Place. The burning of the incense, then, represented the confessions and prayers of God's people ascending to the Lord on the merits of the sacrificial blood. Heaven's acceptance of this incense represented God's acceptance of His covenant people. Consequently, the ceremony by which the incense was offered became a vitally important moment in the temple ritual.

For that reason the priest chosen by lot to offer the incense was given that privilege only once during his lifetime.[1] Once chosen, the priest and his two assistants first approached the altar of burnt offering. One filled a golden censer with incense while the other put burning coals from the altar in a golden bowl. Next they slowly ascended the steps to the Holy Place. When the assistants had spread the coals on the golden altar and arranged the incense, they withdrew and the incensing priest was left alone. Shortly after this, the chief priest gave the signal that the time of incense had come. At this signal, the whole multitude of worshipers withdrew from the inner court and prostrated themselves before the Lord. Then throughout the whole temple complex, all was silent. The Levitical choir stood poised and ready, and priests with silver trumpets waited for the signal to sound their instruments. But all was silent until the incensing priest returned to lead in the blessing and the meal offering of the high priest was presented. Then and only then was the silence broken, with blasts from the silver trumpets and songs of praise.

Now John, who had seen in the earthly temple the copy and shadow of spiritual reality (Heb. 8:5), witnesses this dramatic moment in the heavenly temple. All is silent for about half an hour.

> And I saw the seven angels which stood before God; and to them were given seven trumpets. And another angel came and stood at the altar, having a golden censer; and there was given unto him much incense, that he should offer it with the prayers of all saints upon the golden altar which was before the throne. And the smoke of the incense, which came with the prayers of the saints, ascended up before God out of the angel's hand. And the angel took the censer, and filled it with fire of the altar, and cast it into the earth: and there were voices, and thunderings, and lightnings, and an earthquake (Rev. 8:2–5).

This heavenly scene would have been especially significant to Zacharias and Elisabeth in the bleak years before that very special incensing ceremony in Jerusalem. It would have told them that, after all, their prayers were significant. They were an essential part of God's program to establish His kingdom.

---

[1] A good discussion of the details of this ceremony is in Edersheim, *The Temple*, 157–173 (see chap. 8, n. 5).

Zacharias and Elisabeth were prototypes of the saints of the church age to whom the book of Revelation was written. As a young couple, they had every human reason to believe that God would richly bless their marriage. Not only was Zacharias of the priestly line, but his wife also was "of the daughters of Aaron"—a circumstance which, according to the rabbis, bestowed a twofold honor.[2] So their lineage and calling promised God's blessing, but their exemplary lives did as well. They were a godly couple, "both righteous before God, walking in all the commandments and ordinances of the Lord blameless" (Luke 1:6).

Nevertheless, Elisabeth was barren—a sign of God's disfavor and a reproach in the sight of God's people (Deut. 7:14; Luke 1:25). Year after year they continued to pray, to claim the promises of God, and to hope until they were both "well stricken in years." Their many years of prayers, it seemed, had been of no avail. And in all those years of devout living and faithful service in the temple, Zacharias had not once been favored by the lot for incensing.

This is the same circumstance that church-age saints have faced down through the centuries. When the Pharisees demanded of Christ when the kingdom of God would come, He responded that it would not come "with observation"—that is, you won't be able to see signs of the coming kingdom by carefully watching earthly developments.[3] The Lord then forewarned the disciples of problems His people would have with this circumstance during the church age. "The days will come, when ye shall desire to see one of the days of the Son of man, and ye shall not see it" (Luke 17:22).

It was in this context that the Lord told the disciples the parable of the widow and the unjust judge (Luke 18:1–8)—a parable designed to teach the children of God "that men ought always to pray, and not to faint." In many respects, the church will be like a powerless, disinherited widow in an unjust world. What is her recourse in that case? She will be tempted to follow dynamic visionary leaders who claim to see an earthly kingdom just over the horizon, but the Lord warns, "Go not after them, nor follow them" (Luke 17:23b). In fact, her greatest resource will be persistent, determined prayer—prayer based on the realization of her own weakness.

---

[2] Edersheim, *Jesus the Messiah*, 1:135 (see chap. 1, n. 10).

[3] The word translated *observation* (*parateresis*) in Luke 17:20 was used by medical writers of carefully watching the symptoms of disease and was used also of astronomical observations. A. T. Robertson, *Word Pictures in the New Testament*, 2:228.

But given these conditions—of the church like a helpless widow in an unjust, antagonistic world—will that kind of faith be easy to find in the last days? Will the Son of Man find *the* faith—that kind of faith—when He comes (Luke 18:8*b*)?[4] The fact that the Lord Himself introduced the question reveals the message He intended to convey. His intention, announced at the beginning of the parable, was to convince men to persevere in prayer whatever the obstacles. He concludes the message by saying, in effect, that the type of faith required to do this will become very rare in the last days. So the message of the parable is this: as the wickedness and antagonism of the world increases in the last days, recognize that your best weapon for overcoming the world is the rare quality of prevailing prayer.

John now watches as a designated angel receives and offers much incense, added as a special ingredient of grace to the prayers of the saints; and he sees the smoke of the incense ascend from the angel to the throne of God. Then, as if in response to the ascending prayers, the angel fills the censer with burning coals from the altar and throws them toward the earth. "And there were voices, and thunderings, and lightnings, and an earthquake."

THE TRUMPET JUDGMENTS

We must remind ourselves again of the vital connection between the world's judgment and its rejection of Redemption. The judgments emanate from the heavenly temple, the place of God's revelation to man and the pattern for man's approach to God. The Lamb, Who came to take away the sins of the world, opened the seal judgments. Now the coals that begin the trumpet judgments are scattered on the earth from the altar, the place of God's reconciling sacrifice.

---

[4] Literally, the Greek expression reads "Shall he find *the* faith in the earth?" This could be interpreted as a reference to the Christian faith: Will the Christian faith be on earth when the Lord returns? But the context suggests that it is more natural to read the article as a demonstrative pronoun ("*that* faith") with reference to the kind of faith the parable has just illustrated. The implication that the Christian faith may be nearly obliterated from the earth in the last days clashes with such passages as Rev. 7:9–17, to say nothing of the covenant promises. According to Dana and Mantey, the Greek article "was originally derived from the demonstrative pronoun . . . and . . . it always retained some of the demonstrative force. This fact is evidenced by its frequent use in the papyri purely as a demonstrative pronoun." The New Testament writers use it this way quite often (e.g., Matt. 13:4; Gal. 5:14, and John 4:11). H. E. Dana and Julius R. Mantey, *A Manual Grammar of the Greek New Testament* (New York: MacMillan, 1955), 136–40.

Furthermore, these judgments illustrate man's declining sovereignty over the earth. His original commission was to subdue the earth and have dominion over it, and that command has never been revoked. But when man rebelled against his Lord, the earth rebelled against its appointed sovereign. And as man's rebellion increases, his control over the earth decreases. In a sense, the trumpet judgments are intensifications of the curse God put upon the earth at the fall of man. Nevertheless, there are redemptive as well as judicial aspects to the curse of the earth (Ps. 107:33–34; Exod. 15:25; Deut. 8:2–3; 11:10–15). Even the trumpet judgments are designed to bring men to repentance (Rev. 9:20–21).

The revelation of God on the throne at the Council of War focused on Him as Creator of all things. "Thou art worthy, O Lord, to receive glory and honour and power: for thou hast created all things, and for thy pleasure they are and were created" (4:11). At the sound of the seventh trumpet judgment, there is a song of praise in heaven and the twenty-four elders fall into an ecstasy of worship, praising God that, among other things, the time had come for the Lord to "destroy them which destroy the earth" (11:17–18).

The trumpet blasts, as they begin, result in the devastation of the corrupted earth. At the first trumpet, hail and fire mingled with blood fall, and one-third of the trees and all the green grass are burned. At the second, what appears to be a great burning mountain falls into the sea, and a third of the sea becomes blood. At the third, a great burning star falls, and a third of the rivers and fountains become fatally bitter. Then, at the fourth trumpet, a third of the light of the sun, moon, and stars is darkened, resulting in the light of day being shortened by a third. After this fourth trumpet judgment, a flying eagle catches the John attention. He hears it proclaim with a loud voice, "Woe, woe, woe, to the inhabiters of the earth by reason of the other voices of the trumpet of the three angels, which are yet to sound!"[5]

When the fifth angel sounded, John saw "a star" that had fallen from heaven (Rev. 12:7–9), "and to him was given the key of the bottomless

---

[5] The KJV reads "an angel." The NASB, the ESV, and *The Greek New Testament According to the Majority Text* all have "an eagle." Swete points out that had John written *angel*, he probably would have used *another* (*allos*) with it (as he did, e.g., in 8:3) instead of *an* (*henos*, literally one). *The Apocalypse*, 113 (see chap. 25, n. 2). It was the fourth living creature (which was "like a flying eagle," 4:7) who announced the climactic fourth seal judgment (6:7–8). Cf. Matt. 24:28; Deut. 28:49; Job 9:26; Hosea 8:1; Hab. 1:8).

pit" (9:1). The prophet first sees what appears to be a fallen star on earth. Then he sees the star take shape as a person he later identifies as a king named Abaddon, or Apollyon (v. 11).

Satan with his demonic army now finds himself exiled to the earth. This is the fulfillment, or perhaps the beginning of the fulfillment, of the Lord's prophetic words to His disciples, "I beheld Satan as lightning fall from heaven" (Luke 10:18).

At his expulsion from heaven, Apollyon, in the frenzied rage of impending defeat, began flailing indiscriminately at the nation that gave birth not only to the Messiah but also to the Antichrist—a nation that as a whole had willingly followed the Deceiver, with many still enlisted in his cause. Later, in what appears to be a more controlled anger, he began waging a systematic campaign of destruction against "the remnant" of the seed of Israel, the followers of Christ. But even this war was instigated by his bitter anger with the covenant nation, the ultimate source of his problems.[6]

But though Satan's hatred of God and His program may provide some rationale for his persecution of Israel, we are hard pressed to find a reasonable explanation for his actions at the sound of the fifth trumpet. When this trumpet sounds, the fallen star Apollyon "was given the key of the bottomless pit." With this key he opens the bottomless pit where certain demons have been confined. Upon his opening this prison abyss, massive billows of black smoke rise, darkening the sun and contaminating the air. Out of the smoke, hosts of demons in the form of locusts pour forth.

These demonic hordes then receive their commission.

And it was commanded them that they should not hurt the grass of the earth, neither any green thing, neither any tree; but only those men which have not the seal of God in their foreheads. And to them it was given that they should not kill them, but that they should be tormented five months" (Rev. 9:4–5).

---

[6] In Rev. 12:12 and 17, the inspired writer uses two different words for anger. In v. 12, immediately after Satan's expulsion from heaven, John describes him as "having great wrath [*thumos*]." In v. 17, he depicts the dragon as "wroth [*orgidzo*] with the woman" and as going "to make war with the remnant of her seed, which keep the commandments of God, and have the testimony of Jesus Christ." The first word (v. 12) depicts an outburst of wrath. A. T. Robertson (*Word Pictures*, 6:395) defines it as "boiling rage." The second word (v. 17) "suggests a more settled or abiding condition of mind, frequently with a view of taking revenge." W. E. Vine, *An Expository Dictionary of New Testament Words* (London: Oliphants Ltd., 1953), 1:55–56. See also Richard C. Trench, *Synonyms of the New Testament* (Grand Rapids: Eerdmans, 1963), 130–34.

How are we to understand this commission? These are demonic hordes released by Apollyon himself; yet they are given no power to afflict the enemies of Satan. They have power only to torment, not to kill, his slaves.

Who gave them this commission? John doesn't tell us, as he did on other occasions (e.g., Rev. 6:6; 7:2–3; 11:1–2). It is natural to assume that God (or an angel under His orders) gave the command, since the demons are restricted from tormenting the people of God or from destroying the foliage of the earth beyond the judgment already pronounced (8:7). However, we might assume from the context that throughout the vision Satan commands this vile horde—though of course he is, as he always has been, under the sovereign control of God (Job 1:12; 2:5–7; Luke 22:31–32; II Cor. 12:7).

But would Satan torment his own followers, as he does in this plague? If we go by the divine record of his actions, we would have to say yes, indeed he does torment his own (e.g., Mark 5:4–5; Luke 8:29). Satan is a cruel taskmaster; though he appears often as an angel of light, his modus operandi is fear.

We must remember that the kingdom of darkness stands on feet of clay—or more precisely, on feet that are part of iron and part of clay. However much power this kingdom may gather, it will ultimately fall because it stands on unregenerate and infirm human nature. Its soldiers are self-centered and rebellious at heart. These are not qualities on which powerful armies are built.

So if the "iron" in the kingdom of darkness is to dominate, it must forcibly subjugate the "clay," the self-centered and rebellious nature of man. Satan accomplishes this by various means but chiefly by fear. In this case, the fifth trumpet restricts him from afflicting the people of God or the foliage of the earth, but he is not restricted from intimidating his own to crush all thought of renouncing allegiance to him and his cause.

The sixth angel trumpets the second of the three final "woes" (Rev. 9:13–21) that are to come upon the inhabitants of the earth. When the angel sounded, John heard a voice from the golden altar instructing the angel, "Release the four angels who are bound at the great river Euphrates." (v. 14, ESV).

The Euphrates marked the boundary between the Far East and the West. Since these angels are "bound," they are evidently evil angels who wish to obey their master and wreak destruction on the lands west of the Euphrates. But instead, God has reserved them for His purposes. God,

Who orchestrates even the wrath of His enemies for the accomplishment of His plans, has been preparing these demonic forces for a particular hour, day, month, and year, and that time has come. A third of mankind is to be slain. In the judgment of the fourth seal, one-fourth of the population will die (6:8). This means that after this judgment, only half of the original population will remain.

The instrument of judgment is an army of two hundred million demon-possessed warriors. John's description of this army, cast in the language of biblical times, may well depict the horrors of modern warfare.

> And thus I saw the horses in the vision, and them that sat on them, having breastplates of fire, and of jacinth, and brimstone: and the heads of the horses were as the heads of lions; and out of their mouths issued fire and smoke and brimstone. By these three was the third part of men killed, by the fire, and by the smoke, and by the brimstone, which issued out of their mouths. For their power is in their mouth, and in their tails: for their tails were like unto serpents, and had heads, and with them they do hurt (9:17–19).

It is a somber testimony to sin's power that even in the face of devastating judgment, men insanely cling to the sin that is the source of their destruction.

> And the rest of the men which were not killed by these plagues yet repented not of the works of their hands, that they should not worship devils, and idols of gold, and silver, and brass, and stone, and of wood: which neither can see, nor hear, nor walk: neither repented they of their murders, nor of their sorceries, nor of their fornication, nor of their thefts (9:20–21).

THE VIAL JUDGMENTS OF WRATH

The inspired writers often refer to the Day of Judgment as a day of God's wrath. The wrath of God is His response to the angry rebellion of His subjects on earth. "The nations were angry, and thy wrath is come" (Rev. 11:18). In standard dictionaries, one of the definitions given for *anger* is "a strong feeling of displeasure." The capacity to love deeply carries with it the capacity for deep grievance at scorned love. The love of God expresses itself in the riches of His goodness and longsuffering. The dark side of this is that when a man ignores or spurns God's love, His capacity for noble love becomes instead a cache for indignant anger.

> Or despisest thou the riches of his goodness and forbearance and longsuffering; not knowing that the goodness of God leadeth thee to repentance?

But after thy hardness and impenitent heart treasurest up unto thyself wrath against the day of wrath and revelation of the righteous judgment of God (Rom. 2:4–5).

In rapid-fire order, the angels pour their bowls of wrath upon the earth until the things the world clings to for life become instead harbingers of death. The mark of the beast, which had been a token of their security, makes them now a target for "noisome and grievous" sores. The sea that had been the source of life and prosperity now becomes "as the blood of a dead man." Life-giving rivers and fountains of water also turn into blood. The sun, men's source of light and life, now scorched them with fiery pain; and on the throne of the Antichrist, their last hope for glory, the fifth angel pours a vial of wrath that plunged his kingdom into darkness (Rev. 16:2–11).

As they pour out their judgments, the angels, as if in response to the psalmist's commission (149:6), have the high praises of God in their mouths.

And I heard the angel of the waters say, Thou art righteous, O Lord, which art, and wast, and shalt be, because thou hast judged thus. For they have shed the blood of saints and prophets, and thou hast given them blood to drink; for they are worthy. And I heard another out of the altar say, Even so, Lord God Almighty, true and righteous are thy judgments (Rev. 16:5–7).

In stark contrast to the angels, the people of the earth give vent to the lowest passions of their hardened hearts.

And men were scorched with great heat, and blasphemed the name of God, which hath power over these plagues: and they repented not to give him glory . . . and they gnawed their tongues for pain, and blasphemed the God of heaven because of their pains and their sores, and repented not of their deeds (16:9–11).

With the pouring out of the fifth vial, the end of God's day of wrath is on the horizon. The sixth and seventh vials bring about the climactic battle of all time and the destruction of Babylon.

THE FALL OF BABYLON

The book of Revelation is essentially a chronicle of war. It is a prophetic record of the consummation of the battle of the ages, the war between the kingdom of heaven and the kingdom of the world. Even in the opening chapter, the war format of the book is evident. John, a prisoner on the Isle of Patmos, presents Christ as "the prince of the kings of the earth" Who is coming soon to assume His glory and dominion. He characterizes the saints as "kings and priests" destined to reign with God, and he declares that his own relationship with the saints is that of a fellow soldier—a "companion in tribulation, and in the kingdom and patience of Jesus Christ" (1:5–9).

The seven churches are comparable to beleaguered camps of soldiers in a life-and-death struggle with the enemy. The battle cry to the saints in these churches is always, "Overcome by being faithful unto death, and you shall reign with Christ in the everlasting kingdom" (2:7, 10, 17, 26; 3:5, 12, 21).

The Identity of Babylon

The Bible presents Babylon as the embodiment of the world's rebellion against God. In the Bible's first reference to Babylon (Gen. 10:8–10), Nimrod is identified as a "mighty one" (*gibbor*). This designation, in the context of the developing story in Genesis, associates him with the "mighty men" (*gibborim*) of Genesis 6:4, the leaders of the rebellion of the pre-Flood world. The biblical record designates Babel as "the beginning" of Nimrod's kingdom (Gen. 10:10).

Though the designation *Babel*, by divine design, has come to represent confusion (Gen. 11:9), originally the word meant "gate of God." This meaning suggests that, ostensibly, the tower was built as a memorial to God. In reality it represents the pride of man, for the tower was built in insolent disregard of God's will (Gen. 9:1; 11:4–6). Like Cain, the patriarch and prototype of the kingdom of the world, Nimrod and his followers offered God the fruit of their own willful ways, yet expected God's approval and blessing. From this time on in the inspired record, Babylon symbolizes the spirit and power of the world in rebellion toward God.

In its essence, Babylon represented not simply an anti-God kingdom but an antichrist religion. It came into being, not because its founding fathers needed security or power, but because they convinced themselves, having eaten heartily of the Tree of Knowledge, that there was a better way for man to achieve his destiny than the one God had ordained. The political and commercial power of Babylon that came later was the result of its religious philosophy.

Because of all that Babylon represents, the age-old question as to whether John uses "Babylon" as a symbolic name for Rome in Revelation is, in my mind, not a major issue—though I am convinced that the scriptural evidence supports the view of many Bible scholars that the city of Babylon will be rebuilt on its ancient site in Iraq.

Symbolic or real? The universal linguistic practice of symbolism is not (as Bible students often seem to assume) an either-or matter. A thing is not necessarily *either* symbolic *or* real. Symbolism is based on reality. We use "Wall Street" to represent the financial markets because of the real events that have taken place on that avenue in New York City.

On the basis of the universal laws of language, then, John could legitimately call Rome "Babylon" on the assumption that his readers were familiar with the characteristics of the city of Babylon. In fact, when John sees a great angel announcing the fall of Babylon, he testifies, "And I heard another voice from heaven, saying, Come out of her, my people, that ye be not partakers of her sins, and that ye receive not of her plagues" (Rev. 18:1–4). Does this mean that the appeal he heard was only for the people of God who lived in the city of Babylon on the Euphrates River? Doesn't it mean, rather, that in view of the coming destruction of the world system represented by Babylon, God's people should "come out from among them" and be separate from the world system?

The Great Harlot of Babylon

Of all the phenomenal things John saw in his visions on the Isle of Patmos, the revelation of the great harlot of Babylon was the only one which made him testify, "When I saw her, I marveled greatly" (17:6, ESV). The apostle John, now an old man, had seen the power of the world—including its apostate religious network—at its worst. As a young man, he had witnessed these vicious powers conspire to crucify the Lord of Glory. In his later years, he had warned his spiritual children,

> Love not the world, neither the things that are in the world. If any man love the world, the love of the Father is not in him. For all that is in the world, the lust of the flesh, and the lust of the eyes, and the pride of life, is not of the Father, but is of the world (I John 2:15–16).

But for all that, he wasn't prepared for the vision to which one of the judgment angels summoned him.

> Come hither; I will shew unto thee the judgment of the great whore that sitteth upon many waters: with whom the kings of the earth have committed fornication, and the inhabitants of the earth have been made drunk with the wine of her fornication. So he carried me away in the spirit into the wilder-

ness: and I saw a woman sit upon a scarlet coloured beast, full of names of blasphemy, having seven heads and ten horns. And the woman was arrayed in purple and scarlet colour, and decked with gold and precious stones and pearls, having a golden cup in her hand full of abominations and filthiness of her fornication: and upon her forehead was a name written, MYSTERY, BABYLON THE GREAT, THE MOTHER OF HARLOTS AND ABOMINATIONS OF THE EARTH. And I saw the woman drunken with the blood of the saints, and with the blood of the martyrs of Jesus (Rev. 17:1b–6a).

A Picture of the Filthiness of Apostate Religion

Though John may have wondered specifically who or what this woman represented, he would probably have perceived that she symbolized apostate religion. He was well aware of the abundant references in the Old Testament to the Lord being the husband and Israel being His wife. And he was well aware also of the prophets' scathing condemnations of Israel as an apostate, unfaithful wife, guilty of gross harlotry (e.g., Isa. 54:5–6; Jer. 3:14; Ezek. 16:8; Hosea 1:2; 2:2, 19–20).

A Picture of the Controlling Power of Apostate Religion

When I was a boy, some centuries before video games and space ships, I was absolutely fascinated with cowboys and especially with their horses. On rare occasions, when our family visited relatives down south, I actually got to ride on a real horse! That for me was the stuff dreams were made of. These ecstatic experiences (tinged with a bit of fear) never lasted very long. I never really learned the first thing about horsemanship. In fact, when I was on one of these massive beasts, the horse was always in control. I wasn't. This is not the case for a real horseman: he is in control of the animal, not vice versa.

One of the striking features of John's vision was that the harlot was riding on a huge, fearsome beast—a scarlet-colored creature "having seven heads and ten horns." Yet she was in charge! The beast represents the revived Roman Empire under the dynamic leadership of the Antichrist—who is, in effect, the personification of the Empire. But for all his, and his Empire's, fearful power, he is under the control of the harlot. This is a picture of the controlling power of apostate religion.

There is perhaps no better illustration of the developing scene in this chapter than the saga of the Roman Catholic Church. In the Christian era, the history of Europe has been largely a record of wars—and many of these battles have, in effect, been little more than religious power plays.

Kings and religious potentates have waged war incessantly, kings being deposed by popes and popes by kings. Examples from history abound.

In AD 800, Pope Leo III crowned Charlemagne Holy Roman Emperor. One of the successors to that throne, Henry IV of Germany, was excommunicated by Pope Gregory VII. Reeling under papal power, Henry crossed the Alps and stood barefooted, in penitential garb, before Gregory's palace at Canossa. Finally Gregory granted him an audience and reinstatement. Later, Henry seized power by conquering Rome and installing a new pope. In the sixteenth century, Henry VIII of England waged war for power with Pope Clement VII and eventually removed his kingdom from the pope's supervision. In 1804, Napoleon, at his coronation ceremony in the church of Notre Dame, took the crown of the Holy Roman Empire from the pope and placed it on his own head—a symbol of who he felt was really in charge.

During the Tribulation, the same kind of power struggle will take place between the Emperor and the potentate of harlot religion—only with much higher stakes. As he is rising in power, the Antichrist will need the religious potentate. However, the slaying and resurrection of the Emperor will upset the entire power structure. No longer will the Emperor need organized religion. He becomes the world religion—and the only religion the world needs.

It will be easy then to win the malicious support of his ten confederate kings. For years they have been nurturing a seething hatred for "the whore" (Rev. 17:16) They are all of one mind, the writer tells us—unified in their opposition to the heavenly King, unified in their enmity against this earthly potentate, and oblivious to the direction of God in their plans (vv. 13–14, 17). Unwittingly, they become instruments of the King they have rejected, to destroy the great harlot city that has ruled over nations and the kings of the earth.

The expression "after these things" (18:1) distinguishes between the events of chapter 17 and those of chapter 18. In chapter 17, "mystery Babylon," representing apostate religious power, is destroyed. In chapter 18, the political-commercial city of Babylon is destroyed. Premillennialists commonly place the events of chapter 17 about the middle of the Tribulation and those of chapter 18 toward its end.

The Victory Cry of the King

The official announcement of the fall of Babylon comes with a preview of the glorious light that would come to Earth after its fall.

And after these things I saw another angel come down from heaven, having great power; and the earth was lightened with his glory. And he cried mightily with a strong voice, saying, Babylon the great is fallen, is fallen (18:1–2*a*).

Centuries before, the prophet Isaiah had heard this cry (Isa. 21:9). Now at last comes the fulfillment! This is the victory cry for the King of kings as the capital of the Antichrist's kingdom collapses.

THE GREAT WAR OF ARMAGEDDON

Divine Preparations for the War

When the sixth angel pours out his vial upon the great river Euphrates, its waters dry up "that the way of the kings of the east might be prepared" (Rev. 16:12). Though it certainly must appear otherwise on earth, this is part of the master plan of the heavenly King to culminate His judgment of the earth and to bring salvation to His covenant nation Israel. Some eight centuries before John's Patmos visions, the Lord revealed His plan for this great war to the prophet Joel.

For, behold, in those days, and in that time, when I shall bring again the captivity of Judah and Jerusalem, I will also gather all nations, and will bring them down into the valley of Jehoshaphat, and will plead with them there for my people and for my heritage Israel, whom they have scattered among the nations, and parted my land (Joel 3:1–2; cf. Zech. 14:2).

Satanic Preparations for the War

The Dragon, likewise, has been preparing for this war.

And I saw three unclean spirits like frogs come out of the mouth of the dragon, and out of the mouth of the beast, and out of the mouth of the false prophet. For they are the spirits of devils, working miracles, which go forth unto the kings of the earth and of the whole world, to gather them to the battle of that great day of God Almighty (Rev. 16:13–14).

When he was expelled from heaven three years before, the Dragon was in a frenzied rage because he knew that he had but a short time (12:12). Has anything changed for him? Has he accomplished anything in his vicious war with God that would give him a ray of hope? No on both counts. Nothing has changed for the better. Nothing has happened that would give him the slightest glimmer of hope that he might after all succeed.

True, he has won some victories. His henchman, the Antichrist, has made war with the saints and has overcome them (13:7). But the Dragon is much too perceptive to count these as real victories. In this regard, Satan is like Ahithophel, the perceptive advisor and friend of David who betrayed him for Absalom. When Absalom overruled his strategically sound advice, Ahithophel saw right away that all was lost. His suicide was no rash decision. The inspired writer tells us that he saddled his donkey, traveled several hours to his home in Giloh, and put his house in order—and then he hanged himself. These are not the actions of a rash man. They are the actions of a man perceptive enough to know that if Absalom led an army against David and his mighty men, all would be lost (II Sam. 16:20–17:23).

Why then does the Dragon continue to prepare for war? Because of the nature of sin. Neither impending judgment nor final judgment will relieve the soul of its rebellious nature. Even the doomed in hell will gnash their teeth (Matt. 13:42), a reaction of anger, not of pain (Job 16:9; Lam. 2:16; Acts 7:54). The fires of hell are eternal because the eternal soul will continue to be angry with God and therefore will continually have to be punished. Like the Dragon, rebellious souls cannot cease fighting against God—even in judgment.

The Purging and Salvation of Israel through the War

After Daniel had seen something of the terrors of the time of Jacob's Trouble, he heard a heavenly being ask a question that must have resonated in his own heart: "How long shall it be to the end of these wonders?" In answer,

> the man clothed in linen . . . raised his right hand and his left hand toward heaven and swore by him who lives forever that it would be for a time, times, and half a time, and that when the shattering of the power of the holy people comes to an end all these things would be finished (Dan. 12:7b, ESV).

Until when? Until the power of the holy people is shattered! Once this is accomplished, once the covenant people of God lose their sense of self-sufficiency, then the purpose of God will be accomplished. The final stage in God's program to shatter His people's self-sufficiency will be the war of Armageddon.

Zechariah received the revelation of this war of the nations against Jerusalem. He described it as "the burden of the word of the Lord for Israel" (Zech. 12:1a):

> Behold, I will make Jerusalem a cup of trembling unto all the people round about, when they shall be in the siege both against Judah and against Jerusalem. And in that day will I make Jerusalem a burdensome stone for all people: all that burden themselves with it shall be cut in pieces, though all the people of the earth be gathered together against it (12:2–3).

Just a few weeks before, the armies of the world were at each other's throats. Now, driven by demonic power and malicious hatred for God, they have gathered as one, determined to wipe the Holy City off the face of the earth—and thus thwart the plan of God. They have every reason to expect an easy victory, but they soon find otherwise. They have envisioned the ruins of Jerusalem as providing the foundation stone for their new world; but as sometimes happened to builders in ancient times, their foundational stone rolls back on the would-be builders, crushing them beneath its weight.

The most common of the Jewish soldiers seem to have the power and skill of David, and the "Davids"—the champions—among them to fight as God Himself (Zech. 12:8). But greater things are happening to the soldiers.

> And I will pour upon the house of David, and upon the inhabitants of Jerusalem, the spirit of grace and of supplications: and they shall look upon me whom they have pierced, and they shall mourn for him, as one mourneth for his only son, and shall be in bitterness for him, as one that is in bitterness for his firstborn (Zech. 12:10).

Spiritual work is taking place. The Messiah has not yet returned, so they are not literally looking on the One they have pierced. They are looking with spiritual eyes, as the Lord through His prophets had appealed to them. "Look unto me, and be ye saved, all the ends of the earth: for I am God, and there is none else" (Isa. 45:22; cf. 51:1; Mic. 7:7).

Their long-stifled conscience now awakes to the Word of God, and their sense of pain and sorrow for their crimes against their Messiah becomes overwhelming. As if lamenting for the dead, members of families separate from each other for one purpose: to search their own hearts and find forgiveness for their sins. In response, the Lord opens a fountain of life "for sin and for uncleanness" (Zech. 12:11—13:1).

Many, however, do not look on Him Whom they have pierced—in fact, two of every three see no need for such repentance.

And it shall come to pass, that in all the land, saith the Lord, two parts therein shall be cut off and die; but the third shall be left therein. And I will bring the third part through the fire, and will refine them as silver is refined, and will try them as gold is tried: they shall call on my name, and I will hear them: I will say, It is my people: and they shall say, The Lord is my God (Zech. 13:8–9).

Isaiah, who for over sixty years had preached to a people who heard but understood not, saw this day coming.

Who hath heard such a thing? who hath seen such things? Shall the earth be made to bring forth in one day? or shall a nation be born at once? for as soon as Zion travailed, she brought forth her children. Shall I bring to the birth, and not cause to bring forth? saith the Lord: shall I cause to bring forth, and shut the womb? saith thy God (Isa. 66:8–9).

But even yet the work of shattering the power of the holy people has not been accomplished. God allows the city to be taken, "the houses rifled, and the women ravished" and half the people taken captive. Then, when their most heroic efforts have failed,

shall the Lord go forth, and fight against those nations, as when he fought in the day of battle. And his feet shall stand in that day upon the mount of Olives, which is before Jerusalem on the east, and the mount of Olives shall cleave in the midst thereof toward the east and toward the west, and there shall be a very great valley; and half of the mountain shall remove toward the north, and half of it toward the south. And ye shall flee to the valley of the mountains; for the valley of the mountains shall reach unto Azal: yea, ye shall flee, like as ye fled from before the earthquake in the days of Uzziah king of Judah: and the Lord my God shall come, and all the saints with thee (Zech. 14:3–5).

But from Patmos, John can see an even more glorious climax.

And I saw heaven opened, and behold a white horse; and he that sat upon him was called Faithful and True, and in righteousness he doth judge and make war. His eyes were as a flame of fire, and on his head were many crowns; and he had a name written, that no man knew, but he himself. And he was clothed with a vesture dipped in blood: and his name is called The Word of God. And the armies which were in heaven followed him upon white horses, clothed in fine linen, white and clean. And out of his mouth goeth a sharp sword, that with it he should smite the nations: and he shall rule them with a rod of iron: and he treadeth the winepress of the fierceness and wrath of

Almighty God. And he hath on his vesture and on his thigh a name written, KING OF KINGS, AND LORD OF LORDS (Rev. 19:11–16).

Then John sees the blatant arrogance of the beast and the armies of the earth as they, gathered together, imagine they can actually fight the coming King of kings. And the beast and the false prophet are taken captive and "cast alive into a lake of fire burning with brimstone" (19:19–20).

And what has this fearsome beast, the Antichrist, accomplished in his dazzling career? For all the wonder of his accomplishments and the worship of his subjects, he has been at the top echelon of human success for less than four years—less than the tenure of a one-term president!

CONCLUSION

FROM FOUNDATION TO FULFILLMENT

REMEMBER THE STORY OF THE Leaning Tower of Pisa? The architects built the edifice according to standard specifications, but somehow in the process they lost sight of their foundational parameters.

Having examined various aspects of the edifice of the marvelous Revelation of God, we must ask ourselves now if our perception of the edifice is indeed aligned with the foundation. Our plumb line has been the Creator's first recorded words about man:

> Then God said, Let us make man in our image, after our likeness. And let them have dominion over the fish of the sea and over the birds of the heavens and over the livestock and over all the earth and over every creeping thing that creeps on the earth. So God created man in his own image, in the image of God he created him; male and female he created them. And God blessed them. And God said to them, Be fruitful and multiply and fill the earth and subdue it and have dominion over the fish of the sea and over the birds of the heavens and over every living thing that moves on the earth (Gen. 1:26–28, ESV).

These words were written initially to fallen men and for fallen men, and they have never been revoked. From these words the whole story of the

Bible unfolds. They contain a statement of the created nature of man ("let us make man in our image") and of the Creator's purpose for mankind ("let them have dominion"). In embryonic form, they speak of the kingdom God prepared for man "from the foundation of the world" (Matt. 25:34); for the commission for man to have dominion over the earth carries with it the authority to reign over the earthly kingdom of God.

Implicit also in this passage is an extended time period for the development and multiplication of mankind, for man's commission is to fill the earth and subdue all of it. This would involve a process of conquest by which man would gain increasing knowledge of the details of God's creative works—and, by necessity, an increasing knowledge of the Creator.

The fall of man disrupted and retarded this process, but it did not and could not frustrate the eternal purpose of God. God's eternal purpose "in Christ Jesus our Lord" (Eph. 3:11) included a people for Himself. "Where sin abounded, grace did much more abound" (Rom. 5:20). Even the sinfulness and weakness of man cannot thwart the purpose of God, for God's eternal plan emanates from His gracious and all-powerful nature. "A bruised reed shall he not break, and the smoking flax shall he not quench: he shall bring forth judgment unto truth. He shall not fail nor be discouraged, till he have set judgment in the earth: and the isles shall wait for his law" (Isa. 42:3–4).

But the fall of man brought about the inauguration of another kingdom, the kingdom of the world. The objectives of the two kingdoms were fundamentally the same: to reign as lords over the earth. The process by which their objectives were to be achieved was diametrically opposed. For the citizens of the kingdom of the world, the process involved eating of the Tree of Knowledge and assuming a "godhood" independent of the Creator. For the citizens of the kingdom of God, the process involved renouncing man's self-sufficiency and submitting to the sovereign Savior.

The Fulfillment of the Process

"To every thing there is a season, and a time to every purpose under the heaven" (Eccles. 3:1). Let me repeat a statement that may sound radical to some, even at a second hearing: sin and righteousness are largely matters of timing. Virtually every promise of sin—pleasure, possessions, prestige— God would have fulfilled for man had he only been willing to wait for His timing.

The very first sin involved this principle. The serpent's appeal was for man to be "like God, knowing good and evil" (Gen. 3:5, NASB). From the beginning, it was God's plan for man to be like Him (Gen. 1:26–27; Ps. 17:15; Rom. 8:14–15, 29; I John 3:2; II Pet. 1:4). But Satan lured man into thinking he could have God's likeness immediately, independent of his Creator. Why wait? Why go through an agonizing process of preparation and development? Simply eat of the Tree of Knowledge and you will be like God, discerning for yourself what is good and what is evil.

Man has been eating of the Tree of Knowledge ever since that day, never quite getting it that this way has never worked and never will. In the final kingdom, when redeemed mankind reigns with God and when the earth is filled with the knowledge of the Lord, there will be no Tree of Knowledge from which men will eat—but there will be a Tree of Life (Rev. 22:2, 14; cf. 2:7).

So when will God's process be fulfilled? In his great resurrection chapter, Paul argues, among other things, that the resurrection of the body is necessary if the child of God is to receive his full inheritance:

> Now this I say, brethren, that flesh and blood cannot inherit the kingdom of God; neither doth corruption inherit incorruption. Behold, I shew you a mystery; We shall not all sleep, but we shall all be changed, in a moment, in the twinkling of an eye, at the last trump: for the trumpet shall sound, and the dead shall be raised incorruptible, and we shall be changed. For this corruptible must put on incorruption, and this mortal must put on immortality (I Cor. 15:50–53).

The Lord's process of developing man in His image will not be completed until the resurrection—or the Rapture—when mortal man puts on immortality. The Lord Himself will not assume His kingdom throne until He comes in glory (Matt. 25:31), and it is at this time that thrones will be set up for the glorified saints to reign with Him (Dan. 7:9, NASB; Rev. 4:4; 5:10).

During the millennial kingdom there will be mortal rulers on earth as well. The nations, including Israel, will have mortal leaders (e.g., Isa. 49:7, 23; 60:3, 10–11, 16; 62:2; Ezek. 45:8–9, 16–17, 22; 46:16–18).[1] As long

---

[1] The prince Ezekiel refers to in his description of the millennial temple (44:3; 45:7ff.; 46:8ff.; 48:21–22) is evidently not the resurrected David, though the prophet calls him a prince too (34:24; 37:25). The prince in the millennial temple description offers sin-offerings for himself as well as for the people, is warned not to oppress the people, and has earthly sons as heirs (45:17–18, 22; 46:1–10, 16–18).

as there are mortals on earth, there will be the need for human leadership. Furthermore, the foundational principles of submission and supervision established in the opening pages of the Bible will continue to be in effect during the Millennium.

However, the ultimate fulfillment of God's purpose for man to reign with Him is reserved for the redeemed and glorified saints. The elders in the book of Revelation, representing the redeemed saints, will have crowns signifying that God has made them kings and priests to reign over the earth (Rev. 4:4; 5:10). The apostles will sit on thrones ruling the twelve tribes of Israel (Luke 22:29–30). The King will even delegate important matters of judgment to the glorified saints. In fact, John pictures the saints as ruling with a "rod of iron" (Rev. 2:26–27; cf. Ps. 149:6–9; I Cor. 6:2–3), just as the inspired writers characterize the Messiah (Ps. 2:9; Rev. 12:5; 19:15).

"IN THE MIDST OF THE THRONE . . . STOOD A LAMB"

It was through tears that this vision first appeared to John. He had been weeping "much," because no man had been found worthy to open the seven-sealed scroll through which the final kingdom would be inaugurated. Then one of the elders said, "Weep not: behold, the Lion of the tribe of Juda, the Root of David, hath prevailed to open the book, and to loose the seven seals thereof." Then he looked again at the throne and he saw the Lamb of God standing in the midst of it (Rev. 5:1–6).

We could say that on this occasion John's tears were unnecessary, but they were nevertheless understandable. For John was a brother and "companion in tribulation . . . in the kingdom and patience of Jesus Christ" (Rev. 1:9). His tears, which the Lord chose to include in the Revelation, represent the "much tribulation" through which the saints enter the kingdom.

The Final Victory of the Lamb

The fact that John saw a Lamb standing in the midst of the throne is also significant, for the war of the ages between the two kingdoms this Book depicts as a battle between a dragon and a lamb. What a contest! It would be difficult to imagine a more uneven battle—and that is what gives the symbolism here special significance. The war between the two kingdoms has always been—outwardly at least—ludicrously uneven.

The kingdom of Satan, the Dragon's kingdom, has always dominated in the world. The world marches to Lucifer's drumbeat: the lust of the flesh, the lust of the eyes, and the pride of life. The mighty ones of the earth, the *gibborim*, have virtually all been citizens of the Dragon's kingdom. Nevertheless, the kingdom of the world is doomed to destruction and shameful obscurity, and the kingdom of God is destined for eternal glory. It is "the meek," our Lord declared, who shall inherit the earth.

> And the great dragon was cast out, that old serpent, called the Devil, and Satan, which deceiveth the whole world: he was cast out into the earth, and his angels were cast out with him. And I heard a loud voice saying in heaven, Now is come salvation, and strength, and the kingdom of our God, and the power of his Christ: for the accuser of our brethren is cast down, which accused them before our God day and night. And they overcame him by the blood of the Lamb, and by the word of their testimony; and they loved not their lives unto the death. . . .

> And I heard as it were the voice of a great multitude, and as the voice of many waters, and as the voice of mighty thunderings, saying, Alleluia: for the Lord God omnipotent reigneth. Let us be glad and rejoice, and give honour to him: for the marriage of the Lamb is come, and his wife hath made herself ready. And to her was granted that she should be arrayed in fine linen, clean and white: for the fine linen is the righteousness of saints. And he saith unto me, Write, Blessed are they which are called unto the marriage supper of the Lamb. And he saith unto me, These are the true sayings of God (Rev. 12:9–11; 19:6–9).

SELECTED BIBLIOGRAPHY

Augustine. *The City of God*. In vol. 2, *Basic Writings of Saint Augustine*. Edited by Whitney J. Oates. New York: Random House, 1950.

Barrett, Michael P. V. *Beginning at Moses: A Guide to Finding Christ in the Old Testament*. Greenville, SC: Ambassador-Emerald International, 1999.

Beasley-Murray, G. R. *Jesus and the Kingdom of God*. Grand Rapids: Eerdmans, 1986.

Beecher, Willis Judson. *The Prophets and the Promise: Being for Substance*. Grand Rapids: Baker, 1963.

Biederwolf, William Edward. *The Millennium Bible*. 1924. Reprint, Grand Rapids: Baker, 1964.

Blaising, Craig A., and Darrell L. Bock. *Progressive Dispensationalism*. Wheaton, IL: Victor, 1993.

Bright, John. *The Kingdom of God: The Biblical Concept and Its Meaning for the Church*. New York: Abingdon-Cokesbury, 1953.

Dyer, Charles H., and Angela Elwell Hunt. *The Rise of Babylon*. Wheaton, IL: Tyndale House, 1991.

Edersheim, Alfred. *The Life and Times of Jesus the Messiah*. 1883. Reprint, Grand Rapids: Eerdmans, 1971.

Froese, Arno, James Rizzuti, and Wim Malgo. *Saddam's Mystery Babylon*. West Columbia, SC: The Olive Press, 1998.

Goldsworthy, Graeme. *According to Plan: The Unfolding Revelation of God in the Bible*. Downers Grove, IL: InterVarsity Press, 1991.

Ice, Thomas, and Randall Price. *Ready to Rebuild: The Imminent Plan to Rebuild the Last Days Temple*. Eugene, OR: Harvest House, 1992.

Kaiser, Walter C. *The Messiah in the Old Testament*. Grand Rapids: Zondervan, 1995.

McClain, Alva J. *The Greatness of the Kingdom: An Inductive Study of the Kingdom of God*. Winona Lake, IN: BMH Books, 1974.

Oehler, Gustav Friederich. *Theology of the Old Testament*. Translated by George E. Day. 1883. Reprint, Minneapolis: Klock & Klock, 1978.

Pentecost, J. Dwight. *Things to Come: A Study in Biblical Eschatology*. Grand Rapids: Dunham, 1958.

Peters, George N. H. *The Theocratic Kingdom*. 3 vols. 1884. Reprint, Grand Rapids: Kregel, 1988.

Phillips, O. E. *The Kingdom of God*. Philadelphia: Hebrew Christian Fellowship, 1954.

Richardson, Don. *Eternity in Their Hearts*. Revised edition. Ventura, CA: Regal, 1984.

Riley, William B. *The Evolution of the Kingdom*. New York: The Book Stall, 1913.

Saphir, Adolph. *The Divine Unity of Scripture*. Grand Rapids: Kregel, 1984.

Saucy, Robert L. *The Case for Progressive Dispensationalism: The Interface Between Dispensational & Non-Dispensational Theology*. Grand Rapids: Zondervan, 1993.

Saucy, Mark. *The Kingdom of God in the Teaching of Jesus*. Dallas: Word, 1997.

Sauer, Erich. *The King of the Earth: The Nobility of Man According to the Bible and Science*. Grand Rapids: Eerdmans, 1962.

_____. *From Eternity to Eternity: An Outline of the Divine Purposes*. Grand Rapids: Eerdmans, 1954.

_____. *The Dawn of World Redemption: A Survey of Historical Revelation in the Old Testament*. Grand Rapids: Eerdmans, 1963.

Strom, Mark. *The Symphony of Scripture: Making Sense of the Bible's Many Themes*. Phillipsburg, NJ: P&R Publishing, 1990.

VanGemeren, Willem. *The Progress of Redemption: The Story of Salvation from Creation to the New Jerusalem*. Grand Rapids: Baker, 1988.

Vos, Geerhardus. *Biblical Theology: Old and New Testaments*. Grand Rapids: Eerdmans, 1959.

Walvoord, John F. *The Prophecy Knowledge Handbook*. Wheaton, IL: Victor Books, 1990.